Please remember that this is a library book,
and that it belongs only temporarily to each
person who uses it. Be considerate. Do
not write in this, or any, library book.

STUDYING FAMILY AND
COMMUNITY HISTORY
19th and 20th Centuries

COMMUNITIES
AND FAMILIES

This accessible and innovative series will stimulate and develop personal research in family and community history, and set it within a wider framework. You will find practical suggestions for research projects, activities to enhance relevant skills and understanding, and ideas about how to exploit appropriate written, oral and visual sources. The series also brings together specialist contributors who use current developments in demography, social and economic history, sociology, historical geography and anthropology to suggest new insights and lines of enquiry. With its aim of placing individual and localized cases in their social and historical context, the series will interest anyone concerned with family and community.

This volume explores the links between communities and families. It opens with a series of case studies of various occupations and goes on to examine social mobility and aspects of community life such as local politics, religion and leisure activities. Suggestions for your own research are provided throughout the book.

STUDYING FAMILY AND COMMUNITY HISTORY: 19TH AND 20TH CENTURIES

Series editor: Ruth Finnegan

Volume 1 *From family tree to family history*, edited by Ruth Finnegan and Michael Drake

Volume 2 *From family history to community history*, edited by W.T.R. Pryce

Volume 3 *Communities and families*, edited by John Golby

Volume 4 *Sources and methods for family and community historians: a handbook*, edited by Michael Drake and Ruth Finnegan

All four titles in the series are published by Cambridge University Press in association with The Open University.

This book forms part of the third-level Open University course DA301 *Studying family and community history: 19th and 20th centuries*. Other materials associated with the course are:

Drake, M. (ed.) (1994) *Time, family and community: perspectives on family and community history*, Oxford, Blackwell in association with The Open University (Course Reader).

Braham, P. (ed.) (1993) *Using the past: audio-cassettes on sources and methods for family and community historians*, a series of six audio-cassettes with accompanying notes, Milton Keynes, The Open University.

Calder, A. and Lockwood, V. (1993) *Shooting video history*, a video workshop on video recording for family and community historians, with accompanying notes, Milton Keynes, The Open University.

For availability of the video- and audio-cassette materials, contact Open University Educational Enterprises Ltd (OUEE), 12 Cofferidge Close, Stony Stratford, Milton Keynes, MK11 1BY.

If you wish to study this or any other Open University course, details can be obtained from the Central Enquiry Service, PO Box 200, The Open University, Milton Keynes, MK7 6YZ.

COMMUNITIES AND FAMILIES

Edited by John Golby

CAMBRIDGE UNIVERSITY PRESS *in association with* The Open University

Published by the Press Syndicate of the University of Cambridge in association with The Open University

The Pitt Building, Trumpington Street, Cambridge CB2 1RP
40 West 20th Street, New York, NY 10011-4211, USA
10 Stamford Road, Oakleigh, Melbourne 3166, Australia

First published 1994

Edited, designed and typeset by The Open University

Printed in Great Britain by Butler and Tanner Ltd, Frome

A catalogue record for this book is available from the British Library

Library of Congress Cataloguing-in-Publication data applied for

ISBN 0 521 46003 4   hardback

ISBN 0 521 46579 6   paperback

CONTENTS

LIST OF FIGURES AND TABLES

Figures

CONTRIBUTORS

Brenda Collins, Social and economic historian; Tutor-counsellor, The Open University in Northern Ireland; Research Officer, Lisburn Museum

Ian Donnachie, Senior Lecturer and Staff Tutor in History, Faculty of Arts and The Open University in Scotland

Michael Drake, Emeritus Professor and first Dean of Faculty of Social Sciences, The Open University; Visiting Professor of History, University of Tromsø

Clive Emsley, Professor of History, Faculty of Arts, The Open University

Ruth Finnegan, Professor in Comparative Social Institutions, Faculty of Social Sciences, The Open University

John Golby, Senior Lecturer and Staff Tutor in History, Faculty of Arts and The Open University (South Region)

David Murray, Professor of Government, Faculty of Social Sciences, The Open University

Monica Shelley, Lecturer in Community Education, School of Health, Welfare and Community Education, The Open University

Terry Thomas, Staff Tutor in Religious Studies, Faculty of Arts and The Open University in Wales

Kate Tiller, Director of Studies in Local and Social History, and University Lecturer, Department of Continuing Education, University of Oxford

Bernard Waites, Lecturer in European Humanities Studies, Faculty of Arts, The Open University

PREFACE

Many thousands of people are currently exploring their family trees or investigating the history of their localities. It is an absorbing hobby – and more than just a hobby. It combines the excitement of the chase and the exercise of demanding investigative skills. It also leads to personal rewards, among them perhaps an enhanced awareness of identity, achieved through the process of searching out your roots within the unending cycle of the past, and something to hold on to in the confusions of the present.

At the same time scholars within a series of social science and historical disciplines are increasingly realizing the value of small-scale case studies, extending and questioning accepted theories through a greater understanding of local and personal diversities. Sociologists now look to individual life histories as well as generalized social structure; geographers emphasize the local as well as the global; demographers explore regional divergences, not just national aggregates; historians extend their research from the doings of the famous to how 'ordinary people' pursued their lives at a local level.

This volume and the series of which it is a part have as their central purpose the encouragement of active personal research in family and community history – but research that is also linked to more general findings and insights. The series thus seeks to combine the strengths of two traditions: that of the independent personal researcher into family tree or local history, and that of established academic disciplines in history and the social sciences.

Now is a particularly appropriate moment to bring these two sides together. The networks of family and local historians up and down the country have in the past had scant recognition from within mainstream university circles, which (in contrast to the active involvement of further education and extra-mural departments) have sometimes given the impression of despising the offerings of 'amateur researchers'. Explicitly academic publications, for their part, have been little read by independent investigators – understandably, perhaps, for, with a few honourable exceptions, such publications have been predominantly directed to specialist colleagues. But there are signs that this situation may be changing. Not only is there our increasing awareness of the research value of micro studies, but higher education as a whole is opening up more flexible ways of learning and is recognizing achievements undertaken outside traditional 'university walls'. Our hope is to further this trend of mutual understanding, to the benefit of each.

There are thus two main aims in these volumes, overlapping and complementary. The first is to present an interdisciplinary overview of recent scholarly work in family and community history, drawing on the approaches and findings of such subjects as anthropology, social and economic history, sociology, demography, and historical geography. This should be illuminating not only for those seeking an up-to-date review of such work, but also for anyone interested in the functioning of families and communities today – the essential historical background to present-day concerns. The second, equally important aim is to help readers develop their own research interests. The framework here is rather different from traditional genealogy or local history courses (where excellent DIY guides already exist) since our emphasis is on completing a project and relating it to other research findings and theories, rather than on an unending personal quest for yet more and more details. It differs too from most conventional academic publications, in that the focus is on *doing* research, rather than absorbing or reporting the research of others. These volumes are therefore full of practical advice on sources and methods, as well as illustrations of the kinds of projects that can be followed up by the individual researcher.

Given the infinite scope of the subject and the need to provide practical advice, we have put some limits on the coverage. The timescale is the nineteenth and twentieth centuries, a period for which the sources are plentiful and – for the recent period at least – oral investigation feasible. (The critical assessment and exploitation of primary sources within this timescale will, of course, develop skills which can be extended earlier periods.) There is no attempt to give a detailed historical narrative of nineteenth- and twentieth-century history. Rather we present a blend of specific case studies, findings and theoretical ideas, selected with a view to giving both some taste of recent work, and a context and stimulus for further investigation.

In terms of area, the focus is on the United Kingdom and Ireland, or, to put it differently, on the countries of the British Isles (these and similar terms have both changing historical applications and inescapable political connotations, so since we wish to write without prejudice we have deliberately alternated between them). This focus is applied flexibly, and there is some reference to emigration abroad; but we have not tried to describe sources and experiences overseas. Thus while much of the general theoretical background and even specific ideas for research may relate to many areas of the world, the detailed practical information about sources or record repositories concentrates on those available to students working in England, Ireland (north and south), Scotland and Wales.

The emphasis is also on encouraging small-scale topics. This does not mean that larger patterns are neglected: indeed, like other more generalized findings and theories, they form the background against which smaller studies can be set and compared. But small, manageable projects of the kinds focused on in this volume have two essential merits. First, they link with the emerging appreciation of the value of research into diversities as well as into generalizations: many gaps in our knowledge about particular localities or particular family experiences remain to be filled. Second, they represent a form of research that can be pursued seriously within the resources of independent and part-time researchers.

This third volume focuses on family- or community-based activities that can be studied at a small-scale level such as work, social mobility, local politics, religion, or leisure. It can be read on its own, but it is also linked to the other volumes in the series, which complement and amplify the topics considered here. The companion volumes (listed on p.ii) turn the spotlight on individual families and the broader patterns of family history revealed by recent research (Volume 1); on migration and community (Volume 2); and, in Volume 4, on some of the many sources and methods that can be used to conduct and communicate research in family and community history.

This book forms one part of the Open University course DA301 *Studying family and community history: 19th and 20th centuries* (the other components are listed on p.ii). DA301 is an honours-level undergraduate course for part-time adult learners studying at a distance, and it is designed to develop the skills, methods and understanding to complete a guided project in family or community history within the time constraints of a one-year course – comparable, therefore, to the dissertation sometimes carried out in the final year of a conventional honours degree. It also looks forward to ways in which such a project could be extended and communicated at a later stage. However, these volumes are also designed to be used, either singly or as a series, by anyone interested in family or community history. The introduction to recent research, together with the practical exercises, advice on the critical exploitation of primary sources, and suggestions for research projects, should be of wide interest and application. Collectively the results of such research should not only develop individuals' investigations but also enhance our more general understanding of family and community history. Much remains to be discovered by the army of amateur and professional researchers throughout the British Isles.

Since a series of this kind obviously depends on the efforts of many people, there are many thanks to express. As in other Open University courses, the material was developed collaboratively. So while authors are responsible for what they have written, they have also been both influenced and supported by other members of the course team: not just its academic contributors, but also those from the editorial, design, and production areas of the university. There was also the highly skilled group who prepared the manuscript for electronic publishing, among them Molly Freeman, Maggie Tebbs, Pauline Turner, Betty Atkinson, Maureen Adams, and above all Dianne Cook, our calm and efficient course secretary throughout most of the production period. For advice and help on various points in this volume we would especially like to thank Janet Arnison (for her unstinting and enthusiastic help with information about the Arnison family), Jacqueline Eustace, Dr Barrie Trinder and Wendy Webster. For the series generally we are greatly indebted to four external critical readers who provided wonderfully detailed comments on successive drafts of the whole text: Brenda Collins, particularly for her informed advice on Ireland; Janet Few, both in her own right and as Education Officer of the Federation of Family History Societies; Dennis Mills, with his unparalleled command not only of the subject matter but of the needs of distance students; and Colin Rogers of the Metropolitan University, Manchester, for sharing the fruits of his long experience in teaching and furthering the study of family history. Finally, particular thanks go to our external assessor, Professor Paul Hair, for his constant challenges, queries and suggestions. Our advisors should not be held responsible for the shortcomings that remain, but without them these volumes would certainly have been both less accurate and less intelligible.

Our list of thanks is a long one and even so does not cover everyone. In our case its scope arises from the particular Open University form of production. But this extensive cooperation also, we think, represents the fruitful blend of individual interest and collaborative effort that is typical in the field of studying family and community history: a form of collaboration in which we hope we can now engage with you, our readers.

USING THIS BOOK

Activities

This volume is designed not just as a text to be read through but also as an active workbook. It is therefore punctuated by a series of activities, signalled by different formats. These include:

(a) *Short questions*: these provide the opportunity to stop and consider for a moment before reading on. They are separated from the surrounding text merely by being printed in colour.

(b) *Exercises*: these are activities to be carried out as part of working through the text, requiring anything from ten minutes to an hour to complete. Follow-up discussion comes either immediately after in the main text or (when so indicated in the exercise) in the separate comments and answers at the end of the book.

(c) *Questions for research*: these are suggestions for longer-term research projects to follow up selectively according to personal interest or opportunity *after* working through the relevant chapter(s). Note that although there are frequent references to 'your family', in practice any family (or set of families) in which you are interested will do equally well. In fact taking a family on which there are *locally* available records may be more practicable, as a first stage at least, than chasing the details of your own.

Schemas

These are lists of questions, factors or key theories which can help in formulating research, providing a kind of model or template against which research findings can be compared.

References

While this book is free-standing, there are cross-references to other volumes in the series which appear, for example, as 'see Volume 4, Chapter 6'. This is to aid readers using all the books.

The lists of books or articles at the end of each chapter follow the scholarly convention of giving details of all works cited; they are not intended as obligatory further reading. The asterisked items in these lists are useful starting points for those wishing to go further into the subject.

RUTH FINNEGAN
(Series editor)

INTRODUCTION

by John Golby

Volume 2 of this series looked at what we mean by community and how we go about investigating community history. It is true that community is by no means an easy concept to define, but one particularly helpful starting point has proved to be the indicators of community suggested by Dennis and Daniels in their article ' "Community" and the social geography of Victorian cities' (1981). They suggest that researchers into community and community history could usefully focus on the features of: residential stability; distance between residence and workplace; kinship and marriage links; and affiliation with local clubs, churches and other interest groups.

All of these have, to a greater or lesser extent, already been explored in the earlier volumes of this series. In this volume we pay special attention to the fourth feature, namely affiliation with local clubs, churches and other interest groups. The latter part of the volume, Chapters 6–9, concentrates in particular on local politics, religion and leisure activities. As well as providing some historical background and discussing recent research carried out in these areas, the aim of these chapters is to provide questions and suggest possible methods of approach that will enable you to carry out further research. Involvement in local politics, connections with local churches, and participation in leisure activities provide opportunities for people to meet together, worship together and play together, but politics, religion and oppostailing cultural values can also divide families and communities. Conflict as well as co-operation is an aspect which has to be investigated in any study of communities and families.

The second of Dennis and Daniels' indicators of community is distance between residence and workplace. This aspect was discussed in Volume 2, but the role played by work itself has only been touched on in passing. Yet work can provide an essential link between communities and families. Most families have to work and most do so, not in isolation, but among others who live within the locality. The first half of this volume is devoted to discussing ways in which an examination of work and occupations can help us understand the behaviour of families in communities. As with other local activities, work has the potential for establishing ties within the community, with men and women working together with a community of interests; but work can also give rise to divisions resulting from different occupations, standards of living and lifestyles.

One of the ways in which we explore work and occupations is through a series of case studies. The first set of studies looks at a particular family, a factory worker, and a policeman. The second set examines particular occupations and roles – domestic service, married women and work, and entrepreneurship and business enterprise. Clearly, we are unable to cover all the occupations and roles in which you may have a particular interest, but one of our aims is to offer exemplars for your own projects. In the process we show the wide range of sources that can be used to explore different occupations in both the nineteenth and twentieth centuries, and we focus on particular questions that can be asked of these sources. We also suggest a number of methods and approaches by which you can go about your research projects.

After the case studies we go on to look at a number of communities and the occupational structures and changes that occur within them. Finally, we investigate occupational hierarchies and consider why and how people rose or fell in the social scale. We do this by looking at some of the studies that have attempted to measure social mobility over the past one hundred and fifty years. In fact, a major theme of the volume is to make you aware of some of the theories and debates relating to work and community, so that you can set your local research projects in a wider context.

Much of this volume is devoted to examining the kinds of activities and organizations that were and are available to families in various localities and to investigating what part, if any, these activities play in linking families to communities. Consequently, you will find that many of the case studies concentrate on particular localities and come within the category of local history. Your own research is also likely to be concerned with some aspect of local studies and, if conducted properly, may result in an original contribution towards the study of your community.

A well researched local study can be of immense value, especially if attempts are made to compare the findings with similar but larger-scale or national projects. We have adopted this approach throughout this series. Volume 1 started off by looking at a single family but then moved on to studying families in general. In other words, we attempted to ask, 'Is our particular family typical or not, and if not why not?' In this volume we ask similar questions, for example in relation to work. Were the particular work patterns and other activities in one particular locality similar to others in the region or in the country as a whole? In what ways did they differ, and why? These questions are repeated time and time again in this volume; they are also the questions you must keep asking in the course of your own local research.

REFERENCE

Dennis, R. and Daniels, S. (1981) ' "Community" and the social geography of Victorian cities', *Urban History Yearbook*. Reprinted in Drake, M. (ed.) (1994) *Time, family and community: perspectives on family and community history,* Oxford, Blackwell in association with The Open University.

PART I

WORK AND OCCUPATIONS

CHAPTER 1

IDEAS AND DEBATES ON WORK

by John Golby

Let me start this chapter by posing a question.

Why should we devote so much time to 'work' in a volume on family and the community?

Nowadays, for the vast majority of people, work is something we do away from home and family. It often means we spend some 35 to 48 hours of our lives each week in a factory, workshop, office, shop, school or some other place of employment. Few people today have occupations that can be carried out entirely from the home. Nevertheless, although there is a spatial gap between the home and work, there are a number of good reasons why work needs to be discussed.

First, work provides a link between the family and the community. Most adult members of a family have to work in order to earn money to live, and very often the income from their work determines their lifestyle and, to some extent, as we shall see in Chapter 5 on social mobility, their position in a social hierarchy.

Second, work often influences demographic factors such as job mortality, age at marriage, seasonality of marriage, and levels of fertility. Work can also determine the location of the family home, so that migration and geographical mobility are often the result of families seeking work opportunities.

Third, from a historical viewpoint, work very often cannot be separated from the home. The idea that the workplace and home are almost inevitably distinct areas of activity is a comparatively recent one. Although there has been a trend towards a separation of workplace and home during the period of our studies, the 'domestic economy' cannot be ignored, for example in relation to married women and work, a subject we shall be looking at in some detail in Chapter 3, section 2 (see also Volume 1, Chapter 4).

Fourth, as I have mentioned in the introduction to this volume, we need to explore the extent to which work and the workplace impinge on the community as well as on the home. It is clear that different occupations and work regimes generate quite specific cultures and behaviour patterns, and we need to explore, for example, in what ways and why a nineteenth-century urban community which developed around a newly built mill or mine was different from a long-established rural community.

Fifth, there have been marked changes in attitudes to, and opportunities for, work during this period. There has been a shift from a situation where all members of a family contributed to its income, to a structure which depended primarily on one income, and then to the two-income family, with resulting changes in family power relationships and family household size and structure.

The aim, therefore, of Part I of this volume is to provide you with another dimension to your investigations into families and communities. After a brief discussion of the major changes in the distribution of the labour force since 1800, this chapter will focus on four particular aspects of the history of work. All these aspects relate work to family and community experiences, and they should, by referring to particular debates and raising a range of questions, provide you with a framework in which you can fit your own investigations. They also provide a background for the various case studies which appear in Chapters 2 and 3 and which, in turn, are intended as exemplars from which you can develop your own case study on work.

1   A BRIEF LOOK AT THE HISTORY OF WORK IN THE BRITISH ISLES

Before we begin to suggest the kinds of questions you might ask in your own studies, we need to look at the development of work in a national context and discuss the structural changes that have taken place in the distribution of the labour force in Britain since the start of the nineteenth century (see Joyce, 1990, pp.131–9). This will enable you to relate the experiences of the families and communities you are investigating to these changes and to see how the development in work patterns links in with other themes discussed in the series, such as urbanization, migration, social mobility and class structures.

―――――――――――――――――――――――― *EXERCISE 1.1* ――――――――――――――――――――――――

Take a close look at Table 1.1 and then try to answer the following questions:

1   What happened to those employed in agriculture, forestry and fishing during this period?

2   Which occupations showed a marked increase in numbers between 1851 and 1901?

3   Which occupations showed a noticeable decline in the twentieth century?

4   What criticisms would you make of this sort of statistical table?

Now read my comments below.

Table 1.1   Estimated industrial distribution of the British labour force, 1801-1951 (millions of persons)

	Agriculture, forestry, fishing	Mining and quarrying	Manufactures[1]	Building	Trade[2]	Transport	Public services and professional	Domestic and personal	Total occupied populations
1801	1.7		1.4		0.5		0.3	0.6	4.8
1811	1.8		1.7		0.6		0.4	0.7	5.5
1821	1.8		2.4		0.8		0.3	0.8	6.2
1831	1.8		3.0		0.9		0.3	0.9	7.2
1841	1.9	0.2	2.7	0.4	0.9	0.3	0.3	1.2	8.4
1851	2.1	0.4	3.2	0.5	1.0	0.5	0.5	1.3	9.7
1861	2.0	0.5	3.6	0.6	1.2	0.6	0.6	1.5	10.8
1871	1.8	0.6	3.9	0.8	1.6	0.7	0.7	1.8	12.0
1881	1.7	0.6	4.2	0.9	1.9	0.9	0.8	2.0	13.1
1891	1.6	0.8	4.8	0.9	2.3	1.1	1.0	2.3	14.7
1901	1.5	0.9	5.5	1.3	2.3	1.3	1.3	2.3	16.7
1911	1.6	1.2	6.2	1.2	2.5	1.5	1.5	2.6	18.6
1921	1.4	1.5	6.9	0.8	2.6	1.4	2.1	1.3	19.3
1931	1.3	1.2	7.2	1.1	3.3	1.4	2.3	1.6	21.1
1951	1.1	0.9	8.8	1.4	3.2	1.7	3.3	0.5	22.6

Source: Deane and Cole (1967) Table 31, p.143

[1] Manufactures 1801–1831 includes mining and quarrying, and building.

[2] Trade 1801–1831 includes transport.

1   Although numbers increased during the first half of the nineteenth century and did not fall below the 1801 level until 1891, the percentage of the total workforce associated with agriculture fell drastically from well over 1 in 3 of the working population in 1801 to under 1 in 10 in 1901 and under 1 in 20 by 1951. By 1971 this ratio had declined to 1 in 50.

2   All the other occupations listed show increases. However, if you compare each of them with the last column, which shows the total of those working, then you find that the *proportion* of those employed in manufactures did not increase markedly, while the major proportional increases were in mining, building, transport and public and professional services. The proportional increase in trade was smaller than in these other areas; nevertheless, there was a steady increase in the consumer market in the first part of the century, and this accelerated from the 1860s onwards with the development of large wholesalers, retail outlets and service industries. The growth of shops and the public sector provided new job opportunities for working women, although they were invariably paid lower wages than their male counterparts and they tended to remain in subordinate posts.

3   The numbers employed in domestic and personal service (which had increased proportionally in the nineteenth century) dropped markedly after the two world wars of 1914–18 and 1939–45. Between 1871 and 1901 approximately 1 in 7 of the working population was employed in domestic service (see Chapter 3, section 1), whereas by 1951 this had fallen to approximately 1 in 50. The mining and quarrying industries, after a considerable growth between 1881 and 1911, shrank in size after 1921. In fact, mining was not the only great staple industry that declined in the twentieth century. The column headed by the umbrella title 'manufactures' includes workers in other major industries such as shipbuilding and engineering; both of these grew rapidly in the second half of the nineteenth century but also declined after the First World War. The same is true of the textile industries. The areas of expansion were the new industries of motor vehicle manufacture, electrical goods and chemicals.

4   Although the statistics relate to Britain as a whole, the population of England in relation to Scotland, Ireland and Wales is of such a size that the tables tend to reflect what was happening in England to the detriment of the other countries. A discussion of the changes in the Scottish labour force, together with full statistics, can be found in Treble (1990); for Ireland see Daly (1981). Compare Table 1.2 below, which provides a percentage breakdown of the industrial structure of Ireland (male and female), with Table 1.1.

Table 1.2 Estimated industrial distribution of the labour force, Ireland 1841 and 1891, and England and Wales 1881

| | Ireland (%) | | England & Wales (%) |
	1841	1891	1881
Agriculture	51.3	44.4	16.6
Building	2.0	2.6	6.8
Manufacture	27.3	17.8	30.7
Transport	0.5	2.6	6.8
Dealing	2.6	5.4	7.8
Industrial service	1.2	6.6	6.7
Public service and professional	1.6	5.8	5.6
Domestic service	9.4	12.2	15.7
Others	4.1	2.6	4.4

Source: Daly (1981) p.104

A second criticism is that the headings are too broad: there is no information concerning particular occupations. However, as Raphael Samuel (1975, p.3) points out, it is extremely difficult to discover what an agricultural labourer actually did on the land during the course of the year, let alone what alternative sources of employment were open to him when not working on the land. The same goes for women employed in agriculture. Most often the census enumerators' books (CEBs) merely record 'field labour', but this hides a myriad of different work experiences. We need to remember too that unpaid voluntary work, which might in practice play a significant role within particular families and communities, does not appear in the figures. Furthermore, there is no break-down in the figures regarding occupation by gender. Again, these figures are available elsewhere. We know, for example, that of the 2.3 million employed in domestic and personal service in 1891, over 2 million were women and that this constituted over 40 per cent of the women who were gainfully employed in that year. Also, under the heading 'manufactures' approximately 50 per cent of those employed in cotton textile mills were women (although in the lower paid jobs). Finally, for women in general, it is not always easy to discover what paid work they undertook. It was often casual and very often went unrecorded in the CEBs (see the discussion in Chapter 3, section 2).

There are two further important structural changes in employment over this period that should be mentioned. First, there was a marked reduction in the number of married women in paid employment during the nineteenth century, a trend which was only reversed from the 1930s onwards (see Chapter 3, section 2). Second, attitudes changed towards the employment of children. In 1851 it was estimated that 28 per cent of children aged between 10 and 15 worked, but it is very likely that these figures underestimate the actual numbers, especially if casual or seasonal work is included. By the time of the 1911 census, when compulsory education was in force, the percentage of children in work had halved from that of 1851 (Hunt, 1981, pp.9–17).

The following points summarize this discussion of changes in the structure of employment in Britain since 1800:

o   There was a decline in the proportion of the population working in agriculture, although this was not so evident in Ireland as it was in England and Wales.

o   The early decades of the nineteenth century witnessed a marked shift towards mining and manufactures, much of which was centred around the cotton industry in the north-west of England and in Scotland.

o   In the second half of the nineteenth century this manufacturing base was widened with the mechanization of other textile industries and the growth in shipbuilding, engineering, transport and building.

o   The last quarter of the century witnessed the rapid development of a mass consumer market, with more people occupied in the food, drink and tobacco industries.

o   In this same period there was a growth in the numbers of people working in the public sector.

o   During the twentieth century, and especially in the years following the First World War, there was a decline in the old major staple industries, with many old, well-established firms collapsing, and a reduction in the numbers employed in domestic service.

o   At the same time there was a further growth in the public sector and in service industries as well as major developments in the metal, machinery, vehicle, electrical and chemical industries. These new industries provided job opportunities for many, including – especially after the Second World War – refugees from eastern Europe and immigrants from the Commonwealth. (For further discussion of the role of outsiders in the working community see Chapter 3, section 3.)

o   Finally – although this has not been mentioned in the discussion so far – as Britain was transformed from a primarily rural to an urban dominated country, so there were changes in working-class consciousness. There was a marked growth in the development of trade unionism from the 1880s, and by the early 1960s some ten million men and women were members of trade unions (Pelling, 1963, p.263).

Consider any examples of families you have investigated and ask yourself whether these generalizations fit in with their experiences. Does your own research echo these changes? If they do not, perhaps the next section will throw further light on your research.

2   FOUR ISSUES IN THE HISTORY OF WORK IN THE BRITISH ISLES

You will want, where possible, to link your own research to that of other researchers. The following discussion – based on that by Patrick Joyce (1990) – suggests some key issues to enable you to do so, and to link these continuing debates with the case studies in Chapters 2 and 3.

2.1   IRREGULARITY OF WORK AND MULTI-OCCUPATIONS

As we have already seen, an 1851 CEB which shows Joe Bloggs to be an 'agricultural labourer', while giving us a good idea of his position in the social hierarchy of the village or area in which he worked, does not necessarily tell us much about what Joe Bloggs actually did during the course of a year. For some parts of the year he may well have been unemployed, while for other periods he may have gone out of the area to seek work. Samuel (1975, p.4) cites the case of Suffolk, where many farm labourers travelled after harvest time to Burton-on-Trent to work in the 'maltings'.

Irregularity of work and diversity of occupations was not confined to rural areas in the nineteenth century. Many town trades were casual, and nearly all trades were subject to seasonal fluctuations and periods of over-production.

The evidence of irregularity of work, the wide variety of 'moonlighting' jobs, and changes in occupation, all in a sense call into question some of the ideas of the nineteenth century as being one of the growth of working-class solidarity, for as Joyce states, 'Occupational exclusiveness and concentration are integral to our understanding of the formation of "traditional" working-class culture and consciousness' (Joyce, 1990, p.147).

2.2   THE IMPORTANCE OF REGIONAL VARIATIONS

W.L. Burn (1964), writing of Britain in the mid nineteenth century, emphasized the vast differences in the quality of life and experiences of men and women working in different occupations in different parts of the country. He pointed out that the wages of an agricultural labourer in Dorset were meagre compared with those of a skilled worker in a factory in Lancashire. The labourer would also have found the daily diet of the factory worker 'sumptuous beyond his wildest dreams, although he would have been astonished at the punctuality required of him in the mills' (Burn, 1964, pp.96–7).

There was also great regional diversity within the same occupations. For example, during the nineteenth century the system of living-in – whereby the farm labourer was boarded by the farmer – survived longer in pastoral districts where there was a real shortage of labour than it did in the south and east of England, where outside labourers were paid weekly wages or by the task. Again, there were marked regional differences in agricultural earnings. Where alternative employment opportunities were plentiful, such as in Lancashire and the West Riding of Yorkshire, wages were higher than in parts of the south and south-west of England which were remote from industrial or large urban areas.

These are only a few examples of the sort of regional variations that existed in the nineteenth century. Much more local research is needed into nineteenth- and twentieth-century work and practices in order to provide a fuller picture of this particular aspect of the history of work.

2.3 THE CONTINUITY AND VITALITY OF SMALL-SCALE PRODUCTION UNITS

Joyce writes that, 'The industrial worlds of 1820 and 1920 were very different: in the latter, workplaces were bigger, machinery more prevalent and sophisticated, the direct wage form had spread widely, and these imperatives involved in turn a more direct managerial involvement in the execution and organisation of work' (Joyce, 1990, p.157). Nevertheless, it is easy to exaggerate the scale of industrial development in the nineteenth century. True, machinery and factories brought changes, but production units remained comparatively small. For example, even within the textile industry, between 1850 and 1890 the average number of people working in spinning mills rose only from 108 to 165, and in weaving mills from 100 to 188 (Joyce, 1990, p.158). The small workshop continued throughout the century and so, consequently, did the master–workman relationship.

As the size of workforces increased, so important structural changes occurred in the workplace. Generally speaking, the small employer or entrepreneur would have less of a division of labour within his workforce than the larger employer. Of course, the division of labour is primarily a device to improve the efficiency of production, but in the process of division the workforce tends to be divided into a series of hierarchies separated by skill or job and income (see the experience of Alfred Williams in Chapter 2, section 2). This separation was becoming increasingly apparent in the nineteenth century and has been a major aspect of industrial production in the twentieth century. Its effects on the family and community, as you will see in Chapter 5 on social mobility, have been far-reaching.

Figure 1.1 The composing room of the *Witney Gazette* in Oxfordshire, *c.*1900 (Source: Oxfordshire County Libraries, Local History Collection)

Figure 1.2 Employees at the Britannia Works, Banbury, Oxfordshire, *c.*1900. The largest firm in Banbury in the nineteenth century, this agricultural engineering business employed some 380 people in 1861 (Source: Oxfordshire County Libraries, Local History Collection)

2.4 THE DIFFERING EXPERIENCES OF WORK

In reviewing recent developments in research on work in this country, Joyce concludes that,

> *We now know much more than we did about work processes … something too about workplace life and its relation to life beyond work, but what may be termed the interior life of the workplace is still largely opaque to us, the everyday arrangements of production and the customs and attitudes shaped in work.*

(Joyce, 1990, p.172)

Historians and social scientists recognize the importance of investigating the various experiences of work and are asking questions such as: What was it like to work in a particular occupation? What exactly was involved? How was the day broken up? What were working conditions like? What were the varying attitudes towards work? What were the attitudes towards the foreman, factory boss, etc.? What time was there for other activities apart from work, and what were these activities? These qualitative questions are difficult to answer, but they are extremely important if we are to capture the *flavour* of what working life was like and if we are to explore the connections between work and the family and work and the community. True, it is difficult to investigate work experience, but there are sources available (e.g. letters, diaries, memoirs, literary and oral sources), some of which are used extensively in the case studies in Chapters 2 and 3.

EXERCISE 1.2

Much of what follows in this volume will, we hope, illustrate the methods and sources that can be used to respond to some of the problems that we have raised so far and shed further light on the links between work, communities and families. Before you go any further, try to compile a list of the questions you should be asking and the sources you could use when you start tracing the activities of families in particular communities.

Comments p.225

3   CONCLUSION

You should use the questions I raised in Exercise 1.2 as the basis for your study in relating work to the community and the family. Remember, nearly all of the questions relate to the four major themes outlined in section 2; these are summarized for easy reference in Schema A.

> *Schema A: Issues to investigate in the history of work*
>
> o   Irregularity of work and multi-occupations.
>
> o   Regional variations.
>
> o   The continuity and vitality of small-scale production units.
>
> o   The different experiences of work.

These various aspects of work will be referred to again in Chapters 2 and 3, which present a series of contrasting case studies on work using a wide variety of source material. The case studies are intended to test and amplify these themes and, at the same time, suggest areas of study which you can develop.

REFERENCES AND FURTHER READING

Note: suggestions for further reading are indicated by an asterisk.

Burn, W.L. (1964) *The age of equipoise: a study of the mid-Victorian generation*, London, Allen & Unwin.

Daly, M.E. (1981) *A social and economic history of Ireland since 1800*, Dublin, Dublin Educational Company.*

Deane, P. and Cole, W.A. (1967) *British economic growth 1688–1959: trends and structure*, Cambridge, Cambridge University Press.

Hunt, E. (1981) *British labour history 1815–1914*, London, Weidenfeld & Nicolson.

Joyce, P. (1990) 'Work', in Thompson, F.M.L. (ed.) (1990) *The Cambridge social history of Britain, 1750–1950*, vol.2, Cambridge, Cambridge University Press.*

Pelling, H. (1963) *A history of British trade unionism*, Harmondsworth, Penguin.

Samuel, R. (ed.) (1975) *Village life and labour*, London, Routledge and Kegan Paul.

Treble, J.H. (1990) 'The occupied labour force', in Fraser, W.H. and Morris, R.J. (eds) *People and society in Scotland*, vol. 2, Edinburgh, John Donald in association with the Economic and Social History Society of Scotland.*

CHAPTER 2

WORK CASE STUDIES: INDIVIDUAL EXAMPLES

Chapter 1 discussed four aspects of the history of work which are important to explore when pursuing your studies in family and community history: irregularity of work and multi-occupations; regional variations; the continuity and vitality of small-scale production units; and the differing experiences of work. In this chapter and in Chapter 3 we present a series of case studies which, we hope, will illustrate, test, and amplify these aspects of work.

The three case studies examined in this chapter all draw on different primary source materials. The first, a study of two branches of the Arnison family, uses all the sources familiar to a family historian in order to discover why one branch of the family became prosperous drapers while another branch ended up in Manchester taking a variety of poorly paid jobs. The second uses one particular qualitative source, a memoir, to build up a picture of the working life of Alfred Williams, a worker at the Great Western Railway works in Swindon. As well as describing his own experiences, Williams tells us a great deal about work traditions in the Swindon area and the wide variety of job interests and attitudes of the other men employed at the GWR works. The third study focuses more narrowly on one particular occupation, policing, and on one particular policeman, William Henry Cooper, PC 25. This study draws heavily, but not exclusively, on documents and records in police archives, but it also illustrates the ways in which we can use other occupational archives in the pursuance of our studies.

The aim of this chapter is not just to inform you about a particular family, factory or policeman. The major concern is to help you in your own researches, by showing the wide range of source materials available to you, exploring how best these sources can be used, and indicating the kinds of questions that can be asked in order to help you learn more about work and its relationship to the family and the community.

1 THE ARNISONS: DRIVER, DRAPER, FARMER, SOLDIER, RICH MAN, POOR MAN

by Monica Shelley

Although Nathan Arnison died over a hundred years ago, his name still dominates the market square from the draper's shop which he bought about 1830 and which enabled him to prosper as a well-to-do, well-established citizen of Penrith. The lives and deaths of his family were documented extensively in all manner of ways. However, not all the Arnisons left such tangible evidence of lives well spent in comfort and security. Another branch of the same Arnison family was a great deal less successful in material terms. This branch moved from farm to farm in Cumberland and Westmorland, eking out a living as agricultural labourers and eventually migrating into Manchester towards the end of the nineteenth century, taking casual work of whatever sort they could find. Both branches produced a varied mix of family members, ranging from pillars of their community to one or two who ended their days in ignominy. In each branch there happened to be a descendant who researched and documented their family history. This case study is described in some detail so as to illustrate its links to the wider themes of work raised in Chapter 1 and to raise questions which might have relevance for your own research.

Most people who collect information about their families find the heaping up of dry lists of births, marriages and deaths ultimately unsatisfying: they want to know more about their forefathers and -mothers and their everyday lives. They ask questions along the lines of: What were they like as people? Why did they behave the way they did? What kind of character traits might have been passed down? Why were some rich and some poor? Why did they do the work they did – did they have any choices? What part did work play in their lives? It is never going to be possible to answer all such questions, but we can know more about the people because as social animals they interacted with others and shared many of their characteristics. By drawing on sources from the periods in which they lived, which related to the livelihoods they were likely to have had, we can get closer to them. And by drawing on what scholars have already discovered and by using the strategies of research they have devised, we can relate our forebears' experience to comparative themes or debates, and set them in a wider framework.

This case study summarizes research along these lines carried out by family members into two branches of the Arnison family. It demonstrates differences in the kinds of evidence and resources that were drawn on to provide information about family members, the work they did, and the kinds of life they led. An attempt is also made to use the sources available to work out why one branch of the family prospered and the other laboured in poverty.

As you read through this case study, you will probably identify more possibilities for further research.

1.1   BACKGROUND

At the start of the nineteenth century, Cumberland was 'a region of unusually small farms and, by contrast, of a few unusually great landowners' (Marshall and Walton, 1981, p.ix). Agriculture was still its major industry, employing the largest single section of the employed population – almost a quarter in 1851 (see Table 2.1).

Other major occupations were domestic service, metal-related industries and the clothing and shoe industries, which by the beginning of the twentieth century gave way to coal mining. The area was also subject to a steady flow of out-migration over the years. By 1891 it was estimated that well over 100,000 people born in Cumbria were distributed over other counties of England and Wales (Marshall and Walton, 1981, p.269). In the period 1871–80, the Penrith area showed Cumberland's greatest net loss by out-migration of 3,180 persons, or 13.4 per cent of the total population at the beginning of the period (Marshall and Walton, p.78).

So where did the Arnisons come from, and how do they fit into the general background of their home county? All the Arnisons in Great Britain can be traced back to one man, George Arnison, whose marriage to Maria Brown was recorded in the Kirkoswald parish register in Cumberland for 1686. Kirkoswald is a small market town in East Cumberland, now Cumbria; it received its first market charter in 1201, some 20 years before Penrith, a dozen miles away to the south. The family stayed in the Kirkoswald area, farming there and in the nearby hamlets of Celah and High Haresceugh until it had grown to such an extent that by 1750 younger sons were forced to move away in search of work. So the Arnisons were reasonably typical of their fellow Cumbrians in that they worked in agriculture and moved away from their original home area. This case study concentrates on just two branches of the Arnison family: I shall call them the Manchester Arnisons and the Penrith Arnisons.

1.2   THE MANCHESTER ARNISONS

My starting point was just the family name and some meagre details of Joseph Arnison, who was known to have come from Cumberland and settled in Manchester, and the memories of several family members, including one ninety-six year old; there was also a photograph of Joseph Arnison (Figure 2.1). Building on the information from the International Genealogical Index

Table 2.1   Occupations of persons employed in the county of Cumberland, 1851, 1871, 1891 and 1911

	1851				1871				1891				1911			
	M	F	T	%[1]	M	F	T	%[1]	M	F	T	%[1]	M	F	T	%[1]
Food and drink	3116	940	4056	4.14	3387	1001	4388	4.18	3621	1678	5299	5.14	4332	2687	7019	6.72
Services	509	–	509	0.51	1303	28	1331	1.26	1369	251	1660	1.62	1718	445	2163	2.07
Shipbuilding	672	–	672	0.68	712	13	725	0.69	362	–	362	0.35	174	–	174	0.16
Building	4480	–	4480	4.57	5063	6	5069	4.83	5604	10	5614	5.45	5510	4	5514	5.27
Cloth manufacture	6028	9211	15239	15.56	2585	3488	6073	5.72	1719	1785	3504	3.40	1367	1986	3353	3.21
Clothes and shoes	4087	5064	9151	9.34	4240	4289	8529	8.13	3656	5080	8736	8.48	2898	4492	7390	7.07
Workers in metal																
Iron manufacture	216	–	216		2310	–	2310		4011	4	4015		3693	–	3693	–
Iron mining	369	–	369		3771	–	3771		4609	4	4613		4849	–	4849	
Blacksmiths	1298	–	1298	3.26	1387	–	1387	9.24	1486	1	1487	12.46	1238	–	1238	13.53
General workers in metals	747	–	747		868	–	868		744	68	812		371	–	371	
Engineers	235	18	253		1359	–	1359		1868	42	1912		3946	15	3961	
Horses and horse transport	852	27	879	0.89	1490	13	1503	1.43	2108	14	2129	2.06	2086	4	2090	2.00
Coal	3721	83	3804	3.88	5016	183	5199	4.95	7513	173	7686	7.45	9808	314	10122	9.69
Glass, pottery, chemicals	504	169	673	0.68	281	84	365	0.34	273	32	285	0.27	80	1	81	0.07
Sea and boatmen	1925	23	1948	1.98	1744	2	1746	1.66	1545	–	1545	1.50	543	1	544	0.52
Agriculture	18399	5227	23566	24.07	21673	2588	24261	23.12	13556	1251	14807	14.37	12710	819	13529	12.15
Government service	204	9	213	0.21	308	41	349	0.33	494	105	599	0.58	772	267	1039	0.99
Labourers (unclassified)	1964	158	2122	2.15	3578	280	3858	3.67	5972	64	6036	5.86	1851	–	1851	1.77
Lead mining	1840	–	1840	1.87	1082	–	1082	1.03	517	–	517	0.50	439	–	439	0.42
Teachers	456	478	934	0.95	419	650	1069	1.01	563	1252	1815	1.76	612	1536	2148	2.05
Domestic servants	6333	7330	13663	13.95	615	13631	14246	13.58	521	15410	15931	15.46	933	10701	11434	10.94
Railway service	877	–	877	0.89	3299	4	3303	3.14	4232	7	4239	4.16	4452	26	4478	4.28
Quarrymen	235	–	235	0.23	385	–	385	0.36	779	–	779	0.75	933	2	935	0.89
Wood and timber workers	1211	54	1265	1.29	550	12	562	0.53	503	5	508	0.49	635	15	650	0.52
Others occupied	3969	359	4328	10.39	5632	1448	7080	6.74			8117	5.03			17358	15.51
Total occupations			97921				102738				103007				104445	
Total population (all ages)			195492				220253				266549				265756	

Notes

[1] Percentage of all persons over ten years of age given as occupied.

There were numerous changes in classification of occupations during the period covered; for this reason, for example, general labourers diminished in numbers after 1891.

M = males.

F = females.

T = totals.

Source: Marshall and Walton (1981), based on occupational tables in the published census volumes

Figure 2.1   Joseph Arnison (1871–1924)

(IGI) and subsequent research in the Cumberland census for 1861, 1871 and 1881, details of Joseph Arnison's immediate family were gathered from the indexes at the General Register Office at St Catherine's House, and eventually Joseph's birth and marriage certificates were obtained.

The CEB entries from 1861, 1871 and 1881 provide a useful guide to where the Arnisons were in those years (see Table 2.2). Joseph was born several months after the census of 1871 on 4 October at Newbiggin Dacre, a couple of parishes away from Edenhall, where the Arnison family had been on census night (2 April). Note the typical discrepancy in the ages of John and Mary Arnison between the earlier censuses and that of 1881.

Table 2.2   Summary of entries relating to the Arnison family in the CEBs for Brownrigg, Lazonby West (1861); Edenhall, Penrith (1871); and Penrith (1881)

1861			
John Arnison	Head 38	Ag Lab	born Westmorland Bongate
Jane Arnison	Wife 25	Ag Lab Wife	born Westmorland Temple Sowerby
James Arnison	Son 4		born Cumberland Edenhall
Sarah Arnison	Daughter 2		born Westmorland Brougham

1871			
John Arnison	Head 48	Farm Lab	born Westmorland Bongate
Jane Arnison	Wife 37	Farm Lab's Wife	born Westmorland Temple Sowerby
James Arnison	Son 14	Scholar	born Cumberland Edenhall
Sarah Arnison	Daughter 12	Scholar	born Westmorland Brougham
Ellen Arnison	Daughter 10	Scholar	born Cumberland Plumpton
Mary Ann Arnison	Daughter 8	Scholar	born Westmorland Askham
John Arnison	Son 6	Farm Lab's Son	born Westmorland Askham
Thomas Arnison	Son 3	Farm Lab's Son	born Cumberland Catterlen

1881			
John Arnison	Head 55	Farm Lab	born Westmorland Bongate
Jane Arnison	Wife 47	Farm Lab's Wife	born Westmorland Temple Sowerby
Mary Arnison	Daughter 16	Dressmaker	born Westmorland Askham
Thomas Arnison	Son 13	Scholar	born Cumberland Catterlen
Joseph Arnison	Son 10	Scholar	born Cumberland Newbiggin
Elizabeth Arnison	Daughter 8	Scholar	born Cumberland Penrith

Source: Public Record Office, refs RG9/3905, RG10/5202 and RG11/5141

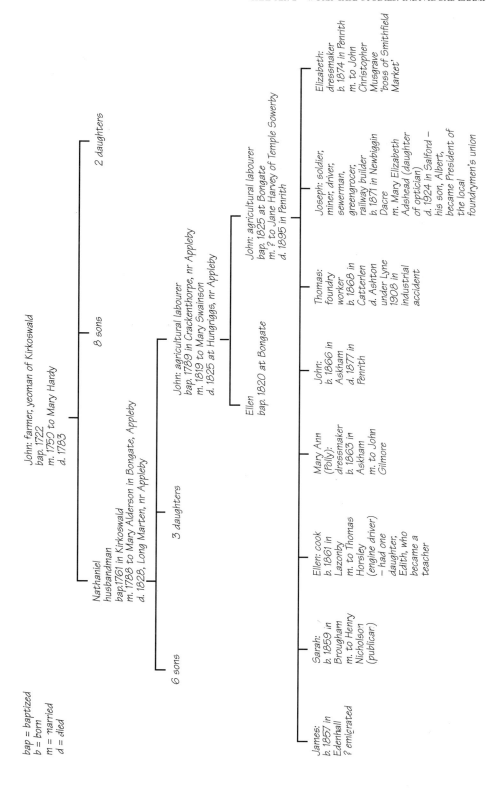

Figure 2.2 Family tree of the Manchester Arnisons

Of this generation of this branch of the Arnisons, Sarah, Mary Ann (known as Polly), Thomas, Joseph and Elizabeth all moved into the Manchester area, probably for mutual support. Only one, Ellen, stayed in Cumberland, marrying a train driver from Braithwaite called Thomas Horsley in 1889; her niece Edith remembers Ellen making occasional visits to Manchester. Nothing more is known of the eldest son, James, who may have emigrated to another country, since his death is not recorded at St Catherine's House. Their parents, John and Jane Arnison, remained in the Penrith area till their deaths.

How did the Manchester Arnisons support themselves? Most of the information here comes from Edith Seddon, born in 1896 and the eldest surviving child of Joseph Arnison. The information was recorded in 1992, when Edith was 96, and she had considerable and, apparently, sound recall of much of the past. Her youngest sister, Alice, born in 1914, also provided some information. Edith recalls that they all took jobs where and how they could, often for very short periods. She remembers that on different occasions her father worked as a sewerman, on the roads, as a greengrocer, on the railway and as a driver for the transport company Carter Patterson. A tremendous patriot, Joseph also served in the army, particularly during the 1914-18 war, when he went to France to help bury the dead bodies of soldiers. He eventually received an army pension, dying of cancer at the early age of 52. Records at the War Office and the Public Record Office at Kew should tell us more about his army career and that of his sons, James and Albert.

Of Joseph's brothers and sisters, Edith said that Sarah and her husband kept the Gaping Goose public house, where Joseph and Polly both worked part-time in the bar. Polly married John Gilmore in 1896 and worked as a dressmaker. Elizabeth, the youngest and also a dress-maker, married John Christopher Musgrave in 1904 – Musgrave was known to the family as Uncle Boss, because he was the boss of Smithfield market. The other Manchester Arnison, Thomas, was killed in an explosion in the foundry where he worked in Ashton under Lyne in 1908.

After working part-time serving and cleaning in a toffee shop, Edith herself left school at thirteen and a half: 'I went halftime as I knew how to work the machine, the treadle machine, so I had a job waiting for me when I left school. I left school on a Thursday and went to work on a Friday, with me dinner under me arm across the field.' As the eldest daughter in a large family (Joseph and his wife had thirteen children, of whom six survived into adult life) Edith was kept at home to mind the children for at least half of most days; even after she started work she recalls her father coming to fetch her away from a job opposite Piccadilly Station to come home and look after the younger children.

Edith's mother ran a tripe shop – she cooked tripe dishes, and meat and potato pie in a big dish – where Edith had to serve on Saturday nights. When Edith had two young children, she continued to work, paying her mother to mind the babies. The money this provided to support the Arnison family – by this time her father had been in hospital for some time during his final illness – was so essential that when Edith's employer failed to pay her wages, she had to go to the local money-lender to borrow thirty shillings to pay her mother; for this, she had to repay him three pounds.

Edith claimed in all her recollections that there was nothing unusual about her circumstances. Every family she knew in Manchester was the same. Jobs were mostly of very short duration, and in the garment trade, where she mainly worked, it was very seasonal. The whole family had to be prepared to take on a wide variety of occupations and to help each other.

EXERCISE 2.1

Which aspect of the history of work highlighted in Chapter 1, section 3, is illuminated in the work histories of the Manchester Arnisons?

Answer/comments p.225.

Eventually, and over a period of some years, a reasonable amount of information had been built up from a variety of sources which fleshed out the basic history of this branch of the family. But what about the rest of the family?

1.3   BACK TO KIRKOSWALD

Halfway through my research I had a stroke of luck which made the rest of the research a lot easier and more enjoyable. I got in touch with a fellow Arnison researcher, Janet Arnison, from Penrith. Janet, I discovered, had collected Arnison data, records, memorabilia, photographs, press cuttings, legal documents, copies of wills and actual wills, business records, letters and visiting cards. Besides researching the whole family back to its earliest recorded appearance in Kirkoswald in 1686, Janet had made a particular study of the branch, headed by Nathan Arnison, which settled in Penrith. She is married to a local solicitor, a direct descendant of Nathan Arnison, and has access to all the legal documents that have accumulated over the years. Because the Arnison name is so prominently displayed on the draper's shop in Penrith, people who have a connection with the family naturally gravitate to the shop and are put in touch with Janet.

Figure 2.3   N. Arnison and Sons' draper's shop has dominated the Market Square in Penrith for over 150 years

Together, Janet and I were able to fill in the missing links of the Arnison family tree, showing how the Manchester Arnisons were descended from the main body of the family in Kirkoswald. By research in parish registers, wills, buildings owned by the Arnisons, manor court records, monumental inscriptions, obituaries and miscellaneous family papers, Janet had been able to build up a picture of a reasonably prosperous farming family owning land at High Haresceugh and Celah near Kirkoswald. The property was passed down in most cases to the eldest son, leaving the younger brothers to move away and make their living elsewhere in Cumberland and Westmorland.

In the case of the branch which produced the Manchester Arnisons, Nathan was born in 1761 in Kirkoswald, had moved to Appleby and married there in 1788 (see the family tree in

Figure 2.2). He was not named in the will of his father, John Arnison, though all eight of his brothers and his two sisters were. In his turn, Nathan produced a family of 10 children; he left no will. On his death at the age of 70 in 1828, Nathan was described as a husbandman. The major part of John Arnison's will reads as follows:

First I give and bequeath to my son John the New house that stands at the East end of this house and the loft that is over the same but not to possess and enjoy the same until he is thirty years of age unless he marries and has a needful occasion for the same. Also I give and bequeath to my daughter Ann the sum of thirty pounds but not to be paid till she is thirty years of age. Also I give and bequeath to my son Thomas the sum of thirty pounds but not to be paid him till he is thirty years of age unless he goes to be an apprentice and has a needful occasion for some of it. Also I give and bequeath to my son Christopher the sum of thirty pounds but not to be paid him till he is thirty years of age unless he is made a scholar and then he is to have it as he stands need. Also I give and bequeath to my son William the sum of thirty pounds but not to be paid him till he is thirty years of age. Also I give and bequeath to my daughter Hannah the sum of thirty pounds but not to be paid her till she is thirty years of age. Also I give and bequeath to my son Samuel the sum of thirty pounds but not to be paid him till he is thirty years of age. Also I give and bequeath to my son Isaac the sum of thirty pounds but not to be paid him till he is thirty years of age unless he is made a scholar and then to have it as he stands in need of it. Also I give and bequeath to my son Joseph the sum of thirty pounds but not to be paid him till he is thirty years of age and lastly it is my will and pleasure that if any of the above dye before they have received their fortunes it is to be divided equally amongst them. Also I give and bequeath to my beloved wife and my son George all the rest of my worldly goods and effects whatsoever whom I appoint the executors of this my last will and testament.
John Arnison (his mark) August 2 1780

Nathan's son John, born in Appleby in 1798, married in 1819 and had two children before he died in 1824, aged 26. One of these children, another John born in the year of his father's death, was the John Arnison listed in the censuses shown in Table 2.2, the father of Joseph who settled in Manchester. Left a young widow, John's mother had an illegitimate baby, eventually marrying the father in 1832. Although no records have yet been uncovered which illuminate John Arnison's early years – no record of his marriage has been found – it seems likely that his family circumstances forced him to make an early start on his adult life as an itinerant agricultural labourer.

What factors could be identified as contributing to the poverty of this branch of the Arnisons?

The factors that I have identified are as follows:

o   Nathan was the only child omitted from his father's will, which meant that he didn't benefit, as did the others, from the 'fortune' of thirty pounds. Although he might have received the money before his father's death, it is perhaps more likely that there had been some kind of family falling out which led to Nathan's exclusion. John's father, George, who had died in 1759, had left a will which divided his property equally between his only son, John, and his two married daughters. While it would be unwise to draw conclusions from the wording of John's will, it does have a very directive and dictatorial air.

o   Nathan had a large family; this was fairly typical of Cumberland and Westmorland, where there was a high birth rate and low crude mortality. It did mean, however, that he had a great many children to support on an agricultural labourer's wage.

o   Nathan's son, John, died very young, leaving his widow with two small children. Parish records tell us that she eventually married again, and had more children. Children of the first marriage might have come off second best.

o   Life for itinerant agricultural labourers was hard, which was presumably why so many of them migrated to the cities such as Liverpool and Manchester, and to other countries. As Marshall and Walton say (1981, p.68), Cumbria's own agricultural institutions and farming practices, far from 'tying the labourer to the soil, tended of their very nature to make him footloose'.

So far I have concentrated on the Manchester Arnisons and their history. What about their more well-to-do distant cousins, the Penrith Arnisons?

1.4   NATHAN ARNISON – THE MAN WHO LEFT HIS MARK ON PENRITH

Like his namesake, the Nathan who went to Appleby, the linen draper Nathan Arnison was a younger son. He was born in 1795. His father, one of the many Georges in the Arnison family, had been born in 1744 and lived all his life at High Haresceugh, a tiny hamlet where he farmed and ran the Horse's Head inn. The Horse's Head was the home of a Friendly Society, formed for the benefit and edification of its members, who were expected to conform to a set of severe rules. Although George died intestate, his older son, yet another George, never married and so Nathan eventually inherited the family land at High Haresceugh.

According to his obituary in the local Penrith paper, Nathan, who had been educated at the local school, moved down to Penrith, a dozen or so miles to the south of Kirkoswald, and learned the drapery business at Mr James's shop in Devonshire Street. In 1827 Nathan married Ruth Burra, from a yeoman family, who eventually inherited money and property. He set up on his own account in 1828, with a partner from Manchester. In 1831 Nathan bought the shop in the Market Square which still bears his name. He died in 1886, having fathered a large, successful family, invested in land in the town which benefitted at this time from the building of the railway, and had built for himself an imposing house in Lowther Street. His family tree appears as Figure 2.4.

Two of Nathan's sons became solicitors, setting up their business originally in the back room of the draper's shop in the Market Square. Another founded a further Arnison shop in Sheffield, where one of his sons became the mayor of Sheffield. Another son worked in the Penrith shop (and his descendant is the current owner). One daughter married a businessman from Salford and the other remained unmarried, living on in the mansion in Lowther Street. William Burra Arnison, the elder of the two solicitor sons and well known in the area as Clerk to the Guardians of the Penrith Union and Superintendent Registrar of Births, Deaths and Marriages, obtained a grant of arms. The motto is *Ditat servata fides* ('Keeping faith enriches').

A brief study of the Penrith Arnisons' family tree gives plenty of clues as to how Nathan and his family became prosperous:

o   Nathan was in line to inherit the family property, as his older brother never married. Although he was well established by the time it came down to him after his brother's death, he would have known he had expectations.

o   He married well, as did several of his children.

o   As his obituary makes clear, he was a hard worker and willing to take risks; he entered into business deals which profited him in the long run.

o   Nathan bought land and property in Penrith at a time when improved communications (the Lancaster–Carlisle railway reached Penrith in 1846) meant that goods and people, including tourists, could reach Cumberland more easily than before.

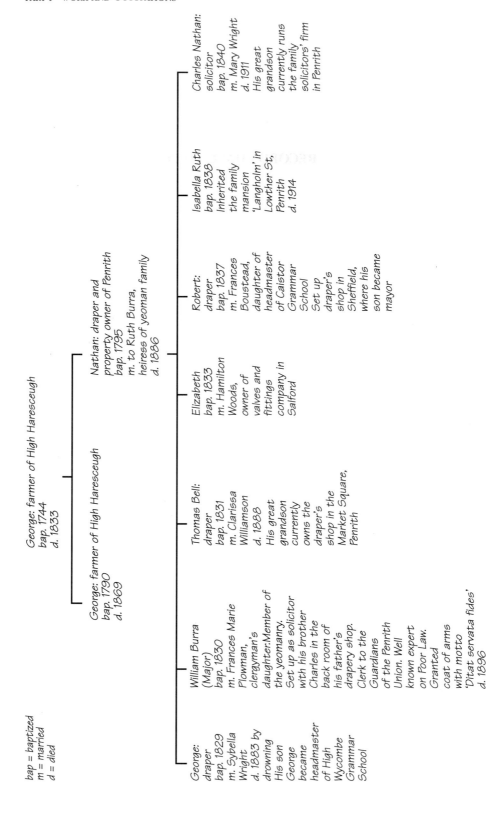

Figure 2.4 Family tree of the Penrith Amisons

This is a fairly general family history, typical of those built up by many researchers. Which particular aspects of the early history of the Manchester and Penrith Arnisons do you think could be developed by means of further research and applied to, or compared with, the experiences of other families?

Comments p.225.

1.5   WHAT RECORDS HAVE THEY LEFT?

The Penrith Arnisons and their lives are amply documented in both public and private records. Sources such as obituaries even give some idea of their nature and behaviour (William Burra Arnison's obituary from the local newspaper indicates that his manner was not particularly pleasant). Letters that have been preserved give further insights into their lives (Nathan's eldest son George, who drowned in the river Petteril on the 21 January 1883 after visits to several public houses, appeared to have had a drink problem, referred to in family letters as 'George's unfortunate habit').

The Manchester Arnisons, on the other hand, have left comparatively few written records behind them. Generally illiterate till the effects of Forster's Education Act of 1870 made themselves felt, their memorial is in public records and fragments of family history passed down from one generation to another. The reminiscences of Joseph Arnison's daughters Edith and Alice provide a unique and lively record, containing both information and subjective assessments. Joseph Arnison's grandson, journalist Jim Arnison, has published an autobiographical work, *Decades* (1991), in which he recounts stories about his grandfather told to him by his father.

Most families can draw on records on some kind – local newspapers can provide particularly valuable clues, even for those not particularly well documented elsewhere.

Which experiential, or personal, aspects of work – the kind you don't find in statistics – did you pick out from these accounts of the Arnisons' working lives? And which were the most useful sources for this evidence?

Comments p.226.

1.6   IN CONCLUSION

Collecting all these facts and reminiscences, newspaper reports and information from public records, letters and legal documents has certainly added to our knowledge of the Arnison family and their working and private lives. As so many family history researchers have found, the actual process of collection is enjoyable: getting in touch with other family members, recording memories of the past, following a unique and individual line of research, has a pleasure all its own.

Much of what has been discovered relates not to major world events, but to the everyday life of Cumbrians, later Mancunians, at various stages in their history. Their work, the way the Arnisons conducted their family lives, their behaviour, their standards, are all part of our family lives as they are today. This Arnison research has enabled us to put the present-day Arnison family into context, to have some better idea of where we have come from, so as to balance the present and offer a context for the future.

The family history research outlined in this case study was undertaken over a number of years (albeit not full-time!) and by two people, drawing on different kinds of records. We are not suggesting that you use this case study as a model for your own research, but rather that you use it to give you ideas about how you might develop your own family or local history research, and what records you might draw on. Take one of the families or places you are currently researching and note down any new approaches or sources that have been suggested by the Arnisons, based on the answers to the exercises.

2   ALFRED WILLIAMS, RAILWAY FACTORY WORKER

by John Golby

In order to build up her history of the Arnison family, Monica Shelley drew upon a wide variety of sources, one of which was a book of family reminiscences, *Decades*, written by a present-day member of the Arnison family. This sort of personal, qualitative evidence has to be used with care. Nevertheless, the genre of autobiography, memoirs and reminiscences is extremely important for the family and community historian.

More detailed references are made to autobiographies and memoirs in Volume 4, Chapter 4, section 8, but it is worth mentioning here that recent research (Burnett, Vincent and Mayall, 1984, 1987, 1989) has revealed that there are more autobiographies and memoirs in existence, written by working men and women, than was believed only a few years ago. Over 1,800 autobiographies and memoirs, written between 1790 and 1945, have now been recorded, and doubtless there are more yet to be discovered. Autobiographies, memoirs and reminiscences can give us important insights into working life in the past. They can put meat on the stark information obtained from sources such as census enumerators' books (CEBs) and birth and marriage certificates. They can help us to explore what work experiences and conditions were like – what was involved in particular occupations and what were the attitudes of individuals to work. The aim of this section is to look in some detail at one qualitative source and see what sort of useful information we can get from it, whilst at the same time pointing out the problems of using such a source.

2.1   LIFE IN A RAILWAY FACTORY

The source we are examining is a memoir, a book, *Life in a railway factory,* written by Alfred Williams and first published in 1915. The factory he writes about is the Great Western Railway (GWR) works at Swindon, which in 1915 employed over 10,000 men. It was here that the rolling stock of the GWR was built, maintained and repaired. Swindon itself had grown enormously, largely as a result of its close links with the GWR and the railways, and by 1911 the population of the town was around 50,000.

Alfred Williams was born in 1877 at South Marston in Wiltshire, a village situated a few miles from Swindon. He attended a local school on a fairly sporadic basis and left at the age of 11 to work on local farms. At the age of 15 he followed in the footsteps of his two brothers and entered the Great Western Railway works at Swindon. He started as a rivet-hotter, became a furnace boy and then at the age of 26 worked as a hammerman. He became chargeman of his gang at the age of 30. Altogether he worked for 22 years at the Swindon works. He left in 1914 to become a market gardener.

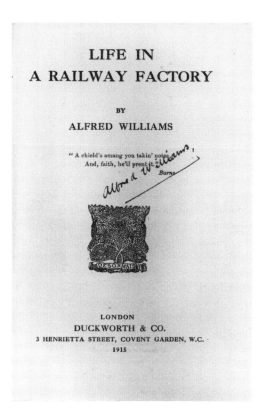

Figure 2.5   Frontispiece of the first edition of *Life in a railway factory*, with Alfred Williams's signature (Source: Rural History Centre, University of Reading)

Williams could not be regarded as a typical factory worker. He showed a great interest in the local folklore of Wiltshire, wrote poetry, taught himself Latin and Greek, and before writing *Life in a railway factory* he had already published two other books, *Round about the Upper Thames* (1912) and *Villages of the White Horse* (1913).

_____ **EXERCISE 2.4** _____

Read the following extracts from Williams (1915) and write down what you learn about the place of the GWR factory in the lives of the men working there. What sort of information do you find untrustworthy?

Comments p.226.

At an early hour the whole neighbourhood within a radius of five or six miles of the factory is astir; there is a general preparation for the coming day's work. The activity will first begin in the villages furthest from the town. Soon after four o'clock, in the quiet hamlets amidst the woods and lanes, the workmen will leave their beds and get ready for the long tramp to the shed, or to the nearest station touched by the trains proceeding to the railway town. Many of the younger men have bicycles and will pedal their way to work. They will not be forced to rise quite as early as the rest, unless they live at a very great distance. A few workmen I know have, for the past twenty years, resided at not less than twelve miles from the town and have made the journey all through the year, wet and dry together. The only time at which they cannot get backwards and forwards is when there are deep floods, or after a heavy snowstorm. Then, if the fall has been severe and the water or snow lies to any depth on the roads, they will be compelled to walk or to lodge in the town. Sometimes the fall of snow has taken place in the night and the workman, under these circumstances, will be forced to take a holiday until it melts and he is able to journey along the road again.

I have heard many accounts, from workmen who had long distances to walk to the factory, of the great and terrible blizzard of 1881, when the drifts in many places along the highways were from sixteen to twenty feet deep. One sturdy fellow took great pride in relating how he made the journeys daily – of six miles each way – during the whole time the snow lay on the ground, though many were frozen to death in the locality …

Very often, in the remote villages, where there is no access to the stations at which the factory trains call, a party of workmen club together and hire a conveyance to bring them daily to the town; or they may subscribe the money and buy a horse and cart and contribute equally towards the expense of keeping them. An arrangement is made with the proprietor of a public-house in the town. The horse is stabled and the vehicle stored for a small sum, and the men ride backwards and forwards, comfortable and independent. It was the custom, years ago, during haymaking and harvest-time, for farmers to come in with conveyances from the out-lying villages and meet the men and drive them home. They went straight from the factory to the farmyard or hayfield, and, after a hearty tea in the open air, or a square meal of bread, cheese and ale, turned in and helped the farmer, both enjoying the change of work and earning a couple of shillings a night as additional wages. This practice was very popular with the factory men, who never ceased to talk about it to their town mates in the shed and rouse them to envy with the frequent narration. Of late years, however, the custom has died out. Labour is too cheap and machinery too plentiful for the farmer to have any difficulty in getting his crops together nowadays.

The majority of the villagers, though compelled to leave home for the town at such an early hour, will yet rise in time to partake of a light breakfast before starting for the shed. The country mothers are far more painstaking in the matter of providing meals than are many of those in the town; they think nothing of rising at four a.m. in order to boil the kettle and cook food for their husbands and sons. Though the goodman may protest against it and declare that he would rather go without the food than give his wife so much trouble, it makes no difference …

Very often the village resident will work for an hour in his garden or attend to his pigs and domestic animals before leaving for the railway shed. If the neighbouring farmer is busy, or happens to be a man short, he may help him milk his cows or do a little mowing with the scythe and still be fresh for his work in the factory. I have known those who, during the summer months, went regularly to fishing in the big brook, or practised a little amateur poaching with the ferrets, and never missed going to gather mushrooms in the early mornings during autumn …

By five o'clock the people of the inner circle of the radius without the town are well awake, and twenty minutes later the dreaded hooter bellows out, like the knell of doom to a great many. The sound travels to a great distance, echoing and re-echoing along the hills and up the valley seventeen or twenty miles away, if the wind is setting in that direction. This is the first warning signal to the workman to bestir himself, if he has not already done so …

At ten minutes to six the hooter sounds a second time, then again at five minutes, and finally at six o'clock. This time it makes a double report, in order that the men may be sure that it is the last hooter. Five minutes' grace – from six till six-five – is allowed in the morning; after that everyone except clerks must lose time. As soon as the ten-minutes hooter sounds the men come teeming out of the various parts of the town in great numbers, and by five minutes to six the streets leading to the entrances are packed with a dense crowd of men and boys, old and young, bearded and beardless, some firm and upright, others bent and stooping, pale and haggard-looking, all off to the same daily toil and fully intent on the labour before them. It is a mystery where they all come from. Ten thousand workmen! They are like an army pressing forward to battle ...

A great many of the crowd bring their breakfast and dinner with them, either to eat it in the shed, or in the mess-rooms provided for the purpose. Some of the men carry it in a canteen, held under the arm or slung with a string over the shoulder and back. Others bring it tied up in red handkerchiefs, and very many, especially of the town dwellers, wrap it up in old newspapers. The country workmen are more particular over their food than are their mates of the town. Though their fare will be plainer and simpler – seldom amounting to anything more tasty than bread and butter, cheese or cold boiled bacon – they will be at great pains to see that it is very fresh and clean.

(Williams, 1915; extract from 1969 edn, pp.120–8)

In Chapter 1, section 3, I picked out four important aspects of work which you could explore when pursuing your studies. In what ways does this short extract from Williams shed light on these four aspects?

I identified the following points:

o   Multi-occupations: Williams mentions some of the men from the GWR works helping out with haymaking and harvesting, but that the practice was dying out around Swindon by 1914.

o   Regional variations: some of the railway workers living outside Swindon kept chickens, pigs and cows. Was this the case for industrial workers in other parts of the country at this time?

o   Continuity of small-scale production units: there is no evidence of this in the extract. Indeed, the GWR works were massive by the standards of 1900, and much of the life within and around the town of Swindon was dominated by the railway works.

o   The differing experiences of work: although the bulk of Williams's book deals with the working conditions in different workshops within the GWR works, there is not much on this aspect in the short extract presented here, although he does draw some interesting comparisons between the workmen living in the town and those living in the surrounding villages.

_____ *EXERCISE 2.5* _____

Now read the two further short extracts from Williams's book below, and then look at Table 2.3. What do we learn about (a) work practices, (b) industrial relations and (c) class divisions among the workforce?

Comments p.227.

Great consternation fell upon the carriage finishers, painters, and pattern-makers, several years ago, when it became known that piece rates were to be substituted for the old day-work system, especially as the change was to be introduced at a very slack time. It was looked upon as a catastrophe by the workmen, and such it very nearly proved to be. Many journeymen were discharged, some were transferred to other grades of work – that is, those who were willing to suffer reduction rather than to be thrown quite out of employment – and the whole department was put on short time, working only two or three days a week, while some of the men were shut out for weeks at a stretch. Several who protested against the change were dismissed, and others – workmen of the highest skill and of long connection with the company – had their wages mercilessly cut down for daring to interpose their opinion. The pace was forced and quickened by degrees to the uttermost and then the new prices were fixed, the managers themselves attending and timing operations and supervising the prices. Feeling among the workmen ran high, but there was no help for the situation and it had to be accepted. Few of the men belonged to a trade union, or they might have opposed the terms and made a better bargain; as it was they were completely at the mercy of the managers and foremen.

The carriage finishers and upholsterers are a class in themselves, differing, by the very nature of their craft, from all others at the factory. As great care and cleanliness are required for their work, they are expected to be spruce and clean in their dress and appearance. This, together with the fact that the finisher may have served an apprenticeship in a high-class establishment and one far more genteel than a railway department can hope to be, tends to create in him a sense of refinement higher than is usually found in those who follow rougher and more laborious occupations. His cloth suit, linen collar, spotless white apron, clean shaven face, hair carefully combed, and bowler hat are subjects of comment by the grimy toilers of other sheds. His dwelling is situated in the cleanest part of the town and corresponds with his personal appearance …

Transfers from one shop to another are seldom made, and never from department to department. One would think that the various divisions of the works were owned by separate firms, or people of different nationalities, such formidable barriers appear to exist between them.

The chiefs of the departments are usually more or less rivals and are often at loggerheads, each one trying to outdo the other in some particular direction and to bring himself into the notice of the directors. The same, with a little modification, may be said of the foremen of the several divisions, while the workmen are about indifferent in this respect. For them, all beyond their own sheds, except a few personal friends or relations, are total strangers. Though they may have been employed at the works for half a century, they have never gone beyond the boundary of their own department, and perhaps not as far as that, for trespassing from shed to shed is strictly forbidden and sharply punished where detected. Thus, the workman's sphere is very narrow and limited. There is no freedom; nothing but the same coming and going, the still monotonous journey to and fro and the old hours, month after month, and year after year. It is no wonder that the factory workmen come to lead a dull existence and to lose interest in all life beyond their own smoky walls and dwellings. It would be a matter for surprise if the reverse condition prevailed.

(Williams, 1915; extract from 1969 edn, pp.38–43)

The fitters are usually looked upon as the men *par excellence* of the shed …

The majority of the fitters are members of Trades Unions, and of all other classes at the works, perhaps, they take the greatest pains to protect themselves and their interests. By contributing to the funds of their organisations they are insured against accidents, strikes, or dismissal, and are thus placed in a position of considerable independence. They are required to serve an apprenticeship of five or seven years' duration before they are recognised as journeymen and they are, by a common rule, compelled to go further afield in order to obtain the standard rate of wages. Nearly all the foremen of the different sheds are appointed from among the fitters; whatever qualities an outsider may discover he stands but little chance of being preferred for the post.

(Williams, 1915; extract from 1969 edn, pp.102–3)

Is there any evidence, from letters, diaries, memoirs or newspaper articles, of what working conditions were like in the factories or workshops in which members of your family or community worked? (For further comment on these sources see Volume 4, Chapter 4.)

Is there evidence of class differences and hierarchies within the workplaces you are studying? (For further comments on this aspect see Chapter 5 of this volume.)

What were industrial relations like in the industries within your community or in one particular industry? Were there any major disputes? Are they recorded in local newspapers? In what ways did the disputes affect feeling within the town? To what extent were the workers unionized in the factories and works within your area?

Williams shows how the town of Swindon was dominated by the GWR works. Is this true to the same extent of other railway towns – Crewe, York and Wolverton (see Kitchen, 1993)? Was the town you are studying dominated by one company? Is there evidence from CEBs, directories and newspapers of the continuation and vitality of small-scale production units?

2.2   CONCLUSION

What wider issues does this case study recall?

If we return to the four aspects of the history of work discussed in Chapter 1, namely irregularity of work and multi-occupations, the importance of regional variations, the continuity of small-scale production units and the differing experiences of work, we can see how the extracts from Williams's book can contribute towards these issues.

With reference to irregularity of work and multi-occupations, Williams reveals that short-time work was taking place in some sections of the GWR works, while other sheds might be working full-time. Therefore at a time when some workers at the factory were earning quite good wages, others could well be suffering hardships. We must also remember that the average wages as detailed in Table 2.3 are only rough indicators of the income coming into any family. There will be bad and good weeks as well as periods of unemployment.

Table 2.3   Table of average day wages per 54-hour week paid to men employed at Swindon Railway Works, July 1914

Foremen	70s	Coppersmiths	30s
Foremen, Assistant	50s	Tinsmiths	30s
Draughtsmen	35s	Moulders	26s
Clerks, Monthly Staff	30s	Wheel Turners	24s
Clerks, Shop	25s	Machinemen, General	24s
Forgemen	33s	Carriage Body-makers	30s
Smiths	33s	Carriage Finishers	28s
Rolling Mills Men	30s	Waggon-builders	28s
Furnacemen	28s	Road-Waggon Builders	28s
Stampers	28s	Carpenters	28s
Stampers' Assistants	22s	Painters	26s
Smiths' Strikers	22s	Saw Mills, Timber	24s
Pattern-makers	35s	Riveters	26s
Boilermakers	34s	Bricklayers	28s
Fitters and Turners	34s	Labourers, Skilled	22s
Fitters, Engine	34s	Labourers, Unskilled	20s
Fitters, Carriage	28s	Labourers, Fitters'	21s
Die-sinkers	34s	Storekeepers	23s

Source: Williams (1915); table from 1969 edn, p.309

Figure 2.6   Alfred Williams, hammerman, at the Great Western
Railway Works (Source: Swindon Museum and Art Gallery)

In the extracts, there is no mention of 'moonlighting', other than occasional agricultural work, and this too seems to have largely died out by 1915.

The problem of regional variations is relevant when looking at Swindon. Swindon was a railway town and the economy of the town was dependent on the GWR and the railway factory.

The GWR works was one of the largest in the country. The information concerning the divisions of labour and the series of hierarchies within the workforce separated by skills and income, is one of the most interesting aspects of Williams's book.

Finally, with regard to the differing experiences of work, Williams gives clear accounts of the various shops in the GWR works. He describes the noise, duties and machinery well. Indeed, he gives many examples of the differing work experiences of the men within the works as well as referring to the works in relation to the workers' homes and life within their communities.

As we have seen, not all Williams's statements can be accepted without qualification. Qualitative sources do have to be handled with care. Nevertheless, as you develop your research it may be necessary at some stage to use the wide range of qualitative sources available to you. If used properly these sources should highlight the experiential nature and complexities of people's lives, and in so doing have the potential to enable us to come closer to understanding and answering the sorts of questions we raised at the start of this section.

3   POLICE CONSTABLE 25

by Clive Emsley

Alfred Williams, as well as describing his own work, gave a vivid account of the varying experiences and skills of workmen in the many workshops existing at the GWR works in Swindon. In this section we focus more narrowly on one particular occupation – that of policing. As well as using sources with which you are now familiar, i.e. memoirs and oral interviews, we are going to explore (a) what other sources are available for those interested in pursuing their researches into this particular occupation (or, by extension, into other comparable occupations), (b) the kinds of questions which can be asked of the primary source materials and the sort of information that can be gathered from these sources, and (c) what light these sources throw, in particular, on our understanding of the occupation of policing and its relationship to the community.

3.1   POLICE AND THE COMMUNITY: SOME QUESTIONS

As you are probably aware, the issue of the police officer's relationship with the community in which he or she lives and works can today excite much debate.

_____ *EXERCISE 2.6* _____

What do the following extracts tell you about community attitudes to the police in the past? My comments follow immediately after the extracts.

The one constable stationed at Candleford Green had plenty of leisure in which to keep his garden up to the standard which ensured him his customary double-first at the annual Flower Show for the best all-round collection of vegetables and the best-kept cottage garden. After the bicycle came into general use, he occasionally hauled up before the Bench some unfortunate who had exceeded the speed limit, or had been found riding lampless after lighting-up time; but, still, for three hundred days of the year his official duties consisted of walking stiffly in uniform round the green at certain hours by day and taking gentle walks by night to meet his colleague on point duty.

Though not without a sense of the dignity due to his official position, he was a kindly and good-tempered man; yet nobody seemed to like him, and he and his wife led a somewhat isolated life, in the village but not entirely of the village. Law-abiding as most country people were in those days, and few as were those who had any personal reasons for fearing the police, the village constable was still regarded by many as a potential enemy, set to spy upon them by the authorities.

(Flora Thompson, *Lark Rise to Candleford*, p.484; first published 1939)

How did [the villagers] view the policeman? In those days the public were very friendly with the police … if there was a stranger about, the villagers would say, 'Ah constable did you see those two men walking about the village the other day?' The relationship was marvellous those days because, well, I can't say anything other. It was marvellous. I think the relationship between the police and public changed with the introduction of the Road Traffic Act in 1930. Most members of the public were just real good citizens and if there was a crime committed they were out to help you. I think we fostered that by (unofficially, of course) warning a person for minor offences. A good beat officer would warn the person concerned. You didn't issue an official caution, but you warned them so they wouldn't do it again. So, if you got a crime near where that person lived at a later date, you felt quite in order to approaching that person and see if they could help you, and if they could they would do so. With the introduction of the motor patrol the motorist used to get upset; as you know, there is nothing more aggravating if you're in a hurry to get anywhere and you are stopped for a trivial offence by the traffic patrol. Well, there was one person on one of my beats said to me once, he'd finished with helping the police. He'd been reported by the traffic police for what I consider a very trivial offence. If I'd have come across it, I'd have just warned him.

(Taped interview with Horace Rogers, ex-Inspector, Bedfordshire Police, 1929–64; the interview was conducted by Clive Emsley on 11 February 1987)

This was not intended as a trick question, but the two extracts illustrate the problems of assessing police–public relations. Of course, you might argue that a man looking back over his career giving a taped interview would be inclined to give a rosy picture of the past; by the same token you could argue that a book of reminiscences may be more interested in dramatic effect than historical truth. Another point which I hope you noted is that both extracts deal with rural policing. Since the middle of the nineteenth century a majority of the population in Britain has been urban, and many people would maintain that towns and cities have been more unruly and less deferential than the countryside.

There is a traditional historical image of the British 'bobby' which suggests that, after some initial hostility arising from a misunderstanding of his intended role, he was soon accepted as a part of the community and that the relationship between the police and the public rapidly became one of mutual respect and support. Much of the recent research has forced a reassessment of this comfortable view.

It is now clear that working-class hostility to the police did not soon evaporate. The middle classes probably had little to do with the police before the coming of the motor-car, and the subsequent enforcement of motor-vehicle legislation soured relations here. But while it would be wrong to see the police as popular with all except 'criminals' (however 'criminals' might be defined) from the early Victorian period, it would be equally wrong to portray police–public, or specifically police–working-class relations as marked purely and simply by mutual hostility and suspicion. Much depended on the nature of individual communities. Looking at late Victorian London, for example, the relations between the police and the public in the central, wealthy district of St James's or the respectable, leafy suburb of Dulwich Village were probably very good and characterized by deference on the part of the police. In an Irish immigrant area which the police and the courts labelled as 'violent', such as Jenning's Buildings in Kensington, or in those parts of the East End considered to be the haunts of 'the criminal class', attitudes on both sides were different; yet this did not prevent the local inhabitants from calling upon the police when they considered it to be in their interest. Rural communities could be equally different; some of these, where there was an industrial working class like a mining village or a quarry village like Headington just outside Oxford, could be similarly stigmatized as 'violent' and 'criminal'. Once a community was so stigmatized it tended to be policed as such, and it tended to live up to its stigma. It is important in this kind of historical study that you know your community, and that you know your police.

Analysis of a community has to be built up from a variety of sources, which might, but not necessarily, include some created by the police. An analysis of policemen might draw upon sources such as newspapers – from the early nineteenth century the local press generally gave very detailed accounts of police and court matters – but it can also draw on the kind of material specific to police archives.

―――――――――――――――――― *EXERCISE 2.7* ――――――――――――――――――

Look at Figure 2.7. What is it? What information can you get from it? My comments follow below.

Form 2.

WORCESTERSHIRE CONSTABULARY.

DESCRIPTIVE REGISTER AND RECORD OF SERVICE OF

PC. No 25 William Henry Cooper

Date of Appointment as Constable ...	2nd October 1882
Warrant Number	1534
Divisional Number	25
Age	19
Height	5 feet 11
Weight	13 stone
Chest Measurement	10 inches
Head Measure for Helmet	7 5/8 × 6 5/8 full
Complexion	Fair
Eyes	Brown
Hair	Brown
Particular Marks	cut mark on forefinger of left hand about an inch long
Where Born { in the Parish of	Kingham
in or near the Town of	Chipping Norton
in the County of	Oxford
Religious Persuasion	Established Church of England
Trade or Calling	Labourer
Education	
Last Place of Residence	Lower Brailes, Shipston on Stour
What Public Service	Nil
Regiment, Corps, Police, &c.	
Length of Service	
Amount of Pension	
When Discharged	
If in Army Reserve	
With whom last Employed	H J Sheldon Esqr
Where last Employed	Brailes House, Shipston on Stour
If Vaccinated	Yes
If in any Sick Club or Benefit Society	No Foresters
Weekly Amount when Sick	10/-
Single or Married	~~Single~~ Married
Maiden Name of Wife, and Date of Marriage	Emma Stewart 14th February 1884
Native Place of Wife	Coven, Staffordshire
Number of Children and Dates of Birth	Elizabeth 1884 William 1890

I hereby declare that the above particulars relating to me are to the best of my belief fully and truly stated.

Signed *William Henry Cooper*

Figure 2.7 Descriptive register and record of service of PC25, 1882–1906 (Source: West Mercia Constabulary)

This document is the physical description and record of service of a member of the Worcestershire Constabulary. It gives the man's physical appearance, his place of birth and previous trade. The alterations at the bottom of the first page suggest that he married and joined a Benefit Club after he joined the police. The subsequent pages (not shown here) detail his career in the police: promotions, demotions, rewards and disciplinary charges – Cooper seems to have been a character, but discipline in the nineteenth-century police was ferocious! The record lists the police stations in which he served (in a county force he was probably the only man in some 'stations') and the length of time he served in each.

The records of the Worcestershire Constabulary, now held by the West Mercia Police, are among the most detailed surviving. Sometimes police registers are only half the size of this with, correspondingly, only half the information – often just the man's physical description and much shorter career details. Usually, but unfortunately not in Cooper's case, the records give the date on which a man left the force, the reasons for his departure, and whether or not he received a pension or gratuity.

How could you use the volume or file from which this document came to assess the extent to which William Henry Cooper was a typical recruit to the Worcestershire Constabulary, with a typical police career?

You could make a survey of the men joining in the same decade as Cooper to see where they came from, their trades, their ages, etc. This would enable you to assess the number of men in the Worcestershire Constabulary who were 'labourers' and what kinds of trades were generally represented, the average age of recruits, how many were locally born, how many came from a neighbouring county, how many from a distant county or country (e.g. Ireland or Scotland). It would be sensible to think about the results you come up with in terms of general migration: remember that some counties had a major road running through them to London, for example, or a developing industrial area. Could some of the recruits have been picked up from these migrants? Other counties would have had very little such traffic.

In addition, the documents could be used to examine questions relating to promotion and career prospects in the police. How long did men serve in the different ranks? How long did they serve in the police, and why did they leave? What was the typical career structure of the policeman? What was the typical pattern of postings during a policeman's career? (On occasions men were moved, at their own expense, as punishment.) Was there a typical disciplinary record?

At the Open University we have been conducting research along these lines, notably with a computer study of police recruits between 1840 and 1940 (Emsley and Clapson, 1993). We found that three-quarters of the recruits to the East Suffolk force were born in that county, half of the recruits to the Worcestershire force were natives to the county, but only a quarter of the recruits to the Metropolitan Police had been born in London or Middlesex. Trades might be explored similarly. The traditional argument has always been that, at least up until the First World War, most police recruits were drawn from agricultural labourers. The police recruitment books suggest that a little more care is needed in making such assertions. Agricultural work was one of the largest employers of labour during the nineteenth century, and perhaps the largest single employer throughout. By far the largest single term used under previous trade in the recruitment books is 'labourer', but 'labourer' was a catch-all term, and it would be wrong to assume that every man who gave his trade as such was an agricultural worker. Local forces also seem to have drawn on the local labour pool, so it is important to ask how many of the recruits were drawn from clearly local trades. Different forces appear to have had different attitudes towards recruiting former military men, and therefore in working through the recruitment books it is worth examining how many of the men had been soldiers.

_____ *QUESTIONS FOR RESEARCH* _____

The use of police records, in conjunction with other sources which you have come across during your studies, could enable you to explore more general questions relating to families and communities. For example:

o   The police service made certain demands as to height and weight when recruiting. It would be interesting to analyse a number of personal records like that of William Henry Cooper and compare these men with recruits to the Boer War and the First World War, which were more representative of men in the country as a whole.

o   The police had strict rules about a man's marital status (permission to marry was required, and the future wife, like the police recruit, was subjected to character investigation). It would be interesting to compare policemen's ages at marriage with the ages of men in other occupations. Similarly, the ages of the wives on marriage, and their ages on the birth of the first child (was Elizabeth Cooper conceived out of wedlock?) might be compared. Police pay rates, and the significance of the pension, could also be examined in comparison with other occupational groups.

Rather more difficult to follow up, but still worth some effort and very relevant to a study of families, would be to explore how many of the recruits were following in a family tradition of being policemen. It seems clear from other evidence that sons often followed fathers and grandfathers, and that brother followed brother into the police.

3.2 POLICE AND THE COMMUNITY: SOURCES

There is frequently a problem in historical research that, while you might have a fascinating question to explore, the sources are insufficient to allow you to follow it up. Police archives have rarely been used for anything other than the most obvious historical questions about the police themselves or about crime and disorder; and even then much of the surviving material has never been used. The biggest problem, however, is that the police archives that have survived from the nineteenth and early twentieth centuries are fragmentary and scattered. They survived by accident rather than design; a brief survey of the development of the police will help to explain.

Police forces became obligatory for local authorities in England and Wales under the County and Borough Police Act of 1856; a similar Act was passed for Scotland the following year. This legislation was the culmination of a series of Acts passed in the second quarter of the nineteenth century which had enabled local government to experiment with different models of policing. Among the models on which the localities could draw were the Metropolitan Police of London, established by Act of Parliament in 1829, and the Royal Irish Constabulary, which evolved from a police created for the troubled parts of rural Ireland in 1814, and which was formalized by Act of Parliament into a constabulary covering the whole country in 1822. Both of these forces (and the Dublin Metropolitan Police as established by Act of Parliament in 1808) were responsible not to local government, but directly to central government – the Home Secretary in the case of the Metropolitan Police, and the central authorities in Dublin Castle in the case of the two Irish police forces.

While the Metropolitan Police and the Irish Police were 'national' forces, answerable to central government, the provincial police in England, Scotland and Wales were answerable to local government. From the 1830s, in the towns and cities, this meant the watch committees appointed by, and often drawn from, the elected town councillors. In the counties the responsible bodies were first the police committees made up of local magistrates (commissioners of supply in Scotland), but after the reorganization of county government and the creation of county councils (in 1888 for England and Wales, in 1889 for Scotland) unelected magistrates sat, in equal numbers, side-by-side with elected county councillors on standing joint committees. In the towns and cities, where watch committees sometimes met once a week or more, there could be very tight operational control of the police and direct orders were given to head constables. The head constables in the towns were often men who had risen from the ranks, and well into the twentieth century there were elements on the watch committees who considered such men as their borough's servants rather than independent officers of the crown. In the Victorian and Edwardian periods in particular, the domination of some watch committees over their police could lead to partiality in policing orders; this was especially the case in places where temperance was a vital local issue, and where temperance Liberals lined up against Tory brewers in the local elections. Control over chief constables in the counties was much more attenuated, since a standing joint committee might meet only quarterly; moreover, from the first creation of county forces the chief constables were invariably drawn from the gentry and were regarded more as an equal than the servant of the police committees. Problems arose, notably during the inter-war period, when stiff-necked ex-military, or ex-colonial police, chief constables confronted Labour county councillors on the standing joint committees.

The number of separate police forces in England, Scotland and Wales varied from 1856 to the Second World War, but there were around two hundred for much of the period. Those in the big cities and largest counties contained several hundred men, but others were tiny. In England in 1910, for example, besides the Metropolitan Police and the separate City of London Police, there were 46 county forces (including those of the Isle of Ely and the Liberty of Peterborough), 30 city forces, and 93 borough forces; in Wales there were 12 county and 5 borough forces. The largest force by far was the Metropolitan Police, with 17,400 men; Lancashire was the next largest with 1,652, and included within that county's boundaries there were another twelve separate forces including Liverpool (1,508 men) and Manchester (1,249 men); apart from Rutland (15 men) and the Liberty of Peterborough (10 men), the smallest English county force was Huntingdonshire (54), while the smallest boroughs were Louth (10) and Tiverton (11). Half of the Welsh county forces were smaller than that of Huntingdonshire. His/Her Majesty's Inspectors of Constabulary, who were appointed under the 1856 Act and whose duty it was to make an annual report to parliament on the efficiency of each force, regularly complained about the irrationality of very small forces. But while parliament was reluctant to upset local sensibilities and compel amalgamations, events prompted the increasing centralization of the police in all but name. From the late nineteenth century Home Office officials began by-passing the local police committees and dealing directly with chief constables, particularly when they perceived national emergencies, as in the case of strikes in key industries, and then with the First World War. The agitation and unrest of the inter-war years continued this process, and when chief constables clashed with Labour councillors on their police committees, they were able to rely on support from the Home Office. The Second World War brought some forced amalgamations and, in the immediate aftermath, legislation provided for a few more. But the major amalgamations came as a direct result of the Police Act of 1964, which reduced the number of forces to around 50. The 1964 Act also led to the abolition of watch committees and standing joint committees and saw them replaced with police committees (still composed of magistrates and councillors) whose tasks were largely confined to providing half of the finances necessary for 'efficient' policing and receiving an annual report from the chief constable.

Tragically the big amalgamations of the 1960s and early 1970s appear at times to have been conducted by the light of the bonfires of archival material from disappearing forces. Furthermore, a problem remains over who has responsibility for the preservation of the records that remain, and those that are currently being generated. The records of local government are the responsibility of local government, but the ambiguous position of the police (the police are not a department of local government, and the new police committees cannot give operational orders to the police as the old watch committees did), has left it unclear as to whether local government is responsible for the preservation of police records. Some police archives have been deposited with county record offices (e.g. South Wales, East Sussex), some are to be found in force museums (e.g. Cambridgeshire, Greater Manchester, West Mercia), some remain scattered in police headquarters or police stations; there is, unfortunately, no hard and fast rule.

The problem is not so marked with the 'national' police forces. Since the Metropolitan Police and the Irish Police were answerable to central government, many of their archives found their way into the Public Record Office at Kew; there is additional material on the Royal Irish Constabulary in the Public Record Office (Northern Ireland). Information leaflets are available from Kew giving details of what these police archives contain. However, even for these forces it would also be worth consulting other archives such as county record offices (e.g. Middlesex and Surrey for London), and borough record offices; the Metropolitan Police also has a valuable archive as part of its, as yet, embryonic museum.

Probably the most common records to have survived are the recruitment books and/or personnel registers such as those from Worcestershire discussed above. Police orders also commonly exist for the largest forces. These give an insight into policy, with their instructions to constables about what they should be looking out for at particular times. They sometimes also give details of collections for death and benefit clubs within individual forces, and of disciplinary charges and rewards. Station books and charge books exist for some areas. These can be used for drawing a picture of the kinds of offences (generally petty, but occasionally serious) that affected a community. Regulatory books registering cab drivers, publicans, pedlars and street-sellers are all illustrative of both police work and the lives of the communities in which they worked. A few force archives have copies of constables' beat books or note books – these are the daily journals kept by constables noting their patrols and any particular events or problems. Those for constables working in rural districts are generally the most detailed; since it was rarely possible to maintain a strict supervision of these policemen, they were required to keep detailed daily journals which were periodically inspected, and signed, by their superiors. Again, such journals are marvellous sources for the life of a community, particularly, of course, its problems. Occasionally there might be miscellaneous documentation that could be useful for research topics suggested elsewhere in these volumes. Some forces, for example, especially in the big towns and industrial districts, ran charities for the poor, for widows and orphans; the records of such a charity would be invaluable.

Some printed sources are also helpful in investigating the police in the community. Local newspapers are an obvious example. For the nineteenth and most of the twentieth century these give detailed reports of the proceedings of local courts. It might be necessary at times to read between the lines if you are examining policing in local communities, but evidence will certainly be there. From the 1860s there were some police 'trade' newspapers, notably the *Police Service Advertiser* (from 1867) and the *Police Review* (from 1891). Among other things these contain lively letters columns which often highlight problems in the police service and how these affect police families. The best archive of these 'trade' papers is the National Newspaper Library at Colindale, North London (see Volume 4, Chapter 12), but they can also be found elsewhere.

Parliament has, from time to time, established committees of enquiry into the police. Some of these have useful information on the policeman in the community and on the policeman and his family as members of communities. The most detailed of these enquiries was that of the commission appointed under Lord Desborough in the aftermath of the police strikes of 1918 and 1919. The minutes and report of the Desborough Committee contain extremely detailed information on police earnings, family budgets, and accommodation: see the *Report of the Committee on the Police Service of England, Wales and Scotland* (1919–20).

Further useful publications on the history of the police include the following:

Research tools

Bridgeman, I. and Emsley, C. (1989) *A guide to the archives of the police forces in England and Wales,* Police History Monograph No. 2, Cambridge, Police History Society.

Waters, L.A. (1987) *Notes for family historians,* Police History Monograph No. 1, Cambridge, Police History Society.

Prochaska, A. (1986) 'Irish history from 1700: a guide to sources in the PRO', *Archives and the User,* 6, British Records Association.

General histories

Emsley, C. (1991) *The English police: a political and social history,* Hemel Hempstead, Harvester-Wheatsheaf.

Palmer, S.H. (1988) *Police and protest in England and Ireland, 1780–1850,* Cambridge, Cambridge University Press.

Steedman, C. (1984) *Policing the Victorian community: the formation of English provincial police forces, 1856–1880,* London, Routledge & Kegan Paul.

Autobiographies and oral histories

Brewer, J.D. (1990) *The Royal Irish Constabulary: an oral history,* Belfast, Queens University of Belfast, Institute of Irish Studies.

Brogden, M. (1991) *On the Mersey beat: policing Liverpool between the wars,* Oxford, Oxford University Press.

Daley, H. (1986) *This small cloud: a personal memoir,* London, Weidenfeld & Nicolson.

Wainwright, J. (1987) *Wainwright's beat,* London, Macmillan.

3.3   CONCLUSION

With regard to regional variations, there were clearly different work practices in rural as against urban areas, and attitudes towards the police varied from community to community. Are these factors discernible in other occupations?

The case study also raises issues concerning the differing experiences of work. Some of these are discussed in the Questions for Research at the end of section 3.1 – for example, pay and pension rates, and the extent to which succeeding generations within families entered the force. In addition, questions concerning recruitment (previous employment), origins (place of birth), career opportunities and length of service can be compared with other occupations.

REFERENCES

Arnison, J. (1991) *Decades,* J. Arnison, 7 Wentworth Avenue, Manchester M6 8BG.

Burnett, J. (1966) *Plenty and want: a social history of diet in England from 1815 to the present day,* Harmondsworth, Penguin.

Burnett, J., Vincent, D. and Mayall, D. (eds) (1984, 1987, 1989) *The autobiography of the working class: an annotated critical bibliography*, Brighton, Harvester; vol. 1, *1790–1900* (1984); vol. 2, *1900–1945* (1987); vol. 3, *Supplement, 1790–1945* (1989).

Clarke, L. (1945) *Life and times of Alfred Williams*, Oxford, Blackwell.

Emsley, C. and Clapson, M. (1993) 'Recruiting the English policeman *c.1840–1940*', *Policing and Society*, 3.

Kitchen, R. (1993) 'Class and community in Wolverton', audio-cassette 1A in Braham, P. (ed.) *Using the past: audio-cassettes on sources and methods for family and community historians*, Milton Keynes, The Open University.

Marshall, J. D. and Walton, J. K. (1981) *The Lake Counties from 1830 to the mid-twentieth century – a study in regional change*, Manchester, Manchester University Press.

Report of the Committee on the Police Service of England, Wales and Scotland (1919–20) (Chair: Lord Desborough), Cmd. 253 (Part 1), Cmd. 574 (Part 2) and Cmd. 874 (Evidence), London, Home Office (British Parliamentary Papers).

Thompson, F. (1973) *Lark Rise to Candleford*, Harmondsworth, Penguin. First published 1939.

Williams, A. (1915) *Life in a railway factory*, London, Duckham. New edition published in 1969, Newton Abbott, David and Charles.

CHAPTER 3

WORK CASE STUDIES: SOME OCCUPATIONS AND ROLES

In Chapter 2 we looked at some individuals and the occupations they undertook. In this chapter we continue our study of work, but here we will be asking questions about particular occupations and roles and exploring ways in which we can use source materials to answer these questions.

Again, we have taken three case studies. The first looks at domestic service, an occupation that involved some 14 per cent of the population of England and Wales in the mid nineteenth century. The study suggests areas for research that involve the use of census enumerators' books (CEBs), census reports and oral history techniques.

The vast majority of domestic servants were female and single. So what kind of work, if any, was undertaken by married women? The second case study examines the changing pattern of paid employment for married women over the past hundred years and attempts to discover, by using CEBs, the extent to which they found paid employment in 1851.

The third study examines entrepreneurship and business enterprise. It considers the sources and methods that can be used for undertaking such a study and suggests a series of possible research topics.

The key aim of this chapter, as that of Chapter 2, is to suggest ways in which you can use particular sources to ask pertinent questions about occupations in the communities and families that you are studying and to relate these to the wider academic literature.

1   DOMESTIC SERVANTS

by Michael Drake

Have you been living in the British Isles since the end of the Second World War? If so, you will have witnessed the rapid decline, indeed the virtual demise, of some of the country's great nineteenth-century industries. Occupations with workers once numbered in the hundreds of thousands are now in the tens of thousands, for example coal-miners, cotton textile workers, merchant sailors, steelworkers, and shipbuilders.

_____ **QUESTION FOR RESEARCH** _____

Perhaps now is the time to do a service for future historians by making a record of the working lives of some of the men and women who toiled in these jobs whilst they are still with us and their memories still fresh. For a checklist of the various sources and techniques you might employ in this task, see Volume 4, Chapter 7.

_____

To have witnessed the decline of the greatest of all nineteenth-century industries, you would have had to be around a little longer – since around the end of the First World War. The number of domestic servants probably peaked in the 1890s, although changes in census classifications make it difficult to be certain. At the 1891 census, one-third of occupied females in the United

Kingdom were engaged in domestic service, making it 'not only the largest women's industry, but the largest single industry for either men or women' (Board of Trade, 1899, p.iii).

Table 3.1 shows both the numbers of male and female indoor domestic servants in the constituent countries of the United Kingdom in 1891 by age group, and the proportion they constituted within each age group. The table is taken from the 1899 Board of Trade report by a Miss Collett that is referred to above.

Table 3.1   Number and ages of domestic servants in the United Kingdom, according to the census of 1891

Ages of indoor domestic servants	England and Wales	Scotland	Ireland	United Kingdom
Females				
10 years and under 15	107 167	10 258	9 293	126 718
15 years and under 25	791 709	92 111	93 404	977 224
25 years and under 45	361 189	46 312	52 333	459 834
45 years and under 65	104 932	13 433	30 315	148 680
65 years and upwards	21 170	2 771	12 557[1]	36 498[1]
Total 10 years and upwards	1 386 167	164 885	197 902	1 748 954
Males				
10 years and under 20	22 544	884	4 747	28 175
20 years and upwards	35 983	2 737	8 446	47 166
Total 10 years and upwards	58 527	3 621	13 193	75 341
Female servants per 10,000 females living in each age group				
10 years and under 15	665	460	345	602
15 years and under 25	2 744	2 320	1 890	2 588
25 years and under 45	902	857	913	898
45 years and under 65	479	421	736	509
65 years and upwards	276	231	803	349
Total 10 years and upwards	1 209	1 031	1 039	1 169
Male servants per 10,000 males living in each age group				
10 years and upwards	73	20	85	69
20 years and upwards	48	27	67	48
Total 10 years and upwards	55	25	72	54

[1] Including 148 of unspecified age.

Source: Board of Trade (1899) Table III, p.48

EXERCISE 3.1

Look carefully at Table 3.1.

1   What do the constituent countries of the United Kingdom have in common regarding the numbers, sex and age distribution of indoor domestic servants?

2   What is the major difference between the situation in Ireland and the rest of the United Kingdom?

Answers/comments p.227.

If the number of domestic servants peaked in the 1890s and declined rapidly during and after the First World War, when and how fast did it grow? Prior to 1841 we can get little help from the censuses. Furthermore, changes in census classifications make comparison difficult over the period as a whole. However, for the years 1851 to 1871 the classification system remained the same. In this period the number of servants increased by 57 per cent, twice the rate of population growth and considerably in excess of the 36 per cent growth in the number of separate occupiers (the nearest we can get from the census reports to a measure of growth of servants per household) (Banks, 1954, pp.83–4).

From this brief foray into the national statistics, it will be apparent that in studying domestic service we are dealing with an industry that touched the lives of many. Indeed, few people who can trace their family tree to the mid nineteenth century in any part of the United Kingdom will not find a domestic servant or two (or an employer of domestic servants) dangling from one branch or another. This surely provides the motivation for family historians to research into the history of domestic service, though, as yet, remarkably few have done so. As for community historians, there is an additional incentive: the fact that behind the national aggregates lies much variability. Only by analysing this will we be able to tease out the many gaps in our understanding that remain. In the rest of this chapter I shall therefore suggest exercises you might carry out with a view to filling some of the gaps.

1.1 WHEN IS A SERVANT NOT A SERVANT?

Remarkably, there is still a lot of mileage left in this most basic of all questions. A Workers' Educational Association (WEA) class analysing the 1851 CEBs for Swaledale and Arkengarthdale in North Yorkshire discovered that of the 302 women who described themselves as servants, as many as 40 per cent were related to the head of the household and were 'really indistinguishable from the 273 daughters living at home with no occupation [stated]' (Reeth WEA Local History Class, 1970). Carole Pearce and I found that for the ancient market town of Ashford (Kent) at the same date, 13 per cent fell into this category of family members. Not only is this a much lower proportion than that found in Swaledale, but it is also out of line with the 40 per cent figure found by Higgs for Rochdale (Higgs, 1982, p.61). Higgs's figure is based on a 1-in-4 sample and includes those described as lodgers in the CEB's relationship to head of household column, as well as kin ('used … in the widest sense to indicate any relationship by marriage or birth').

───────────────── *QUESTIONS FOR RESEARCH* ─────────────────

Because living-in domestic servants were considered by many in the nineteenth century to be members of the family/household in which they lived, as well as employees, they *can* appear as such in two columns of the census schedule. Higgs (1982) explores this issue and is, therefore, a useful starting point for research on this interesting dichotomy. Among questions to be explored further are:

o   Differences in the proportion of 'kin' servants in different places at the same census and between censuses. Thus in 1851 in the borough of Blackburn (Lancashire), 38 per cent of the entire servant population were described as 'housekeepers'. By 1861 the proportion was down to 3 per cent. In nearby Oldham, however, the number virtually trebled (cited in Higgs, 1982, p.64).

o   Differences in the type of servants within the 'kin'/'non-kin' categories. Higgs, for instance, found that in his 1-in-4 Rochdale sample in 1851, of 38 'nurses' living with kin, 18 were under 10 years of age and only three of these were not members of the nuclear family. Probably, he surmises, this reflected the high level of child-minding necessary in a community where so many married women worked outside the home – a conjecture supported by the fact that households with such 'nurses' contained more children under 10 years of age than was the case generally (Higgs, 1982, p.62).

You too could explore questions like these quite easily by taking two contrasting CEBs (one rural, one urban) at the same census, or the same enumeration district over two or more censuses.

1.2 NOW YOU SEE 'EM, NOW YOU DON'T

Change in domestic service in Britain since the Middle Ages is characterized by three main features. First, there was a widening of the gap in social status between servants and those they worked for. Second, the proportion of male servants fell, so that by 1891 they accounted for only 4 per cent of all servants (see Table 3.1). Third, employers of servants, especially those who employed large numbers, insisted on more and more privacy. This was not simply a matter of 'upstairs-downstairs'; it also concerned back and front stairs, with servants increasingly confined to the former, so that the 'gentry walking up the stairs no longer met their last night's faeces coming down them' (Girouard, 1980, p.138). But it wasn't just a matter of keeping faeces out of sight. Victorian servants were to be both as invisible and as inaudible as possible. In fact the 'Duke of Portland (admittedly eccentric, if not mad) sacked any housemaid who had the misfortune to meet him in the corridors' (Girouard, 1980, p.285). Blythe reports of a stately home in Suffolk in this century where the gardeners should never be seen from the house: 'If people were sitting on the terrace or on the lawn, and you had a great barrow-load of weeds, you might have to push it as much as a mile to keep out of view' (Blythe, 1972, p.118).

_____ *QUESTION FOR RESEARCH* _____

Among people over 60 years of age there are still considerable numbers who were themselves domestic servants or who grew up in households that employed servants. Their world is unlikely to return. It is, therefore, that much more important to attempt to recapture some of it before it is too late. Oral interviewing and recording would be invaluable (see Volume 4, Chapter 7) simply because so little of that experience has been recorded. Apart from the census material, there is little official information – in fact just two reports (Board of Trade, 1899; Ministry of Reconstruction, 1919). Other material has tended either to be written by, or for, employers (for example Mrs Beeton and similar manuals) or is biased towards the experiences of servants in upper-class houses (Higgs, 1986a, p.5; Burnett, 1974). Novelists give some clues: Dickens, for instance, portrays some memorable servants; E. M. Forster, on the other hand, manages to use servants to carry forward the plot without breaching their anonymity – see his *Howards End*.

If you want to conduct an oral history project on domestic service, how should you go about it? I suggest you tackle some of the questions put by Paul Thompson, Thea Thompson and Trevor Lummis in an unpublished project they carried out for the Open University in 1974. They sought to examine the quality of personal contacts between servants and their employers; the degree of deference expected of servants; and the effect of the presence of servants on family relationships, especially on the upbringing of children. These are 'big questions' which you will need to break down into smaller, realistic ones, i.e. questions that are down to earth, immediately meaningful. For example, if you wish to examine the deference expected of servants, you might ask, 'What did you call your mistress or master?' 'Did this change when non-household members were present (i.e. first name terms most of the time, 'ma'm' or 'sir' on other occasions)?' Or you could ask, 'What did you, as a master or mistress of servants, call them?' Note that in some households all maids were called Mary or Jane irrespective of their actual first names. There is some evidence that the presence of young children in a servant-keeping family was important for the servant–master/mistress relationship. You might therefore try to test the hypothesis *that the presence of young children reduced the social distance between masters and mistresses*. One way of doing this is to see whether servants were more likely to eat with the family when young children were present. Thompson, Thompson and Lummis found that this was indeed the case: 68 per cent ate with the family when children were present, but only 14 per cent when they were not. But they also found a strong correlation between the *number* of servants in a household where children were present and the incidence of meals shared with the family. Thus in 80 per cent of households where there were young children and but a single servant, meals

Eliza Young, Emma Clark and Mary Buckland: Domestic Servants

Eliza Young *(top left)*: 16 years old; born in Penn; single; father dead; last residence: Penn; offence: stealing a pair of shoes from her master in Burnham; sentence: one month's hard labour.

Emma Clark *(top right)*: 24 years old; born in Great Missenden; unmarried; father a labourer living in Stoke Common; last residence Slough; offence: concealment of birth in Slough; sentence: 14 days.

Mary Buckland *(left)*: 20 years old; born in Upton-cum-Chalvey; unmarried; father a labourer living in Slough; last residence Slough; offence: obtaining goods by false pretences in Slough (an offence for which she had served three months' hard labour in 1870 and again in 1871); sentence: nine months' hard labour.

It is very unusual to find photographs of servants from this period (1872–3), out of uniform and not in the workplace. But are they representative of domestic servants generally – in looks, dress and the other features given above? The question must be asked since these servants came before the assizes or magistrates' courts of Buckinghamshire, and each received a custodial sentence. Does this introduce a bias into the record, and if so what is it? The Aylesbury Gaol Receiving Book for 1872–3 contained nine photographs of female domestic servants (including those shown above) – and many more of prisoners with other occupations. In the main the servants were young, with a modal and median age of 20. Four reported their fathers as being labourers and one said he was a bricklayer. The fathers of the other four were said to be dead. None of this is surprising given what we know of domestic service from other sources. Nor does the distance travelled between place of birth and place of last residence appear out of the ordinary. That only one was married is not unexpected either, given what we know of age at marriage in this period. That six of the nine were called Elizabeth or Eliza suggests an amazing coincidence, or that it was 'the' name in the 1840s and 1850s, or a surprising lack of imagination on the part of their parents. As for the circumstances in which we come across them, note Emma Clark's offence against 'Victorian values'; that she and the others were subject to the 'short, sharp, shock' treatment; and that it doesn't seem to have worked in the case of Mary Buckland.

were taken in common. Where there were two servants the percentage dropped to 34. Age too turned out to be a factor. A young girl in her first job was more likely to be treated as a child herself and, if the parents ate with their children, she would do so too.

With all these investigations your results will be more meaningful if you are able to talk to a number of former servants or mistresses. You might therefore explore the possibility of conducting interviews with members of clubs for retired people, or residents of retirement homes.

Several other factors contributed to the near invisibility of servants in spite of the fact that they existed in such vast numbers. For instance, because it was a relatively short-term job for most people, few appeared in more than one census enumerator's book. The vast majority of servants also occupied one-servant households, again making it difficult to 'get at them'. For example, when Miss Collett sought to investigate the wages of domestic servants she noted that whereas 'in the case of the Cotton Trade, schedules received from 542 employers gave information as to the wages of 143,000 cotton operatives, in the present inquiry no fewer than 2,067 schedules were required in order to arrive at the wages of 5,568 indoor domestic servants' (Board of Trade, 1899, p.iii).

Miss Collett also encountered the problem of distributing her schedules. This was her solution: 'It was found that returns could be more freely obtained by distributing these forms through the medium of private persons sufficiently interested in the matter to hand a few of them to their friends, than by any system of wholesale distribution' (Board of Trade, 1899, p.1).

EXERCISE 3.2

Can you envisage any problems regarding the representativeness of the data acquired by such a sampling procedure?

Comments pp.227–8.

In her fascinating report Miss Collett also discussed a matter which helps to explain the 'invisibility' of servants generally, namely their length of service in the same household. As Table 3.2 indicates, this was generally very short, and uniformly so across the United Kingdom as a whole. Servants moved principally in order to 'better themselves', i.e. secure higher wages and better conditions. Moving seems to have been the only way of doing so. At the bottom end of the market – in the single maid-of-all-work, or general servant, household – many mistresses would dismiss their servants rather than raise their wages, and then recruit a younger, less trained one. Thus Carol Pearce, in an unpublished study of servants in Ashford (Kent), found that of 312 servants enumerated in 1841 and 1851, only seven survived long enough with the same family to be enumerated twice (i.e. were with them from at least 1841–51 or 1851–61) and only one was with the same family in 1841 (described as a 'servant'), 1851 ('cook') and 1861 ('housekeeper'). From this evidence we cannot even be sure that the period of employment between censuses was a continuous one. William Trevor, the Irish novelist, has noted that Kitty, the maid in his childhood home whom he remembers best, had at least two separate periods of service with his family (Trevor, 1993, pp.31–3).

Table 3.2 Percentage of female servants who at the date of Miss Collett's inquiry (carried out between 1894 and 1898) had been in the service of the household making returns, for the undermentioned periods[1]

	London	England and Wales (excluding London)	Scotland	Ireland
Number of servants	1864	2443	638	358
Percentage of servants who at the date of inquiry had been in service in the same situation:				
Under 1 year	36	35	35	37
1 year and under 2 years	18	19	20	17
2 years and under 3 years	13	13	13	12
3 years and under 4 years	10	10	7	10
4 years and under 5 years	4	5	6	6
Total under 5 years	81	82	81	82
Average years of service	1.3	1.4	1.3	1.4
Total over 5 years and under 10 years	11	10	12	10
Average years of service	6.1	6.4	6.5	6.4
Total 10 years and upwards	8	8	7	8
Average years of service	15.6	16.7	17.9	15.9

[1] 'It is to be understood that the years of service stated are those already completed in one situation at the date of inquiry. The average length of time during which the servants remain in one situation would naturally be about twice as great.'

Source: Board of Trade (1899) p.25

The 'large' houses with many servants also appear to have experienced a considerable turnover of staff, even though these houses employed far more career servants.

_____ *QUESTION FOR RESEARCH* _____

It would be interesting to explore further the question of servant mobility – its speed, causes, geographical extent, link with wages and career, variability from one period to another, from one area to another, and between general servants in one- or two-servant households and specialist servants in larger establishments.

How much you can do will depend on the time available, as there are few financial costs involved. You might, for instance, examine the number and turnover of servants in a single street, part of a town or village, a complete community, a 'big' house, or several 'big' houses between censuses (1841–91 in England, Wales and Scotland; 1901–11 in Ireland). If you follow up either of these last two suggestions, keep an eye out for changes of ownership and occupancy – not, of course, necessarily the same thing. When I looked at the nearest 'big' house to where I live (Milton Keynes Village) I was able to discover the following from the CEBs for Wavendon parish alone:

o   The house (Wavendon House, Lower End, Wavendon, Bucks) remained from 1841 to 1891 in the hands of the Hoare family.

o   The total number of occupants at the censuses was:

    1841 = 12
    1851 = 26
    1861 = 9
    1871 = 4
    1881 = 10
    1891 = 10

o   The number of servants in the house was:

1841 = 8 (of which 2 male)
1851 = 18 (of which 8 male)
1861 = 8 (of which 3 male)
1871 = 0
1881 = 8 (of which 3 male)
1891 = 6 (all female)

o   Not one of the *occupants* was enumerated at the house on more than a single occasion.

o   The mean age of the servants was:

	female (years)	male (years)
1841	23.2	36
1851	24.9	26.1
1861	23.8	19.5
1871	–	–
1881	29.6	24.3
1891	25.7	–

o   The birthplaces of the servants were:

1841   Outside Bucks (7); in Bucks (1). Note that Wavendon House is very close to the borders of Northamptonshire and Bedfordshire, so these figures do not necessarily indicate long-distance migration. However, read on!

1851   Surrey; Ireland (6); Middx; Bucks (3); Northants; Staffs; Sussex (2); Kent (2); Leicester (1).

1861   Beds (2); Hants; Northumberland; Bucks (2); Middx; London

1871   –

1881   Suffolk; Banffshire; Lincs; Cambs; Staffs; Somerset; Hants; Bucks

1891   Suffolk; Oxon (3); Middx; Surrey

This distribution of birthplaces shows a considerable spread, though with something of a concentration on the southern half of England. In this regard it contrasts with the much narrower recruitment area for servants employed in Ashford (Kent) in 1851 and 1861:

Place of birth:	1851 (%)	1861 (%)
In Ashford	15	12
Within 10 miles of Ashford	69	69
Elsewhere	16	19
Total number	251	276

Source: Carole Pearce, calculated from CEBs

o   The head of household at Wavendon House was:

1841   Richard Hoare, retired Royal Navy captain, aged 48
1851   Henry Charles Hoare, magistrate, farmer of 500 acres employing 48 labourers (*sic*), aged 61
1861   No head given. House occupied by servants and a visiting dressmaker
1871   Joseph Ball, gardener, aged 48
1881   Frederick W. Bigge, drawing income from dividends, aged 63
1891   Henry Hugh Arthur Hoare, landowner, aged 25

Another way of finding out more about the extent and causes of the movement of servants between households is through an oral history project. The following summary provides one illustration of this from the project mentioned earlier.

Mrs McLelland ... was born in 1900, the second of altogether thirteen children ... in a poor waterside district of Greenwich. Her father was a skilled man in a regular job, a waterman, and many other members of her family had been 'water people'. She thought her mother might have been in service, but was unsure. She thus came from the upper working class, but from a poor community which, with her father's very traditional trade, helped to explain her attitudes – in contrast to those which one might expect, for example, from the family of a highly paid industrial worker. She was unusual in gaining a scholarship for training in domestic science and service. She therefore started work in 1916 at sixteen instead of fourteen (although she was still very small at this age). Her first job was for the Countess of Kinnull, Pont Street, London ... Like most of her jobs it only lasted a few months. From there she went to Colonel Karslake (West End and Hampshire country house) where she 'had the honour of being confirmed with one of the daughters'; to a Harley Street doctor; to the Marchioness of Salisbury in about 1918 (London and Hatfield); to the Mansion House (where the Lord Mayor's establishment was on an especially large scale, with casual butlers brought in for banquets); to Sir Marcus Samuel (London and Kent); to the Honourable Mrs Bailey, whose husband was an MP (London and Wiltshire); and so to the Duchess of Rutland at Belvoir Castle in 1924.

At Belvoir she met her husband, who was groom of chambers – a supervisory office job. He came from a middle-class background in Belfast. They married in 1926 and then worked briefly together for Agatha Christie. This proved unsuccessful because they were bored by the small house and annoyed by the Christies' 'trying to be big' by entertaining on a large scale with too few staff. They then acted as caretakers for Lord Faringdon until Mrs McLelland's first child was born. After trying to be a butler at a small private school at Ham Common, Mr McLelland took another joint post, probably in 1928, with a Gloucestershire colonel. It resulted in a legal case when he refused to saw up firewood because he had been engaged as a footman. This ended their career in domestic service. Mr McLelland became a clerk in the civil service. Lucy herself did not go out to work again.

(Source: Paul Thompson in an unpublished project carried out for the Open University in 1974)

For me this brief passage touches on many aspects of domestic service, each of which could be developed. If this thought hasn't struck you, re-read the passage, underline areas of potential research, and reflect upon them.

1.3 THE TOUCH OF CLASS

In his study of poverty in York in the closing years of the nineteenth century, Seebohm Rowntree remarked that 'the keeping or not keeping of domestic servants has in this inquiry been taken as marking the division between the working classes and those of a higher social scale' (Rowntree, 1901, p.35). Trevor (1993, p.32) also remarks that '"Have they a maid?" was a question often asked, the answer supplying instant social status'. If these statements have a general applicability, then the keeping or not of servants could be a very useful marker for social analysis. For instance, it could be used to indicate the 'better' areas of town, as in Figure 3.1. Here Ashford (Kent) households with servants in 1861 have been plotted on a map. The result is doubly interesting. First, it shows a very considerable degree of concentration. Second, the concentration was greatest in the heart of this ancient market town, indicating that the medieval/pre-industrial residential pattern still prevailed, as opposed to the present-day situation where the better-off usually live in the suburbs, with town centres becoming either bereft of domestic accommodation, or the abode of some of the poorest members of the community.

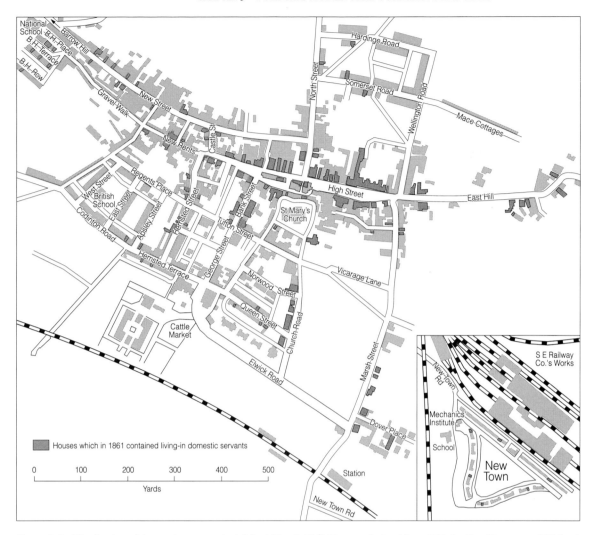

Figure 3.1 Distribution of domestic servants in Ashford (Kent), 1861 (Source: derived from CEBs by Carol Pearce and Michael Drake)

A problem with using servant-keeping as a surrogate for middle class arises from the variation in the proportion of women employed in domestic service in different areas. Take England in 1851. In that year, in about half the counties, over 30 per cent of women aged 15–19 years were in domestic service (including those described as 'farm servants – indoor'), but of the southern counties Bedfordshire had only 19.5 per cent, Dorset and Cornwall 24 per cent; of Midland counties, Staffordshire had 27 per cent in service as against neighbouring Shropshire with 42 per cent. In the North, Lancashire and Yorkshire's West Riding had around 18 per cent in domestic service, whilst Lincolnshire had 46 per cent; Yorkshire's North Riding had 42 per cent, Westmorland 41 per cent. By 1871 all counties had a higher proportion of 15–19 year old women in domestic service than in 1851 (calculated from *Census of Great Britain 1851* and *Census of England and Wales 1871*).

Unfortunately, it is not possible to calculate quite so easily the proportion of women aged 15–19 years who were domestic servants in the registration districts. This is a pity, as these smaller areas correspond in many places to the communities you probably want to study. However, it is possible that an approximate figure can be obtained as follows. The published report of the 1851

Table 3.3 Female servants aged 15–19 years as a percentage of the age group in Yorkshire registration districts, 1851

Registration district	Females 15–19 years	Servants 15–19 years	% servants of females 15–19 years
Yorks, West Riding			
Sedbergh	191	63	33.0
Settle	620	194	31.3
Skipton	1447	285	19.7
Pateley Bridge	351	76	21.7
Ripon	901	309	34.3
Knaresboro'	1257	550	43.8
Otley	1441	274	19.0
Keighley	2631	177	6.7
Todmorden	1532	159	10.4
Saddleworth	989	94	9.5
Huddersfield	6451	962	14.9
Halifax	6534	830	12.7
Bradford	10798	1012	9.4
Hunslet	4569	746	16.3
Leeds	5339	1347	25.2
Dewsbury	3746	368	9.8
Wakefield	2317	585	25.3
Pontefract	1394	304	21.8
Hemsworth	376	132	35.1
Barnsley	1628	290	17.8
Wortley	1318	247	18.7
Eccleshall Bierlow	1866	555	29.7
Sheffield	5004	941	18.8
Rotherham	1502	358	23.8
Doncaster	1691	589	34.8
Thorne	737	161	21.8
Goole	690	149	21.6
Selby	761	177	23.3
Tadcaster	867	317	36.6
Total	68948	12251	17.8
Yorks, North Riding			
Scarborough	1260	589	46.7
Malton	1007	434	43.1
Easingwold	488	184	37.7
Thirsk	557	239	42.9
Helmsley	571	202	35.4
Pickering	439	158	36.0
Whitby	1045	457	43.7
Guisborough	534	224	41.9
Stokesley	399	195	48.9
Northallerton	572	181	31.6
Bedale	393	198	50.4
Leyburn	438	181	41.3
Askrigg	234	103	44.0
Reeth	300	70	23.3
Richmond	711	312	43.9
Total	8948	3727	41.7
Yorks, East Riding			
York	2978	1548	52.0
Pocklington	750	226	30.1
Howden	662	206	31.1
Beverley	913	411	45.0
Skulcoates	2375	903	38.0
Hull	2522	915	36.3
Patrington	439	154	35.1
Skirlaugh	464	170	36.6
Driffield	839	299	35.6
Bridlington	681	231	33.9
Total	12623	5063	40.1

Source: *Census of Great Britain 1851*

census tells me that in the West Riding of Yorkshire there were 12,251 female domestic servants aged 15–19 and 20,761 over 20 years of age. Thus the group aged 15–19 was 59.0 per cent as big as that aged 20 years and over (i.e. 12,251 ÷ 20,761 x 100 = 59.0 per cent). (For more on the published census reports see Volume 4, Chapter 3.) The corresponding percentages for the North and East Ridings were 65.7 and 63.2. If we now apply these proportions to the registration districts (for which the census report gives us the number aged 20 years and above), we can estimate the number of female domestic servants in each who were aged 15–19 years. Given that the census report tells us the total number of women in this age group, a relatively simple calculation gives us the percentage who were domestic servants (Table 3.3). The percentages varied dramatically, especially within the West Riding; they were especially low in the industrial areas, presumably because alternative occupations outside the home were available for women or because family incomes were sufficient to keep unmarried children in the parental home.

QUESTION FOR RESEARCH

This brings us back to the point made earlier: does the designation 'domestic servant' vary from one place to another? If so, what does this mean for social relationships? How can we use the servant/non-servant households as a marker for social class? These are important questions waiting to be answered. As a first step I would be interested to know how close my estimates of the percentage of domestic servants in the 15–19 year age group are to reality – a question that can be answered by totalling the number of women so designated in the CEBs.

1.4   CONCLUSION

Although a considerable amount of research into domestic service has been done in recent years (Burnett, 1974; Ebery and Preston, 1976; Higgs, 1982, 1983, 1986a, 1986b, 1987; Horn, 1975; McBride, 1976; Malcolmson, 1981; Marshall, 1968; Richardson, 1967), I hope I have said enough to indicate that much remains to be done. The opportunities range across the entire spectrum of the research endeavour, from an analysis of sources (notably the CEBs and census reports) to the refinement of techniques (qualitative in the case of oral history, quantitative – as Miss Collett discovered – when statistical work is involved). There is also a contemporary relevance issue: the dramatic rise in recent years of the number of married, or cohabiting women, in paid employment outside the home, has increased the numbers of nannies and childminders and revived issues faced by earlier generations of mothers, when domestic service first began to decline.

2   MARRIED WOMEN AND WORK

by John Golby

Throughout the nineteenth and twentieth centuries, very many married women have contributed to the family income by taking on a whole host of jobs, often temporary or casual in nature – washing, sewing, childminding, taking in lodgers, and so on. Such jobs carried out by women in their own homes are not easy to investigate for the past, if only because they are rarely recorded in the returns of the census enumerators. They are a form of work, nevertheless, and even when unpaid in monetary terms they could still make a significant contribution in kind to the family economy (see Pennington and Westover, 1989; also Volume 1, Chapter 4, section 1).

This section, however, will start from explaining the percentage of married women recorded in the censuses as having occupations other than housewife and suggest why these percentages have changed during the period of our study. Also, questions will be asked which you can develop in your own research.

EXERCISE 3.3

Read the two extracts below carefully and note the different attitudes to work.

Comments p.228.

Q   Did she work after she was married?
A   I couldn't say. No, I couldn't say. I wouldn't think so 'cause – let me see, mam was married – I have it in a book, she was married at High Street Chapel 1897. I was born 1898 and my sister was born 1901, so she'd have enough with two children, wouldn't she? Yes, and there wasn't much work really. Then tradesmen were very proud of being able to keep their wives you see. M' father was nicely brought up and I think he wouldn't want her to go to work. I can't remember mother ever working.
(Source: interview with Mrs S, quoted in Roberts, 1984, p.138)

I feel that it should always be possible – things *should* so be arranged that no woman need feel that marriage is going to drive her into domesticity. There should be just as many openings for women as for men ... men will do their damnedest to push women back into it [domestic work] and keep them from 'outside' jobs – and women must fight hard to hold their present positions.
(Source: Mass-Observation questionnaire, 1944, quoted in Sheridan, 1990, p.216)

If we were to take these two pieces of evidence alone as the basis for a generalization about national attitudes (but of course we cannot), then it might seem that attitudes towards married women seeking paid employment outside the home had changed considerably between 1900 and 1944. The aims of this section are (a) to discover if this was so; (b) if it was, to find out why this change had come about; (c) to go further back into the nineteenth century to examine both the attitudes towards married women working and the extent to which they worked then; and (d) to raise questions that will enable you to take part in this research.

I am going to pursue these four aims by different methods. With regard to the nineteenth century, I have undertaken a small research project based on the 1851 census enumerators' books. In the attempt to explain the changes in attitude in the twentieth century, I am putting forward a set of general explanations which you should be able to examine and test for yourselves when carrying out interviews or reading diaries and letters of the period.

2.1   MARRIED WOMEN AND WORK IN THE NINETEENTH CENTURY

The question this study sets out to explore is, did the vast majority of married women in the mid nineteenth century remain in their own homes and not obtain paid employment? In an attempt to try and answer this for my own community I used the 1851 CEBs for Eynsham, an agricultural parish situated about eight miles west of Oxford with a population of 1,941. The exercise I undertook was a straightforward one, and apart from the time spent travelling to and from Oxford Central Library, where copies of the CEBs are lodged, it took me about five hours to assemble the information from them that is listed in Schema A.

Schema A: Investigating married women and work from the CEBs – a checklist of information found for Eynsham (Oxon)

o   The percentage of married women in Eynsham entered in the census as having an occupation other than housewife.

o   Their occupations.

o   The occupations of the husbands of the married women in paid employment.

FINDINGS

The results of my investigations into married women and employment in Eynsham in 1851 are shown in Tables 3.4–3.7. Table 3.4 shows that 43.6 per cent of married women in Eynsham were in paid employment. The 1851 census figures show that, for the country as a whole, the figure was just under 25 per cent (Hunt, 1981, p.18).

Table 3.4 Married women in Eynsham, 1851

Age	Working		Not working	
	No.	%	No.	%
Under 25	8	36.4	14	63.6
25–45	94	49.5	96	50.5
Over 45	37	34.6	70	65.4
Total	139	43.6	180	56.4

Table 3.5 Occupations of married women in Eynsham, 1851

	Under 25	25–45	Over 45
Dressmaker	2	8	0
Slop-maker		2	1
Glover	4	43	12
Seamstress	1		
Tailoress		2	
Waistcoat-maker		1	
Milliner		1	
Spinner		1	
Housekeeper		18	13
Laundress	1	4	1
Servant		5	
Governess		1	
Nurse			1
Field worker		4	3
Shoe-binder/maker		3	
Bark thatcher		1	1
Schoolmistress			2
Grocer			1
Fruitseller			1
Licensed victualler			1

As I have mentioned, Eynsham in 1851 was primarily a farming community, as is indicated by the occupations of the men living in the parish. From Table 3.6 we can calculate that approximately 55 per cent of married women who were entered in the census as having an occupation were married to agricultural labourers, while of those married women not working, 33 per cent were married to agricultural labourers. However, few of the married women were themselves directly involved in agricultural work (at least, not in their own eyes or those of the census enumerator), and it is clear that the majority were employed inside their homes in the clothing industries, as dressmakers and especially glovers.

Table 3.6 Number of working and non-working women married to agricultural labourers in Eynsham, 1851

Age	Total	Number married to agricultural labourers
Working married women:		
Under 25	8	6
25–45	94	54
Over 45	37	16
Non-working married women:		
Under 25	14	3
25–45	96	29
Over 45	70	28

Finally, by adding up the numbers of single, married and widowed women working in Eynsham, I was able to obtain overall figures for the composition of the female labour force – see Table 3.7.

Table 3.7 Numbers and percentages of working women by marital status, Eynsham, 1851

Single		Married		Widowed	
No.	%	No.	%	No.	%
169	49.8	139	41.1	31	9.1

EXERCISE 3.4

Note down three major conclusions you might draw from this use of the 1851 census for Eynsham.

Comments p.228.

Bearing in mind the issues discussed in Chapter 1, why do you think the percentage of married women in Eynsham with occupations was higher than the national average?

Eynsham was an agricultural community but, as we have seen, most of the married women did work which was unconnected with agriculture and which could be carried out within their own homes.

Pennington and Westover (1989, p.44) identify four major location factors that 'determined the availability of a female labour force for recruitment to the sweated home industries' in the mid nineteenth century: areas most likely to have a high proportion of female labour in such industries were those where (a) men's wages were low; (b) seasonal or casual labour was marked; (c) there was little alternative work available to women; and (d) there was a surplus of women. At least three of these factors applied to Eynsham in 1851.

Glove-making, the major occupation for married women in Eynsham, was indeed a major home industry in the county of Oxfordshire (see Figures 3.2.and 3.3). Woodstock, situated about five miles from Eynsham,

> *was famous for a hardwearing glove made from deerskin or sheepskin. Up to the First World War the army provided the main market for gloves to the Woodstock industry: they wore strong leather gloves of English sheepskin which were pipe-clayed to give them a very white appearance. These were hand-sewn by the homeworkers, mainly the daughters and wives of agricultural labourers.*

(Pennington and Westover, 1989, p.54)

It would be interesting if you were to carry out a similar exercise with an agricultural parish in another part of the country or in an industrial town. My guess would be that in many urban areas the percentage of married women registered as working in the 1851 census would be lower than that of Eynsham. In industrial towns the home and the workplace were becoming increasingly spatially separated during the nineteenth century. For women with young families it was always difficult to go out to work, even if there was work available, which very often was not the case. Consequently, it is perhaps not surprising that during the course of the century the census returns show a declining proportion of married women working.

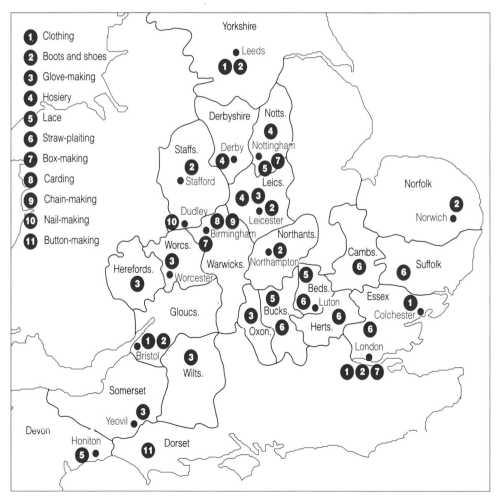

Figure 3.2   Map showing the distribution of the major home industries, 1850-1901 (Source: Pennington and Westover, 1989, p.45)

Figure 3.3 Mrs Brackenborough, a glover, outside her house in Main Road, Woodstock, *c.*1900 (Source: Oxfordshire County Libraries, Local History Collection)

Nevertheless, the figure of approximately 1 out of every 4 married women having an occupation other than housewife in 1851 seems very low. Can you think of any other reasons why these census figures are low?

I can think of three:

o   There is the usual problem of accuracy with census information. For example, can we be sure that the householder always bothered to enter the wife's occupation?

o   We must also bear in mind the point made earlier that very many married women did casual work in the home which, quite understandably, did not get recorded in the census. (Elizabeth Roberts, writing about married women in parts of Lancashire at the turn of the century, estimated that between 40 and 50 per cent of the women she interviewed worked for wages at some time in their married lives – Roberts, 1994, p.131.)

o   The 1851 census was conducted in late March/early April; consequently in rural communities many women did not appear to have employment, yet would frequently have been at work later in the year helping with the harvest.

If you wish to carry out a similar exercise with the 1851 census in your own locality, you should appreciate that the returns will tend to underestimate the percentage of married women working.

However, we can't blame the census enumerators and their informants for everything. There were other important reasons why the percentage of married women working was so low compared with today. As we have seen, with the transference of work outside the home to workshops, factories and offices, together with the decline in farm employment, it became much more difficult for married women to work and look after their young and often large families. Futhermore, work opportunities varied in different localities. Roberts (1994) has pointed out the wide variations in the employment of married women in the towns of Barrow and Preston in 1911. There were similar differences in other parts of the country. Generally speaking, for married women seeking to work outside the home, the major centres of employment were the textile towns (hence the high numbers employed in Preston). But in areas dominated by heavy industries such as mining, and iron and steel, there were few opportunities for women to work even if they wished to do so. Finally, as Paul Thompson has pointed out when writing about the early twentieth century, there is another important demographic factor that must be taken into account:

> *Edwardian women married later, had more children and died earlier. They married in their mid rather than their early twenties and had three or four children. Large families were still very common. A working-class mother was not usually free of her children before she was fifty-five, by which time she had a dozen years to live. Today with a typical family of two children, independent when she is little above forty, a wife now has more than thirty independent years ahead. If Edwardian husbands did not like their wives to go out to work when they could not afford to, it was partly because they had a full job at home.*
>
> (Thompson, 1977, p.84)

This last point about Edwardian (or for that matter Victorian) husbands not liking their wives to work cannot be seen solely as the imposition of dominant male attitudes. It was a very real problem confronting many working-class families. For many married women their role was not that of paid worker but, as we have seen, they were key figures in the management of households. The idea that women's place was in the home was one that grew in the nineteenth century and has only gradually declined, and certainly not disappeared, in the twentieth century (for further discussion see Volume 1, Chapter 4).

2.2 MARRIED WOMEN AND WORK, 1911 ONWARDS

Table 3.8 shows the numbers and proportion of women in work between 1911 and 1981. One clear feature is that the percentage of married women in work rose significantly between 1931 and 1981. Why did this happen?

PART I WORK AND OCCUPATIONS

Table 3.8 Female labour force by marital status, Great Britain, 1911–1981

Year	Single		Married		Widowed/ Divorced		All (000s)
	No. (000s)	%	No. (000s)	%	No. (000s)	%	
1911	4058	77.7	712	13.6	455	8.7	5225
1921	4470	78.8	733	12.9	469	8.3	5672
1931	4885	77.9	953	15.2	426	6.8	6264
1951	3733	53.7	2653	38.1	570	8.2	6956
1961	3220	41.4	3908	50.2	655	8.4	7783
1966	3044	34.3	5063	57.1	756	8.5	8863
1971	2593	28.4	5761	63.1	783	8.6	9137
1981	2686	27.2	6286	63.6	906	9.2	9878

Source: Halsey (1988) pp.169–70

Perhaps we need go no further than accepting the demographic reasons given by Paul Thompson. However, other explanations for this increase have been given; for example, Arthur Marwick (1968 and 1974) has argued that a significant factor, although not the only one, has been the part played by the two world wars in the lives of British women. He points out that as resources in Britain became increasingly stretched in both world wars, women were called upon to participate in the war effort in a number of ways, including taking over work previously regarded as the domain of men. This in turn had a number of effects, including making women realize that they could do men's jobs and giving them confidence and expectations which they did not have previously. It also helped to break down the widely held view that women's place was in the home. Marwick concludes, therefore, that the total wars of 1914–18 and 1939–45 were significant events in changing the attitudes of both men and women towards the role of women in society and especially in relation to work.

Certainly it is true that before 1914 men's and women's work were seen as separate spheres. E.H. Hunt states that before the First World War,

There were very few instances where men and women were engaged on identical tasks. What constituted women's work was determined partly by physiological characteristics: it was believed, for example, that certain work could be performed by none but nimble-fingered females and that various other tasks required physical strength beyond their capacity. Some occupations, including many of those that were well-paid, were barred to women because the likelihood that girls would cease work when they married made it unprofitable to give them extensive training and made the girls themselves reluctant to accept responsibility. But the greater part of both 'women's work' and 'men's work' was reserved exclusively to one sex not as a result of real or imagined physiological characteristics but by long-standing custom. Women were restricted to certain tasks because they always had been, because men were not anxious to yield any of their monopolies, and because few women felt strongly that there was much wrong with things as they existed.

(Hunt, 1981, pp.23–4)

There have been many critics of Marwick's thesis. Gail Braybon has pointed out that although the number of women working rose dramatically during the First World War, the numbers fell equally dramatically afterwards. The opportunities in terms of range of occupations were not widened, and in a country where unemployment never fell below one million between 1921 and 1939, Braybon has argued that 'women wage-earners in the 1920s had to face far more hostility than they had before the war' (Braybon, 1981, p.14). Again, immediately after the Second World War there was a decline in the number of married women working, but not to the extent of 1918 – largely because the post-1945 period was one of comparatively full employment.

56

Nevertheless, from 1931 there was a large increase in the number of married women in paid employment, and it has been estimated that in 1943 43 per cent of all women working were married (Summerfield, 1989, p.196). Harold Smith (1986) attributes this increase to the widening of job opportunities for women from the 1930s onwards, and concludes that the participation of women in the war effort of 1939–45 had no long-term effect. Feminist historians, including Penny

Figure 3.4   Women at work in the Second World War: some women (*top*) took on work that was previously done by men; however, for many women (*bottom*) war work was 'the same as usual' but in uniform (Source: Hulton-Deutsch Collection)

Summerfield, have stressed that the war did not have the influence that Marwick suggests, but nevertheless Summerfield does admit that important changes did take place. In particular, she believes that the war did contribute to the growth of job opportunities for older and married women, mainly because of the establishment of part-time working arrangements. However, her overall conclusion is that there is little evidence to show that the changes during the war did much to break down sexual divisions either at work or at home (Summerfield, 1988, p.114).

Elizabeth Roberts does not agree completely with Summerfield. Her views concerning paid work opportunities for married women coincide more with those of Marwick. She states that the

> *demands made of women during the war … symbolize a bridge between the pre- and post-war world of women. During the war they were expected to be, as they had been earlier in the century, household managers par excellence: they were required to feed their families on meagre rations and to clothe them with an inadequate supply of clothing coupons. The war can be regarded as the apogee of the period of married women as household managers. But the other role of women at this time was as important participants in the men's world of work.*
>
> (Roberts, 1994, p.132)

Roberts (1994) also summarizes what she sees as the major changes affecting the lives of married women since 1945 (see Schema B).

Schema B: Married women at work, 1945–1990 – a summary of changes

o The hopes of wider job prospects for married women did not last long after the war; many women lost their jobs.

o The idea that women should work outside home was increasingly accepted by both men and women from 1945 on.

o The labour shortage at the end of the 1940s produced a renewed demand for women to work outside the home.

o There was a steady increase in the numbers of women working from 1951 onwards, but with local variations.

o Fewer and fewer women were earning money at home.

o Women's wages were less important to family survival than in the nineteenth century.

o Married women worked increasingly for other than financial reasons.

o Very few worked to build a career. Most still took jobs that were casual, poorly paid, gender-related and with few prospects.

o Women's role as budget controllers and in the domestic economy weakened, and they lost control of the family budget.

QUESTIONS FOR RESEARCH

1 Set up a project similar to the one that I did in Eynsham (pp.50–4). To what extent do your findings differ from my study of Eynsham? If they do differ, what reasons can you give for this? What was the role of married women in paid employment in your area in the mid nineteenth century?

2 From the discussion above it is clear that there is a wide range of disagreement concerning the role that the Second World War played in the lives of British women. What

effect do you think participation in the war had on married women? This is an area of enquiry which those of you who are working on recent family or community history can explore in your oral interviews or when reading diaries, letters, newspapers and magazines.

3 In addition, you can investigate the developments which Elizabeth Roberts claims have altered the lives of married women over the last forty years. Ask yourself whether your studies fit with her conclusions, and if not, why not.

3 ENTREPRENEURSHIP, BUSINESS AND OUTSIDERS: SOME QUESTIONS

by Ruth Finnegan

It is easy to forget that economic developments – including the famous Industrial Revolution – are not just mechanical and impersonal forces, but ultimately depend on the actions and experiences of vast numbers of ordinary people. There were the early railway workers, the women in textile factories, apprentices in the steel industry, or mid-nineteenth-century Yorkshire mining entrepreneurs (simultaneously owner-carters, farmers, beersellers – and more; see Samuel, 1977, p.19); there were the Arnisons, who moved from agriculture to industry (see Chapter 2, section 1); the Ulster food importer and mill owner (one of my great grandfathers) with his unbusiness-like son; the Methodist worsted manufacturer in Halifax (another great grandfather) building his fortune on his father's machine-making enterprise; or, more recently, the immigrant owners of 'cut, make, and trim' firms in Manchester. Clearly many factors are at play, but one crucial element has to be the individual innovators and their families who, whether at a high or quite modest level, founded and developed these many enterprises.

Although much has been written about general economic trends, there is still research to be done on specific businesses, individuals and families over time, above all for small businesses. This section provides some background and suggestions both on economic entrepreneurship and, more especially, on family businesses, relating these to continuing debates about the nature of entrepreneurship and business enterprise.

The theory that entrepreneurs are typically 'marginal' is one that could be investigated. This 'marginality' may be because particular family circumstances or values ('family microclimates', as Elliott, 1990, p.71, puts it) produce 'non-conforming' members who go their own way. It could be interesting to relate this to social mobility (see Wilken, 1979, p.10; also Chapter 5 below). Did entrepreneurs starting up businesses see their children rise or fall in the social scale in the next and subsequent generations? What role was played by their families?

Individuals or families may also be 'marginal' because of particular obstacles keeping them out of 'mainstream' opportunities, encouraging them to adopt alternative, entrepreneurial channels. Such barriers sometimes rest on formal legal prohibitions, but can be informal too, for example lack of access to education or capital. For those without the apprenticeship or professional training for entry into many occupations, entrepreneurship was sometimes the only way they could make a mark:

My great uncle Walter Scrimshaw is a marked case. As a Lincolnshire farm labourer he decided to 'follow' the potatoes he grew to the place where they were consumed, so he walked the 70 miles to Doncaster about 1895. He finished up in the 1930s owning the town's chief potato merchant's business, sundry houses, a cinema, a shop and two garages, as well as the whole of Braithwell parish (900 acres).

(Dennis Mills, personal communication to the author, 1992)

Or the background could be a 'success story' resulting from turning against the established employment channels or even a personal disagreement with the authorities. Brenda Collins recalls the family story of her Ulster great grandfather in this light:

He was a successful businessman. He had founded a sweet factory in the 1870s/1880s, which became W.J.Shaw and Sons. Family story has it that it started from a small shop in the front room of his house in Sandy Row (where my gran was born) after he was dismissed from his job as spinning master (foreman) at Durham Street Mill for having spoken out against cruel treatment of a young girl by their employer. It's interesting that the family story of his rise to prosperity begins with the reasons why he turned to 'being his own boss'.

(Brenda Collins, personal communication to the author, 1993)

It also depends on what opportunities there happen to be at a given time. Some lines of business may be impossible for those without capital or establishment backing, but other openings exist for those exploiting the 'cost-free' labour input within small family businesses. It could be interesting to investigate this role of families. What was their own social background, and were their own entrepreneurial activities related to openings or to barriers in the established mobility channels?

There are already some studies of such questions. Charlotte Erickson (1959) analysed a thousand biographies of British industrialists in steel and hosiery between 1850 and 1950. About 500 were biographies of Nottingham hosiers drawn from obituaries in local newspapers, together with 'marriage notices, parish registers, birth and death certificates, local directories, poll sheets, school records and local church and political chronicles' (p.4). She found recruitment more open in the hosiery industry (i.e fewer fathers of new entrants were in social class I) than in the heavily capitalized steel industry (for classifications of social class see Chapter 5; Erickson broadly followed the categories used in Glass, 1954). More recently the Business History Unit of the London School of Economics has conducted a computer-assisted analysis of entrepreneurs in England and Wales in the period 1860–1980, based on data from the *Dictionary of Business Biography* (Jeremy and Shaw, 1984–6). One report (Shaw, 1989) focuses on entrepreneurs in the distribution trades, and suggests again the importance of family connections over time. There were good openings in the distribution trades (especially retailing) for an individual from a relatively humble background to set up a business with comparatively little capital.

Another strand in the 'marginality' theory is the suggestion that entrepreneurs often come from a foreign or immigrant background or are 'outsiders' belonging to a subordinate or minority group (Wilken, 1979, Chapter 1; Pollins, 1989). For example, there were the Jewish financiers and nonconformist businesses established when other channels were barred; and more recently there have been Chinese and Italian restaurants, fish-and-chip shops, and ice cream vans; Indian shops and restaurants; and women entrepreneurs who have gone it alone rather than remaining below the 'glass ceiling' in larger enterprises. So is there a relationship between 'immigrant and/or minority status and a disposition towards business and entrepreneurship' (as it is put in Pollins, 1989, p.252)? Definitive answers are elusive, if only because the terms are unprecise ('minority' or 'outside' groups in whose terms, for instance; 'entrepreneur' as innovator, as founder or as business manager?). But the basic idea is certainly a stimulating one to explore in further research.

One interpretation is that the marginal position of entrepreneurs from religious, cultural, ethnic or migrant minority groups prepares them psychologically for innovatory roles. Alternatively, incomers may take up unattractive openings or gaps in the economy which local people are unwilling to fill themselves (the Irish in nineteenth-century Britain, perhaps, or Asians more recently – see Ward, 1985). Maybe it is *because* they are disadvantaged that minorities move into new businesses. Again, economic segregation or discrimination can lead to minority groups developing particular specializations to their own mutual advantage – like Jewish food or clothing sold to other Jews – often exploiting effective family, kinship or religious networks.

The Pakistani migrants who have settled in Manchester from the mid twentieth century are one interesting example (described in Werbner, 1987; see also Werbner, 1979, 1990). The first post-war settlers began in factory work, gradually shifting to petty entrepreneurship in the garment industry, first as pedlars in the 1950s, then market trading, wholesaling, and manufacturing (see Figure 3.5). These activities had the advantage of low starting-up costs (particularly market trading) and the help from information networks built up by migrants. The availability of family labour was also crucial, for few successful businesses could be started without the work of at least two family members. The expansion of small businesses gathered momentum as second-generation Pakistanis became involved as workers or business partners, and as the economic recession in Britain limited opportunities in the broader labour market. Eventually they were operating within a single economic niche or 'enclave': a connected network of businesses throughout the local garment industry, linked by kinship, neighbourhood and communal-political ties.

Several points can be drawn from this example for further investigation. One is the role of family links. Are these especially valuable for 'outsider' businesses? Or are they perhaps important in *all* small businesses, both for (often unpaid) family labour, through which output could be expanded without necessarily increasing labour costs, and for fostering kinship links with business as well as family benefits (see Jenkins, 1984, p.235)? Here, perhaps, is where studies of family history and of business history converge.

Consider, too, the social links in business. The mutually supportive networks built up by a group regarded as outsiders or marginal by others are well worth investigating. This may be true too of networks within a self-conscious *majority*, as with business links among Ulster Protestants (Jenkins, 1984).

Figure 3.5 A market stall in Longsight, Manchester: most British Pakistani wholesalers, and some manufacturers, started out as market traders (Source: Werbner, 1990, p.299)

Cultural or religious aspirations may also be relevant. Do particular groups hold ideologies that encourage entrepreneurship? This has often been suggested, from the nonconformist 'Protestant ethic', to Jewish or Asian interests in business. We need to beware of simple stereotyping, of course, given the variations not only within particular groupings, but also over space and time. Jamaican migrants, for example, are commonly pictured as uninterested in business within the British Isles, but are renowned for their entrepreneurial success in New York, where they are characterized as 'Black Jews' (Foner, 1977, p.132). With that proviso, this question too is worth investigating at a local and individual level.

Finally, a couple of other provisos. First, it is tempting to dwell on the positive aspects of outsider entrepreneurship. But 'ethnic enclaves' are not necessarily economically viable, and there have been failures – for example among the Manchester Pakistani settlers (Werbner, 1987, p.225). Further, as Ladbury (1984) points out for Turkish Cypriots in small-scale clothing factories in London, ethnic clustering can be because of first-generation migrants being educationally or linguistically blocked from higher-status jobs: 'most immigrants in the small business sector probably took jobs there because that was all they could get' (p.106). Even the second and third generations may be trapped, due both to lack of alternative jobs and to parental or group 'pressures to stay within the ethnic business sphere, [where] at least it is "safe" and familiar' (Ladbury, 1984, p.123). So a further set of questions could relate particular families or small businesses to changing mobility patterns over the generations.

You should also be aware that particular expectations and ideologies are not necessarily welcome to *all* members of a specific category. For example, before the Second World War many Jewish refugees came to Britain with the expectation (from others even if not themselves) of starting up small enterprises. Some no doubt did so successfully. But for others, given their own backgrounds and personalities, this was *not* the obvious course, and there could be painful personal costs. Indeed a study of failed or unhappy businesses would be as interesting as the successes. So though the theories about 'outsiders' and entrepreneurship provide a useful stimulus and testing ground for research, we must beware of taking them so seriously that we try to lump everything together under one head, and ignoring the perhaps equally important negative cases.

Provided we proceed with care, there is certainly scope for 'micro-level studies of the development of individual businesses over time' (Jenkins, 1984, p.236), whether or not classed as 'minority' or 'outsider' businesses, as well as of the role of individuals and families in this process, and of the business make-up of particular local communities. The issues in this section provide one framework within which studies of particular firms and the individuals or families associated with them can be pursued.

———————————————— *QUESTIONS FOR RESEARCH* ————————————————

If you are already knowledgeable about some family involvement in business or about a local enterprise, you could exploit this to investigate the following:

1   A particular family whose members were involved in a specific business. Questions to explore might include:

o   What sort of people were they?

o   Did they differ from others around them in circumstances or personalities?

o   Did they perhaps *not* differ much from the majority? Or did their success (if any) partly lie in access to a network of like-minded people for supplies, markets or information?

o   What role did other members of their family play at the start or in later generations?

o   Did any descendants carry on the business (if so, which?) and did the family generally rise or fall in the social scale over the generations?

2   A particular grouping or network that interests you. Many of the same questions as in (1) would be worth exploring. Also, how far do shared perceptions and experience (e.g. kinship links, 'ethnic enclave' marketing, their own cultural expectations or those of others) fit with the theories summarized above? Are similar processes at work in other small businesses *not* usually labelled 'minority' or 'ethnic'?

3   The history of a particular business(es): how far does it fit any of the theories, or throw new light on them?

4   Business leaders in a particular locality (similar to Erickson's 1959 study and using similar sources, but on a smaller scale).

5   Particular types of business in a local community (e.g. small firms, retailing generally, corner shops.)

You could select your sources from the following: oral memories (for twentieth-century studies); CEBs (mainly nineteenth century); personal letters or diaries (often important in family businesses); business records; your own knowledge of a particular area, group, shop or firm, supported perhaps by interviews or observation; trade directories (though these may not include small family firms/shops); local newspapers (difficult, but possibly useful for trade advertisements or obituaries); local audio recordings (e.g. on particular immigrant groups). For further discussion of these sources, see Volume 4 and Armstrong (1993).

4   STUDYING WORK AND OCCUPATIONS: A REVIEW

by Ruth Finnegan

Finally, look back over Chapters 1, 2 and 3. They present examples of many different localities, historical periods and types of work.

What relevance do these examples have for your own needs and interests?

You will have your own views, but the way to make the most of the examples is to consider the lessons for your own research. Looking back at Chapter 1 and the introductions to Chapters 2 and 3 will remind you of three important threads: (1) the nature, availability and critical use of *sources*; (2) some *methods and research strategies* and (3) possible *questions, themes and theories* which link the study of specific examples to work by other researchers.

It is worth quickly reviewing each of these.

_____ *EXERCISE 3.5* _____

1   List nine sources mentioned in Chapters 2 and 3, and note briefly what they were used for.

2   Note any others you consider could or should be exploited.

3   Which do you (a) have access to, and (b) intend to explore further?

Comments pp.228–9.

The examples also illustrate how such sources can be *used*: they indicate the questions or theories you can tackle through them, and the importance of evaluating and interpreting them critically (see also Volume 4, Chapter 2). These points – essential in serious research – can be learned both through observing the practice of others (as in these examples), and, equally important, through developing your own skills in the course of your research.

_____ **EXERCISE 3.6** _____

Look back through Chapters 2 and 3 and note down two methods or research strategies that struck you as potentially useful.

Comments p.229.

Which *you* chose is what matters, for the point is now to look forward to your own research. The value of that research will always be enhanced if you can bring out the links between the unique characteristics of a specific case and a more general question or theory.

_____ **EXERCISE 3.7** _____

Glance back through Chapters 1–3 to identify some *general* questions or theories to which research on specific cases could be linked. Note down two possibilities worth considering further.

Comments p.229.

Why are such links important? You will have your own ideas. But a couple of answers are (a) that they make both the individual cases *and* the general theories more interesting (comparison is always illuminating); and (b) that they provide vehicles not only for stimulating your own research but also for contributing to the general understanding of aspects of family and community history within a framework that is also meaningful to other researchers.

REFERENCES AND FURTHER READING

Note: suggestions for further reading are indicated by an asterisk.

Armstrong, J. and Jones, S. (1987) *Business documents: their origins, sources and uses in historical research*, London, Mansell.*

Armstrong, J. (1993) 'Local directories: exploring change and continuity in business activity', in Braham, P. (ed.) *Using the past: audio-cassettes on sources and methods for family and community historians*, Milton Keynes, The Open University.

Banks, J.A. (1954) *Prosperity and parenthood: a study of family planning among the Victorian middle class*, London, Routledge and Kegan Paul.

Barker, T.C., Campbell, R.H. and Mathias, P. (1971) *Business history*, Helps for Students of History, 59, revised edition, London, The Historical Association.*

Blythe, R. (1972) *Akenfield: portrait of an English village*, Harmondsworth, Penguin.

Board of Trade (Labour Department) (1899) *Report by Miss Collett on the money wages of indoor domestic servants*, London, HMSO, British Parliamentary Papers, 1899, XCII, pp.i–vii and 1–50.

Braybon, G. (1981) *Women workers in the First World War*, London, Croom Helm.

Burnett, J. (1974) *Useful toil: autobiographies of working people from the 1820s to the 1920s*, London, Allen Lane.*

Bythell, D. (1993) 'Women in the work force', in O'Brien, P.K. and Quinault, R. (eds) (1993) *The industrial revolution and British society*, Cambridge, Cambridge University Press, pp.31–53.

Census of England and Wales 1871 (1871) British Parliamentary Papers, vol. LXXI, part 1, pp.xxxvii–xxxviii.

Census of Great Britain 1851 (1854) British Parliamentary Papers, vol. L, pp.ccxxii–ccxxvii.

Central Office of Information, Wartime Social Survey (1944) *Women at work*, London, Central Office of Information.

Davidoff, L. (1974) 'Mastered for life: servant and wife in Victorian and Edwardian Britain', *Journal of Social History*, 7, pp.406–28.

Drake, M. (ed.) (1994) *Time, family and community: perspectives on family and community history*, Oxford, Blackwell in association with The Open University (Course Reader).

Ebery, M. and Preston, B. (1976) *Domestic service in late Victorian and Edwardian England 1871–1914*, Reading, Reading University Geography Papers No. 42.

Elliott, B. (1990) 'Biography, family history and the analysis of social change', in Kendrick, S. *et al.* (eds) (1990) *Interpreting the past, understanding the present*, Basingstoke, Macmillan. Reprinted in Drake (1994).

Erickson, C. (1959) *British industrialists*, Cambridge, Cambridge University Press.

Foner, N. (1977) 'The Jamaicans: cultural and social change among migrants in Britain', in Watson, J. L. (ed.) (1977) *Between two cultures: migrants and minorities in Britain*, Oxford, Blackwell.

Forster, E.M. (1989) *Howards End*, Harmondsworth, Penguin (first published 1910).

Girouard, M. (1980) *Life in the English country house: a social and architectural history*, Harmondsworth, Penguin.

Glass, D. (ed.) (1954) *Social mobility in Britain*, London, Routledge.

Halsey, A.H. (1988) *British social trends since 1900*, London, Macmillan.

Hearn, M. (1989) 'Life for domestic servants in Dublin, 1880–1920', in Luddy, M. and Murphy, C. (eds) *Women surviving*, Dublin, Poolbeg.

Higgs, E. (1982) 'The tabulation of occupations in the nineteenth century census, with special reference to domestic servants', *Local Population Studies*, 28, pp.58–66.

Higgs, E. (1983) 'Domestic servants and households', *Social History*, 8, 2, pp.201–10.

Higgs, E. (1986a) *Domestic servants and households in Rochdale 1851–71*, New York, Garland.*

Higgs, E. (1986b) 'Domestic service and household production', in John, A.V. (ed.) *Unequal opportunities. Women's employment in England 1800–1918*, Oxford, Blackwell, pp.125–52.

Higgs, E. (1987) 'Women, occupation and work in the nineteenth century census', *History Workshop*, 23, pp.59–80.

Horn, P. (1975) *The rise and fall of the Victorian servant*, Dublin, Gill and Macmillan.*

Hudson, P. and Lee W.R. (1990) *Women's work, family income and the structure of the family in historical perspective*, Manchester, Manchester University Press.

Hunt, E. (1981) *British labour history 1815–1914*, London, Weidenfeld & Nicolson.

Jenkins, R. (1984) 'Ethnic minorities in business: a research agenda', and 'Ethnicity and the rise of capitalism in Ulster', in Ward and Jenkins (1984).

Jeremy, D. and Shaw, C. (eds) (1984-86) *Dictionary of business biography*, 5 vols and supplement, London, Butterworth.

Jordan, E. (1988) 'Female unemployment in England and Wales 1851–1911: an examination of the census figures for 15–19 year olds', *Social History*, 13, pp.175–90.

Ladbury, S. (1984) 'Choice, chance or no alternative? Turkish Cypriots in business in London', in Ward and Jenkins (1984).

Lewis, J. (1984) *Women in England 1870–1950*, Sussex, Wheatsheaf.*

McBride, T.M. (1976) *The domestic revolution. The modernisation of household service in England and France 1820–1920*, London, Croom Helm.*

Malcolmson, P. (1981) 'Laundresses and the laundry trade in Victorian England', *Victorian Studies*, 24, pp.439–62.

Marshall, D. (1968) *The English domestic servant in history*, reprint of 1949 edition, Historical Association Pamphlets, General Series No. 13, London, Historical Association.

Marwick, A. (1968) *Britain in the century of total war: war, peace and social change 1900–1967*, Boston, Little Brown.

Marwick, A. (1974) *War and social change in the twentieth century*, London, Macmillan.

Marwick, A. (ed.) (1988) *Total war and social change*, London, Macmillan.

Ministry of Reconstruction (1919) *Report of the women's advisory committee on the domestic service problem*, London, British Parliamentary Papers, 1919, XXIX, pp.7–42.

Pearce, C. (1969) 'The domestic servants of Ashford', unpublished paper from ESRC project, *Ashford 1840–1870: a socio-demographic study*.

Pennington, S. and Westover, B. (1989) *A hidden workforce, homeworkers in England, 1850–1985*, Basingstoke, Macmillan Education.

Pollins, H. (1989) 'Immigrants and minorities – the outsiders in business', *Immigrants and Minorities*, 8, 3, pp.252–70.

Reeth WEA Local History Class (Tutor: R. Fieldhouse) (1970) *Domestic servants in Swaledale*, Richmond, Workers' Educational Association.

Richardson, S.J. (1967) *'The servant question': a study of the domestic labour market 1851–71*, MPhil thesis, London, University of London.

Roberts, B., Finnegan, R. and Gallie, D. (eds) (1985) *New approaches to economic life*, Manchester, Manchester University Press.

Roberts, E. (1984) *A woman's place: an oral history of working-class women 1890–1940*, Oxford, Blackwell.*

Roberts, E. (1994) 'Women and the domestic economy, 1890–1970: the oral evidence', in Drake (1994).

Rowntree, B.S. (1901) *Poverty: a study of town life*, London, Macmillan.

Samuel, R. (ed.) (1977) *Miners, quarrymen and saltworkers,* London, Routledge.

Shaw, C. (1989) 'British entrepreneurs in distribution and the steel industry', *Business History,* 31, 3, pp.48–60.*

Sheridan, D. (ed.) (1990) *Wartime women: an anthology of women's wartime writing for Mass-Observation 1937–45*, London, Heinemann.

Smith, H.L. (1986) *War and social change: British society in the Second World War,* Manchester, Manchester University Press.

Summerfield, P. (1988) 'Women, war and social change: women in Britain in World War II', in Marwick (1988).

Summerfield, P. (1989) *Women workers in the Second World War: production and patriarchy in conflict,* London and New York, Routledge.*

Thompson, P. (1977) *The Edwardians,* St Albans, Paladin.*

Tilly, L.A. and Scott, J.W. (1978) *Women, war and family,* New York, Holt Rinehart & Winston.

Trevor, W. (1993) 'Kitty', in Ingrams, R. (ed.) *The Oldie Annual,* London, Bloomsbury.

Ward, R. (1985) 'Minority settlement and the local economy', in Roberts *et al.* (1985).

Ward, R. and Jenkins, R. (eds) (1984) *Ethnic communities in business: strategies for economic survival,* Cambridge, Cambridge University Press.*

Werbner, P. (1979) 'Avoiding the ghetto: Pakistani migrants and settlement shifts in Manchester', *New Community,* 7, pp.376–89. Reprinted in Drake (1994).

Werbner, P. (1987) 'Enclave economies and family firms: Pakistani traders in a British city', in Eades, J. (ed.) (1987) *Migrants, workers, and the social order,* London, Tavistock.

Werbner, P. (1990) *The migration process: capital, gifts and offerings among British Pakistanis,* New York, Oxford and Munich, Berg.

Westwood, S. and Bhachu, P. (eds) (1988) *Enterprising women: ethnicity, economy and gender relations,* London, Routledge.*

Wilken, P. H. (1979) *Entrepreneurship: a comparative and historical study,* Norwood, NJ, Ablex.

CHAPTER 4

WORK AND COMMUNITY: CHANGING OCCUPATIONAL PROFILES

by Ian Donnachie

Historically, work and work-related activities occupied a large proportion of a family's time and helped to shape its own history and that of the community. Work opportunities and skills not only determined occupation, income, status, social class, and social mobility within the community, but also the potential for geographical mobility or migration elsewhere. We might just note that different occupations and work regimes generated quite specific cultures and behaviour patterns – for instance, the strong sense of bonding, religious commitment, or lively popular culture in some fishing or colliery communities. Occupation certainly influenced, if it did not wholly dominate, communal lifestyles.

Occupation tells us a lot about a family's social and economic position, and while some families stayed in the same occupation, many didn't. Limited occupational (or social) mobility might be expected in farming or fishing communities, but, even in these contexts, moves into mining, textiles and other industrial occupations occurred well before 1800 (see the Arnison case study in Chapter 2, section 1). In many parts of the British Isles there was a surprising degree of occupational, geographical and social mobility, prompted partly by improved educational opportunities and training for both established and new industries and by better and cheaper transport.

Some industrial communities were established by landowners or entrepreneurs to exploit local resources, such as water power, minerals, wool or flax, or were perhaps developed as service centres (e.g. transport towns, ports, turnpike or canal communities, even seaside resorts or spas). In the later stages of industrialization, new technologies spawned new communities, often on a larger scale than before. All had distinctive occupational profiles which shaped the lives of those individuals and families living and working there.

Some early communities were formally planned and this planning tradition, with ever widening social and economic objectives, continued, notably in the development of the new towns in the post-1945 period. Like earlier examples of the classic Industrial Revolution era, these communities had clearly defined functions and occupational profiles which much influenced their class structure and the role individuals and families played as they developed.

This chapter aims to show how work stamped its mark on families and communities, by looking at occupational profiles, just one of numerous approaches to work-related projects. It introduces four brief case-studies, using a variety of sources chosen to illustrate the potential for further investigations involving work, skills, occupations, occupational mobility, working conditions, the rewards of labour, as well as wider issues such as labour relations and the growth of the labour movement. Sources used in these examples include parish records, registers of birth, marriage and death, census records, valuations rolls, rent rolls, poor rolls, business and estate archives, newspapers, maps, plans, prints, photographs, and a wide range of secondary material such as trade journals, commercial and Post Office directories – some of which could be deployed on a project. As it happens, the specific examples here are Scottish, but they are used to illustrate the kinds of questions, sources and methods which could be used on studies elsewhere.

Does your occupation differ from that of your parent(s) and grandparent(s) and, if so, why?

1   HIERARCHY AND LABOUR IN A RURAL COMMUNITY, *c*.1800

Historically the rural community – often associated with an estate – was small, relatively little urbanized and its prime economic activity was agriculture. Until the First World War, landed estates, great and small, predominated throughout much of the British Isles – and no more so than in the south-west of Scotland. For example, the vast patrimony of the Earls of Stair in Wigtownshire covered thousands of acres. The life and work of numerous farming and village communities in this extreme south-west corner of Scotland revolved around this estate, and an important historical source is the extensive collection of family and estate papers assembled over the years by the Stairs and the stewards charged with the management of their lands. There we find an almost complete record of the day-to-day detail of estate supervision, farm leases, rent rolls, crop yields, tree plantations, ditching and dyking, house and road building – as well as a vast archive of material relating to more general social and economic conditions. This documentation, preserved in the Scottish Record Office, together with similar collections housed in archives up and down the country, provides a valuable insight into past community life (Donnachie and Macleod, 1974). Other local archives include those of the Murrays of Broughton and Cally, who developed, adjacent to their Palladian mansion, the planned village of Gatehouse-of-Fleet, a fascinating community which combined cotton spinning and a range of processing industries, and whose products were exported by sea through a riverside harbour (Donnachie, 1971).

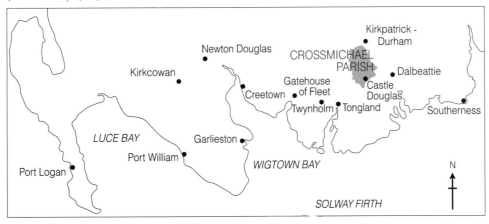

Figure 4.1   Planned estate villages and location of the Parish of Crossmichael, south-west Scotland (Source: based on Donnachie and Macleod, 1974, p.63)

However, our first case study of the parish of Crossmichael (see Figure 4.1) uses information on the social and economic structure of rural communities that can be obtained from secondary sources in many localities. Basic research could be followed up for a wide range of family and community history projects by more detailed investigation of parish, census, valuation, estate and other records.

EXERCISE 4.1

Look at the data in Table 4.1 overleaf (reproduced here as in the original) from the 1791 *Statistical Account* of Crossmichael parish, Stewartry of Kirkcudbright, and comment on the social and occupational profile revealed. My comments follow below.

Divifion of the Inhabitants—According to,

1ſt, Place of Birth.		3d, Occupations.	
Natives of England	4	The ſtewart depute	1
———— Ireland	10	The miniſter	1
———— Iſle of Man	5	The fchoolmaſter	1
———— Highlands	1	Farmers renting L. 15—	
———— Edinburgh	3	L. 170	41
———— Galloway and		Farmers under L. 15	27
Dumfries	749	Weavers	5
	——	Shoemakers	4
Total	772	Taylors and 3 apprentices	7
		Blackſmiths and 1 do.	3
		Maſons and 5 do.	10
		Joiners and 1 do.	6
2d, Religious Perfuaſions.		Dyer and 1 do.	2
		Shopkeepers	3
Cameronians	14	Small innkeepers	2
Their children	12	Male ſervants	51
Antiburghers	15	Female ſervants	54
Their children	9	Millar	1
Epiſcopalians	2	Labouring cottagers	55
Roman Catholic	1	Paupers	7
Eſtabliſhed church	719	Families of the above, &c.	491
Total	772	Total	772

Character

Table 4.1 Data on the population of Crossmichael parish, 1791 (Source: *Statistical Account of Scotland*, 1983, Volume 5, p.103)

Your response could begin with the point that even this simple table tells us a great deal about the social structure of the parish: typically, a hierarchy with the landowner's steward, the minister and the schoomaster (or dominie) at the peak and 7 paupers at the base of the pyramid. On other intermediate rungs of the social-occupational ladder were 68 farmers of varying degrees of affluence, 38 tradesmen, 5 service sector workers (i.e. shopkeepers and innkeepers), 55 labouring cottagers, and 105 servants – a total of 281 persons. Discounting the paupers, there were 274 persons, or 35 per cent, in employment out of a total population of 772. Assuming a relatively small number of strictly domestic servants (those employed by the more prosperous farmers would presumably also work on the land), a high proportion of the labour force – over 80 per cent – was absorbed by agriculture. The annual value of the farms was around £3,500, giving an average income of about £50 per farm. The 38 tradesmen must have made Crossmichael virtually self-supporting in terms of occupational skills, and the proportionately high number of masons suggests much building activity, perhaps associated with the agricultural 'improvement' then much in vogue. Note that the parish had also experienced a little 'proto-industrialization' in milling and textiles, hence feeding into general trends. The other statistics are not without their interest, especially the evidence of some modest immigration to Crossmichael, the majority from Ireland, another indication of socio-economic changes elsewhere.

Not bad for a few figures! But clearly much more information could be got by further research, particularly from the rest of this entry in the Statistical Account (which is particularly good on 'the State of the Population' and other community concerns), and from parish, estate and census records, all of which would fill in more detail of the individuals and families who lived and worked in the parish. The population of Crossmichael parish in 1801, by the way, was 1,084, so if the 1791 statistics are accurate, Crossmichael was a growing and prosperous agricultural community, clearly benefiting from demand for primary products from surrounding urban, industrial communities, notably the Scottish Lowlands to the north and Cumbria and Lancashire across the Solway Firth to the south. Its population, in common with many other rural districts, continued to expand until the 1860s but thereafter continuous decline became the norm (Donnachie and Macleod, 1974).

How does this compare with your own community and what sources would you use to find out?

2 AN INDUSTRIAL VILLAGE: THE TEXTILE COMMUNITY OF NEW LANARK AND ITS WORKFORCE IN 1885

Let's move on now and look at an industrial community. New Lanark presents a classic example of a factory village developed to house the workforce of a spinning mill dating from the water power stage of the Industrial Revolution. The community was founded in 1785 by the Scottish entrepreneur, David Dale (briefly partnered by Richard Arkwright), but it became famous under the management of his son-in-law, the savant and social reformer, Robert Owen. During the first quarter of the nineteenth century, Owen used New Lanark as a test-bed for his economic and social ideas, which by paternalistic methods sought to raise efficiency and produce conforming characters. Owen, like his friend and partner, Jeremy Bentham, talked much about 'happiness'

Figure 4.2 New Lanark villagers *c.*1890 (Source: New Lanark Conservation Trust)

but he really meant docility. At any rate, he made New Lanark, with its schools and well-disciplined children, a place of resort for the enquiring middle and upper classes before he left in 1824 for another community experiment in the United States.

The story of the community after Owen's departure and under later owners has been much neglected despite the existence of a voluminous archive, the Gourock Ropework Co. Mss., documenting its subsequent history and now preserved in Glasgow University Business Records Centre. This collection is clearly of great interest to the business historian, but it also has considerable value as a source for family and community history – both of New Lanark and Port Glasgow, where the 'Gourock' had its main plant (Donnachie and Hewitt, 1993).

We'll look now at one interesting document from the Gourock Mss., a statement of wages at New Lanark dating from 1885, which provides valuable data on the structure of the labour force and rates of pay in the different occupations in the mills. (NB. For reasons of space, the first two pages have been reproduced as a facsimile of the original, but the remainder of the document has been typeset in the form of a table.) As you examine it, think about its strengths and weaknesses as a source, the sorts of questions it raises in your mind, and the other sources you might want to consult to clarify the picture it presents.

EXERCISE 4.2

Look carefully at the document 'Statement of wages paid at New Lanark, 13 March 1885' in Figure 4.3 on pages 73–6, and then answer the following questions. (Note that calculations of average wages included in the document are not directly relevant to the questions below. The last paragraph in the statement of wages refers to marginal jottings, not relevant to this exercise, which have been omitted in the section of the document which has been typeset.)

1   What principal departments and occupations are identified?

2   Tabulate for each of the above the numbers employed.

3   What do the wage rates tell us about the occupational hierarchy at New Lanark?

4   What strengths and weaknesses does this document have as a source for family and community history?

My comments follow on pages 77–8.

UGD/42/22/2

Statement of Wages paid.

Blowing Room.

Robt. Wilson,	Master.	28/. p week,		2/
Jno. Black,	Assistant & Lap Carrier	14/. "		1/.
Women,	1 @	7/6. "		
	3 "	8/. "		
	2 "	8/6 "		
	2 "	9/. "		6
Pickers. (Village)		7d. per bag of 8 lbs,		(till June '82 5½)

1st Mill Preparation.

Wm Howe,	Master.	25/. p week,	1/6	2/-
Wm Stewart,	Setter	17/. "		1/
Jas. Purdie,	Sharper	16/. "		1/
Wm Watson,	Lap Carrier,	12/. "	6	1/
Card Tenter,	1 @	8/. "		6
Drawing Frames,	3 "	8/. "		6
Duplex "	1 "	9/6 "		6
Intermediate "	2 "	10/. "		6
Fly "	2 "	10/. "		6
Back Flyers,	1 "	7/6 "		6
do.,	1 "	8/- "		1/

3rd Mill Preparation.

Hugh Elder,	Master,	26/. p week,	1/-	2/-
Wm Christie,	Setter,	17/. "		1/
Jas Lennox	Sharper,	17/. "		1/
John Hepburn,	"	17/. "		1/
Jas. Campbell	"	16/. "		1/
Danl. Thomson	"	16/. "		1/
Wm Graham.	Rove Carrier,	15/. "		1/-
Thos. Steele	do.,	13/. "		
Thos. Hislop	Dust Boy	6/. "		

(over)

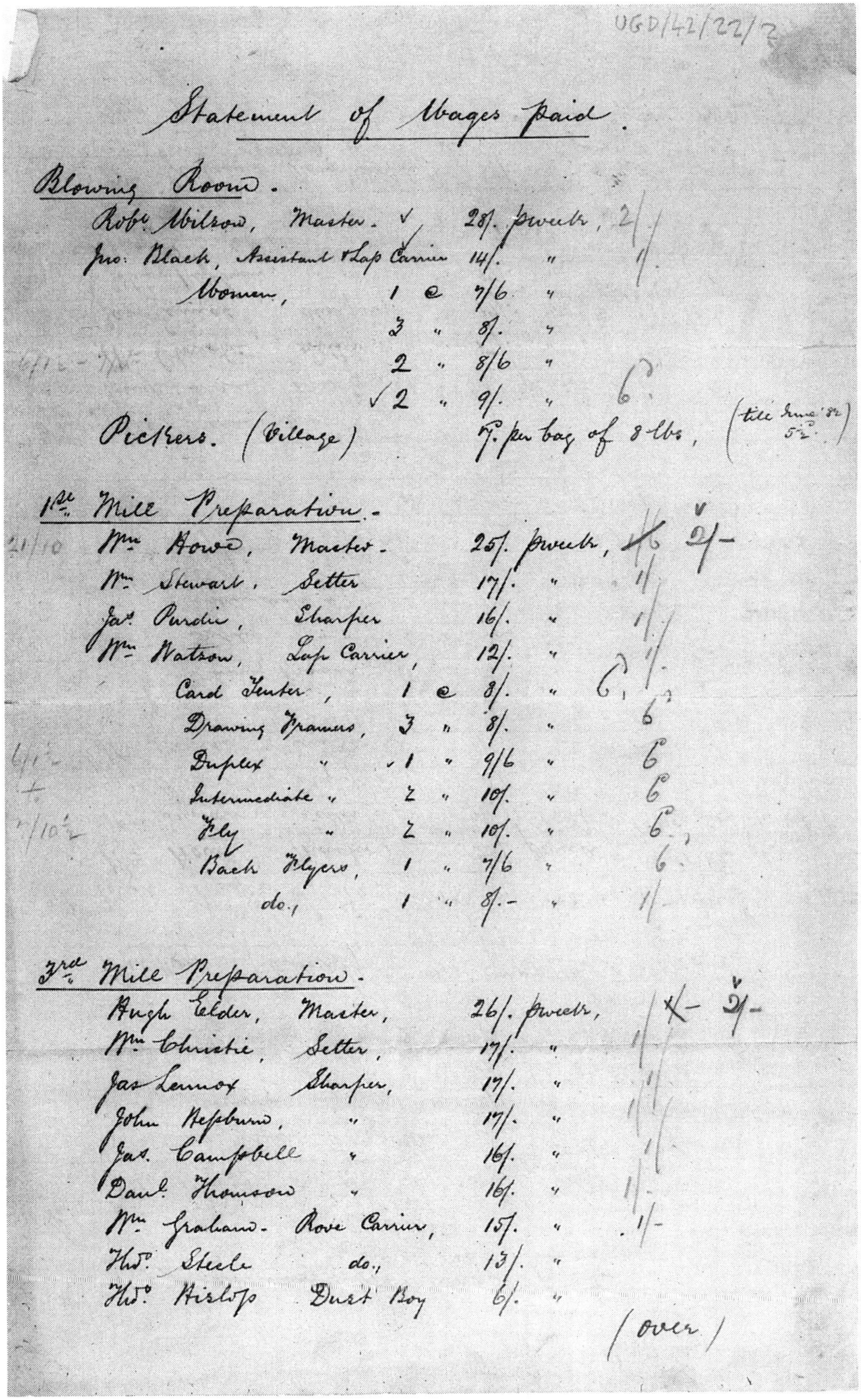

Figure 4.3 Statement of wages paid at New Lanark, 13 March 1885 (Source: Gourock Ropework Co. Mss., Business Records Centre, Glasgow University Archives)

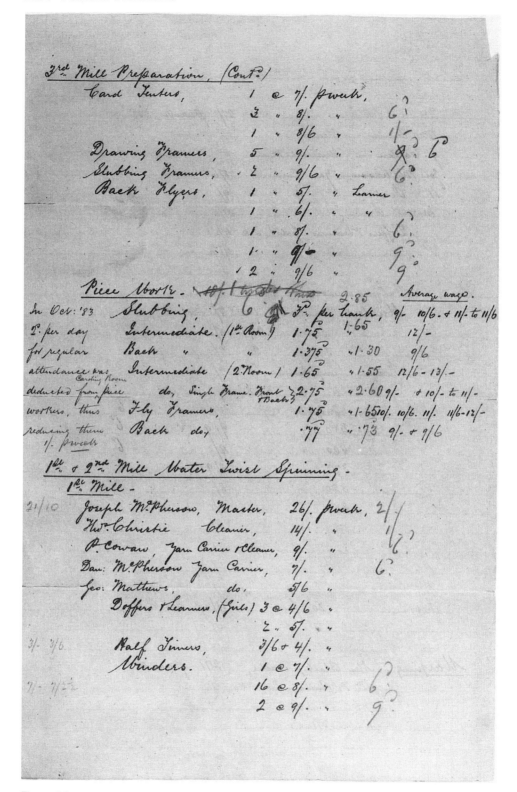

Figure 4.3 Statement of wages paid at New Lanark, 13 March 1885 continued

Statement of wages paid at New Lanark, 13 March 1885 (continued from Figure 4.3)

Twist Spinning (contd)

2nd Mill

David McPherson, Master		27/-	p.week
Wm Smith, Cleaner		18/-	"
J. Calderwood, Unsworths Machiner		17/-	"
Joe McPherson,	Yarn Carrier	8/6	"
Wm Peat,	do.,	9/-	"
Matth^w Brown,	do.,	6/-	"
Doffers and Learners (Girls):	3 @	4/-	"
	1 @	4/6	"
	4 @	5/-	"
Half Timers		3/6 & 4/-	"
Winders	4 @	7/-	"
	21 @	8/-	"
	2 @	9/-	"
Reelers (Large Reels)	2 @	9/-	"

Spinners

460 spdles & up	10/-	p.week
450 spdles & up	9/9	"
400 spdles & up	9/-	"
372 spdles & up	8/9	"
350 spdles & up	8/-	"
300 spdles & up	7/-	"
250 spdles & up	6/-	"
220 spdles (New Frame)	9/-	"
110 spdles (New Frame)	5/-	"

Twist Reeling

		Average Wage
20^S and finer	4/- per 100 Reels	10/6
18^S/14^S	4/3 per 100 Reels	

Warping

Alex. Black, Master	27/-	p.week
W^m McPhillamy, Beam Setter	14/-	"
John Bennett, Assistant	13/-	"
Warpers and Beamers (17)	9/6	"
Bankers (2)	8/-	"

Mule Spinning

3rd Mill

John Dickson, Master		27/-	p.week
Wm Muir and D. McPherson, Cleaners		17/-	"
Wm Fisher, Yarn Carrier		8/-	"
H. Waddell, Yarn Carrier		7/-	"
Mrs Gibson, Waste Picker		8/-	"
Piecers, Endwheels	3@	7/-	"
	1@	8/-	"
Slippers and Learners	1@	4/6	"
	1@	5/-	"
	7@	5/6	"
	3@	6/-	"
	2@	6/6	"
Half Timers		3/-, 3/6 & 4/-	"

Waterhouse & 2nd Mill Garret

Alex. Johnstone, Master		22/-	p.week
Piecers (Top flat W'house)	2 @	8/6	"
	1 @	9/-	"
Slippers and Learners	1 @	4/-	"
	1 @	4/6	"
	2 @	5/-	"
Half Timers		3/6 & 4/-	"

Piecers rates

		Average Wage
3rd Mill, Platt's Mules, per 100 lbs 50^S	4/2	11/- to 11/6
3rd Mill, McGregor's Mules, per100 lbs 50^S	4/5	from 9/- to 11/-
2nd Mill Garret, per 100lbs 50^S	4/7	8/6 & 9/6
Waterhouse (bottom flat), per 100 lbs 50^S	4/7	9/- & 10/-

Reeling and Bundling

W[m] Kilpatrick, Master	25/-	p.week
John Dale (Calcutta Yarn etc.)	16/-	"
J. Laidlaw (Damper and Sizer)	8/-	"
R. Mathews (General Jobber)	8/-	"

Reeling		*Average Wage in Mill*
40 End Reels, per 100 Reels	4/-	
40 End Reels (Platt's), per 100 Reels	3/9	from 6/- to 10/6
32 End Reels, per 100 Reels	3/6	
32 End Reels (Platt's), per 100 Reels	3/4	

Bundling		*Average Wage*
Lappers, per 1000 knots	5[d]	9/- to 10/-
Bundlers (3), per Dozen Bundles	4½[d] lb	20/- to 22/-
" " "	5[d] Mule	

Mechanic's Department

Engineers,	J. Ritchie	28/-		p.week
	J. Thomson	26/-		"
	Ja[s] Kent	26/-		"
Apprentices,	1 @ 9/-,	2 @ 10/-,	& 1 @ 11/-	p.week
	3rd	4th	& 5th year	
Joiners,	Jno. Mathews	26/-		p.week
	R. Kirkhope	24/-		"
	R. Grieve	24/-		"
Blacksmith, Templeton		26/-		"
Hammerman, Meikle		16/-		"
Moulder, Munro		27/-		"
Moulder Labourer, Rae		16/-		"
Masons,	Ja[s] Purdie	20/-		"
	Jno. Purdie	18/-		"
	T. Somerville	17/-		"
Fireman, D. Stewart		16/6		"
Carter, J. Tennent		19/-		"
Gas Man, C. Hislop		18/-		"
Greaser, J. McCallum		14/-		"
Labourers,	2 @ 15/-	& 2 @ 16/-		p.week
Banding, J. Laidlaw		15/-		p.week
Roller Coverers, Smith		19/-		"
	Black	18/6		"
	Mrs Mount	8/-		"

Net Department

Tho[s] Norcross		27/-	p.week
And[w] Love		17/-	"
W[m] Ritchie, Boy		7/-	"
Mrs Love, Fore Woman		15/-	"
Guarders and Learners	1 @	7/-	"
	1 @	8/-	"

	Average Wage
Weaving – If 4 nets p.fortnight, 4/- each net of 60 yds	10/6 to 13/6

If 5 nets p.fortnight, 4/2½ each net of 60 yds
If 6 nets or up p.forthight, 4/6 each net of 60 yds
Guarding – (Village) 1/5 each net of 60 yds

Sundries

Gateman	14/-	p.week of 60 hours
Night Watchman	22/-	p. week of 7 nights
Sunday Watchman	3/-	per day
Food Warmer	8/-	p.week

All the Masters are now paid steady wages, receiving no overtime –

Mechanics etc. when working overtime get time & quarter till 10 o'clock, after that time & half & 8[d] of allowance – Before 6 in morning, time & half & 8[d] of allowance –

The Rates marked in blue on left side of sheet are the Wages paid when the Mills were taken over, the rates in Red being the wages paid previous to last reduction, in Oct: '83 –

New Lanark,
13th March '85

This is a lot trickier than the previous exercise and requires a bit of close analysis and fiddly arithmetic.

1   The main departments are the blowing room, numbers 1 and 3 preparatory mills, numbers 1 and 2 twist mills, number 3 mule spinning mill, the waterhouse, reeling and bundling, the mechanics' department, and the net department. Principal occupations are masters, winders, spinners, warpers, beamers, reelers, bundlers, carriers, cleaners, doffers, learners, weavers and mechanics.

2   Your table should look something like this:

Department	No. of employees	Total
BLOWING ROOM:		
Master	1	
Operatives	9	10
NOS 1 AND 3 PREPARATORY MILLS:		
Master	2	
Operatives	40	42
NOS 1 AND 2 TWIST MILLS:		
Masters	3	
Cleaners/carriers	9	
Doffers/learners	13	
Half-timers	4	
Winders	43	
Reelers	2	
Spinners	9	
Warpers/beamers/bankers	21	104
NO. 3 MULE SPINNING MILL:		
Master	1	
Cleaners/carriers	4	
Piecers etc.	19	
Half-timers	3	27
WATERHOUSE:		
Master	1	
Operatives	9	10
REELING AND BUNDLING:		
Master	1	
Operatives	3	4
MECHANICS' DEPARTMENT:		
Engineers, joiners, masons, etc.	29	29
NET DEPARTMENT:		
Operatives	6	
Sundries	4	10
TOTAL WORKFORCE		236

3   The highest wages were paid to masters and skilled workers, notably the time-served tradesmen in the mechanics' workshop, on whom the smooth running of the operation, particularly the machinery, so obviously depended. All the *named* operatives, save three, were male, with Mrs Love, forewoman in the Net Department, apparently being the highest paid woman. The bulk of anonymous workers were female and the best wage they could expect was 10 shillings as a spinner. Piece rates could probably bring higher returns. There was also a clear hierarchy among the overwhelmingly female workforce, with the experienced at the top of the ladder and the learners at the bottom – typically men were in supervisory roles. The presence of half-timers suggests the employment of women with families who chose to work part-time.

4   The obvious strengths of the document lie in the detailed picture it paints of the occupational structure of a textile community, together with the levels of remuneration for the respective trades. Unfortunately, it does not detail all the workers, so it would need to be supplemented by other sources (e.g. census enumerators' books (for, say, 1881), rent books, valuation rolls, trade directories, and further data from the Gourock Mss. on labour conditions at New Lanark).

Clearly, this document raises many questions which are not answered immediately by the evidence it provides. For example, what was the total population of New Lanark, and how many of them had been born in the village? What proportion was employed in the mills? How many followed in their father or mother's footsteps? What was the male-female ratio? How many women were single and how many married? If married, did their husbands work in the mill? If their husbands did not work in the mill, where did they work and in what occupations? What were the hours of work? How did housing and other social conditions compare with those elsewhere and were the policies of Dale and Owen still maintained? The search for answers would, I suspect, raise still more questions!

For the family and community historian, places like New Lanark – with its extensively documented history – are dreams come true. Because business archives are now much more readily accessible than before, there are enormous possibilities for the pursuit of similar work-related topics using these sorts of records, and thanks to the work of bodies like the Business Archives Council and the National Register of Archives it is easy to find out what can be obtained locally. Records not held by companies have often found their way into local and regional archives for safe keeping, so these are invariably the best places to start a search (for further comments on business records, see Volume 4, Chapter 4, section 5).

────────────────── **QUESTION FOR RESEARCH** ──────────────────

Are there any major firms in your neighbourhood and what is the likelihood of them maintaining potentially interesting records on which to base a project? How would you find out and resolve questions of access? If you can resolve these questions, the likelihood is that an interesting project could be built around such topics as occupations and working conditions, or the relationship of a firm and its workforce to the community.

3   NEW COMMUNITIES IN THE VICTORIAN ERA: OCCUPATIONS AND OCCUPATIONAL MOBILITY IN THE SHALE-OIL INDUSTRY OF WEST LOTHIAN

This case study derives from the work of one of my research degree students, John McKay, whose thesis (1985) examined the social history of the Scottish shale-oil industry from 1850 to 1914. The industry was established to exploit discoveries of the great Victorian chemist turned entrepreneur, James 'Paraffin' Young, who patented processes to distil oil from shale ores which abounded with coal measures in West Lothian and adjoining areas of the Scottish Lowlands. The shale-oil industry developed on what we would now call 'greenfield' sites and expanded very rapidly on quite a large scale. Hence it attracted a considerable labour force – both skilled and unskilled – who migrated into the shale-mining and processing districts, mainly in the Almond Valley around Bathgate and Linlithgow to the west of Edinburgh. A high proportion of the labour force was at first recruited locally, but the 1871 census showed a high level of inward migration. While West Lothian and Midlothian accounted for 24 per cent of the workforce, other industrial counties of the Scottish Lowlands represented no less than 41 per cent and Ireland 28 per cent, with a further 7 per cent from the north or south of Scotland and from England and Wales.

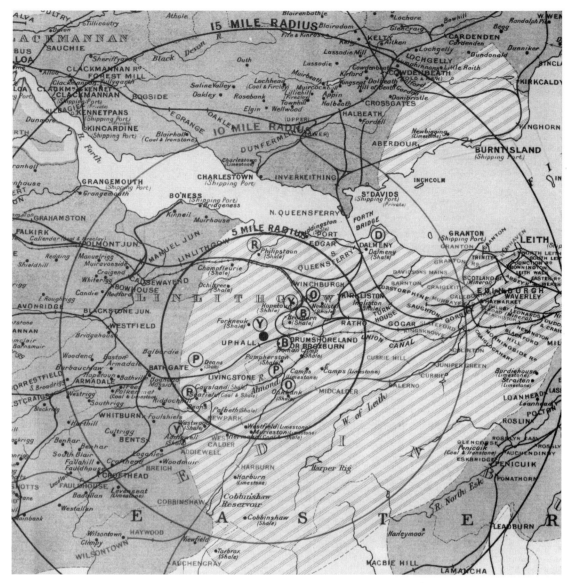

Figure 4.4 Map of West Lothian shale-oil districts, centred on Broxburn and Uphall (Source: *Minutes of arbitration on shale miners' wages*, Glasgow, 1903)

This influx, which continued during the heyday of the industry in the 1880s and 1890s, created a series of distinctive communities around the shale mines and shale-oil plants. Some adjoined older centres, while others were new company villages. John McKay's own family history illustrates a pattern of in-migration and occupational shift typical of the district at the time. His great grandfather, John Mackay, a cotton spinner at New Lanark (where my own research shows Mackays from Caithness had settled as early as the 1790s), and so recorded in the 1861 census, moved sometime thereafter to Oakbank, where a major shale-oil plant was established. According to the 1891 census, Mackay, then aged 57, was working as a mineral oil refiner, while his son, Daniel, 27, was an oil stillman. Both were in skilled and responsible occupations, but as the shale-oil industry was new, neither was a time-served (apprentice-trained) tradesman in the strictest sense. McKay used his own family's oral history to good effect in his research, building on the personal contacts it provided to interview many other survivors of a now abandoned industry.

This new technology generated an interesting occupational profile, and John McKay's work shows how census enumeration and other data can be deployed to reconstruct a detailed picture of the tasks and skills found in the shale communities. This particular exercise also shows how data from registers of birth, marriage and death, newspapers and other sources, obtainable in record offices, can be used to chart inter- and intra-generational movement between occupations (McKay, 1985; for further general discussion of inter- and intra-generational mobility, see Chapter 5).

_____ **_EXERCISE 4.3_** _____

Examine Table 4.2 on pages 80–2, a list of occupations of shale-oil workers in Mid Calder and Kirknewton parishes in 1871, together with their previous occupations and the occupations of their fathers, where known.

Then construct two tables. The first should show the total numbers of individuals in each of the five occupational groups in 1871, and then, for each of these totals, give a breakdown showing the numbers occupying each of the five occupational groups according to the nature of their previous occupations. To save you time counting, 102 instances of occupations in 1871 are given in Table 4.2, and previous occupations are listed for 96 of these. In compiling the first table, do not count the six individuals whose previous occupations are unknown.

Your second table should also show the total numbers of individuals in each occupational group in 1871, but this time only for those 78 individuals whose fathers' occupations are listed in Table 4.2. You should then, for each of these totals, give a breakdown of the fathers' occupations according to the number in each occupational group.

In compiling both tables, you will need to make quick qualitative judgements in order to classify previous occupations and occupations of fathers according to the descriptions of the occupational groups given in the note at the end of Table 4.2.

Comment on (i) the occupational structure and its possible influence on family and community life and (ii) the shifts of employment which emerge from your calculations.

_____

Table 4.2 Occupations of shale-oil workers in Mid Calder and Kirknewton parishes in 1871, together with previous occupations and occupations of fathers, where known

Occupation given in census enumerator's book, 1871	Previous occupations given in children's birth registration	Occupation of father as given in marriage register
Occupational group II [*]		
Colliery manager	Coal mine manager, Coal mine overseer, Coal miner, Engine keeper	
Oil work manager	Millwright	Carter
Oil manufacturer	Carpenter	Blacksmith
Occupational Group IIIA		
Engine fitter	Engine fitter	
Engine fitter	Engineer	
Engine fitter	Engineer	Labourer
Fitter	Agricultural labourer, Coachman	
Engineer	Engine keeper, Miner	Labourer
Time keeper	Weigher at chemical works, Picture liner	Candlemaker
Joiner	Forester, Miller	Ploughman
Joiner	Labourer, Lime burner	
Joiner	Joiner	
Joiner	Joiner	Farm servant
Cooper	Cooper	Tailor
Cooper	Master cooper	Brewer
Blacksmith	Blacksmith	Blacksmith
Contractor, oil works	Labourer, Drain contractor	Drain contractor
Shale mine foreman	Blacksmith	Stocking weaver

Occupation given in census enumerator's book, 1871	Previous occupations given in children's birth registration	Occupation of father as given in marriage register
Occupational group IIIB		
Storekeeper	Overseer, Land steward	
Oil refiner	Cotton spinner	
Oil refiner	Agricultural labourer, Furnaceman, Engine keeper	Farm servant
Oil maker	Agricultural labourer, Railway surface-man	Agricultural labourer
Shale miner	Coal miner	Miner
Shale miner	Coal miner, Iron miner	Coal miner
Shale miner	Coal miner	Gardener
Shale miner	Coal miner, Iron miner	Miner
Shale miner	Coal miner	
Shale miner	Iron miner	Miner
Shale miner		Miner
Shale miner	Coal miner	Miner
Shale miner	Coal miner	Coal miner
Shale miner	Iron miner	Miner
Shale miner	Coal miner	Coal miner
Shale miner	Coal miner	Coal miner
Shale miner	Coal miner	Flax dresser
Shale miner	Shale miner	Iron miner
Shale miner		Agricultural labourer
Shale miner	Iron miner	Coal miner
Shale miner	Fireclay miner	Labourer
Shale miner	Fireclay miner	Labourer
Shale miner	Coal miner	Miner
Shale miner		Surfaceman (roads)
Shale miner		Labourer
Shale miner	Agricultural labourer, Quarryman	Sawyer
Shale miner	Coal miner	Labourer
Shale miner	Labourer, Quarryman	Sawyer
Shale miner	Coal miner, Iron miner	Iron miner
Shale miner	Coal miner	Coal miner
Shale miner	Coal miner, Iron miner	Sailor
Shale miner	Labourer, Agricultural labourer, Quarry-man	
Shale miner	Carter	
Shale miner	Labourer	Quarryman
Shale miner	Coal miner	Labourer
Railway engine driver	Engine keeper	Blacksmith
Engine keeper	Engine keeper, Labourer	Labourer
Engine keeper	Engine keeper	
Engine keeper	Ploughman	
Retortman	Ploughman, Fireman	Farm servant
Retortman	Labourer	Labourer
Retortman	Platelayer	Joiner
Retortman	Labourer	Small farmer
Retortman	Baker	Tailor
Foreman labourer	Retortman, Loadsman, Porter	
Stillman	Pit roadsman, Engine keeper	
Stillman	Carter, Labourer	Farm servant
Stillman	Retortman, oil works	Hand-loom weaver
Occupational group IV		
Platelayer	Platelayer, Railway labourer	Weaver
Paraffin pressman	Chemical works labourer, Miller	Weaver
Paraffin pressman	Chemical works labourer	Weaver
Paraffin worker	Wine & spirit merchant, Gardener	Farmer
Shale mine labourer	Quarryman, Agricultural labourer	Sawyer
Shale mine labourer	Labourer	
Mine roadsman	Labourer	Labourer

Occupation given in census enumerator's book, 1871	Previous occupations given in children's birth registration	Occupation of father as given in marriage register
Occupational group V		
Labourer	Weaver	Weaver
Labourer	Potter's carter	Coal carter
Labourer	Maltman, Chemical works labourer	Agricultural labourer
Labourer	Railway clerk	Labourer
Labourer	Labourer	Labourer
Labourer	Oil works retortman	Oil works retortman
Labourer	Blacksmith	Labourer
Labourer	Chemical works labourer, Boatyard labourer	Farmer
Labourer	Labourer	
Labourer	Chemical works retortman, Ploughman	Ploughman
Labourer	Agricultural labourer	
Labourer	Quarryman, Roads labourer	Labourer
Labourer		Sawyer
Labourer	Ploughman	Farm servant
Labourer	Labourer	Quarryman
Labourer	Agricultural labourer	
Labourer	Quarry labourer, Drainer, Agricultural labourer	
Labourer	Quarry labourer, Tile works labourer	Labourer
Labourer	Agricultural labourer	Labourer
Labourer	Farm servant, Farmer	Farmer
Labourer		Ploughman
Labourer	Oil works fireman, Platelayer	Farm servant
Labourer	Agricultural labourer	
Labourer	Agricultural labourer, Railway labourer	
Labourer	Agricultural labourer, Van driver	Grocer
Labourer	Railway surfaceman, Forester	Agricultural labourer
Labourer	Ploughman	Carter
Labourer	Agricultural labourer, Porter	
Watchman	Baker, Railway checker	

Occupational categories: Group II: professional, entrepreneurial and management (e.g. managers, partners, chemists, contractors); Group IIIA: formally recognized skilled workers or craftsmen (e.g. engineers, fitters, plumbers); Group IIIB: skilled men without recognized craft training (e.g. stillmen, retortmen, engine-keepers, miners); Group IV: semi-skilled workers (e.g. underground workers, furnace stokers, agricultural labourers, ploughmen, farm workers);. Group V: unskilled, requiring physical effort with minimum of skill (i.e. labourers). (These categories are based on the Registrar-General's groupings for 1951.)

Source: McKay (1985) pp.295–9

Your own tables should look something like Tables 4.3(a) and 4.3(b) – percentages have been added as an aid to interpretation.

Table 4.3(a)   Previous occupations of shale-oil workers, Kirknewton and Mid Calder parishes, 1871, by occupational group

Occupational group in 1871			Previous occupational groups									
			II		IIIA		IIIB		IV		V	
	No.	%	No.	%	No.	%	No.	%	No.	%	No.	%
II	3	3.1	-		2	66.6	1	33.3	-			
IIIA	15	15.6	1	6.6	9	60.0	1	6.6	2	13.3	2	13.3
IIIB	44	45.8	1	2.2	1	2.2	27	61.3	8	18.1	7	15.9
IV	7	7.2	1	14.2	-		-		2	28.5	4	57.1
V	27	28.1	1	3.7	5	18.5	2	7.4	14	51.8	5	18.5
	96		4	4.1	17	17.7	31	32.2	26	27.0	18	18.7

Table 4.3(b) Occupations of fathers of shale workers identified in Kirknewton and Mid Calder parishes in 1871, by occupational group

Occupational group, son in 1871			Father's occupational group									
			II		IIIA		IIIB		IV		V	
	No.	%	No.	%	No.	%	No.	%	No.	%	No.	%
II	2	2.5	-		1	50.0	-		1	50.0	-	
IIIA	10	12.8	1	10.0	4	40.0	-		3	30.0	2	20.0
IIIB	39	50.0	-		5	12.8	16	14.0	10	25.6	8	20.5
IV	6	7.6	1	16.6	3	50.0	-		1	16.6	1	16.6
V	21	26.9	2	9.5	2	9.5	1	4.7	10	47.6	6	28.5
	78		4	5.1	15	19.2	17	21.7	25	32.0	17	21.7

Firstly, the data show that a high proportion of shale-oil workers – over 60 per cent – were skilled operatives, while less than a third were engaged in labouring. The high proportion of skilled labour suggests relatively high wages, but this might have been counter-balanced by poor and even dangerous working conditions – both in mines and plant. All individuals were presumably married and heads of families, who would need to be housed quickly as they migrated into the industry. It would not be unreasonable to suppose that shale-oil communities contained many hastily constructed and crowded company dwellings and that the rapid expansion put pressure on other social facilities.

Secondly, you should have noted that the data demonstrate considerable occupational mobility on the part of family heads and between first and second generations. The detail depends on how you classified the various occupations. You're unlikely to have come up with exactly this pattern, but let me summarize the rest of the findings briefly.

Taking intra-generational mobility first (see Table 4.3(a)), the three in Group II had moved up from Groups IIIA and IIIB. In Group IIIA, nine had previously worked on the same group, five had moved up and one down. Many occupations in this group were controlled by apprenticeship, so the five upwardly mobile individuals might suggest a breaking down of barriers and the acceptance of less formally acquired skills. But closer examination reduces the transfers across the craft barrier to three: a fitter, a joiner and an engineer. The fitter had previously been a coachman and an agricultural labourer; the joiner was a labourer and lime burner; the engineer had been a miner and an engine keeper. All three may have gained entry to the jobs held in 1871 on the basis of acquired skills, or they may have been formally skilled men who had adopted intermediate occupations before returning to their original trade. In Group IIIB, 27 had previous work experience in the same group, two had moved down and fifteen up, half of the last being connected in some way with agriculture. The transition from rural employment is also clear in group IV and even more so in Group V, where there were five skilled workers and many Group IV operatives, including ten agricultural labourers, a carter and a maltman. Clearly the transition to the new industry and communities involved the extinction of rural skill in favour of simple labouring.

Occupational mobility was even more marked between the generations (see Table 4.3(b)). Management had all moved up. The fathers of those in Group IIIA included one in II, four in IIIA and five in IV and V. The fathers' occupations were: brewer (II); tailor, blacksmith, stocking weaver, drain contractor (IIIA); candlemaker, ploughman, farm servant (IV); and two labourers (V). Where sons had been enumerated in IIIB, five fathers had been employed in Group IIIA occupations: blacksmith, joiner, small farmer, tailor and weaver. Among fathers in Group IIIB itself, there were fifteen miners and one sailor – indicating a considerable degree of inter-generational job stability among miners. The ten Group IV fathers comprised five agricultural labourers, a flax dresser, a gardener, two sawyers and a quarryman. In the case of the Group IV sons, the fathers' occupations had been: farmer (II), three weavers (IIIA), sawyer (IV) and

Figure 4.5 Broxburn, West Lothian, *c.*1920, showing workers' housing and shale-oil plant. To the right are a shale bing and the chimneys of a crude-oil works. A large refinery can be seen on the left. The vacant lot in the foreground later accommodated a picture house (Source: Dr John McKay)

labourer (V). Of sons enumerated in Group V occupations in 1871, 21 fathers were found: two farmers (II), weaver and grocer (IIIA), retortman (IIIB), two carters, six agricultural labourers, one sawyer and one quarryman (IV), and six labourers (V).

McKay's conclusion is that the transition from the occupational structure of an essentially rural to an industrial community involved both upward and downward movement in terms of occupational classification and family status. It is important not to exaggerate the level of skill required by this new industry and equally we must not underrate traditional agricultural employment. Agriculture and associated activities certainly accounted for a high proportion of the locally recruited labour, while many of the migrants also had relatively skilled family backgrounds. Unfortunately, we don't have space here to assess whether or not the shale-oil industry offered improvement in terms of working conditions, rewards of labour, and family and community life (but see McKay, 1988).

--- **QUESTION FOR RESEARCH** ---

Do the conclusions about occupational mobility apply to either your own community or another known to you and how would you pursue these issues further?

4 PLANNED TWENTIETH-CENTURY COMMUNITIES: CHANGING OCCUPATIONAL STRUCTURES IN NEW TOWNS

A major shift in time and historical perspective takes us to our fourth and final case study which uses data from the archives of new towns, specifically two Scottish examples. East Kilbride, the first Scottish new town, designated in 1947, was built round an old rural community south of Glasgow and was mainly planned to cope with overspill and slum clearance from the city. A later community, dating from 1954, Glenrothes, was built on the Fife coalfield, and thus incorporated older mining communities as well as housing migrants from the cities. Both developed in the halcyon days of post-war planning when on 'greenfield' sites efforts were made to integrate economic and social development as part of the recovery programme.

Historically, these communities are very well documented and the archives contain potentially valuable data on every conceivable aspect of life and work there since designation. I've chosen to look at employment profiles of the kind that would be essential to any further analysis of specific industries or changing work patterns in such communities. This short exercise tells us much about the occupational and social structure of near-contemporary new town communities – a considerable contrast to the eighteenth-century parish we looked at in section 4.1.

EXERCISE 4.4

Examine the tables for employment and occupations in Glenrothes (Tables 4.4–4.6) and East Kilbride (Table 4.7) on pages 86 and 87, then respond to the following questions:

1   What do the occupational data for Glenrothes tell us about the community's economic and social structure?

2   What were the major occupational categories in 1974 and which were the largest employers of female labour? Have you any observations on the latter item?

3   Do the data for East Kilbride present a similar pattern? What points of comparison and contrast can you draw between East Kilbride and Glenrothes 14 years before?

---

1   The tables indicate sustained decline in the traditional industries of paper making and coal mining, as well as construction, the last possibly reflecting the rundown in building houses and infrastructure as the new town matured. There is a corresponding increase in employment in new engineering and electronic industries brought with the development of the new town's economy – in fact the very industries and skills which have become typical in such communities.

2   The predominant occupational categories in 1974 were engineering, professional-technical, and electronic workers – all in the so-called 'sunrise' industries that were attracted by government grants and incentives to locate in new towns. A large service and distributive labour force is evident – again very much the norm. The 'blue collar' workers can be assumed to constitute a large slice of the labour market. The biggest employers of women were (by far) the clerical, professional-technical and electrical sectors – suggesting much secretarial employment in a variety of sectors and semi-skilled assembly-line work in electronic and similar sorts of factories. Women represented well over a third of employees, and nearly 12 per cent of them were part-timers (compare with the position at New Lanark in 1885). Women clearly played an important role in the local economy, especially in the new industries, but as part-timers many were probably less well paid than men. We can also assume that more women were going out to work to enhance family income and that smaller, post-war families and better educational provision facilitated this trend. (We would need further information to tell what proportion were women in single-parent families – another significant social trend of that period.)

3   The data are not strictly comparable, but nevertheless show a similar pattern, particularly when the most recent figures for Glenrothes and those for East Kilbride are compared. Manufacturing accounted for 37 per cent of jobs in East Kilbride in 1988, roughly comparable to the proportion in Glenrothes fourteen years earlier. Another obvious point of comparison is the substantial role played by women in the labour force – more than a third of the total employed females being in public administration and almost another third in manufacturing. Points of contrast include the huge growth in the service sector (again typical of the 1980s), the increase in the skilled labour force, and the corresponding decrease in essentially unskilled manual occupations.

Table 4.4 Glenrothes: employed residents as % of total in 1954, 1968 and 1974

	1954	1968	1974
Paper making	19	5	3
Coal mining	16	8.3	8
Construction	15	11.8	6
Electrical/engineering	no data	24	24
Professional/scientific	no data	9	9

Table 4.5 Glenrothes: main occuption groups, 1968 and 1974 (% of total)

	1968	1974
Engineering workers	16.5	15.7
Professional/technical	14.3	14.1
Clerical	10.0	11.6
Service, sport, recreation	6.5	8.4
Electrical/electronic	7.6	8.2

Table 4.6 Glenrothes: employment status and occupational classes, 1974

Occupational class	Sex and employment status					
	Full-time male	Part-time male	Full-time female	Part-time female	total	total %
Farmers, foresters, fishermen	84	5	4	2	95	0.83
Miners, quarrymen	156	0	0	0	156	1.37
Gas, coke, chemicals	21	0	2	1	24	0.22
Glass, ceramic makers	9	0	0	1	10	0.09
Fur, forge, foundry workers	35	1	2	0	38	0.33
Elect./electronic workers	362	0	387	186	935	8.21
Engineering workers	1 481	3	215	86	1 785	15.67
Woodworkers	257	0	4	0	261	2.29
Leatherworkers	1	0	2	0	3	0.03
Textile workers	48	1	22	5	76	0.67
Clothing workers	16	0	149	21	186	1.63
Food, drink, tob. workers	90	0	52	11	153	1.34
Paper printing works	387	0	64	32	483	4.24
Makers of other products	187	1	108	71	367	3.22
Construction workers	309	1	3	0	313	2.75
Painters, decorators	135	0	2	1	138	1.21
Drivers of cranes etc.	170	0	0	0	170	1.49
Labourers NEC	204	4	5	3	216	1.90
Trans./comm. workers	419	1	32	20	472	4.14
Warehousemen packers	177	1	139	45	362	3.18
Clerical workers	382	1	822	111	1 316	11.55
Sales workers	396	3	220	171	790	6.94
Service sport recreation	299	16	213	431	959	8.42
Administrators/managers	288	0	16	0	304	2.67
Professional/technical workers	1 010	7	468	125	1 610	14.14
Armed forces	163	0	5	0	168	1.47
Inadequately described	0	0	0	0	0	0.00
Total	7 086	45	2 936	1 323	11 390	
%	62.20	0.40	25.78	11.62		100.00

Table 4.7   East Kilbride: employment, economic classification and unemployment, 1988

Employment	Male	Female	Total
Employed inhabitants	19 100	14 400	33 500
Work in East Kilbride	9 200	10 700	19 900
Work elsewhere	9 900	3 700	13 600
Jobs in town (total)	16 300	13 900	30 200
Incoming commuters	7 100	3 200	10 300

Thus 41% of employed inhabitants work outside East Kilbride

34% of jobs in East Kilbride are held by people who live elsewhere.

Categories of jobs in East Kilbride	Male %	Female %	Total %
Manufacturing	43	30	37
Non-manufacturing/service	25	14	20
Public administration	18	37	27
Retail	4	13	8
Others	10	6	8

Estimated economic classification of employed inhabitants	
Skilled/semi-skilled manual	36%
Unskilled manual	4%
Clerical, retail, service	45%
Managerial and professional	15%

Unemployment (April 1988)	Male %	Female %	Total %
East Kilbride (estimate)	10.9	8.6	9.9
Strathclyde region	21.1	10.5	16.5
Scotland	15.3	8.9	12.6
Great Britain	–	–	9.1

Sources: Tables 4.4–4.7: Glenrothes and East Kilbride Development Corporation Archives

Much more can be said about the data relating to occupational profiles, occupational mobility, skill levels, and work patterns – all of which affect family lifestyles in communities like Glenrothes and East Kilbride. Notice that in the latter, 41 per cent commute elsewhere and 34 per cent of the labour force is drawn from outwith the community – features that would have been pretty limited in most nineteenth-century industrial communities and virtually non-existent in rural, agricultural ones. Neither would unemployment be much in evidence in earlier industrial or rural communities – and certainly not on the scale that existed in East Kilbride in 1988. We've talked much about the influence of work on family and community history, but we mustn't forget that lack of work or opportunities (as in the migration studies explored in Volume 2) could have an even more dramatic impact on the lives of our predecessors.

─────────────── *QUESTION FOR RESEARCH* ───────────────

If you live a new town, find out what historical records are available for research of the kind illustrated by the case study above. Could you use them for a similar project?

5   CONCLUSION

As an economist-turned-historian, I'm acutely aware of the shallowness of my economic analysis. And I suspect that the sociologist too will have seen many missed opportunities, relating to such issues as work and social class (see Chapter 5), working conditions and work-related culture. But I hope the case studies here have given some indication of the kinds of questions the historian would want to ask about work and occupations in any community and the sorts of sources that could be deployed to answer some of them in a project.

QUESTION FOR RESEARCH

How did people in your community earn their living over the last century? Have there been major changes in the economic and occupational structure of the community? If so, why, and what have been the results?

Relevant primary sources are available in most local or regional archives and can be supplemented by a variety of secondary works, such as the enormously useful trade and commercial directories, which often provide considerable detail on the local economy and occupations (see Volume 4, Chapter 4, section 1, and Armstrong, 1993). We've said little here about the workplaces themselves, but industrial archaeology can be a useful tool and abandoning one's books for one's boots takes us into the real world of work in the past (discussed in Volume 4, Chapter 6, section 1). As suggested at the outset, there are also many other important aspects of work affecting family and community history which you might also like to explore.

Thinking about work as the basis of a local project opens up a potentially fascinating area of family and community history, regardless of period.

REFERENCES AND FURTHER READING

Armstrong, J. (1993) 'Local directories: exploring change and continuity in business activity', audio-cassette 4A in Braham, P. (ed.) *Using the past: audio-cassettes on sources and methods for family and community historians*, Milton Keynes, The Open University.

Donnachie, I. (1971) *The industrial archaeology of Galloway*, Newton Abbot, David & Charles.

Donnachie, I. and Hewitt, G. (1993) *Historic New Lanark: the Dale and Owen industrial community since 1785*, Edinburgh, Edinburgh University Press.

Donnachie, I. and Macleod, I. (1974) *Old Galloway*, Newton Abbot, David & Charles.

Jackson, S. (ed.) (1988) *Industrial colonies and communities*, Conference of Regional and Local Historians.

McKay, J.H. (1985) *The social history of the Scottish shale oil industry 1850–1914*, unpublished Ph.D thesis, The Open University.

McKay, J.H. (1988) 'Retail cooperatives in the shale mining areas of the Almond Valley 1872–1914', in Cruickshank, G. (ed.) *A sense of place: studies in Scottish local history*, Edinburgh, Scotland's Cultural Heritage.

Moody, D. (1986) *Scottish local history: an introductory guide*, London, Batsford.

Smout, T.C. and Wood, S. (1990) *Scottish voices 1745–1960*, London, Collins.

Statistical Account of Scotland (1983) Volume 5, *Stewartry of Kirkcudbright and Wigtownshire*, Wakefield, E.P. Publishing. (First published 1791–99.)

PART II

CLASS, MOBILITY AND LOCAL POLITICS

CHAPTER 5

SOCIAL MOBILITY

by Bernard Waites, Michael Drake and Ruth Finnegan

Part I of this volume stressed the links between work, families and communities, and in Chapter 4 we saw how a study of occupational profiles could throw light on the social and economic position of families and their communities. In this chapter we are turning the spotlight on the relationship between occupation and social position, linking this to the study of what is known as social mobility. The greater part of the chapter is devoted to a critical examination of some large-scale social mobility surveys of Britain for both the nineteenth and twentieth centuries. This gives you both the national background – the macro view – and a series of questions and concepts against which local and specific studies can be set.

Social mobility takes place when people come to occupy a different social stratum or a different occupational rank from that of their family of origin. Though our Victorian forebears did not use the term social mobility, they certainly recognized the process. Samuel Smiles, in his best-selling *Self-help* (1859), wrote of 'the efficacy of self-respect and self-reliance in enabling men of even the humblest rank to work out for themselves an honourable competency and a solid reputation' (1986 edn, p.23).

In studying families within your community, you may well have gathered occupational information which appears to confirm Smiles's perception of his own society. The photographs in Figures 5.1 and 5.2 suggest that it was not entirely mistaken. The old couple outside their cottage (Figure 5.1) are an illiterate agricultural labourer and his wife, but their daughter (wearing her best dress in the studio portrait in Figure 5.2) was educated under the 1870 Education Act and became a schoolmistress.

Your own research may uncover a similar family history of 'rising from the ranks'. But if this research is to be of more than personal interest, you will need to ask, 'How typical or how significant was this?'. To answer this requires some background knowledge of the national trends in mobility and how they have been studied. This chapter should help you to relate your 'personal' interests to broader sociological and social historical issues and to become familiar with some influential concepts and techniques used in social mobility research in nineteenth- and twentieth-century Britain.

Figure 5.1 John and Elizabeth Summers outside their cottage in Hampshire, *c*.1900. The photograph was taken by an itinerant photographer. Both John Summers and Elizabeth Green were illiterate. He worked as an agricultural labourer, and she as a lacemaker. They moved to Hampshire from Northamptonshire around 1875 and changed their name to Butler, as John was in trouble for poaching. They had 8 children.

Figure 5.2   Eliza Susannah, youngest daughter of John and Elizabeth 'Butler'. Eliza Susannah (born in 1868) profited from the first Education Act and went to school, becoming a pupil teacher in Hampshire. She later travelled widely in the South of England as a lady's maid and eventually married Walter Bartholomew, a painter and decorator from Reigate, in 1894. Her granddaughter, Monica Shelley, is a Lecturer in the Institute of Health, Social Welfare and Community Education at The Open University.

1   STUDYING SOCIAL MOBILITY

Since social mobility research assesses change and stability in society over time, a moment's reflection shows that we have to define our categories with some care. Unless these are precisely stated, the results will carry little credence. Let us start, therefore, by outlining briefly some basic concepts.

Inter-generational and intra-generational mobility   You will recall these terms from Chapter 4. A young person entering the labour force at a different point in the occupational hierarchy from his or her father – for example where the daughter of a hospital porter trains to be a doctor – has experienced *inter-generational* mobility. In this example the parental and filial occupations differ greatly in material reward and social cachet, so her mobility is *long-distance*; had she trained to be a nurse it would have been comparatively *short-distance*. Mobility within someone's lifetime is *intra-generational*: for example, the son of a bricklayer training to be a bricklayer, but in the course of his career becoming a successful property developer.

As formal qualifications are required for entry into more and more occupations, the balance between inter-generational and intra-generational mobility may alter, facilitating the former as against the latter.

Rank, class and stratification: the varying scales   Studying social mobility depends on the assumption that society is stratified into a hierarchy of grades or 'classes': mobility is up or down this scale.

How do you define this scale and separate out the steps within it if you are doing research on social mobility?

Unfortunately the answer is by no means self-evident. Indeed, even the members of the community being studied may not all see their social hierarchy in the same way. Furthermore, social rankings (of people, groups, occupations) change over time, and may vary from place to place.

So what should you and other researchers do? There are a number of well-established frameworks – none of them perfect, perhaps, but useful to know about as a basis both for individual research and for comparative studies. The main frameworks referred to in this chapter are listed in Table 5.1.

Which framework you use will affect your research plan and likely findings. A scale designed to test Marx's class theory, for example, would probably have only two classes on the assumption that the basic division lies between those possessing property (the means of production) and the propertyless. This scale would reveal much less mobility than one designed to test movement between status groups (whose members are defined by the honour they enjoy in the wider community), for there is a multiplicity of status groups and consequently more 'status mobility'.

Perhaps the most common approach is to focus on *occupations*. These can (up to a point) be ranked according to size and source of income, together with such factors as workplace authority. Similar occupations can then be aggregated into classes or strata. Occupation is a reasonable guide to a person's position in the economic system and helps to determine the social status of his or her family. Occupation is also reasonably easy to identify and investigate. In particular, many thousands of occupations were entered in the census returns (for examples, see Volume 4, Chapter 3, section 2.1.1; see also Chapter 3, section 2 above). These were then aggregated into larger categories during the census processing. From 1911 and (more explicitly) from 1921, the Registrar-General classified the occupations listed into five main 'social classes', adapting this from census to census to fit the changing occupational picture. For nineteenth-century studies, historians have applied these twentieth-century 'social class' classifications to the earlier occupations. Although this is perhaps not wholly satisfactory, it is convenient for comparison; one particularly useful example of this (Armstrong, 1972) is reproduced in Volume 4, Chapter 3, section 2.1.1.

Using occupational scales as the framework for studying mobility has problems as well as advantages. The categories have to be broadly defined so as to cover the typical experiences of masses of individuals; consequently they do not identify separately the elites in whose hands wealth and power are concentrated. Furthermore, the ranking between occupations may be neither widely agreed nor stable. It can be misleading to think of mobility between many types of 'white-collar' employment and skilled manual labour as up or down. Lastly, we should note that concentrating on individuals moving 'up' or 'down' between occupations misses the fact that historically much mobility has been accomplished by occupational *groups*. Typically, these have been professions whose control of training and accreditation has restricted recruitment and who have closed their ranks. Medicine in the nineteenth century and accountancy in the twentieth are good examples of upwardly mobile professions.

Table 5.1 Some alternative ranking frameworks used in social mobility studies[1]

	Number of ranks or categories used	Terms frequently used	Some of the researchers using these categories[2]	Notes
A	3	Upper, middle and working (or lower) classes		Commonly used in everyday speech, and as rather vaguely defined terms by researchers
B	2	Class: (a) working class (proletariat); (b) upper class (bourgeoisie)	Marx and Marxist writers	Regarded as two opposed and antagonistic classes
C	5	Class, or occupational group, or socio-economic group (SEG)	Miles and Vincent (1991); McKay (1985); Armstrong (1972); Pearce (1969); Mills and Mills (1989)	Based on occupations; ranking of these often derived from 20th-century classifications by Registrar-General of the occupations in census returns[3]
D	7	Status, rank, class	Glass (1954); Erickson (1959)	Occupation not irrelevant, but other factors important too, especially status (following Weber's approach[4])
E	7	Class	Goldthorpe *et al.* (1980)	An extension and adaptation of C
F	Multiple	Occupations, status groups, classes (plural), social identities, subjective ideas	Booth (1902); Lockwood (1966)	A set of disparate approaches, but sharing a scepticism about clearly separated unitary or homogeneous divisions, emphasizing instead multiplicity, complexity and variations according to people's locality, circumstances (including gender), and the effects of imagery and language

[1] Note that these alternative frameworks not only vary over time and among different researchers, but can also coexist in people's own views of themselves and in how they speak about their own society. How these and similar divisions work out and are understood at local level may remain an open question (and perhaps the focus for research), irrespective of the aggregate findings at a national level.

[2] Most of the specific examples of research listed here (in the fourth column) are taken from those referred to in this volume, especially Chapters 4 and 5.

[3] The Registrar-General's listing has varied over the years, as both the nature and the status of particular occupations have changed; in the twentieth century many thousands of occupations were aggregated and translated into five basic classes. Armstrong's (1972) application of these to occupations listed in the 1851 CEBs has provided a useful resource for researchers (see Volume 4, Chapter 3, section 2.1.1); but see also Mills and Mills (1989), who have more to say on the ranking of rural occupations.

[4] For an account of the Marxist and Weberian traditions see Giddens (1989, Chapter 7) and the useful overview of the term 'class' in Williams (1983, pp.60–9).

'Closure' and 'closed' social groups   These expressions are used in two related senses. The *specific* meaning refers to the ways in which social groups restrict their membership to a limited circle. A gross instance would be the obligation to dine regularly at one of the Inns of Court to qualify for the Bar. Its effect is to exclude new entrants from lower social strata and ensure that this elite profession has a high degree of self-recruitment. Social closure can operate in plebeian circles too: the recruitment of London dockers was once confined to the sons and relatives of dockers, and craft unions have a history of excluding women.

'Closure' in a more general sense refers to the systematic restriction of 'life chances' experienced by people in certain social situations, say by a manual wage-earner or a member of a minority group that is subject to discrimination. Here, the closure takes the form of barriers that people encounter, especially to occupational change and social advancement. (As must be evident to you, the two meanings are connected because these barriers can result from some groups' 'exclusion strategies', although more usually they stem from restricted access to scarce resources like higher education.)

'Closure', in both its senses, can connect the ideas of 'mobility' and 'class'. The partial 'closure' of mobility chances, both in the individual's lifetime and inter-generationally, can give rise to common funds of experience, a shared outlook on society, and class consciousness – a sense of solidarity, say, from belonging to the 'working-class' as against 'upper-class' closure through primogeniture or privileged access to independent education.

Such concepts may seem rather abstract, but an empirical example may highlight their relevance to the type of research you might undertake. In their study of a Yorkshire mining village ('Ashton') in the mid twentieth century, three sociologists provided a graphic account of 'closure' both in the individual miner's lifetime (intra-generational) and through family genera-tions (inter-generational). Over 60 per cent of the community's male labour force were employed as manual wage-earners by the National Coal Board, and though there were significant economic differences between grades of miner (and surface workers), this had only a limited impact on the solidarity of a workforce in a dangerous occupation where the managerial officials were commonly seen as enemies (Dennis *et al.*, 1956, p.31). The only forms of career mobility for manual workers within the industry were either to become a 'pit deputy' or an official within the miners' union; the opportunities for movement to another occupation were restricted by the local employment structure. Although most fathers said they did not want to see their sons follow them down the pit, most sons did, chiefly because the good wages they could earn at the age of 18 were well above those enjoyed by young men in apprenticeships or without technical training. Upward mobility for sons into white-collar occupations was restricted by the fact that few 'Ashton' children received a grammar school education – a prerequisite for most forms of higher education – while 'very few develop[ed] interests broader than those of their parents whose interests [were] satisfied by life in Ashton' (Dennis *et al.*, 1956, p.235). The effects of 'closure' in the miner's life and that of his family produced a militant class identity and consciousness.

This example is of an 'extreme' occupational community. It is nevertheless an illustration of how the concepts and questions within social mobility research can be used in a specific empirical study. It may also help you to pose questions about the community you are studying.

How far does the history of a specific community or set of families known to you fit with either the Smiles view of mobility (illustrated, for example, in the Summers family history on p.90) or that exemplified in the Ashton study – or is it different from both of these?

2   SOCIAL MOBILITY IN NINETEENTH-CENTURY BRITAIN

How do we study nineteenth-century social mobility? Contemporary social researchers can ask a representative sample of the population about their parents' occupation and their own occupa-tional experiences. Historians of the nineteenth century have no such living 'documents' to interrogate and have to find a substitute for the researcher's questionnaire and interview. One such substitute exists in the nineteenth-century census returns, which give the occupations of named individuals. Thus tracking individuals between census dates is possible provided they remained resident within the same census district. However, nominal record linkage between censuses can be enormously time-consuming, and there is also the problem that it may well be the socially mobile – up, down or sideways – who leave the district and disappear from the local census.

Partly for this reason, historians of nineteenth-century Britain until recently knew rather more about social mobility into elite groups, such as steel and hosiery industrialists (see Erickson, 1959) and the super-rich, than they did about that of the common people. There is a handful of local studies, however, including McKay's (1985) study of occupational mobility among Scottish shale-oil workers, using CEBs, civil registers and local newspapers (see Chapter 4, section 3). There is also Michael Sanderson's notable (1972) analysis of school and marriage registers to chart the mobility of two samples of workers' sons in late eighteenth- and early nineteenth-century Lancashire in the context of the relationship between early industrialization and mobility. Sanderson's conclusion that the coming of the factory system drastically reduced the chances of social promotion for working-class men has carried great weight with historians. Generally, however, British local studies have focused on occupational mobility *within* the working class. Many have attempted to test the thesis that around 1850 an exclusive 'labour aristocracy' of skilled workers emerged, relatively well paid compared with the unskilled and semi-skilled below them, whose sons tended to 'inherit' their father's trade, and whose children showed a strong propensity to marry within the group (Foster, 1974; Gray, 1976; Crossick, 1978).

Do either Sanderson's conclusions or the 'labour aristocracy' thesis throw any light on the specific community, group or family you are studying?

The local studies need to be seen in the wider context of inter-generational class mobility in Victorian society at large. In 1991 the first results were published of a national mobility study based on a representative sample of the population (regrettably confined to England). This places the discussion of nineteenth-century mobility on a broader and firmer basis. The research-ers, Andrew Miles and David Vincent, used the information given in the civil marriage registers on the occupations of the partners and their parents (on civil registers, see Volume 4, Chapter 5, and also section 3.1 below). They extracted from ten registration districts occupational data on 10,000 grooms marrying between 1839 and 1914, their fathers and fathers-in-law. These were then coded according to the Registrar-General's 1951 ranking of occupations into five social classes (*Census of England and Wales*, 1951). These are summarized in Schema A; see also Table 5.1, note 3, above.

Schema A: Registrar-General's 1951 class ranking

Class I: Professional/higher occupations

Class II: 'Intermediate' or petit bourgeois occupations

Class III: Skilled manual

Class IV: Semi-skilled manual

Class V: Unskilled manual

Allocating the often laconic occupational descriptions in the registers to this schema can scarcely have been simple, and one might query its applicability to the nineteenth century, as many Victorian occupations would have been missing from the Registrar-General's 1951 listing. Curiously, however, this still contained such archaic trades as quill-pen cutter and postilion, so the unclassifiable occupation is not a major problem! A more fundamental difficulty is that in comparing the occupations of fathers and grooms, we are looking at men at different points in their work life-cycle. Newly married men are predominantly at the beginning of their careers; they may later experience 'career' mobility that we do not know about. This objection is inherent in marriage records, and can be overcome only by using additional sources, such as autobiographies.

Table 5.2 is an excellent illustration of just how much information can be conveyed, in a small space, by using numbers rather than words. (For more on the advantages – and the disadvantages – of quantification, see Volume 4, Chapter 8.) However, it has to be admitted that the full glory of Table 5.2 is not immediately apparent. The main purpose of the table is to show the relationship between the social class of bridegrooms and that of their fathers. If you look along the bottom row and down the last column, you will see that overall the class distribution is the same between fathers and sons (for example 2 per cent of fathers are in Class 1, and 1.5 per cent of grooms; 42 per cent of fathers are in Class III, and 45 per cent of grooms), but there is a very large difference between the numbers in each of the various classes. Thus the number of grooms in Class I was very small (156) as it was of fathers (208). By contrast, the number of grooms in Class III was very large (4,596) as it was of fathers (4,288). The dominance of Class III is a common feature of nineteenth-century social mobility studies, and a cause of some concern among historians (see Mills and Mills, 1989, pp.64–5, 74), since they suspect that it masks subtle areas of social differentiation. Similarly, the size of Class IV relative to Classes III and V is a worry: there is a widespread view that this group of semi-skilled should be larger.

Table 5.2   Class distribution of grooms by class of father and vice-versa, England 1839–1914

Class of groom's father	Groom's class						
	I	II	III	IV	V	Total	Per cent
I	**89**	69	33	9	8	208	2.0
II	48	**885**	458	216	161	1 768	17.3
III	13	287	**3 126**	437	425	4 288	42.0
IV	5	87	394	**542**	159	1 187	11.6
V	1	77	585	389	**1 704**	2 756	27.0
Total	156	1 405	4 596	1 593	2 457	10 207	
Per cent	1.5	13.8	45.0	15.6	24.1		100.0

Source: based on Miles and Vincent (1991) Table 1, p.51

At a community level these differences can appear even more extreme. You will notice, for instance, that in Carole Pearce's Ashford (Kent) study (see Tables 5.5–5.7 below) the overall configuration was the same as that shown in Table 5.2, but the numbers in Class IV were very small indeed.

That some social mobility did take place is clear from Table 5.2: as we have seen, whereas 208 grooms had fathers in Class I, only 156 grooms ended up in that class. For a shift in the opposite direction you will notice that whereas 1,187 grooms' fathers were in Class IV, some 1,593 grooms ended up in that class. But what was the movement within the body of the table? Let us look at a few examples. Of the sons of the 208 fathers who were in Class I, less than half (89) remained in Class I at the time of their marriage: 69 had dropped to Class II; 33 to Class III; 9 to Class IV; and 8 right down to Class V – black sheep indeed! Now look at Class I from the other direction, that of the 156 grooms in this class. As we have seen, 89 had fathers in Class I; of the rest 48 had fathers in Class II; 13 in Class III; 5 in Class IV and one in Class V – a real high flier. To test your comprehension of Table 5.2, have a go at Exercise 5.1.

_____ **EXERCISE 5.1** _____

1   How many sons in Class II had fathers in Class I?
2   How many fathers in Class IV had sons in Class III?
3   How many sons in Class III had fathers in Class III?
4   How many sons from non-manual backgrounds were in manual jobs? Refer to Schema A to see which classes embraced manual and non-manual workers. Do the same before answering question 5.
5   How many sons in non-manual jobs had fathers who were in manual classes?

Answers p.230.

The example of movement into and out of Class I shows that most of it was relatively short-distance, i.e. down to or up from Class II. In fact the majority did not move at all. This is clear if one looks at the figures in bold which appear from top left to bottom right in Table 5.2. If we add these up we find that 6,346 of the 10,207 grooms remained in the same class as their fathers. Of the rest 1,886 moved upwards (48 + 13 + 5 + 1 + 287 + 87 + 77 + 394 + 585 + 389) and 1,975 moved downwards (69 + 33 + 9 + 8 + 458 + 216 + 161 + 437 + 425 + 159). Although this would suggest more downward than upward mobility, we must remember that we are dealing with a *sample* of marriages. The difference could, therefore, have been caused by chance. (For how to demonstrate this statistically see Volume 4, Chapter 8.) Some downward mobility could stem from the relative youth of newly-weds. Many sons of business owners began their careers 'on the shop floor' and worked at a trade before taking over the business, which could account for some of what appear to be downwardly mobile grooms.

Table 5.2 provides us with the raw data – the actual numbers of grooms and fathers of grooms in the various classes. This is rather limiting, especially if you want to compare the distribution with that in another place or period – something you might wish to do if you undertake a community study like that of Carole Pearce (see Tables 5.5–5.7). To make that comparison easier we turn the actual numbers into percentages. For purposes of clarity this is best done by producing two tables, with one showing the percentage of fathers with sons in the various classes (Table 5.3) and the other showing the percentage of grooms with fathers in the different classes (Table 5.4). The reading of these tables is the same as with Table 5.2. For example, Table 5.3 shows that 12.2 per cent of fathers in Class II had sons who, at marriage, were in Class IV. Table 5.4 shows, for example, that 6.2 per cent of sons in Class II had fathers in Class IV.

Table 5.3   Percentage of fathers with sons in the various classes, England, 1839–1914

Father's class sector	Son's class sector					
	I	II	III	IV	V	Total per cent
I	42.8	33.2	15.9	4.3	3.8	100.0
II	2.7	50.1	25.9	12.2	9.1	100.0
III	0.3	6.7	72.9	10.2	9.9	100.0
IV	0.4	7.3	33.2	45.6	13.4	100.0
V	0.0	2.8	21.2	14.1	61.8	100.0

Source: based on Miles and Vincent (1991) Table 2, p.54

The sharpness of the division between the manual and non-manual classes *for those beneath it* is clearly evident in the data, as is the inter-generational stability of the class structure. Out of 8,231 men of manual origins, 19 were in the 'professional' Class I when they married, and only about one in twenty (5.5 per cent) were upwardly mobile to the 'lower middle' Class II (451 out of

8,231). As we have seen already, the majority of men (six out of ten) experienced no change in occupational classification, with those in the skilled and unskilled manual sectors particularly prone to remain in their occupational category.

Table 5.4 Percentage of grooms with fathers in the various classes, England 1839–1914

Father's class sector	Son's class sector				
	I	II	III	IV	V
I	57.1	4.9	0.7	0.6	0.3
II	30.8	62.9	10.0	13.5	6.5
III	8.3	20.5	68.0	27.5	17.2
IV	3.2	6.2	8.6	34.0	6.5
V	0.6	5.5	12.8	24.4	69.5
Total per cent	100.0	100.0	100.0	100.0	100.0

Source: based on Miles and Vincent (1991) Table 2, p.54

We get more impression of flexibility when we consider the 'inflow' into the different classes in Table 5.4, for one in eight grooms (12.1 per cent) in Class I and three out of ten (32.2 per cent) in Class II were of manual origin. This accords better with the notion of Victorian England as a land of opportunity. But we must remember the huge discrepancy in size between the manual and the non-manual classes: just 19 men accounted for the one in eight from working-class backgrounds in Class I. Otherwise, however, Table 5.4 is striking testimony to a high degree of self-recruitment across the social structure: only the semi-skilled working class was exceptional. Most young men were working in familiar social milieux, and, if not precisely following their father's trade, were in jobs with similar pay, prospects and prestige. Few manual workers worked alongside men from non-manual backgrounds. The sense of class division in everyday working life must have been acute, while there was sufficient movement between the different sectors of the working class to suggest that they were bound together by a common fund of experience.

How far does any local or family investigation you have undertaken support or contradict the above general findings and interpretations?

3 SOCIAL MOBILITY THROUGH MARRIAGE: SOME RESEARCH EXERCISES

In 1872 Anthony Trollope, that well-known master of the Victorian blockbuster, published a short novel, *The golden lion of Granpère,* under a pseudonym. Our interest in the novel lies in the comments made about the marital prospects of the heroine, a beautiful, talented but poor employee – 'Marie Bromer had not a franc of *dot*' (dowry) – in her guardian's country inn:

> *it will be a good match for her … it is impossible that she should do better … How are you to do better? … This marriage was undoubtedly a good marriage … It is well for girls to be disposed of sometimes. It saves them a world of trouble … People say that it is a great match for you … There she is, a bar maid … of course such a marriage as this is a great thing; a very great thing indeed … The man was above her.*

(Trollope, 1872, pp.11–121)

Needless to say the marriage does not take place, in spite of its being approved by family and friends, and offering a helping hand up the social scale. Marie marries her one true love. As he happens to be the son of her guardian and also an innkeeper with prospects, she didn't in the end do badly in social terms.

Marriage may not be the only road to upward mobility (or downward either): others are education, migration, patronage, entrepreneurship – all, of course, to be seen within the varying contexts of social or economic change. But marriage can be one channel – or can it? This section throws some light on the question.

3.1 THE EXTENT AND EFFECTS OF SOCIAL MOBILITY THROUGH MARRIAGE

In Jerzy Berent's (1954) study of social mobility in Britain through marriage in the first half of the twentieth century, around 45 per cent of the sample (2,288 out of 5,100) married within their own social class, and the vast majority did so either in that class or in the class immediately above or below it (Berent, 1954, p.325). Thus of men born into Class I, some 73.4 per cent married women from their own class or from Class II. For men born into Class IV, 83.9 per cent married women in their own class or from Class III.

David Glass's study (of which Berent's work was a part) was a national one conducted in the mid twentieth century. There is nothing to stop it being replicated in the nineteenth century at local level given access to marriage registers covering the whole of a community. Indeed, such a study was done of the Kent town of Ashford using the civil registers for the years 1837–70 (Pearce, 1969). Though these registers are now generally closed for research purposes in England and Wales, there is some access in Scotland and parts of Ireland (on civil registers, see Volume 4, Chapter 5, section 1). It is not absolutely essential to have them, since in most communities the bulk of the population continued to marry in churches or chapels, long after civil registration was introduced (on religious registers see Volume 4, Chapter 4, section 3). Church and chapel registers are more readily available.

Tables 5.5–5.7 show Pearce's findings on the distribution of inter- and intra-class marriages. The allocation of occupations to the different classes is as in Schema A.

EXERCISE 5.2

To check your understanding of Tables 5.5–5.7, try to answer the following:

1 How many brides originating in Class IV found husbands from Class I?

2 How many grooms originating in Class III found wives in the same class?

3 What percentage of brides' fathers in Class II had sons-in-law in Class III?

4 What percentage of grooms' fathers in Class I had daughters-in-law in Class V?

Answers p.230.

Table 5.5 Class origins of brides by that of grooms and vice-versa, Ashford (Kent), 1837–70

Class of groom's father	Class of bride's father						
	I	II	III	IV	V	Total	Per cent
I	10	2	12	0	2	26	2.1
II	6	45	66	6	45	168	13.6
III	10	63	315	18	143	549	44.5
IV	1	5	25	3	8	42	3.4
V	0	28	131	14	276	449	36.4
Total	27	143	549	41	474	1234	
Per cent	2.2	11.6	44.5	3.3	38.4		100.0

Source: Pearce (1969)

Table 5.6 Percentage of brides (by class origins) by class origin of grooms, Ashford, 1837–70

Class of groom's father	Class of bride's father				
	I	II	III	IV	V
I	37.0	1.4	2.2	–	0.4
II	22.2	31.5	12.0	14.6	9.5
III	37.0	44.0	57.4	43.9	30.2
IV	3.7	3.5	4.6	7.3	1.7
V	–	19.6	23.9	34.1	58.2
Total	100.0	100.0	100.0	100.0	100.0

Source: Pearce (1969)

Table 5.7 Percentage of grooms (by class origins) by class origin of brides, Ashford, 1837–1914

Class of groom's father	Class of bride's father					Total
	I	II	III	IV	V	
I	38.5	7.7	46.2	–	7.7	100.0
II	3.6	26.8	39.3	3.6	26.8	100.0
III	1.8	11.5	57.4	3.3	26.0	100.0
IV	2.4	11.9	59.5	7.1	19.0	100.0
V	–	6.2	29.2	3.1	61.5	100.0

Source: Pearce (1969)

Tables 5.5–5.7 do not show the regularity of Tables 5.2–5.4, which we looked at earlier. This is possibly because of the smaller numbers involved; the inappropriateness of the classification; problems associated with using occupation to measure social class differences; errors in allocating bridal couples to their social class; and finally the different classification systems. Even so, some 52.6 per cent married within their own class (649 out of 1,234). This is on a par with the 44.9 per cent who did so in Berent's sample (2,288 out of 5,100) – see Table 5.8 on p.104.

Perhaps we ought to look at other ways of measuring the extent of social mobility through marriage. The pioneer Norwegian sociologist Eilert Sundt (1817–75) made a number of studies based on two classes, those with property and those without (Sundt, 1855). In a society where the vast majority of the population lived in rural areas and where the major social divide was between farmers and farm labourers, such a division would seem an appropriate one.

Can you think of any parts of nineteenth-century Britain and Ireland where Sundt's approach might be the appropriate one?

One of Sundt's findings was that the daughters of farm labourers were more likely to marry the sons of farmers than the sons of farm labourers were to marry farmer's daughters. He also found that in areas where the proportions in each class were not too wide apart (e.g. 40 per cent farmers, 60 per cent labourers) the amount of inter-class marriage was greater than where the proportions differed greatly (e.g. 10 per cent farmers, 90 per cent labourers). It would be interesting to see whether this was true in Britain (for example rural Wales or parts of Eastern Scotland) or in Ireland's rural areas in the second half of the nineteenth century. One might, for instance, compare the situation in the hill country of central Wales with that in the lowlands of central England; or the poorer parts of Connaught with the richer parts of Leinster.

3.2 THE MECHANISMS OF SOCIAL MOBILITY AND MARRIAGE

The results presented in Tables 5.2–5.8 suggest that people tended to marry within their own class and that any movement out of it was limited, being confined to neighbouring classes. If the norm is for people to marry within their social class (however defined), those who do not are in some way deviant. Since in any marriage involving social mobility one partner moves up the social scale and the other down, is it possible to discover patterns of behaviour common to the upwardly mobile partner, the downwardly mobile one, their children, their relations with their in-laws, etc.? And do differences occur on a gender basis, i.e. when the husband or the wife is upwardly/downwardly mobile? Do these differences have an impact on spending patterns, political allegiance, or religious observance?

If you have access to a family tree or, better still, to a number of them, you could trace social mobility through marriage over time (in other words in a longitudinal study) and perhaps follow up some of these questions. Depending on the details available it would be worth exploring whether the children of a family at any one time tended to move – *en bloc* as it were – up or down socially through their marriages, or stayed within the same class or had a mixed experience.

Movement from the bottom to the top of the social scale, or even a move across two classes, was probably relatively rare. That in itself makes it interesting, since deviant behaviour of this kind may cast light on the mechanisms involved in social mobility through marriage. By trawling through a marriage register you could collect instances of this type of movement and be able, from the registers themselves, to say something about it. Are there any patterns to be observed in relation to the ages of the couple marrying, the occupations of their parents, or their addresses (close or far apart)? Since one partner will be high up the social scale, and the marriage itself probably something of a 'talking point' in the community, you may be able to find more details in a local newspaper report. Such an exercise will inevitably be indicative rather than definitive. Yet it could help towards the creation of hypotheses which in the initial stages of any enquiry is an important activity.

Another indicative exercise would be to use biographies and autobiographies. Many of these will be of upper-class families, so you will get an indication of the extent of social mobility to and from that class. But there are now also increasing numbers of working-class autobiographies which could be sampled (on autobiographies/biographies, see Volume 4, Chapter 4, section 8).

In studying social mobility through marriage in more recent times you could do an exercise in oral history. The late Professor K. H. Connell went some way along this road when he drew on material collected by the Irish Folklore Commission for his study of Catholicism and marriage in the century after the famine (Connell, 1968, pp. 113–61). You could prepare a similar set of questions relating to cross-class marriages (you would have to identify how you were going to define class in this context, of course – see Table 5.1 above). Among the questions of interest would be:

o   Who did it (age, occupation, address)?

o   Were comments made at the time, and if so what form did they take?

o   Did cross-class marriages lead to different behaviour patterns from intra-class marriages? For example, is there any evidence that, as sometimes suggested (see Macdonald, 1974, p.73), women who 'married beneath them' played a significant role in seeking the social advancement of their children, e.g. by laying emphasis on education, or paying for elocution lessons, etc.?

o   What about relations with kin? Were partners in cross-class marriages spurned by their socially more elevated kin? Did they socialize more with their higher-class than with their lower-class kin?

Such questions need careful articulation. Though it is unlikely that results from any such exercises can be meaningfully quantified or widely generalized, the results should nevertheless be interesting in their own right and, taken with those of others, may lead to a more general understanding.

Finally, we would like to suggest an examination of so-called 'irregular marriages' in Scotland. To understand the significance of these it is necessary to go back to Lord Hardwicke's Act of 1753. Under this Act, which applied to England and Wales, the only legal marriages were those conducted by a recognized clergyman (usually of the Church of England) after the publication of banns or on production of an ecclesiastical licence. The Act is directly relevant to our current concern since it was aimed at doing away with clandestine marriages (most notably those carried out in London's Fleet Prison, which was outside ecclesiastical supervision). The propertied classes were concerned about such marriages because of instances of 'unprincipalled adventurers' wedding heiresses, which no doubt produced a number of cross-class marriages. How many we do not know. More likely the type of marriage made illegal by the Act was resorted to by people who, probably quite legitimately, wanted a quiet wedding. The Act proved a success and, until modified by Lord Russell's Act of 1836 (which introduced civil marriage), made a properly constituted and recognized religious service the only means of entry to a legal marriage *in England and Wales*.

Scotland, however, 'recognized the concept of *irregular marriage*, which in origin was a marriage simultaneously illegal and valid' (Smout, 1981, p. 205). The number of such marriages rose from the seventeenth century to the early nineteenth century, declined in the mid nineteenth century, and then rose again until the Second World War. At times irregular marriages accounted for a high proportion of total marriages, especially in the larger cities. Thus in 1915, 20.5 per cent of all marriages were irregular, though in Edinburgh in that year it was as high as 42.3 per cent (Smout, 1981, pp. 224–5).

An irregular marriage was based on the conduct of the two parties involved. It

> *did not have to take place in church, nor at any particular time of day or night, nor even before witnesses, for it to be valid, but the consent of freely contracting parties did have to be proved ... By the late nineteenth and twentieth centuries (after the Civil Registration Acts) irregular marriages were usually formally proved by a declaration before the Sheriff, who then provided a warrant which could be shown to the local registrar and which alone could enable him to register the marriage legally; this became especially common in the large burghs and comes very close to the English concept of civil marriage.*

> (Smout, 1981, p.206)

Irregular marriage was therefore similar to civil marriage in England, and after civil registration began in Scotland (in 1855) most marriages of this type were in fact registered. The significant question is whether irregular marriages produced more cross-class marriages than those carried out by the clergy. Certainly the English upper classes saw such irregular marriages as a threat to property, and tried to get the Scots to bring their law into line with the English (Smout, 1981, p.208), but to little effect. A fast coach to Gretna Green, one imagines, must have featured in the nightmares of English fathers with sons and daughters at risk of marrying 'unsuitably', i.e. across class lines.

Today features of Scottish irregular marriage seem to be taking hold in England – indeed, in much of the western world. Though the causes of this are likely to be found in the late twentieth century rather than in the Middle Ages (the Scottish position, according to Smout (1981, p. 210) can be traced as far back as that), a study of cross-class marriages may throw some light upon it. Such cross-class marriages were against the norm that marriage partners should, ideally, be drawn from within the same social group (Borscheid, 1986). It may be the case that couples who cohabit without benefit of a marriage ceremony, choose their partners on a somewhat different basis from those who marry.

Look back through section 3 – which essentially consists of extended suggestions for research – for ideas about possible questions, sources and methods.

4   STUDIES OF TWENTIETH-CENTURY MOBILITY

4.1   SOCIAL MOBILITY IN EARLY TWENTIETH-CENTURY BRITAIN

The first mobility study based on a live representative sample of a national population was undertaken in 1949 by David Glass, when 9,296 British adults were interviewed about their occupational history, educational experience and father's occupation (Glass, 1954). Glass's oldest cohort was born before 1889, so his data overlap with Miles and Vincent's (1991) study of nineteenth-century England (see section 2 above). However, the theoretical perspectives and categories of the two enquiries were significantly different. Miles and Vincent adopted the Registrar-General's 1951 classification, whereas Glass's enquiry focused on the extent of movement in social status or prestige by individuals of diverse social origin, and so adopted a seven-fold hierarchy of status categories (validated by a public opinion survey on the relative prestige of different occupations). This is listed in Schema B.

Schema B: The Glass status hierarchy

Group 1: Professional and high administrative

Group 2: Managerial and executive

Group 3: Inspectional, supervisory and other non-manual, higher grade

Group 4: Inspectional, supervisory and other non-manual, lower grade

Group 5: Skilled manual, and routine grades of non-manual

Group 6: Semi-skilled manual

Group 7: Unskilled manual

_____ *EXERCISE 5.3* _____

On the face of it, the overlap between the studies by Glass (1954) and by Miles and Vincent (1991) should give us the basis for a continuous history of social mobility from the early nineteenth to the mid twentieth century. Note down at least one problem about interpreting the data in this way.

Comments p.230.

Like Miles and Vincent, Glass found more 'skidders' than social 'climbers'. Of course, his categories obscure the manual/non-manual divide, so we must be cautious about making this comparison. But Glass's finding that there was negligible long-distance mobility from categories 5, 6 and 7 to professional and higher administrative positions *is* genuinely comparable. Miles and

Vincent found 0.2 per cent of workers' sons 'making it' to the top, while Glass found 0.6 per cent achieving status category 1. The 'social closure' evident at the top of the Victorian occupational structure persisted well into the twentieth century, but it was not a hermetic seal: one in eight of Miles and Vincent's professional class came from working-class backgrounds; for Glass the figure is nearer one in seven.

Glass's data demonstrate considerable movement upwards and downwards, and dispel any notion of a society in which individual position in the hierarchy of inequality was fixed at birth. Mobility was mostly 'short-distance', however. Where men had achieved a status category different from that of their fathers, they still tended to cluster round the parental category. Glass's figures show less self-recruitment, but it was still marked among the professional elite and (apparently) the skilled working class. However, this is one instance where appearances are deceptive: because skilled workers were such a large proportion of the total, we should expect lots of sons to come from skilled workers' families, and the actual figures are pretty close to expectations. (Incidentally, this last point is a useful reminder of the need to look at individual movements in relation to the wider social context – for example the demographic trends in fertility – as between different classes, or the effects of economic conditions, notably the Depression, on employment opportunities. These are important additional influences on mobility which are not always fully taken into account by those citing Glass's findings.)

There is no reason to question Glass's conclusions concerning educational mobility or – the theme of section 3 – mobility and marriage. In twentieth-century Britain, the family and marriage, together with the educational system, must be considered as among the most important 'channels' for moving up and down the status hierarchy. In the social conditions of early twentieth-century Britain marriage was more likely to enhance the status of women who married outside their group of origin than of men, since the greatest influence on determining a woman's status was her father's or husband's occupation. Few women thought of paid employment in terms of a career, and most gave it up on marriage (see Chapter 3, section 2). Only a handful of women found their way into prestigious occupations, and a woman's occupation before marriage was not necessarily a reliable index of her later social status. The greater frequency of marriage as the twentieth century progressed meant a decline in the number of single women who were capable of pursuing independent careers and acting as role models for their sex. To take one telling statistic, there were 1.1 million single women between the ages of 25 and 34 in 1931, but less than half a million single women in that age group in 1955; as a proportion of the age group, female singletons fell from 33 to 16 per cent (Carr-Saunders *et al.*, 1958, Table 1.6). Glass's respondents were classified according to their *father's* occupation. In 45 per cent of the 5,100 reported cases, husband and wife came from the same social group, while among all husbands, irrespective of origin, 29.8 per cent (1,520) married 'below' themselves as compared with 25.3 per cent (1,292) of women who did so (see Table 5.8). Clearly, the data indicate a relatively fluid social structure, and when analysed by the year of marriage suggest an increase over time in marital social mobility or a fall in intra-class marriage (Glass, 1954, p.329).

The 1949 Glass survey exerted an enormous influence. It emphasized four interrelated points: (i) 'social closure' at the top of the class structure, so mobility was almost exclusively short-range; (ii) a buffer zone around the 'white-collar line', absorbing upwardly mobile manual workers and preventing further movement upwards; (iii) increasing upward mobility through education, 'counterbalanced' by decreasing career mobility; and (iv) no tendency for the mobility rate to increase over time (for further comment and analysis, see Parkin, 1971; Westergaard and Resler, 1975). Glass's findings should not be taken as representing the present-day situation. But they remain an important historical source, based as they were on a survey, most of whose respondents entered the labour force before the Second World War, and a substantial minority of whom began their careers before 1914.

Table 5.8 Distribution of husbands and wives by social group of origin in Glass's survey, 1949[1]

Social group of origin of husbands	Social group of origin of wives				
	I	II	III	IV	All
I	37.4 136 47.4	36.0 131 10.9	20.6 75 3.2	6.0 22 1.7	100.0 364 7.2
II	6.4 81 28.2	34.2 434 36.3	41.4 524 22.5	18.0 228 17.8	100.0 1267 24.8
III	2.6 60 20.9	19.8 451 37.6	53.8 1225 52.5	23.8 540 42.1	100.0 2276 44.6
IV	0.8 10 3.5	15.3 182 15.2	42.6 508 21.8	41.3 493 38.4	100.0 1193 23.4
All	5.6 287 100.0	23.5 1198 100.0	45.7 2332 100.0	25.2 1283 100.0	100.0 5100 100.0

[1] This table uses only four groups. Groups 1 and 2 of the seven-group system have been amalgamated to form Group I of a four-group system; Groups 3 and 4 become Group II; Group 5 becomes Group III, and Groups 6 and 7 become Group IV (see Glass, 1954, p.322)

Source: Berent (1954) p.325

To what extent does any evidence you have discovered about specific individuals, families or relatives within the first half of the twentieth century coincide with Glass's findings?

4.2 THE 'NEW WAVE' OF MOBILITY STUDIES FROM THE 1970s

The next major study was the 1972 Oxford Mobility Survey of men living in England and Wales. This generated two influential monographs: *Social mobility and class structure in modern Britain* (Goldthorpe *et al.*, 1980; second edition, 1987) and *Origins and destinations: family, class and education in modern Britain* (Halsey *et al.*, 1980). Scotland was excluded on the pragmatic grounds that, since it has only one-tenth of the population of Great Britain, a pro rata sample would not have been large enough to make separate analysis worthwhile. Also, there seemed no reason to believe that Scottish mobility rates would diverge significantly from those elsewhere. Fortuitously, this was put to the test by the Scottish Mobility Study, initiated in 1973 and directed by Geoff Payne, using a slightly different occupational scale (see Payne, 1987).

A third study, *Following in father's footsteps: social mobility in Ireland*, undertaken by the American sociologist Michael Hout (1989), was remarkable in several respects: it analysed samples from both the Irish Republic and Northern Ireland; its respondents in the south had lived through a period of rapid economic transformation as Irish governments promoted the industrialization of a hitherto agrarian society; it explored the relationship between mobility, class and religious confession in Northern Ireland; and finally the researchers undertook something closer to 'life history' analysis (as opposed to the British studies, which compared parental and filial occupations at particular points in time).

Goldthorpe and his colleagues did not disguise a political as well as an academic interest in their research, which aimed to relate mobility to class formation: they were committed to the ideal of an 'open' society, but sceptical as to its being achieved without concerted class action.

Their 'interests' required a different occupational scale from that employed by Glass, one more sensitive to market and work situations, and their location within the systems of authority governing production. As you can see in Schema C, Goldthorpe disaggregated routine, largely clerical employees from skilled manual workers, and assigned them to their own 'white-collar class', while he identified as a separate class a 'petty bourgeoisie' whose income came from small businesses and self-employment. (These differences between the two scales again make the extrapolation of long-term mobility trends hazardous.)

Schema C: The Goldthorpe class scheme

Class I: Higher-grade professionals, administrators, managers and officials, self-employed or salaried, together with large proprietors (the 'service class' of modern capitalist society)

Class II: Lower-grade professionals, officials, managers and higher-grade technicians

Class III: The 'white-collar labour force' of routine non-manual employees

Class IV: Small proprietors and self-employed artisans of the 'petty bourgeoisie'

Class V: The 'blue-collar elite' of lower-grade technicians and supervisors of manual workers

Class VI: Skilled manual wage-workers

Class VII: Semi- and unskilled wage-workers

Note: This scheme was not meant to be consistently hierarchical, and it is appropriate to speak of 'upward' and 'downward' mobility only with respect to movement to Classes I and II, and V, VI and VII respectively. Movement of manual workers' sons to white-collar work would be more aptly described as 'sideways'.

In pursuit of their interest in class formation, Goldthorpe and his colleagues turned to the 1970s theorists (such as Parkin) for questions to be empirically tested against their interview data. The most important concerned the 'service class' (Class I in Schema C). Did it, as many theorists claimed, exhibit a marked degree of self-recruitment because of the social 'closure' practised by its members? In other words, did the educational terms of entry to this class enable wealthier parents to secure their own children's future by private education etc., and at the same time restrict upward mobility from the working class? The expectation was that the elite groupings in Class I would contain no more than quite negligible proportions of men whose recruitment had entailed long-range upward mobility.

_____ **EXERCISE 5.4** _____

1 Do either the Oxford mobility data (see Table 5.9) or the Scottish data (see Table 5.10) confirm this expectation?

2 Which section of British society was most homogeneous in terms of common social origins?

Answers and comments follow on below.

Table 5.9 Class composition by class of father[1] at respondent's age 14, from 1972 survey

Father's class[1]	Respondent's class								
	I	II	III	IV	V	VI	VII	Number	Per cent
I	25.3	12.4	9.6	6.7	3.2	2.0	2.4	680	7.9
II	13.1	12.2	8.0	4.8	5.2	3.1	2.5	547	6.4
III	10.4	10.4	10.8	7.4	8.7	5.7	6.0	687	8.0
IV	10.1	12.2	9.8	27.2	8.6	7.1	7.7	886	10.3
V	12.5	14.0	13.2	12.1	16.6	12.2	9.6	1072	12.5
VI	16.4	21.7	26.1	24.0	31.1	41.8	35.2	2577	30.0
VII	12.1	17.1	22.6	17.8	26.7	28.0	36.6	2126	24.8
Number	1230	1050	827	687	1026	1883	1872	8575	
Per cent	14.3	12.2	9.6	8.0	12.0	22.0	21.8		

[1] Or other 'head of household'. The two basic questions in the 1972 inquiry from which the data in the table derive were: 'What is your job now?', following on several questions about earlier occupations; and 'What was your father's (or other head of household's) job at that time (i.e. at respondent's age 14)?', following on several other questions about the respondent's family circumstances at that age. Men occupied in agriculture are not included in this table.

Source: Goldthorpe *et al.* (1980) Table 2.1

Table 5.10 Inter-generational male mobility, Scotland, 1973[1]

Father's occupation when respondent aged 14		Respondent's occupation at time of interview							
		I	II	III	IV	V	VI	VII	Totals
I	Professional; manager; senior administrator	128 (23.3)	71 (10.3)	18 (2.8)	29 (10.9)	14 (1.4)	14 (1.6)	12 (1.8)	286
II	Semi-professional; white-collar supervisor	108 (19.6)	193 (28.0)	62 (9.6)	45 (16.9)	54 (5.8)	72 (8.0)	35 (5.3)	569
III	Foreman; self-employed artisan	76 (13.8)	95 (13.8)	121 (18.8)	26 (9.7)	91 (9.7)	110 (12.2)	75 (11.4)	594
IV	Routine white-collar	41 (7.5)	35 (5.1)	16 (2.5)	15 (5.6)	21 (2.2)	14 (1.6)	11 (1.7)	153
V	Skilled manual	91 (16.5)	128 (18.6)	172 (26.7)	63 (23.6)	400 (42.6)	265 (29.5)	217 (32.9)	1336
VI	Semi-skilled manual	51 (9.3)	92 (13.4)	131 (20.3)	47 (17.6)	193 (20.6)	257 (28.6)	152 (23.0)	923
VII	Unskilled manual	55 (10.0)	75 (10.9)	124 (19.3)	42 (15.7)	166 (17.7)	167 (18.6)	158 (23.9)	787
	Totals	550 (100)	689 (100)	644 (100)	267 (100)	939 (100)	899 (100)	660 (100)	4648 (100)

[1] Numbers represent absolute mobility, percentages are inflows.

Source: Payne (1987) Table 8.7, p.123

1 Both sets of data reveal a wide basis of recruitment in Class I and low homogeneity in its composition. Although approximately a quarter of Class I respondents were the sons of Class I fathers, the remaining three-quarters were drawn from the other six classes in a remarkably even manner, with – in the Oxford survey – each contributing at least 10 per cent. The Scottish data diverge slightly, since only 7.5 per cent of the 'service class' were from routine white-collar backgrounds, but we must note that only 3.3 per cent of the fathers in Scotland were routine white-collar. About 40 per cent of the Oxford 'service class' were men from 'blue-collar' backgrounds; if we count the Scottish foremen etc. as blue-collar, then half (49.6 per cent) of the service class north of the border came from blue-collar families. Both sets of findings dispel the idea of 'closure' at the higher levels of the British class structure.

2   There was far greater homogeneity in terms of social origins among manual workers: four out of five (79 per cent) of Scottish manual workers were from manual backgrounds; elsewhere in Britain the figure was 71 per cent.

Our picture of relative 'openness' at the top is modified if we enquire more closely into the different constituents of Class I in the Oxford data. Self-employed professionals (such as doctors and barristers) proved to be much more exclusive in their social recruitment than salaried professionals, administrators and industrial managers; more than half of the last group had blue-collar backgrounds, compared with only a quarter of self-employed professionals (Heath, 1981, Table 2.3, p.66). The entrance to the self-employed professions – the most highly educated group in Class I – may be skewed in favour of those who inherit 'cultural capital', that is the symbolic and linguistic competences and educational and vocational expectations acquired within the family. Large proprietors, on the other hand, demonstrate the influence of the inheritance of material capital on the recruitment of the entrepreneurial elite: 47 per cent of large proprietors were themselves the sons of proprietors (large and small combined). These discrepancies in the social origins of different groups in Class I underline the fact that it is the bureaucracies of industry and government that provide the main channels of long-distance upward mobility.

The greater degree of upward mobility observed by these newer surveys (as compared with Glass) also has to be interpreted in the light of changes in the *structure* of the labour force between generations. The census data reveal that, whereas 6 per cent of men in England and Wales were recorded as engaged in professional, administrative and managerial occupations in 1931, 16 per cent were in these categories in 1971. Net upward mobility has been determined by this expansion at the top and contraction at the bottom.

This helps to explain the great paradox of the Oxford survey: the data demonstrated considerable long-distance upward movement, but when analysed in terms of the mobility chances of working-class sons relative to the chances of 'service class' sons maintaining their position, they showed that there had been no diminution in class inequality. In other words, the disparities in opportunities had remained much the same throughout the cohorts of the survey (see Table 5.11).

Table 5.11 Disparity ratios showing relative chances, by class of father and birth cohort, of being found in Classes I and II and Classes VI and VII, (a) on entry into work, (b) ten years after entry, and (c) at the time of the enquiry (1972)

Father's class	Birth cohort	Relative chances of being found in Classes I and II (chances of sons of Class VI and VII fathers set at 1)			Relative chances of being found in Classes VI and VII (chances of sons of Class I and II fathers set at 1)		
		(a)	(b)	(c)	(a)	(b)	(c)
I and II	1908–17	9.48	7.65	3.90			
	1918–27	6.73	5.71	3.73		(set at 1)	
	1928–37	5.97	4.72	3.89			
	1938–47	4.97	3.66	3.38			
III–V	1908–17	2.75	2.70	1.75	1.56	2.11	2.18
	1918–27	2.11	2.45	1.89	1.55	2.05	2.19
	1928–37	2.34	2.15	1.98	1.99	2.28	2.50
	1938–47	1.51	1.62	1.61	2.12	2.59	2.84
VI and VII	1908–17				1.99	2.74	3.29
	1918–27		(set at 1)		2.00	3.16	3.71
	1928–37				2.58	3.63	4.47
	1938–47				2.75	4.15	4.60

Source: Goldthorpe *et al.* (1980) Table 3.2, p.75

As Goldthorpe sums it up,

> the increasing 'room at the top' has in fact been shared out more or less *pro rata* among men of different class origins, including those of Class I and II origins, so as to produce no change in their relative chances of access; and, on the other hand ... the contraction of the working class has been accompanied by a decline not only in the absolute chances of men of Class I and II origins being found in manual work but in their relative chances also. Overall, therefore, the picture obtained, once the perspective of relative mobility is adopted, is no longer one of significant change in the direction of greater opportunity for social ascent but, rather, of stability or indeed of increasing *in*equality in class mobility chances.

(Goldthorpe *et al.*, 1980, p.76)

5 SOCIAL MOBILITY, FAMILY AND GENDER

Most of the surveys discussed so far have taken individuals as the main target for study. This focus is a useful one for exploiting the data in such sources as the CEBs or individually completed questionnaires, which can then be related to the (similarly based) aggregate conclusions in, for example, the published census figures. Since information about an individual's occupation tends to be readily accessible, it is not surprising that it is so frequently relied on by researchers on social mobility (see the examples in Table 5.1).

However, despite its rewards, such a focus has limitations too, and some complementary approaches are worth noting. One is to pay more attention to how people experience or speak about 'class' and other forms of ranking – the *plurality* of complex ways these may be perceived depending on culture or circumstances (Joyce, 1991, pp.12, 16).

Another approach is to lay greater emphasis on *the family's* active role in upward or downward mobility – or, indeed, in keeping things the same. Michael Hout's (1989) study of social mobility in Ireland, for example, reveals the family as a key factor in the maintenance of inequality from generation to generation; in his view it is even more important than religion or emigration. Family values, he explains, legitimate employment practices such as 'favouritism in hiring and special favours on the job ... Special treatment for family members aids in the maintenance of privilege (and poverty) from one generation to another' (Hout, 1989, p.322).

The wider family can be important too in keeping up the 'family position'. One form of this is cousin marriage, which, it has been pointed out, can be an effective means to cement business or occupational ties, or to consolidate property within the family (see Davidoff and Hall, 1987; Anderson, 1986). Daniel Bertaux too makes a strong plea for more work on the active role of the family: 'between the level of classes and that of isolated individuals lies ... the level of *families*. That this has not been perceived so far is entirely consistent with the blindness of the founders of sociology to the female half of the population' (Bertaux, 1991, p.90; see also Elliott, 1990, and section 3 above).

Both these strands point towards the importance of specific and local studies, where the macro-surveys and quantitative analyses of official records can be complemented by qualitative sources such as biographies, oral history, or life-course studies.

QUESTION FOR RESEARCH

One possible small-scale project on social mobility would be to collect life histories from a series of parents and children in successive generations and analyse them in relation to questions such as the following:

1 For those who have risen in the social scale, what role, if any, was apparently played by such commonly mentioned factors in mobility as (a) marriage, (b) education, (c) entrepreneurial activity (see Chapter 3.3 above), and (d) migration?

2   It has been suggested by scholars such as Bertaux (1991) and Elliott (1990) that the traditional focus on aggregate measures of occupational movement and on *individuals'* mobility (usually that of men) misses the *family* basis of much social mobility and the qualitative influences of internal family structures and traditions. This possibility opens up some further questions:

o   Do the life histories you have collected indicate that social mobility *is* as much a family as an individual affair?

o   Is it individuals or whole sets of siblings that rise or fall in the social scale? Do birth order and/or gender seem to affect which siblings do well or badly? Can any such patterns be related to wider social factors?

o   Is it true that mothers do more than fathers to establish the family 'microclimates' that encourage or discourage particular forms of mobility (as suggested in Elliott, 1990, p.68)? Similarly, how about grandparents?

o   How do family resources affect social mobility, either in the form of material resources, effective social networks or cultural traditions (religious commitments, or a family tradition of migration or educational aspiration)?

You might wish to start with a short exercise on just one family's fortunes over two or more generations, but for comparative study you would need to take several families. One method would be through oral history investigation, supplemented by any other relevant sources you can locate.

A further and much criticized aspect of many earlier surveys, including the Oxford study, was, as you may already have noticed, their omission of women. Goldthorpe argued that class inequalities in mobility chances were 'gender-blind'. To his critics, however, this was another instance of sociological theory limping sadly behind the reality it seeks to explain: gender and class divisions, they argued, were not discrete, independent processes but mutually reinforcing; the characteristic types of modern class formation could not have happened without a sex-biased division of labour. They pointed to the parallel growth of the predominantly male service class and the 'white-blouse', routine, non-manual labour force whose work was often part-time, had limited career prospects, and rarely involved the exercise of authority. The mobility opportunities for men to rise to the service class depended on the feminization of work in Goldthorpe's Class III (which was, in fact, women's commonest class destination). This process began in the early twentieth century, but accelerated around 1960 with the lowering of the barriers to married women's 'white-blouse' employment. By taking on the routine clerical and secretarial tasks of industry, commerce and government, women 'released' men for managerial and administrative functions. There was also the problem of looking solely at the male breadwinner's occupation to determine a family's class position. Women's jobs make a difference in terms of home ownership and a family's style of life, and the class analyst simply cannot ignore the growth of wives' paid employment (for further details of this debate between Goldthorpe and his critics see Marshall *et al.*, 1988, pp.64–8).

The question of women's mobility was studied in a 1984 survey carried out in Essex, in which a random national sample of about 3,000 individuals were questioned about their work experiences and social attitudes (Marshall *et al.*, 1988). This provided unsurprising confirmation that women's chances of occupational mobility were worse than those of men, notably in access to the service class. The sexual division of labour was especially evident at the top of the class hierarchy: men made up more than four-fifths of the Class I respondents in the sample and while 13 per cent of all male respondents were service class, the proportion of women was only 4 per cent. The paucity of opportunities at the top meant that in terms of their careers, if not their marriages, large numbers of women were downwardly mobile. Only 14 per cent of women from Class I backgrounds had 'made it' into Class I occupations. But the disabilities attached to women's sex were also evident in their exclusion from skilled manual work, i.e. from those jobs commanding the greatest pay, power and respect within the working-class community. Whatever their class origin, women were far more likely than men from similar backgrounds to arrive at the routine non-manual occupations of Class III, and their career or promotion chances within these occupations were about half those of men, whereas men were more likely to arrive at service-class or working-class positions. Men were also more likely than women to be mobile into self-employment (Class IV) or supervisory (Class V) positions (Marshall *et al.*, 1988, pp.75 onwards). Within every class location a man would find his market and work situations superior to those of occupationally similar females.

Goldthorpe's earlier argument that class inequalities are 'gender-blind' is, therefore, unsustainable (for a more recent approach see Erikson and Goldthorpe, 1992). The structure of occupational opportunities into which it is possible for women to be mobile was different from that available to men, and the sexually segregated social division of labour systematically disadvantaged womanhood in mobility terms.

We ought to hesitate before describing the marriage of a working-class woman to a middle-class man as 'upward marital mobility', since it has offensively chauvinist undertones. Nevertheless, the incidence of inter-class marriage may contribute more to social fluidity than women's occupational mobility. The Oxford survey data included information on the occupations of respondents' fathers-in-law: while there was no large-scale net tendency for women to 'marry up', there was a great deal of 'marrying up' that was balanced by other women 'marrying down'. Anthony Heath comments that:

> *The British class structure would appear to be rather more fluid than consideration of father-son mobility alone would have us believe. The typical father from Class I is more likely to see his daughter downwardly mobile than his son, or, to be precise, to have a son-in-law of lower social class than his son. Conversely, the girl from Classes VI and VII is more likely to be upwardly mobile than her brother ... There is both more downward and more upward mobility through marriage for women than there is through the labour market for men. In this sense a woman's 'class fate' is more loosely linked to her social origins than is a man's.*

(Heath, 1981, pp.113–14)

--- *EXERCISE 5.5* ---

As a review of the chapter, as well as a stimulus for research ideas, try the following:

1   Look back through the main studies and note down how social mobility was defined in each, i.e. identify the framework for the ranked steps, classes, etc.

2   Similarly, locate other studies relating to social mobility either elsewhere in this volume or in any other sources and note down (a) which classification was adopted and (b) what main sources were used.

3   If you were considering a project on social mobility, which classification, if any, would you use and why?

Comments p.230.

Mobility is a central process in modern society, and anyone undertaking family and community history must be aware of its significance and dimensions. This chapter will have fulfilled its purpose if it has developed that awareness. We hope, too, that it will help some of you put your own research into a framework that will make it of more than personal interest.

_____ *QUESTIONS FOR RESEARCH* _____

In thinking about questions you might pursue in a project related to mobility, you must bear in mind that gathering aggregate data is *very* time-consuming. However, the following small-scale topics may be worth considering (in addition to those listed earlier), bearing in mind the types of questions, sources and methods discussed in both this and the previous chapter:

1   Research into the social recruitment of local 'elite groups' (whether business, professional or administrative). This is likely to be more feasible than a study of mobility between other strata, as individuals are easily identifiable and biographical data can be obtained through obituaries or valedictory notices in the local press. (Information on eminent members of elite groups will be found in *Who's Who, The dictionary of national biography* and more specialist sources such as *The dictionary of labour biography.*) 'Elite' need not be interpreted too narrowly in this context. For example, one topic suggested by Figures 5.1 and 5.2 is recruitment to the elementary teaching profession in a particular locality after the inauguration of compulsory education during the 1870s. It should be possible, for example, to analyse the social background of headteachers of the local authority and grant-aided schools in your area during particular decades.

2   While you are unlikely to have the time or resources to replicate the type of enquiry undertaken by Miles and Vincent (1991), it should be possible for you to analyse something their data tell us nothing about, namely the 'career' mobility of those living in the Victorian and Edwardian periods. How relevant was the family, or family connections? Did the members of the families you are studying 'hand down a trade' from father to son (or mother to daughter), and did they stick to trades throughout their working lives? Or did they move frequently from unskilled to skilled occupations, even becoming 'petty' capitalists? How about occupational mobility *within* the same broad 'class'? If you are working in the twentieth century, using oral evidence, you could enquire into the implications of mobility for the kin contacts of your respondents. Were family connections maintained by the upwardly mobile? Did kinship lead to cross-class links within the family? Finally, of course, oral historians have the immense advantage of being able to enquire directly about what the experience of mobility meant for the mobile. Did it change their political views? Did they cease to feel that they belonged to a class, or a community, or a family?

This does not exhaust the possibilities. Whatever you decide to focus on, it is important to remember that your researches should be informed by the findings of the major social mobility studies, as well as contributing in a modest way to filling the lacunae in them.

REFERENCES

Note: suggestions for further reading are indicated by an asterisk.

Anderson, N. F. (1986) 'Cousin marriage in Victorian England', *Journal of Family History,* 11, 3, pp. 285–301.

Armstrong, M.E. (1972) 'The use of information about occupation', in Wrigley, E.A. (ed.) *Nineteenth century society: essays on the use of quantitative methods for the study of social data,* Cambridge, Cambridge University Press.

Berent, J. (1954) 'Social mobility and marriage: a study of trends in England and Wales', in Glass (1954).

Bertaux, D. (1991) 'From methodological monopoly to pluralism in the sociology of social mobility', in Dex (1991).

Booth, C. (1902) *Life and labour of the people in London. First series. Poverty. 1 East, Central and South London*, London, Macmillan.

Borscheid, P. (1986) 'Romantic love and material interest: choosing partners in nineteenth-century Germany', *Journal of Family History*, 11, 2, pp. 157–68.

Carr-Saunders, A.M., Caradog Jones, D. and Moser, C.A. (1958) *A survey of social conditions in England and Wales*, Oxford, Oxford University Press.

Census of England and Wales 1951 (1955) *Classification of occupations*, London, HMSO.

Connell, K. H. (1968) 'Catholicism and marriage in the century after famine', in *Irish peasant society: four historical essays*, Oxford, Clarendon Press, pp. 113–61.

Crossick, G. (1978) *An artisan elite in Victorian society: Kentish Town, 1840–1880*, London, Croom Helm.

Davidoff, L. and Hall, C. (1987) *Family fortunes: men and women of the English middle class 1780–1850*, London, Hutchinson.

Dennis, N., Henriques, F. and Slaughter, C. (1969) *Coal is our life: an analysis of a Yorkshire mining community*, London, Tavistock. First published 1956.

Dex, S. (ed.) (1991) *Life and work history analyses: qualitative and quantitative developments*, London, Routledge.

Drake, M. (ed.) (1994) *Time, family and community: perspectives on family and community history*, Oxford, Blackwell in association with The Open University (Course Reader).

Elliott, B. (1990) 'Biography, family history and the analysis of social change', in Kendrik, S. *et al.* (eds) *Interpreting the past, understanding the present*, Basingstoke, Macmillan. Reprinted in Drake (1994).[*]

Erickson, C. (1959) *British industrialists: steel and hosiery, 1850–1950*, Cambridge, Cambridge University Press.

Erikson, R. and Goldthorpe, J.H. (1992) *The constant flux: a study of class mobility in industrial societies*, Oxford, Clarendon Press.

Foster, J. (1974) *Class struggle and the Industrial Revolution: early industrial capitalism in three English towns*, London, Methuen.

Giddens, A. (1989) *Sociology*, Cambridge, Polity Press. See especially Chapter 7.[*]

Glass, D. (ed.) (1954) *Social mobility in Britain*, London, Routledge and Kegan Paul.

Goldthorpe, J.H., Llewellyn, C. and Payne, C. (1980) *Social mobility and class structure in modern Britain*, Oxford, Clarendon Press.

Gray, R.Q. (1976) *The labour aristocracy in Victorian Edinburgh*, Oxford, Clarendon Press.

Halsey, A.H., Heath, A.F. and Ridge, J.M. (1980) *Origins and destinations: family, class and education in modern Britain*, Oxford, Clarendon Press.

Heath, A. (1981) *Social mobility*, London, Fontana.[*]

Hout, M. (1989) *Following in father's footsteps: social mobility in Ireland*, Cambridge, Mass. and London, Harvard University Press.

Joyce, P. (1991) *Visions of the people: industrial England and the question of class 1848–1914*, Cambridge, Cambridge University Press.

Kitchen, R. (1993) 'Class and community in Wolverton', audio-cassette 1A in Braham, P. (ed.) *Using the past: audio-cassettes on sources and methods for family and community historians*, Milton Keynes, The Open University.

Lockwood, D. (1966) *The blackcoated worker: a study in class consciousness,* London, Unwin.

Macdonald, K.I. (1974) 'Downwardly mobile mothers', in Ridge, J.M. (ed.) *Mobility in Britain reconsidered*, Oxford, Clarendon Press.

Marshall, G. *et al.* (1988) *Social class in modern Britain*, London, Hutchinson Education.

McKay, J.H. (1985) *The social history of the Scottish shale oil industry 1850–1914*, PhD thesis, The Open University.

Miles, A. and Vincent, D. (1991) 'A land of "boundless opportunity"? Mobility and stability in nineteenth-century England', in Dex (1991).*

Mills, D. R. and Mills, J. (1989) 'Occupation and social stratification revisited: the census enumerators' books of Victorian Britain', *Urban History Yearbook 1989*, pp.63–77.

Parkin, F. (1971) *Class inequality and political order*, London, MacGibbon and Key.

Payne, G. (1987) *Mobility and change in modern society*, Basingstoke, Macmillan.

Pearce, C. (1969) 'Social mobility through marriage in Ashford (Kent) 1837–70', unpublished paper from ESRC Project, *Ashford (Kent) 1840–70: a socio-demographic study.*

Sanderson, M. (1972) 'Literacy and social mobility in the Industrial Revolution in England', *Past and Present,* 56.

Smiles, S. (1859) *Self-help: with illustrations of conduct and perseverance.* Reprinted 1986, Harmondsworth, Penguin.

Smout, T. C. (1981) 'Scottish marriage, regular and irregular 1500–1940', in Outhwaite, R. B. (1981) *Marriage and society: studies in the social history of marriage*, New York, St Martin's Press, pp. 204–36.

Sundt, E. (1855) *On marriage in Norway.* Reprinted 1980, trans. Drake, M., Cambridge, Cambridge University Press.

Trollope, A. (1872) *The golden lion of Granpère.* Reprinted 1993, Oxford, Oxford University Press, World Classics.

Westergaard, J. and Resler, H. (1975) *Class in a capitalist society,* London, Heinemann.

Williams, R. (1983) *Keywords: a vocabulary of culture and society,* London, Fontana.

CHAPTER 6

PARLIAMENTARY ELECTIONS AND COMMUNITY HISTORY

by Michael Drake

Were you aware that:

o   In 1868 the register of parliamentary electors for the Eastern Division of Kent bore the names of 87 women, and that the revising barrister was complimented on his chivalry in admitting them? (*Kentish Express and Ashford News,* 24 October 1868, p.5; and 7 November 1868, p.5)

o   In 1866 some 69.8 per cent of the Coventry electorate were described, in a report to both Houses of Parliament, as being working class? (*Electoral Returns*, 1866, p.748)

o   Between 1832–3 and 1862–3 the parliamentary electorate of the United Kingdom rose from 813,210 to 1,313,680, without any extension of the franchise? (Martin, 1884, pp.109–10)

o   In 1856–7, some 42 per cent of the *whole* borough electorate of England and Wales sent only 40 members to the House of Commons, while the remaining 58 per cent sent nearly five times as many, namely 195? (Newmarch, 1857, p.317)

o   In 1837 the Liberal candidate in Banbury was said to have contributed £5 to the Old Charitable Society, £5 to the Visiting Society, £10 10s to the National School, £2 to the Infant School, £3 3s to the Clothing Fund, £2 2s to the Bible Society and £5 to the Mechanics Institute? And that his Tory opponent was said to have contributed only £3 11s 6d to these same charities? (Potts Collection, Banbury Public Library, 1837, Volume 4, p.29)

o   In the 1841 election, Edward Barlow of 102 Sydney Place, Bath, voted for the two Liberal candidates, Duncan and Roebuck (Bath was a two-member constituency), both of whom were successful; and in 1837 for the two Liberal candidates, Palmer and Roebuck, both of whom lost? Or that he did not vote in the 1835 election but in that for 1832 he cast his two votes for Palmer and Hobhouse, the former winning a seat, the latter not? Or that the second seat went to the other candidate, Roebuck, who was also described as a Liberal? (*Bath Reform poll book for 1841*)

My purpose in putting to you this list of rhetorical questions is twofold. First, I wanted to bring out the diversity of electoral experience, a diversity that was played out at the community level. To explore that diversity is to reveal some central characteristics of community life, for example its social composition, power structure, public behaviour, economic characteristics, residential segregation, etc. – in other words far more than voting. Second, the questions indicate the wide range of sources – especially in the period 1832–72 – available for this proposed exploration. Over the next few pages I shall say something about these sources, suggest a way of bringing out the electoral morphology of your community and, finally, suggest some exercises which you might care to carry out on your local poll books.

Before the Secret Ballot Act of 1872, those who had the vote cast it in public, for all to see. This was not just to satisfy the public's curiosity, but to emphasize that casting a vote was both a public duty and a way of expressing not just one's individual preference but that of the community to which one belonged. This community element appears to have continued down to the present day, in Britain at least, for one of the arguments against various schemes for proportional representation is that they would entail larger constituencies and so break the link between an MP and his or her community. Could one say, then, that, over the last two centuries, the composition of the House of Commons has been determined by a wish to represent communities, not individuals?

1 SOURCES

Local newspapers, especially after 1855 when the tax on them was abolished, devoted a great deal of space to parliamentary elections (for newspapers as a historical source generally, see Volume 4, Chapter 4, section 7). Some of this took the form of paid advertisements. Candidates would usually publish their manifestos in the form of a letter to the electors (see Figure 6.1). One notes in Meryweather's letter his line on issues of the day (e.g. the vote by ballot, disestablishment of the Irish Church) and on those that are with us still (e.g. the need to cut public expenditure and income tax and make re-adjustments in what, today, we would call social security payments: *plus ça change, plus c'est la même chose!*)

Newspaper advertising columns also carried the names of local notables who were giving their support to a particular candidate. Figure 6.2 shows a part of one such advertisement.

_____ *QUESTION FOR RESEARCH* _____

A parliamentary election often revealed much about a community that was normally hidden. Lists of prominent supporters of the various candidates, as shown in Figure 6.2, are a case in point, for these men can be taken to represent the elite of the community. By linking these names to the CEBs, rate books, directories and other sources of nominative information it is possible to build up a picture of the people who 'ran' the community.

_____

Another feature of nineteenth-century local newspapers was the large amount of space devoted to the public meetings held by parliamentary candidates. Figure 6.3 is an extract from a newspaper article on a meeting in 1868; it gives a flavour of the minute-by-minute reporting of such events.

It is hardly surprising that Parliament devoted a considerable amount of time to discussing elections to it. The *British Parliamentary Papers* (see Volume 4, Chapter 5 for a discussion of these) give information on the number of votes cast for which candidates, at both general and by-elections; returns on specific issues (like the number of working-class voters in each constituency cited above); and often lengthy reports of inquiries into the conduct of elections where allegations of corrupt practices were made. All these are grist to the mill for the community historian, especially the last mentioned, since, as with the newspaper reports, they enter into such detail on the workings of a community. In doing so they can tell us far more about a community than merely its behaviour at election time.

Worth looking for in any local library, record office or the archives of printers and solicitors (for business records see Volume 4, Chapter 4, section 5) are *handbills, posters, broadsheets* and any other ephemera from an election campaign. The charitable donations of the Liberal and Conservative candidates at the Banbury election of 1837, cited above, appeared on a handbill. It is preserved in the magnificent Potts Collection in Banbury Public Library. These documents may contain scurrilous comments, coded references to local personalities and their doings (Figure 6.4), detailed policy statements, cartoons, or an MP's voting record in the House of Commons (Figure 6.5).

TO THE
INDEPENDENT ELECTORS
OF THE BOROUGH OF
HYTHE, WEST HYTHE, FOLKESTONE TOWN AND FOLKESTONE PARISH, SANDGATE, CHERITON, NEWINGTON, AND SALTWOOD.

GENTLEMEN.—It was in the first instance at the request of numerous and influential Electors of your Borough, BOTH Liberal and Conservative, that I sought the honour of your Suffrages at the ensuing election, being assured that I should receive the support of EACH by a very large majority, as they considered that your present representative had not given that strict attention to his Parliamentary duties, and to your local affairs, which they had a right to receive at his hands; and after the very flattering reception you gave me at my meetings, both at Folkestone and Hythe, on hearing my political sentiments, the resolution was come to that I should stand a Candidate for your Suffrages. I responded to that invitation, and I will take an early opportunity of paying my personal respects to every Elector, to solicit his vote; and I have no doubt, from what I am told, that I shall receive a majority of them.

Gentlemen,—From what I stated at the Meetings, you know that mine is a Liberal policy; and, if returned, I should be a staunch supporter of Mr. Gladstone in his general policy.

I am for Vote by Ballot, believing it to be the best means of protecting the voter against intimidation and coercion, and allowing him to vote according to his conscience.

I am for economy in every department of the State, and would give my best attention to cutting down our enormous annual EXPENDITURE, whereby the INCOME TAX, which presses so much upon trade and professions, if not at once dispensed with, might be very materially RE-ADJUSTED.

I am for the Dis-establishment of the Irish Church, believing it to be a just measure to Ireland, and the means of adding to her tranquility.

I would give my support to the most comprehensive measure of general Education, whereby every child should be taught to read and write, without any distinction of creed.

I am for civil and religious liberty in its fullest sense. Myself a Churchman, I would give to others the same freedom of opinion I enjoy.

I would support any well-digested measure for the re-adjustment of Poor Rates, as well as the Poor Laws generally.

If returned your Representative, I would devote my time to my Parliamentary duties and to your Local Interests, which would always receive my unremitting attention; and I would do all in my power to promote the WELFARE and Prosperity of your Borough.

I have the honour to remain,
Gentlemen,
Your faithful and obedient Servant,
MONTAGUE MERYWEATHER.
Junior United Service Club,
London, Oct. 9th, 1868.

Figure 6.1 Letter of Montague Meryweather announcing his candidature for the 1868 election (Source: *Kentish Express and Ashford News,* 24 October 1868, p.4)

EAST KENT ELECTION.

THE following Gentlemen have consented to act on the ASHFORD COMMITTEE for the return of HENRY J. TUFTON, Esq., and Sir F. CROFT, Bart.

HENRY WHITFELD, Esq., Ashford, Chairman.
Carter, G. W. L. P., Esq., Pimlico London
Sir Edward C. Dering, Bart., Surrenden Dering
Sir Richard Tufton, Bart., Hothfield Place
Sir Edward Hoare, Bart., Little Hothfield
The Honourable George Edwardes, Little Chart
E. H. Knatchbull-Hugessen, Esq., M.P., Smeeth
Robert Darell, Esq., Calehill
Edward C. Dering, Esq., Surrenden Dering
Henry Neville Dering, Esq., Surrenden Dering
William Tilden Baldwin, Esq., Stede Hill, Harrietsham

ASHFORD.

John Allen	Samuel Joynson
George Andrew	G. A. Lewis
George Aspin	S. H. Lawrence
Thos. Bates	Alfred H. Langley
James Benton	George Lepine
George Bennett	William Mapperson
David Best	William Marshall
William Biggar	Thos. Nesbit
John Bourne	John Dobson Norwood
John Broad	Francis Pollatt
John Buss	Richard Raben
W. E. L. Buss	Thos. E. Scott
Henry Foster	John Taylor
William Gilford	H. A. Tite
John Goldsmith	George Wanstall
Edward Huyward	John Watson
Henry Harms	Geo. F. Wilks
Henry Headley	Thos. G. Wilkinson
Frederick Hyland	Frederick Worger
Henry Igglesden	

Figure 6.2 Part of the Ashford Committee formed to support the candidature of Tufton and Croft at the 1868 election (Source: *Kentish Express and Ashford News,* 14 November 1868, p.1)

ELECTION MEETINGS.

GREAT DISTURBANCE AT THE CONSERVATIVE MEETING AT ASHFORD.

E. L. Pemberton Esq., M.P., and the Hon. G. Milles, the Conservative candidates for the representation of the Eastern Division of the county, were to address the electors of Ashford and the neighbourhood, in the New Corn Exchange on Tuesday evening last. The hour after two or three changes was ultimately fixed at eight o'clock. We regret to say that so great a disturbance occurred that the candidates could not express their sentiments, and that not the slightest opportunity for discussion was afforded. A large crowd collected outside the doors previous to their being opened, and mingled with the adults was a large proportion of boys, who were evidently ready for any amount of noise and mischief. It was also evident that a great deal of ill-feeling prevailed respecting the introduction of the body of prize-fighters into the town at the last election. After the doors were opened probably about 1,000 persons entered the room, and it was soon apparent that there was a considerable number among them who would allow very little to be heard besides their own sweet voices. On the chairman (Sir E. Knatchbull, Bart.) coming on the platform with the candidates and their more prominent supporters in this district they were received with a chorus of groans. Among the gentlemen present, we noticed Lieut.-Colonel Groves, C. S. Hardy, Esq. (Chilham Castle); the Rev. J. Philpott, C. P. Carter Esq., W. P. Burra, Esq., J. S. Burra, Esq., the Rev. R. Baldock, the Rev. J. P. Alcock, (Vicar of Ashford), T. Thurston, Esq., G. W. Greenhill, Esq., Messrs. G. C. Rolfe, J. Bates, E. Clements, T. Bates, E. Bishopp, Churchill, &c., &c.

Figure 6.3 Report on election meeting at Ashford, Kent, 27 October 1868 (Source: *Kentish Express and Ashford News,* 31 October 1868, p.6)

116

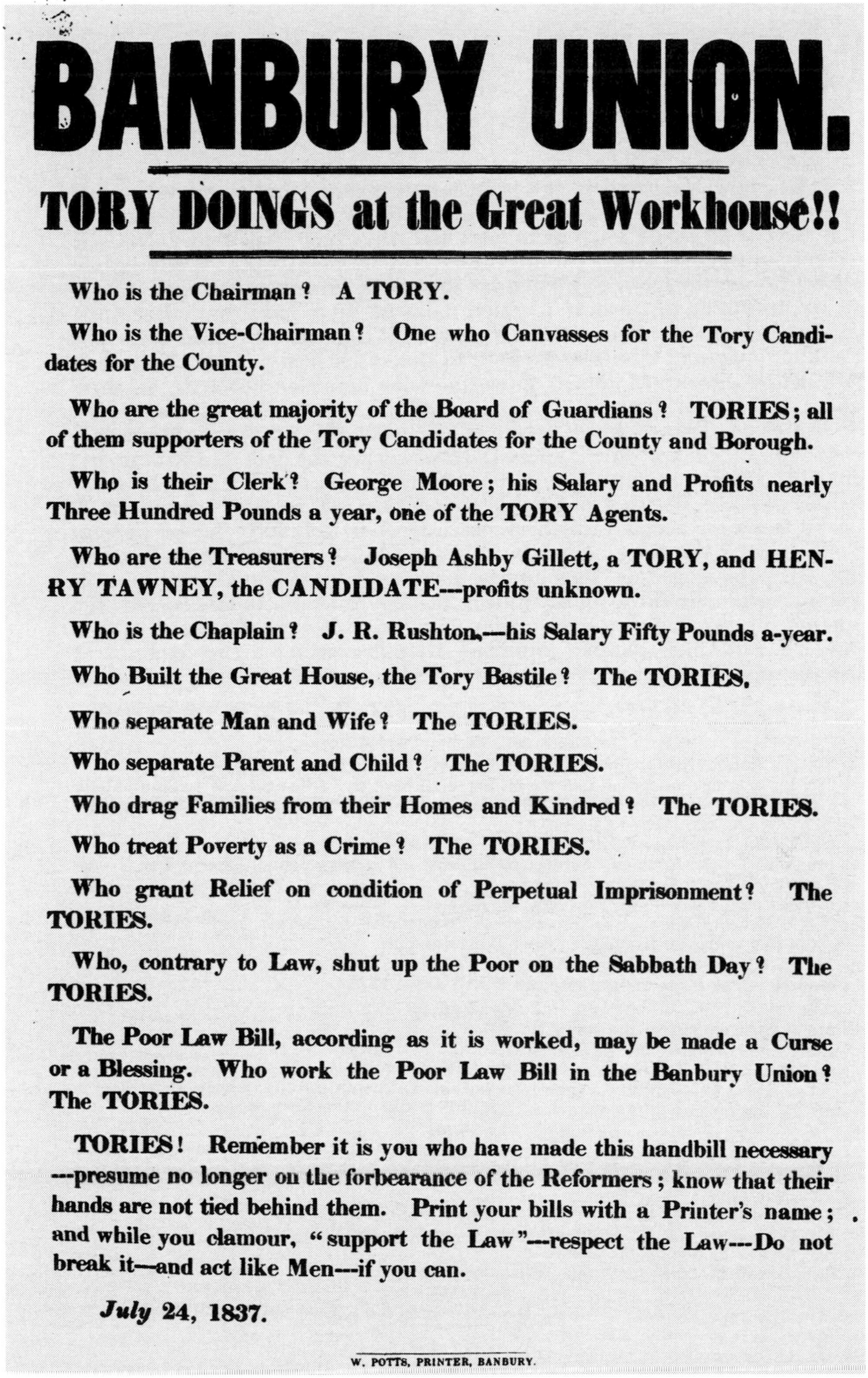

BANBURY UNION.

TORY DOINGS at the Great Workhouse!!

Who is the Chairman? A TORY.

Who is the Vice-Chairman? One who Canvasses for the Tory Candidates for the County.

Who are the great majority of the Board of Guardians? TORIES; all of them supporters of the Tory Candidates for the County and Borough.

Who is their Clerk? George Moore; his Salary and Profits nearly Three Hundred Pounds a year, one of the TORY Agents.

Who are the Treasurers? Joseph Ashby Gillett, a TORY, and HENRY TAWNEY, the CANDIDATE---profits unknown.

Who is the Chaplain? J. R. Rushton,---his Salary Fifty Pounds a-year.

Who Built the Great House, the Tory Bastile? The TORIES.

Who separate Man and Wife? The TORIES.

Who separate Parent and Child? The TORIES.

Who drag Families from their Homes and Kindred? The TORIES.

Who treat Poverty as a Crime? The TORIES.

Who grant Relief on condition of Perpetual Imprisonment? The TORIES.

Who, contrary to Law, shut up the Poor on the Sabbath Day? The TORIES.

The Poor Law Bill, according as it is worked, may be made a Curse or a Blessing. Who work the Poor Law Bill in the Banbury Union? The TORIES.

TORIES! Remember it is you who have made this handbill necessary ---presume no longer on the forbearance of the Reformers; know that their hands are not tied behind them. Print your bills with a Printer's name; and while you clamour, "support the Law"---respect the Law---Do not break it---and act like Men---if you can.

July 24, 1837.

W. POTTS, PRINTER, BANBURY.

Figure 6.4 Anti-Tory poster from 1837 (Source: Potts Collection, Banbury Public Library, 1837, Volume 4, p.22)

TANCRED'S PLEDGES.

TO THE ELECTORS OF BANBURY.

FELLOW TOWNSMEN,

It has been asserted by Mr. Vincent and echoed and re-echoed by his supporters, that Mr. Tancred has *broken all the pledges he ever made.*—— They have been asked to point to one; and they have failed to do so. It has been observed that "the inventors of a lie may repeat it until they believe it to be the truth:" if such be sometimes the effect of repetition on the inventor of an untruth, it is much more likely to have that effect upon those who are merely hearers of it, especially if they have not paid sufficient attention to passing events to be able to detect its falsity. Mr. Tancred's more active supporters appear to consider the assertion unworthy of their notice; but I think it ought to be contradicted, and therefore, as no one else has come forward I will make it my business, for your information, to write down a few of Mr. Tancred's votes during the present Parliament: you will, when you have read them, be able to judge if he has kept his pledges or not. Wishing to be able to ascertain if I was fairly represented, I have kept an account of the most important votes which our present Member has given since he has been in the House of Commons: I notice, now, only those of this Parliament, because I know that *many persons* kept a similar account to mine, during the two first Parliaments that Mr. Tancred represented us; but as they found his votes, *in the main,* so well to accord with their political opinions, they discontinued the register. I have continued mine, and I now give you some extracts from it.

Banbury, June 21, 1841.　　　　**AN OLD REFORMER.**

In 1837, Mr. Tancred Voted for

For Sir W. Molesworth's motion to abolish Property Qualification of Members.
For Mr. Lushington's resolution that the sitting of Bishops in Parliament was unfavourable to the general interests of the Christian Religion, and tended to alienate the affections of the people from the Established Church.
For making the Legislative Council of Canada an elective body.
For providing for the repair of Churches by an improved management of Church Lands: the collection of Church Rates then to cease.
For Mr. Roebuck's motion for repealing the duty on Newspapers.
For Mr. D'Eyncourt's motion for repealing the Septennial Act, which would have had the effect of shortening Parliaments to three years duration.
For the amendment of the Reform Bill.
For a select committee to inquire into the PENSION LIST.

In 1838,

For Mr. Grote's motion for the Ballot.
For going into committee on the Corn Laws.
For the appointment of a committee on Military Punishment.
Against the grant of £80,280 for the support of the Yeomanry Cavalry, for one year.
Against the continuance of the annuity of £21,000 a year to the King of Hanover.

In 1839,

For Mr. Duncombe's amendment to the Address, stating that the Reform Act had disappointed the people, that the measure could *not* be final, and that a further Reform should be taken into consideration.
For hearing witnesses on the Corn Laws at the bar of the House.
For Mr. O'Connell's motion for the extension of the Parliamentary Franchise.
For Mr. Grote's motion for the Ballot.
For the grant of £30,000 for Public Education.

In 1840,

For Mr. Duncombe's motion to relieve Dissenters from the payment of Church Rates.
For Mr. Hume's motion for a return of Registered Electors.
For Mr. Hume's motion for suspending the King of Hanover's Annuity.
For Mr. Villiers' motion for taking into consideration the law relating to Foreign Corn.

In 1841,

For admitting Jews to Civil Offices.
For limiting the continuance of the Poor Law Commission to three years.

W. POTTS, PRINTER, GUARDIAN OFFICE, BANBURY

Figure 6.5 Handbill produced by Tancred's supporters, 1841 (Source: Potts Collection, Banbury Public Library, 1841, Volume 5, p.15)

Poll books provide a record of votes cast at parliamentary elections prior to the Secret Ballot Act of 1872. They were usually produced by jobbing printers soon after the close of the poll, usually in small pamphlet form. They are also to be found as supplements in local newspapers. At their simplest they give the name of each voter and the way he or she voted (as we have seen, there were women on the East Kent electoral register and some did cast their vote). Others give much more than this, for example each elector's precise address, the rateable value of the property enfranchising him, his occupation, and his religion (in Ireland). The names of abstainers, deceased electors, and those who had left the constituency, and occasionally even the previous voting record of voters, appear in the poll books. (For the titles, contents and current whereabouts of poll books see Gibson and Rogers, 1990, and Sims, 1984; for a more detailed examination of poll books and electoral registers see Volume 4, Chapter 4, section 2). An extract from the 1865 poll book for Banbury and Neithrop is shown in Figure 6.6.

2 YOUR COMMUNITY'S ELECTORAL MORPHOLOGY

Because parliamentary elections often get at the heart of community life, it is worth creating a community's electoral morphology. By this I mean the form taken by various facets of the electoral process such as the constituency boundaries, the nature of the franchise, the size and composition of the electorate, the process of registration, voting procedures and the electoral outcome as indicated by the poll books. Some communities will provide a broad range of sources, others will not. Even if an initial trawl for sources proves disappointing, it is worth persisting as there is undoubtedly much that remains to be discovered.

The 1832 Reform Act paid great attention to the redrawing of constituency boundaries in the case of the boroughs. The aim was, as far as possible, to avoid a clash of interests within a constituency, so maintaining its homogeneity. The commissioners who drew the boundaries were carefully briefed to this end. For instance, Moore (1966) notes that for those constituencies that were growing rapidly, the commissioners were told not to set the boundaries of the towns as they existed in 1832 but to project them in 'the direction in which [the] Town [was] increasing … and [to make] a liberal allowance … for the extension of the Town in such direction so that the boundaries determined today may not require alteration tomorrow' (cited in Moore, 1966, p.55).

QUESTION FOR RESEARCH

If the community in which you are interested forms, or lies within, one of the constituencies created or redrawn by the electoral commissioners in 1832, try to judge the extent to which they fulfilled their brief of creating a constituency with a recognizable identity. For constituency maps see Lewis (1833, 1835, 1837, 1846). For other sources of maps see Volume 4, Chapter 6, section 2.

Prior to the Reform Act of 1832 the franchise for the county constituencies was uniform. If a man possessed a freehold valued at 40 shillings or more, he had the right to vote in the county in which it was situated. If he had several such freeholds he could still only vote once at each election unless they were situated in different counties, in which case he could vote as many times as he had freeholds and the energy to move from one polling station to another. This was not excessively demanding, as elections could last for several days and take place at different times. Indeed, votes could be counted and the result declared in one county before polling had begun in another.

1865.

BANBURY AND NEITHROP.

HIGH STREET.

Probably Vote for.			Name of Voter.	How Voted in 1859.					New Voters.
✓	9	B		February.			April.		
				S.	H.	M.	S.	D.	
			John Gazey . . .			1		1	
			William Munton . .	1			1		
			James Stockton . .	1			1		
			Edward Day . . .	1			1		
			Robert H. Brooks . .			1		1	
			Richard H. Rolls . :					1	
			Daniel P. Pellatt . .						1
			Joseph Shayler . .						1
			James Hutchings . .			1		1	
			James Hall . . .			1		1	
			George Watson . .			1			
			Richard Fisher . .			1		1	
			George Cottam . .		1				
			Thomas Draper . .	1			1		
			Thomas Mitchell . .	1			1		
			Robert S. Wise. . .	1			1		
			Frederick Staines . .	1			1		
			William Hobley . .			.1			
			Henry W. Clarke . .						1
			Henry Flowers . .			1	.	1	

Figure 6.6   Extract from *Banbury and Neithrop poll book, 1865* (Source: Potts Collection, Banbury Public Library)

In contrast with the county franchise, that in the borough constituencies was very complicated. Also, since the borough constituencies returned far more members than the counties
(about 80 per cent of the total number in England and Wales in 1830), this meant that more MPs
were elected on widely differing franchises. Thus in a few constituencies – the case of Preston is
usually cited – almost all adult males could vote. In others, for example Bath, only the members of
the municipal corporation could vote. Thus whereas Preston had an electorate of between 8,000
and 9,000, that of Bath numbered around 30. It is impossible to give a precise figure before 1832,
when the Reform Act introduced a system of electoral registration.

The 1832 Reform Act simplified the franchise in the boroughs and complicated it somewhat
in the counties. Thus from 1832 until 1867 the borough franchise went to those possessing a
household valued at £10. (For details of changes in the franchise subsequent to 1867 see Volume
4, Chapter 4, p.66.) In the counties the 40 shilling freeholders continued to have the franchise.
However, it was extended to rural tenants who paid a rent of at least £50 a year. This decision
(known as the Chandos clause after the name of the peer who proposed it) was seen as a method
of extending the influence of landlords in rural areas, for it was assumed – you might care to
investigate whether rightly or wrongly – that such tenants would vote as their landlords wished.

The effect of these changes in the franchise on the size and composition of the electorate
varied enormously from one part of the country to another. The Reform Act of 1832 is believed to
have increased the electorate by around 50 per cent, though a precise figure eludes us since no
register of electors was kept before 1832. As already noted, there was a considerable increase in
the electorate between 1832–3 and 1862–3. Table 6.1 shows this for various parts of the United
Kingdom. The reason for the increase was partly an increase in wealth, which created more £10
householders, and partly an increase in political interest, which led to more of those who were
eligible to vote getting themselves on the electoral register. Note the especially large percentage
increase in the size of the Irish electorate. It would be interesting to know how this was spread
around the Irish constituencies.

Table 6.1 Increase in the number of parliamentary electors between 1832–3 and 1862–3

	Number	1832–3 As percentage of total		Number	1862–3 As percentage of total	
		Electors	Population		Electors	Population
England and Wales	656 622	80.7	4.7	1 003 693	76.3	5.0
Scotland	64 447	7.9	2.7	101 795	7.8	3.3
Ireland	92 141	11.4	1.2	208 192	15.9	3.6
Total	813 210	100.0		1 313 680	100.0	

Source: Martin (1884)

--- **QUESTION FOR RESEARCH** ---

If, as we have seen, part of the increase in the size of the electorate was due to increased
wealth allowing more people onto the electoral register, then by tracing that growth in
individual constituencies, one should get some measure of their changing level of prosperity.
The link between the two was clear to contemporaries, as the following quotations show.
These are taken from a parliamentary report dealing with the rise and fall in the number of
working-class electors (*Electoral Returns*, 1866, pp.215–494), but you need not confine
yourself to this particular report. The rise or fall in the total electorate – available annually for
many places – provides the clues for an enquiry into a community's economic well-being.
You will also note from the passages cited below the enormous differences in economic

conditions, employment, family and household composition that were revealed in the course of an electoral inquiry.

Bridgwater A large number of the working classes on the register derive their support from working at the foundries, railway carriage works, brick and pottery manufacturers, and in connection with the shipping of Bridgwater (p.324).

Birkenhead In Birkenhead there are no works of any consequence in which men are employed in manufacture, except highly skilled and well-paid artificers with wages from 40s to 60s per week. Rents are stated to be exceptionally high, involving the necessity of operatives unskilled and labourers occupying houses in common of a rent sufficiently high to give a vote to one, whereas if rents were lower each family would be occupying a house under £10 (p.316).

Brighton There are nearly 1,500 men employed in the railway workshops exclusive of engine drivers, stokers and porters and upwards of 500 of them are on the Register and come within the description of artizans etc. The town, as the resort of many thousands of visitors, employs a very large number of mechanics of all trades, especially tailors, shoe-makers, journeymen butchers, bakers etc. The amount of building that has gone on for 10 years also has found occupation for a vast number of bricklayers, plasterers, masons, carpenters etc.

With reference to the excess of male occupiers at a rateable value of £10, over electors on the Register, it is stated that 1,634 are compound occupiers, that persons of that class frequently change their place of abode, and that a great many never make a claim to be placed on the Register. 420 houses have been recently erected, and have not been occupied sufficiently long to confer a vote (p.326).

Dorchester With reference to the large number of working classes on the Register it is stated that many of the persons who rent £10 houses in the borough take them with a view of letting out again to lodgers (p.351).

Hythe In Hythe there are a great many men who, although only journeymen mechanics or labourers, live in a better class of house than in many towns, in consequence of their wives earning a portion of their living by letting rooms in the summer to visitors. The South-Eastern Railway Company also employ a large number of men at high wages (p.378).

Launceston The large number of the working class on the register is attributed to the fact that there is a custom prevailing chiefly in the parish of St. Stephen of allowing labourers to occupy a field or two, which gives them the franchise (p.388).

Macclesfield Mr May, Clerk to the Guardians, states with reference to the small number of the working classes on the Register that wages have been lower and much more precarious in Macclesfield than elsewhere for a series of years, and that the distress among the operative class has been severe and trying. In consequence the rents of cottages and houses generally are much lower than in other towns and of late years they have so materially diminished in value as to render them absolutely unprofitable. There are upwards of 4,000 houses in the borough unoccupied. A house of £10 value in Macclesfield would be worth £15 in the prosperous towns of Yorkshire and Lancashire (p.401).

Oxford About 200 of the 1,252 working class electors are college servants (p.422).

Sheffield The large number of the working class on the Register is attributed to the circumstance that many of the workmen of Sheffield earn large wages and can afford to occupy houses of the value of £10 a year. It is stated that there is scarcely another borough in which the earnings of the working class are as high as in Sheffield (p.444).

Shrewsbury With reference to the number of working classes on the Register it is stated that the mode of living in Shrewsbury is widely different from that in the manufacturing districts. Most married men become householders and not lodgers merely, and on the whole are much more provident than in the districts alluded to. There is no staple trade in Shrewsbury, but the persons included in the Return found employment at the various works in the town, and earn sufficient money to enable them to occupy £10 houses (p.446).

After reading these extracts you may have wondered how the definition of 'working classes' was arrived at. The process was no easier then than today. (For a more general categorization of socio-economic groups see Volume 4, Chapter 3, section 2.1.1, and also the discussion in Chapter 5, section 1 above.) Initially the instruction was to include anyone 'coming within the description of *Mechanic, Artisan, or other person supporting himself by daily manual labour*'. A further direction was given that no elector was to be excluded because he had a 'shop which is kept by his wife or other member of the family' (*Electoral Returns*, 1866, p.221). Subsequently, the Board responsible for drafting these instructions had second thoughts. Fearing misunderstandings, the following amplification was issued:

> *The Board direct me to point out that the object of the Return is to show the Number of Electors on the Parliamentary Register now in force who would ordinarily be understood to come within the designation of 'the working classes'. The Board do not intend that the Return should be exclusively confined to journeymen who are employed by masters at daily or weekly wages, but that it should include men who work daily at their own handicraft trade without a master, and even sometimes employ a journeyman or an apprentice, provided they derive their chief support from their own hand labour, and not from the labour of others, or the profits arising from the employment of capital or the supply of materials.*
>
> *The Board have already stated in a note to the Form of Return that no artisan, mechanic, or labourer is to be excluded because he has a shop which is kept by his wife or other member of his family; but it must be distinctly understood, that, as a general rule, shopkeepers and their shop assistants are not to be inserted. The Board think it right to add that overlookers, superintendents, foremen or others employed among or in connexion with operatives, workmen, or other daily labourers are not to be included, unless actually employed in daily manual labour in the same manner [and] in every respect as the men who are under them.*
>
> (Electoral Returns, 1866, p.221)

A later attempt at a definition of the 'labouring classes' also reveals the complexity of the task:

> *the expression 'labouring classes' includes mechanics, artisans, labourers, and others working for wages; hawkers, costermongers, persons not working for wages, but working at some trade or handicraft without employing others except members of their own family; and persons, other than domestic servants, whose income does not exceed thirty shillings a week, and the families of any such persons who may be residing with them.*
>
> (Local Government Provisional Orders Bill, 1890, pp.1–2)

What do you make of these two definitions?

In spite of getting rid of the so-called 'rotten boroughs' (constituencies with just a handful of electors), the 1832 Reform Act did not lay much emphasis on a more equitable relation between the population and parliamentary seats. Thus the 700,000 men of County Cork had two members, the 160,000 men of Cumberland four members. As late as 1852 Tower Hamlets had 23,534 electors, Totnes only 371. The size of the electorate in the community that interests you, both in absolute terms and relative to its population, is an important feature of the community's electoral morphology. Its composition – in terms of social structure and wealth (as measured by the rateable values of the property conferring the vote) – is an important feature of the community's character.

From the variations associated with the post-1832 franchise and the distribution of seats, we now turn to those introduced by the registration system. Again, these demonstrate the hetero-geneity of community experience, the underlying reasons for which are well worth the attention of community historians. The system varied as between the counties and the boroughs. In the former the parish overseer was responsible for drawing up the list of electors, but in order to get on the list, those who believed themselves to be qualified had to put forward their claim. In the boroughs two officials were responsible for the lists. One was the town clerk, who looked after those freemen voters whose rights were reserved under the Acts of 1832 and 1867. The other official was the overseer of the poor. Since the vote in the boroughs was given to £10 house-holders, the overseer had a list of voters to hand in the rate book. Thus it was not necessary for qualified electors to make a formal claim (Thomas, 1950, p.82), although eligible voters had to check that they had been registered. Sometimes this was an easy enough task, but much depended upon the zeal of the local administration. For example, in Bath in 1832, provisional lists of electors were pinned up around the town and those who felt they had been wrongly omitted were directed to a firm of solicitors in order to make their case. As a result of this procedure some 200 names were added, increasing it by 7 per cent. One whose complaint was not upheld was a man born in The Cape of Good Hope in 1793. As this was four years before the colony was conquered by Britain, he was not regarded as a British subject by birth (Wroughton, 1972, p.29).

These registration procedures left plenty of opportunity for political activists to make their presence felt. Thompson notes its differential effect in the mid 1830s:

> Between the 1834 and 1835 registrations, the English county electorate increased by over twenty per cent, an increase by no means evenly distributed over all constituencies. The highest rate of increase was in south Staffordshire, 88 per cent, and the West Riding came second with a growth of 63 per cent in one year, from 18,061 to 29,456 voters. Party enthusiasm on both sides had ferreted out an enormous number of people who had been too lazy or too ignorant to claim the vote, and had found others to fill new voting qualifications expressly manufactured for the occasion by splitting large tenancies into the maximum number of £50 a year 'voting tenancies'
>
> (Thompson, 1959, p.221)

As the registration process was closely tied to the level of political interest and to the skill with which that interest was articulated, variations in the growth of electorates would be expected. Nossiter (1972, p.409) remarks that shopkeepers were often prominent in registration societies because they had developed the 'clerical and organizational skills that were needed'. In areas where the 'shopocracy' was strong one might expect a high proportion of potential electors to be registered. The same would be expected in times of political ferment.

QUESTION FOR RESEARCH

Here are two hypotheses that could be tested in constituencies with appropriate docu-mentary evidence, i.e. newspaper reports, local government records, memoirs of political activists, 'leading family' archives, parliamentary reports and returns on particular constituencies.

1 That where the 'shopocracy' was strong, a high proportion of potential electors were registered.

2 That in times of political ferment, e.g. the early 1840s and the mid 1860s, a high proportion of potential electors were registered.

The process of voting had two main features. First, nomination took place on hustings – temporary open-air stages – on which the candidates would present themselves to such voters and non-voters as cared to come along. Although a show of hands was usually called for, it was rare for it to be taken seriously, and one or other of the candidates would demand a poll. This would take place on one or two days. Electors would be informed where they had to vote. Having established the electors' *bona fides,* the polling clerk would ask them who they wanted to vote for and would put a tick or a cross against the name – or names if it was more than a one-member constituency – of their choice. Voting usually took place between 8 a.m. and 4 p.m.

Whether people voted or not obviously depended on a variety of factors, perhaps the most important being the extent of their political commitment. Polling stations, especially in county constituencies, could be inconveniently situated. The poll itself often took place under what might be described euphemistically as boisterous conditions. An indication of the excitement, not to speak of tumult, caused by elections is indicated in Figure 6.3. Thus the elderly and the timid could well be hesitant about casting their vote. In this context it is interesting to note that of the 31 Ashford women on the East Kent division electoral register for 1868, only four went to the poll (Drake, 1971, pp.483–4). All four voted for the Liberal candidate.

Notice too that the disenfranchised were not entirely without political influence. In his analysis of Oldham politics in the post–1832 period, Foster (1974) has clearly shown how the non-voters could influence the electorate through mass organization, while Vincent (1966) found similar influences operating in other industrial centres. Such organizational pressure could easily spill over into physical intimidation and rioting. Nevertheless, it is yet another way for a community to present its feelings and aspirations.

QUESTION FOR RESEARCH

From a study of turnout (the proportion of the electorate who voted) it should be possible to gauge the political activity level of a community at a point in time, as well as over time. From this you might examine other literary sources to explain whatever level you find, thus giving another insight into community attitudes.

---

3 SOME EXERCISES IN VOTING BEHAVIOUR

The exercises described below were all carried out on Bath poll books. Given poll books of a similar quality, there is no reason why you should not try them yourself.

Bath was a borough constituency before the 1832 Reform Act. Its electorate was very small indeed, being confined to the 30 or so members of the corporation. The Reform Act increased the electorate to 2,825. With almost one-third of the adult male population thus enfranchised, it moved, within the space of a year, from being one of the most undemocratic constituencies in the country to one of the most democratic. However, the electorate grew only slowly from the 1830s to the 1860s, an indication of the town's relative economic decline. The extension of the franchise in 1868 raised Bath's electorate to 5,024. Incidentally, the printed poll book from which this last figure was obtained is particularly informative: it contains not only the names, addresses and occupations of the voters and the way they cast their votes, but it also breaks down the aggregative returns by parish and polling booth, in a two-page analysis. In addition, it indicates, again in part by polling booth, the number of votes promised the Conservative candidate and the actual votes given him.

Given the small size of the pre-1832 franchise, it is not surprising that the freeman vote was of negligible proportions, only 15 being on the register in 1841, of whom five voted, in each case for the two Conservative candidates. The electorate was, then, a very new one. Another feature of the Bath electorate in the period 1832–68 was that few had a dual qualification: 172 out of 3,000 electors fell into this category in 1842, 284 out of 3,172 in 1859, and 223 out of 5,024 in 1868.

Possession of the franchise by different socio-economic groups can be gauged from several sources. For instance, the parliamentary return of 1866 (*Electoral Returns*, 1866) showed only

15.1 per cent of the Bath electorate to be 'working class'. The six poll books covering the elections of 1841, 1847, 1851, 1852, 1855 and 1868 all give the occupations of the individual electors. The *Bath poll book 1855* also gives us a measure of the wealth of the individual voters by showing the rateable value of the property enfranchising them (which in turn was used to assess their contribution to the support of the poor). This provides us with our first exercise. Note that if you have a rate book and a poll book for the same year, you can do this exercise, though because you will have to match the two it will take longer.

EXERCISE 6.1

In Table 6.2 you will see the number of votes cast for each of the two candidates at the Bath parliamentary by-election of 1855, the number of electors who abstained and the total poor rate assessment of each. Work out the mean poor rate assessment for each and comment on the result.

Answers/comments p.230.

Table 6.2 Number of votes cast for each candidate and number of abstainers at the Bath parliamentary by-election of 1855, together with the total poor rate assessment for each category

Voted for	Number of votes	Total poor rate assessment	Mean assessment per voter
Whately (Conservative)	1,129	£61,249	
Tite (Liberal)	1,176	£39,227	
Abstained	455	£21,793	

Source: *The Bath poll book 1855*

Why should such a relatively large and well-off body of electors abstain? As it turns out, it was no new phenomenon in 1855. Table 6.3 shows that turnout was consistently higher in the 'central artisan populated' parish of St James than in the 'wealthy suburban parish' of Bathwick. The descriptions are Neale's (1972, pp.51–2).

Table 6.3 Percentage of the electorate voting in the Bath parishes of St James and Bathwick at the parliamentary elections of 1832, 1835, 1837 1841 and 1847

Year	St James	Bathwick
1832	88.0	74.2
1835	76.7	62.1
1837	73.8	62.7
1841	74.7	67.4
1847	78.2	72.8

Source: *The Bath Liberal poll book 1847*

Note that the highest turnout in both parishes occurred at the elections generating the most heat, namely those of 1832 (parliamentary reform) and 1847 (Corn Law repeal).

Another exercise might well appeal to family historians who have worked on their family trees. I refer to the creation of what I call a psephological tree in Figure 6.7.

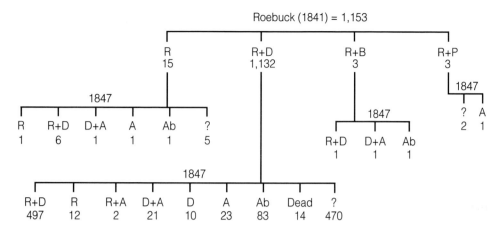

R = John Arthur Roebuck
D = Lord Viscount Duncan
A = Lord Ashley
Ab = Abstained

B = Harold Ludlow Bruges
P = Lord Viscount Powerscourt
? = Dead, disappeared etc. and not in poll book

Figure 6.7   The distribution of those of Roebuck's 1841 voters who participated in the 1847 election (Source: *The Bath poll book 1847)*

EXERCISE 6.2
---

1   What percentage of those who cast at least one of their votes for Roebuck in 1841 did so in 1847?

2   What percentage of voters deserted him altogether by voting for other candidates?

3   What percentage of Roebuck's 1841 supporters did not participate in the 1847 election?

4   What do you make of your answers to the above three questions?

Answers/comments p.231.

Exercise 6.2 brings out yet again what I hope has emerged from this chapter, namely that electoral behaviour tells us far more about nineteenth-century community life than might at first appear. Here it is a matter of the physical replacement of the population, something not confined, one assumes, to those who enjoyed the franchise. Earlier, however, we saw that an examination of the electoral system brings out the heterogeneity of community life in Britain and Ireland. The belief which underlay the 1832 Reform Act, namely that it was possible to create constituencies with overall common interests by a skilful drawing of their boundaries, proved impossible. There were too many class divisions, religious hostilities, clashes between 'incomers' and the established population, and so on. Much of this was mirrored in political behaviour, especially at election time. The sources mentioned here have been little explored, the questions rarely put. There is much that remains to be done!

REFERENCES AND FURTHER READING

Note: suggestions for further reading are indicated by an asterisk.

Bath Reform poll book for 1841, Bath, S. Gibbs.

The Bath poll book 1847, Bath, W. Pocock.

The Bath Liberal poll book 1847, Bath, S. Gibbs.

Bath poll book 1855, Bath, R.E. Peach.

Davis, R.W. (1972) *Political change and continuity: a Buckinghamshire study,* Newton Abbot, David and Charles.*

Drake, M. (1971) 'The mid-Victorian voter', *Journal of Interdisciplinary History,* 1, 3, pp.473–90.

Electoral Returns. Boroughs and Counties 1865–66. Return B Working classes on the Parliamentary Register (1866) British Parliamentary Papers, 1866, LVII, pp.215, 220–2, 303–495.

Fisher, J. R. (1981) 'Issues and influence: two by-elections in south Nottinghamshire in the mid-nineteenth century', *Historical Journal,* 24, pp.155–65.*

Fisher, J.R. (1981) 'The limits of deference: agricultural communities in a mid-nineteenth century election campaign', *Journal of British Studies,* 20, pp.90–105.*

Foster, J. (1974) *Class struggle and the Industrial Revolution: early industrial capitalism in three English towns,* London, Weidenfeld & Nicolson.*

Fraser, D. (1972) 'The fruits of reform: Leeds politics in the 1830s', *Northern History,* 7, pp.89–111.*

Fraser, D., (1976) *Urban politics in Victorian England,* Leicester, Leicester University Press.*

Gibson, J. and Rogers, C. (1990) *Poll books c.1696–1872: a directory to holdings in Great Britain,* 2nd edn, Birmingham, Federation of Family History Societies.

Gibson, J. and Rogers, C. (1993) *Electoral Registers since 1832; and Burgess Rolls: a directory to holdings in Great Britain,* 5th edn, Birmingham, Federation of Family History Societies.*

Hanham, H.J. (1959) *Elections and party management: politics in the time of Disraeli and Gladstone,* London, Longman Green.*

Hanham, H.J. (1971) *The reformed electoral system in Great Britain 1832–1914,* London, The Historical Association.*

Jones, I.G. (1964) 'The elections of 1865 and 1868 in Wales, with special reference to Cardiganshire and Merthyr Tydfil', *Transactions of the Honourable Society of Cymmrodorian,* pp.41–68.*

Joyce, P. (1975) 'The factory politics of Lancashire in the late nineteenth century', *The Historical Journal,* XVIII, 3, pp.525–54.*

Jupp, P. (1972) 'County Down elections, 1703–1831', *Irish Historical Studies,* XVIII, 70, pp.177–206.*

Lewis, S. (1833) *Topographical dictionary of Wales,* 2 vols, London, S. Lewis & Co.

Lewis, S. (1835) *Topographical dictionary of England,* 3rd edn, 5 vols, London, S. Lewis & Co.

Lewis, S. (1837) *Topographical dictionary of Ireland,* 2 vols, London, S. Lewis & Co.

Lewis, S. (1846) *Topographical dictionary of Scotland*, 2 vols, London, S. Lewis & Co.

Lloyd, T. (1968) 'Uncontested seats in British general elections 1852–1910', *Historical Journal*, VIII, pp.260–5.*

Local Government Provisional Orders Bill to confirm certain provisional orders of the Local Government Board relating to the Urban Sanitary Districts of Brighouse, Bromley, Burnley, Dover, Folkestone, Mountain Ash and Trowbridge (1890) British Parliamentary Papers, 1890, VI, pp.1–14.

Martin, J.B. (1884) 'Electoral statistics: a review of the working of our representative system from 1832 to 1881, in view of the prospective changes therein', *Journal of the Statistical Society*, London, 47, pp.75–124.

Mitchell, J.G. and Cornford, J. (1977) 'The political demography of Cambridge, 1832-1868', *Albion*, 9, pp.242–72.*

Moore, D.C. (1966) 'Concession or cure: the sociological premises of the first Reform Act', *Historical Journal*, IX, 1, pp.39–59.

Moore, D.C. (1976) *The politics of deference*, Hassocks, Harvester Press.*

Neale, R.S. (1972) *Class and ideology in the nineteenth century*, London, Routledge & Kegan Paul.*

Newmarch, W. (1857) 'On the electoral statistics of the counties and boroughs of England and Wales during the twenty-five years from the Reform Act of 1832 to the present time', *Journal of the Statistical Society*, 20, pp.169–234.

Nossiter, T.J. (1972) 'Shopkeeper radicalism in the nineteenth century', in Nossiter, T.J. *et al.* (eds) *Imagination and precision in the social sciences*, London, Faber.

Nossiter, T.J. (1975) *Influence, opinion and political idioms in reformed England. Case studies from the North-east 1832–74*, Hassocks, Harvester Press.*

O'Gorman, F. (1986) 'The unreformed electorate of Hanoverian England: the mid-eighteenth century to the Reform Act of 1832', *Social History*, 2, 1, pp.33–52.*

O'Gorman, F. (1989) 'Electoral behaviour in England, 1700–1872', in Denley, P. *et al.* (1989) *History and computing II*, Manchester, Manchester University Press.*

Olney, R. J. (1973) *Lincolnshire politics 1832–1885*, Oxford, Oxford University Press.*

Phillips, J.A. (1982) 'The many faces of reform: the Reform Bill and the electorate', *Parliamentary History Yearbook*, 1, pp.115–35.*

Sims, J. (1984) *A handlist of British parliamentary pollbooks*, Leicester, Leicester University Press.

Thomas, J.A. (1950) 'The system of registration and the development of party organization 1832-70', *History*, new series, XXXV, pp.81–98.

Thompson, F.M.L. (1959) 'Whigs and Liberals in the West Riding 1830–1860', *English Historical Review*, LXXIV, pp. 214–39.

Vincent, J.R. (1963–4) 'The electoral sociology of Rochdale', *Economic History Review*, second series, XVI, pp.76–90.*

Vincent, J.R. (1966) *The formation of the British Liberal Party 1857–68*, London, Constable.

Vincent, J. (1968) *Pollbooks: how Victorians voted*, Cambridge, Cambridge University Press.[*]

Walker, B.M (1989) *Ulster politics: the formative years, 1868–86*, Belfast, Ulster Historical Foundation and The Institute of Irish Studies.[*]

Whyte, J.H. (1960) 'The influence of the Catholic clergy on elections in nineteenth century Ireland', *English Historical Review,* LXXV, pp. 239–59.[*]

Wright, D.G. (1969) 'A radical borough: parliamentary politics in Bradford, 1832–41', *Northern History,* 4, pp.132–66.[*]

Wroughton, J. (ed.) (1972) *Bath in the age of reform 1830–41,* Bath, Morgan Books.

CHAPTER 7

LOCAL ELECTIONS IN THE 1920s AND 1930s: NORTHAMPTON

by David Murray

The richness of poll books as a source for studying how individuals voted contrasts with the apparently bare electoral data available for the end of the nineteenth century and the first half of the twentieth century.

Remembering what you know about poll books from Chapter 6 (and from Volume 4, Chapter 4, for example), compare this with the following list of limitations of data on local elections. I have taken the period between the two world wars for the sake of illustration.

o   After the Ballot Act of 1872, voting was carried out secretly, with no records kept of how individuals cast their votes either in national or local elections.

o   Individual votes in an electoral division like a ward or parliamentary constituency were aggregated (as they are still). Votes were shuffled together before the count began and results were recorded, and declared, for the division as a whole, so preventing us from finding out the distribution of votes in a locality smaller than an electoral division.

o   Sample surveys have become a valuable source for understanding political attitudes and voting intentions, and the information from them can be set alongside the results of elections. Surveys are now part of the historical record, but the first Gallup Poll in Britain was for the general election in 1945. For the period between the wars – and earlier – surveys are not available to provide information that adds understanding to bare election figures.

o   Limitations in the national census restrict its use in conjunction with electoral data. Only since 1966 have the sample and full censuses made data available by parliamentary electoral division (thus allowing census data to be correlated with data on voting in parliamentary elections, constituency by constituency). There are other limitations with earlier censuses: for example, for those trying to relate voting behaviour to social class, the means available for measuring class were limited in the censuses up to 1951.

o   A practical difficulty is that information on local elections has not been made widely available, in contrast to the published electoral data on parliamentary elections in the United Kingdom (Craig, 1974, 1983). In England and Wales the Registrar-General's annual *Statistical Review of England and Wales* includes information on the voters turning out in local elections and on the seats contested, but this information only started to be included with the 1945–46 *Review*. Anyone seeking to use local electoral data has to go back to original sources for each town and district. It may be difficult to find the information, and what is found may not be as complete as you would hope. Then there are problems in using it. If, for example, you want to see the trends in voting over a period of years, you may be disappointed to find electoral divisions disappearing or boundaries changing, whilst a sequence of elections in which a candidate is returned unopposed may hinder some lines of inquiry.

Having listed these points, you may now think that poll books are singularly illuminating as a source in contrast to local government elections, and that data from local elections might be best left untouched. But before reaching that conclusion, consider some advantages of exploiting them:

o   In many – indeed most – localities little work has been done on these data. They offer an opportunity and a challenge.

o   Information on local elections is readily available and accessible locally.

o   The electoral divisions for local elections have always been much smaller than for parliamentary elections. You can see the distribution of votes – and numbers not voting – in an area that often has the character of a distinct (or partly distinct) local community, and this enriches the data.

o   The relatively small size of local government electoral divisions allows connections to be made more easily between what happens in local elections and other features of communities. You do not have attitude surveys to help understand electors but you may be able to make connections between local elections and what is happening in local churches or trade unions, new housing developments, or changes in local industry. When taken with other events in a local community, the data from local elections can be not simply fruitful, but revealing. (I should add that at a national level, and using data for parliamentary elections, there have been important studies of voting behaviour – see Miller, 1977; Ross, 1953; Turner, 1993).

To demonstrate what can be done I have collected data from local newspapers on local elections in Northampton between the wars. I hope your reaction will go beyond just understanding what is contained in these data between the wars and that you will want to collect information yourself and see what you can do with it.

Let me, then, express three aims for this chapter: (a) to show what local electoral data comprise, their potential use and how they can be exploited both in hypothesis-led inquiry and in more open-ended investigations which question sources; (b) to show how to use some simple techniques to analyse the data; and (c) to interest you in collecting and using local government electoral data for your town or district.

1   NORTHAMPTON ELECTORAL DATA, 1919–38

As a start, take a look at Tables 7.1 and 7.2, which present the basic electoral data for the borough of Northampton between 1919 and 1938, i.e. the period between the two world wars. I explain later (in section 4) how I collected it. If you glance at the tables you may think they look rather daunting. In fact they contain a lot of potentially interesting information about the town in an ordered form.

After the First World War local elections started again in 1919; the first run of data in Table 7.1 ends in 1930. In 1931 the boundaries of Northampton borough were extended to take in some of the surrounding area, and the local government electoral divisions – the wards – were redrawn (see Figure 7.1). Some ward names remained the same but with different boundaries, and some redrawn wards were given new names. The first elections in the new wards were deferred from November 1931 to March 1932. Table 7.2 starts with the elections in 1932, when each elector had three votes and wards returned three members each. This table runs to 1938. By the time elections should have been held in 1939 the Second World War had begun and borough-wide elections were suspended.

Table 7.1 Local electoral data for the borough of Northampton, 1919–1930

	1919	1920	1921	1922	1923	1924	1925	1926	1927	1928	1929	1930
Abington												
Electors	2872	2874	2884	2905	2935		3052		3083	3164		3361
M					1385		1440		1461	1496		1548
W					1550		1612		1622	1668		1813
Conservative				684	960		978	C[1]	858	925	C	1127
Liberal	W647	*1629	*1305	681	786	L	1023	L[1]	*947	*933		*993
Labour		346	460	599	W403				427	439		
Other	1122[2]											
Total votes	1769	1975	1765	1964	2149		2001.		2232	2297		2120
% poll	61.59	69.37	61.20	67.61	73.22		65.56		72.40	72.60		63.08
Castle												
Electors	3641	3683	3723	3817	3856	3859	3941	4254	3939	3905	4166	4020
M					1926		2006	2017	2018	2004	2047	1942
W					1930		1935	2237	1921	1901	2119	2078
Conservative	*1197	1267	*1338	*1197	*1141	*1584	1227	1050	*1303	*1252	1203	*1313
				454								
Liberal												
Labour	1170	1056	860	1029	1018	876	956	1087	W1236	W1274	1300	1158
Other												
Total votes	2367	2323	2198	2680	2159	2460	2183	2137	2539	2526	2503	2471
% poll	65.01	63.07	59.04	70.21	55.99	63.75	55.39	50.24	64.46	64.69	60.08	61.47
Delapre												
Electors	2053	2136	2201	2439	2584	2849	3032	3231	3255	3242	3510	3560
M					1352		1573	1682	1697	1679	1695	1727
W					1232		1459	1549	1558	1563	1815	1833
Conservative	*406	*895		*893	*936		852	*1034		*889	1173	
Liberal			*963			*1076	535		*953			*1295
Labour	1050	643	W477	695	741	626	574	686	765	879	1509	776
Other												
Total votes	1456	1538	1440	1588	1677	1702	1961	1720	1718	1768	2682	2071
% poll	70.92	72.00	65.42	65.11	64.90	59.74	64.68	53.23	52.78	54.53	76.41	58.17
Kingsley												
Electors	2689	2732	2739		3037	3226		3691	4099	4892	5492	5842
M					1517			1852	2050	2481	2569	2716
W					1520			1839	2049	2411	2923	3126
Conservative												
Liberal	1259	*1379	*1235	L	*1304	*1521	L	*1542	*1652	*1838	1602	*1816
Labour	693	W599	W687		579	549		636	749	970	W1026	1085
Other												
Total votes	1952	1978	1922		1883	2070		2178	2401	2808	2628	2901
% poll	72.59	72.40	70.17		62.00	64.17		59.01	58.58	57.40	47.85	49.66
Kingsthorpe												
Electors	2872	2904	3038	3080	3162	3290	3443		3618	3649	4012	4590
M					1582		1715		1819	1836	1888	2168
W					1580		1728		1799	1813	2124	2422
Conservative		*1252			1180	1103	972	C	*855	*797	828	1093
Liberal	*953		1061	1089		*404	404		835	1028	792	W612
Labour	708	632	580	765	788	697	*679		527	767	925	1192
Other												
Total votes	1661	1884	1641	1854	1968	2204	2055		2217	2592	2545	2897
% poll	57.83	64.88	54.02	60.19	62.24	66.99	59.69		61.28	71.03	63.43	63.12

Table 7.1 Local electoral data for the borough of Northampton, 1919–1930 *continued*

	1919	1920	1921	1922	1923	1924	1925	1926	1927	1928	1929	1930
North												
Electors	3385	3484	3637	3560			3681	3695	3660	3692		3946
M							1805	1821	1800	1834		1846
W							1876	1874	1860	1858		2100
Conservative		732	952	921			W980	W889	1208	1198		W1312
Liberal												
Labour	W1077	*1048	*1314	W*1403	Lab	Lab	1323	*1447	*1446	*1577	Lab	*1367
Other	652[2]											
Total votes	1729	1780	2266	2324			2303	2336	2654	2775		2679
% poll	51.08	51.09	62.30	65.28			62.56	63.22	72.51	75.16		67.89
St Crispin's												
Electors	2870	2957	3039	3024	3048	3125	3152	3103	3109	3091	3193	3161
M					1489		1538	1511	1515	1504	1478	1458
W					1559		1614	1592	1594	1587	1715	1703
Conservative		1085	1189		*926	*1250		867	*1077		868	*1097
Liberal	889			*1220			1299			*938		
Labour	*938	878	*856	913	1015	1020	763	*1094	907	835	1197	W922
Other												
Total votes	1827	1963	2045	2133	1941	2270	2062	1961	1984	1773	2065	2019
% poll	63.66	66.38	67.29	70.54	63.68	72.64	65.42	63.20	63.81	57.36	64.67	63.87
St Edmund's												
Electors	2948	3013	3029		3181	3158	3223	3203	3191	3138	3239	3220
M					1520		1519	1509	1505	1475	1473	1475
W					1661		1704	1694	1686	1663	1766	1745
Conservative	*1068	1284	*1292	C	871	1065	1008	*987	*996	*945	875	1122
Liberal					768	757	536		785			
Labour	667	703	550		804	744	627	660		731	812	922
Other												
Total votes	1735	1987	1842		2443	2566	2171	1647	1781	1676	1687	2044
% poll	58.85	65.95	60.81		76.80	81.25	67.36	51.42	55.81	53.41	52.08	63.48
St James'												
Electors	3696	3721	3824	4013		4242		4362	4371	4501	4833	4820
M								2207	2202	2259	2297	2289
W								2155	2169	2242	2536	2531
Conservative								1086		1406		
Liberal	1283	*1711	*1374	*2048	L	*1855	L	*1423	*1381	*1282	1683	*1648
Labour	1050	755	622	652		804		688	810	755	1103	1153
Other												
Total votes	2333	2466	1996	2700		2659		3197	2191	3443	2786	2801
% poll	63.12	66.27	52.20	67.28		62.68		73.29	50.13	76.49	57.65	58.11
St Lawrence's												
Electors	2843	2969	2986	2921	3016	3119	3156	3142	3207	3239	3403	3388
M					1456		1519	1508	1541	1530	1552	1554
W					1560		1637	1634	1666	1709	1851	1834
Conservative	*680	1037	1104	1121	703	*1087	799	645	*788	*757		906
Liberal					740	516	618	*942	729	624	1683	
Labour	1018	734	774	*743	690	720	789	769	W655	796	651	1177
Other												
Total votes	1698	1771	1878	1864	2133	2323	2206	2356	2172	2177	2334	2083
% poll	59.73	59.65	62.89	63.81	70.72	74.48	69.90	74.98	67.73	67.21	68.59	61.48

Table 7.1   Local electoral data for the borough of Northampton, 1919–1930 *continued*

	1919	1920	1921	1922	1923	1924	1925	1926	1927	1928	1929	1930
St Michael's												
Electors	3629	3718	3804	3742	3791	3795			3742	3749	3874	
M					1799				1763	1755	1756	
W					1992				1979	1994	2118	
Conservative	*1380	*1727		*1614	*1432	1423	C	C	*1319	*1235	1293	C
Liberal			*1657			*834			1231	1195		
Labour		636	482	680	790	556					W881	
Other	1355											
Total votes	2735	2363	2139	2294	2222	2813			2550	2430	2174	
% poll	75.37	63.56	56.23	61.30	58.61	74.12			68.15	64.82	56.12	
South												
Electors	2504	2587	2639	2699	2749	2729	2715		2696	2674	2793	2688
M					1365		1343		1347	1335	1325	1303
W					1384		1372		1349	1339	1468	1385
Conservative	*747	*941	*819	*1080	977	*1045	1087	C	*787	843	909	869
Liberal									692	214		
Labour	494	504	513	545	637	W541	W496			576	560	452
Other												
Total votes	1241	1445	1332	1625	1614	1586	1583		1479	1633	1469	1321
% poll	49.56	55.86	50.47	60.21	58.71	58.12	58.31		54.86	61.07	52.60	49.14
Mean turnout, all wards	62.44	64.21	60.17	65.15	64.69	67.79	63.21	61.07	61.87	64.65	59.95	59.95

Notes

Numbers in bold indicate candidate returned
* = Sitting councillor standing for re-election
W = Woman candidate
C, L, Lab = Candidate returned unopposed
[1] Abington 1926, two candidates returned (one in by-election)
[2] Other candidates: Abington 1919 = Ex-serviceman; North 1919 = Independent (Ex-serviceman)
Source: data published by *Northampton Herald, Northampton Mercury, Northampton Independent* (weeklies), *Northampton Chronicle* (daily), 1919–30

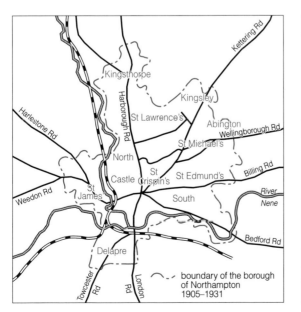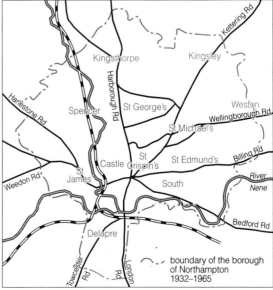

Figure 7.1   Local government wards, borough of Northampton, 1920s (*left*) and 1930s (*right*)

Table 7.2 Local electoral data for the borough of Northampton, 1932–1938

	1932[1]	1933	1934	1935	1936	1937	1938
Castle							
Electors	5096		4246	4240	4061	3816	3708
M	2457			2037	1934	1833	1786
W	2639			2203	2127	1983	1922
Conservative	1004	951		866	**720**		993	
Liberal	1109						
Labour	W*1500	**1475**	*1377	Lab	*1509	W*1441	Lab	*1191	W*1191
Other[2]					91[2]		27[2]	59[2]
Total votes			2015		2375	2252		2211	1250
% poll			39.54		55.93	53.11		57.94	33.71
Delapre							
Electors	3577			3800	3947	4071	4223
M	1739			1845	1920	1977	2047
W	1838			1955	2027	2094	2176
Conservative	W982	937					902	
Liberal	*1309				*1089			*1162
Labour	**1039**	W**984**		Lab	Lab	923	Lab	*1216	**970**
Other								241[2]
Total votes			2226		2012		2118	2373
% poll			62.23		52.95		52.03	56.19
Kingsley							
Electors	3712			5213	5397	5594	5733	5790
M	1736			2551	2652	2703	2711
W	1976			2836	2942	3030	3079
Conservative	*1133		C		*1079	1194	
Liberal	*1348	*1245		1354	*1602	1002	*897	*1289
Labour	510			1036	780	887	892	
Other								793[2]
Total votes			1849	2390	2382	2968	2983	2082
% poll			49.81	45.85	44.14	53.06	52.03	35.96
Kingsthorpe							
Electors	3000			3183	3450	3819	4111	4182
M	1439			1646	1841	1950	1994
W	1561			1814	1978	2153	2188
Conservative	**744**		C		780	*1183		991
Liberal	*812	485		*1166			1025	
Labour	*900	*728	690	809	*1135	1133	**1042**	*1339
Other					134[2]			
Total votes			1887	1975	2049	2316	2067	2330
% poll			62.90	62.05	59.39	60.64	50.28	55.71
St Crispin's							
Electors	5035			5773	5685	5546	5423	5288
M	2743			2647	2577	2506	2445
W	3192			3038	2969	2917	2843
Conservative	*1773	**1578**	C	*1681		*2023	*1556	1667
Liberal	*1421				796			
Labour	*1855	1561	1446	1784	*2109	1434	1535	*1843
Other								
Total votes			3566	3465	2905	3457	3091	3510
% poll			70.82	60.02	51.10	62.33	57.00	66.38

Table 7.2 Local electoral data for the borough of Northampton, 1932–1938 *continued*

	1932[1]			1933	1934	1935	1936	1937	1938
St Edmund's									
Electors	4155				4179	4146	4156		4026
M	1908					1893	1891		1821
W	2247					2253	2265		2205
Conservative	*1335	1204	*1199	C	*1198	*1343	*1272	C	*1250
Liberal									
Labour	694	684			944	899	1109		983
Other									
Total votes			1985		2142	2242	2381		2233
% poll			47.77		51.26	54.08	57.29		55.46
St George's									
Electors	4609				4768	4788	4785	4990	
M	2150					2192	2189	2294	
W	2459					2590	2596	2696	
Conservative								917	
Liberal	*1698	1350	1121		1374	L	1299	*684	L
Labour	*1235	*908	818	Lab	1092		*1386	1048	
Other									
Total votes			2626		2466		2685	2649	
% poll			56.98		51.72		56.11	53.09	
St James'									
Electors	4361				4360	4357	4463	4401	4527
M	2075					2072	2122	2040	2146
W	2286					2285	2341	2361	2381
Conservative	1175			C			C	958	
Liberal	*1571	1452			1392	L		*895	*1334
Labour	W1019				765			785	
Other									645[2]
Total votes			2462		2157			2638	1979
% poll			56.45		49.47			59.94	43.72
St Michael's									
Electors	5634				5613	5517	5522		
M	2535					2483	2484		
W	3099					3034	3033		
Conservative	*1753	*1742		C	*1667		C	C	
Liberal	1776					*1735			L
Labour	1319	964			1221	1035			
Other									
Total votes			3192		2888	2770			
% poll			56.66		51.45	50.21			
South									
Electors	2731				2693	2663	2497		2440
M	1271					1234	1146		1112
W	1460					1429	1351		1328
Conservative	*852	*835	809	C	*801	900	*788	C	*702
Liberal									
Labour	554				554	463	388		
Other									380[2]
Total votes			1361		1355	1363	1176		1082
% poll			49.84		50.32	51.18	47.10		44.34

Table 7.2 Local electoral data for the borough of Northampton, 1932–1938 *continued*

	1932[1]	1933	1934	1935	1936	1937	1938
Spencer							
Electors	4047		3974	3933	3962	3974	4270
M	1940			1911	1918	1916	2007
W	2107			2022	2044	2058	2263
Conservative	W**1194** *1187		858	W***1281**	**1123**	903	W***1316**
Liberal	W948						
Labour	***950** W***874** 847	Lab	***1321**	1019	1085	W**1211**	**1381**
Other				57[2]			
Total votes	2270		2179	2357	2208	2114	2697
% poll	56.09		54.83	59.93	55.73	53.20	63.16
Weston							
Electors	2175		2621	3325	3580	3683	4055
M	1056			1599	1731	1862	1918
W	1119			1727	1859	2001	2137
Conservative	C C			**1053**	C	**871**	***782**
Liberal	L		***614**			817	
Labour			366	544			
Other			420[2]				**969**[2]
Total votes			1400	1597		1688	1751
% poll			53.41	48.03		45.83	43.18
Mean turnout, all wards	55.37		53.30	52.41	56.04	53.48	49.78

Notes

Numbers in bold indicate candidate returned

* = Sitting councillor standing for re-election

W = Woman candidate

C, L, Lab = Candidate returned unopposed

[1] 1932, three candidates returned in all wards

[2] Other candidates: Weston 1934 = Ratepayer; Castle, Kingsthorpe and Spencer 1935 = Workers' representative; Castle 1937 and 1938 = Fascist; Delapre, Kingsley, St James', South and Weston 1938 = Ratepayer

Source: data published by *Northampton Mercury and Herald, Northampton Chronicle and Echo,* 1932–8

If you refer now to Table 7.1, I will describe what the table contains. The left-hand column lists twelve wards into which the borough was divided. The vertical columns give data for each year in which there was an election to the borough council. Nine rows for each ward provide the following raw data:

o   Row 1 gives the number of local government electors registered to vote in the ward. If you look along the first row in Abington ward you will notice the change in the number of electors over the eleven years from 1919 to 1930. You will see that there was an increase of nearly 500 voters. If you look at the equivalent line for the South ward you will see that the increase over the period was only 184 – the smallest increase in a ward in this period.

———————————————— *EXERCISE 7.1* ————————————————

Which ward had the largest increase?

Answer p.231.

o   Rows 2 and 3 give the breakdown of electors according to the number of men (M) and women (W). These data are only readily available for some years. The breakdown was not always reported in the local newspapers (though it would be possible to fill in the figures for the missing years by going through the laborious process of counting in the relevant electoral register the number of men and women local government electors). If you look at the column for 1923 – the first year for which this breakdown is available – you will note that there are differences from one ward to another in the proportions of men and women. In Delapre there were 120 more men than women, while in Abington there were 165 more women than men. (In percentage terms men constituted 52.32 per cent of the electors in Delapre and 47.19 per cent in Abington.)

o   In the columns headed 1928 and 1929 you can see the effect of the Representation of the People (Equal Franchise) Act 1928. This extended the vote to women aged between 21 and 30, so that their eligibility matched that of men. In parliamentary elections the right to vote was based on adult status; for local government elections occupation of rateable property was the basis of the franchise. In 1928 five wards had more men than women electors; in 1929 (and using the 1930 figures for Abington and North wards) women were in a majority in every ward.

EXERCISE 7.2

In which ward did women have the smallest majority over men in 1929, and in which the largest?

Answer p.231.

---

o   Rows 4–6 give the votes cast for candidates of the three main parties. The single letters 'C' or 'L' or 'Lab' in place of numbers indicates that the candidate from the party indicated was returned unopposed in that ward.

o   Row 7 is used for the votes cast for candidates of minor parties.

o   You will have noticed that there was an annual election in the borough. This was because each ward was represented by three councillors, with each being returned for a staggered three-year term and one retiring each year. With this electoral system we get an annual series recording the changes in voting in every ward in which an election took place. The local election results are, for this reason, a richer source than the periodic parliamentary elections.

o   Two additional pieces of information appear in rows 4–7. First, where a candidate was a woman, this is indicated by the letter 'W' next to the votes received. Second, where a member of the borough council stood for re-election this is indicated by an asterisk in front of the number of votes cast. Thus you can see that the candidate elected in Delapre ward in 1921 for the coalition Liberals was re-elected as a Liberal in 1924, 1927 and 1930. (He was in fact the chemist at the corner shop in the ward.)

o   Row 8 records the total of valid votes cast (the number of lost or spoiled ballots was too infrequently recorded to be worth reporting in the table) i.e. the sum of the votes recorded in rows 4–7.

o   Row 9 gives the percentage of the electors in the ward who cast valid votes that were counted. Based on the figures in rows 1 and 7, it shows considerable variations in voter turnout – from 81.25 per cent in St Edmund's in 1924 to 47.85 per cent in Kingsley in 1929.

The mean turnout in all the wards contested is given at the foot of each column. An alternative and slightly different figure could have recorded the overall percentage turnout by calculating the total turnout as a proportion of all the electors.

If you have, as I hope, looked at Table 7.1 and at the different columns and rows, I expect that you will have been spotting things and been thinking to yourself 'that's interesting' or 'why was that?' or 'I wonder what effect that had?' or 'I wonder how the community in which I am interested compares with this?' Indeed, such reactions may offer you the germ of a project.

EXERCISE 7.3

I suggest that at this point you immediately jot down some reactions under the three headings:

o   That's interesting.

o   Why was this?

o   What effect did something shown in the table have?

The tables throw up lots of interesting questions. You may have looked at patterns of voting for party candidates, the relationship between turnout and voting, gender and turnout, the rise and fall of support for the parties, and so on. You will almost certainly have thought of points that have not occurred to me – ones that are well worth pursuing in a project. It may also have struck you that the information raises questions about the community: who were the candidates and what was their standing in the town? Let me say, though, where I am headed in the rest of this chapter.

I will investigate two among many possible topics involving the use of electoral data for Northampton. The first concerns the way electors did or did not exercise their right to vote in local elections, i.e. voter turnout. The second concerns the fortunes of the Liberal Party. I will approach these using two different strategies: one might be termed hypothesis-led inquiry, the other questioning sources.

2   TURNING OUT TO VOTE IN LOCAL ELECTIONS

'Never within living memory has there been such an appalling apathy concerning the municipal election in Northampton ... nine-tenths of the population neither seemed to know nor care about the elections': so ran the report of the local election results in the weekly *Northampton Independent* in 1925. Levels of participation in elections were then, and have remained, a matter of interest. The right to vote is central to representative democracy, and the numbers of those who exercise that right has been a continuing matter of concern. Turnout is also taken to carry other messages. It is often thought to reflect on the level of interest taken by ordinary people in the local community. In addition, at a practical level, who is elected is, in one sense, as much determined by who votes and who abstains as by the distribution of the votes that are cast. Consequently, who does and does not vote, why people vote and what influences them to do so, why they vote in one election and not in another, and what the differences are between local and national elections have been extensively researched on a cross-national basis. The general literature is substantial (a review of it up to 1977 is contained in Milbrath and Goel, 1977) but that on local government elections in Britain is much more sparse, and on such elections between the two world wars it is particularly thin (it is reviewed in Miller, 1986).

2.1   PERSONAL CHARACTERISTICS AND TURNOUT

A person who votes takes a decision. What sort of people take that decision? What relationship is there between, on the one hand, such characteristics as age, gender, type of house or other domestic accommodation lived in, employment and, on the other hand, voter turnout? For relatively recent local government elections there could well be surveys of electors to give us answers. We do not have these for electors in the 1920s and 1930s and it is therefore more difficult to gather information that enables us to understand turnout – difficult but not impossible. We can start by seeing if electoral data give us any leads on the characteristics of those who decided to vote as against those who did not.

GENDER

Let's begin by asking whether there is anything significant to be found out about the turnout of women as against men.

Is gender relevant to turnout in the 1920s and 1930s? In one of the very few studies of municipal elections in the 1920s and 1930s, one hypothesis investigated was that turnout varied according to gender. The test devised was to compare the level of turnout with the percentage of males in the local government electorate in Leeds before and after the Act of 1928 (see Table 7.3).

Table 7.3   Level of turnout and male percentage of local electorate, City of Leeds, 1921–37

Year	Percentage turnout	Male electors as percentage of electorate	Year	Percentage turnout	Male electors as percentage of electorate
1921	50.8	49.7	1930	48.6	46.3
1922	51.1	49.8	1931	46.7	46.3
1923	50.1	49.7	1932	44.4	46.3
1924	48.1	49.6	1933	45.6	46.2
1925	53.1	49.3	1934	51.7	46.2
1926	59.3	49.2	1935	53.6	46.2
1927	58.9	49.3	1936	48.9	46.2
1928	53.8	49.4	1937	44.0	46.2
Average	51.9		Average	48.0	

Source: Rhodes (1938) p.275

The conclusion drawn was: 'the fact that the average [percentage turnout] is less for the years 1930–37 than it was for the years 1921–28 is probably linked with this change in the sex composition of the body of electors, and we may conclude that the voting percentage of male electors is higher than that of female electors' (Rhodes, 1938, pp.274–5).

Although Tables 7.1 and 7.2 do not provide as full information as that available to Rhodes, how does Northampton compare with Leeds?

―――――――――――――――――――――― *EXERCISE 7.4* ――――――――――――――――――――――

Let me ask you to make a limited comparison using the same method as for Table 7.3. In order that the task is not too time-consuming, simply take the two years before and after the change in the franchise. Look to see if there was a change in the turnout in the two pairs of years, 1927/28 and 1929/30, and whether this corresponded with a change in the proportion of men and women electors. Before you try to do anything it would help to have a calculator. Then repeat the calculation reported in the article:

1   Prepare a table with the same columns as in Table 7.3, entering in column 1 the years 1927, 1928 and in column 4 the years 1929, 1930.

2   Add up the total number of electors in 1927 in those wards only where there was a contested election (i.e. row 1 for each contested ward in the 1927 column).

3   Add up the total number of votes cast in each contested ward (the figure in row 7 in each ward contested in 1927).

4   Turn the figure for the total number of voters into a percentage of the total number of electors in the contested wards (by multiplying the number of persons voting by 100 and dividing this number by the number of electors – stage 2 above) and enter this figure in your table as the voting percentage for 1927.

5   Add up the total number of male electors in the wards contested in 1927 (i.e. the top figure for row 2 in the contested wards).

6   Turn this total of male electors into a percentage of the total electors (by multiplying your total of male electors by 100 and dividing this number by your total number of all electors; express this percentage to one figure after the decimal point) and enter the result in your table as the male electors as a percentage of the electorate for 1927.

7   Repeat these steps for the other three years.

8   Calculate the average, or strictly the mean, of the voting percentages for the two pairs of years and enter these at the bottom of columns 2 and 5 as shown in Table 7.3 (for column 2 do this by adding the figures you have calculated for the voting percentages in the years 1927 and 1928 and already entered in column 2 and dividing this by two; then repeat this for the figures in column 5).

Having completed your own table ask yourself:

(a)   Is the mean voting percentage in column 2 higher than that in column 5?

(b)   Are the male electors as a percentage of the electorate in column 3 higher than in column 6?

Do you conclude that the change in voting percentage – the percentage turnout – parallels the change in the percentage of male voters among the electors, and that Northampton is similar, in this regard, to Leeds? Needless to say, the figures may not support this statement. Looking now at your own table, what conclusion do you reach?

If you want to check your calculations against someone else's, mine, together with my conclusions, are on p.231.

You have now used one hypothesis to cast light on gender and turnout. You can make a very tentative statement about the personal characteristics of electors who voted in local government elections.

What other personal characteristics do you think might have affected turnout?

OTHER PERSONAL CHARACTERISTICS

Is age relevant? Does the sort of employment or employment status correlate with turnout? Is the sort of house or other accommodation occupied significant? What about class, education, church attendance or length of local residence in the town? Most of these questions can be explored, but it will often be necessary to use other sources in conjunction with the electoral data. That means finding facts about age distribution, levels of church attendance or employment status and then seeing how the information correlates with electoral data.

Let me illustrate this by considering the connection between housing and voter turnout. A thesis by Dickie (1987; see also Dickie, 1989–90, 1992) reported an investigation made into housing in each ward differentiated by rateable value. The source used was the rate books for

Figure 7.2   Styles of housing in the Northampton wards of Kingsley (*top*) (Source: Northampton Public Library) and North (*bottom*) (Source: Northampton Borough Council). Similar houses to those shown in Kingsley were described by the *Northampton Independent* at the time of construction as 'charming residences', with back gardens 'enclosed by brick walls instead of the very flimsy fences so often supplied'

Northampton for 1925 (these are potentially available for all local authorities). Dwellings were categorized according to their rateable value: up to £13, between £14 and £26, and over £27. This showed that the three wards with the highest proportion of dwellings with a rateable value up to £13 were North (92.8 per cent), Delapre (91.28 per cent) and St James' (88.16 per cent), while the three wards with the lowest proportion of dwellings in that category were South (68.27 per cent), St Michael's (63.54 per cent) and Kingsley (54.31 per cent). South with 13.66 per cent and Kingsley with 12.43 per cent were the two wards which were somewhat apart from the others because they had at least 5 per cent more dwellings with a rateable value of £27 and above than the other wards.

The exercise was in part founded on the judgement that dwellings indicate the class of people living in them. Based on a study of housing nationally from 1919 to 1944 (Bowley, 1945), the three categories of house in Northampton were allocated to a classification labelled as working class, lower middle class and middle class.

EXERCISE 7.5

Look again at Table 7.1 and find the six wards for which I gave the percentages of dwellings with a rateable value of up to £13 in the text above. Look at the level of turnout in these six wards and consider whether there is any obvious connection between turnout and distribution of housing by ward. It will help here to calculate the mean turnout in these six wards in, say, the five years 1923–27 and to compare these means with the proportions of 'working class' dwellings in each ward.

Answers/comments p.232.

My own conclusion is that nothing striking is revealed; even if, as will be outlined later, you take account of the differences between elections with two and three candidates standing, there is no pattern suggesting a link between turnout and type of housing in the two groups of wards (i.e. those with the highest and lowest proportions of 'working-class' housing). This itself may be of interest because it indicates that there was no obvious relationship between the decision to vote and the category of house occupied in these years or, by extension, between the decision to vote and this particular way of differentiating electors by social class.

2.2 POLITICAL PARTIES AS INSTRUMENTS FOR MOBILIZING VOTERS

For a person to cast a vote involves a decision to do so, and it is possible that political parties mobilize electors to reach that decision. Political parties believe that they can stimulate electors to vote. They do so by providing information and persuading electors to identify with them. Electoral data cannot prove whether people did or did not have a sense of identification with a political party, but they may show some relationships between parties and turnout. Here I suggest two hypotheses which have been thought useful. Both are taken from work done on local elections in a later period.

In 1969 an article reported an investigation of ward turnout in local elections held between 1964 and 1967 in a sample of 59 English local authorities (Fletcher, 1969). The aim was to assess whether the presence or absence of action by political parties could explain variations in voter turnout. A number of different hypotheses were explored. I have taken two to see if they illuminate turnout in local elections in Northampton thirty to forty years earlier. Both rest on the premise that political parties canvass for support and mobilize electors to vote.

Hypothesis 1   The first hypothesis I have taken is that *voter turnout was higher where there were candidates from three parties than where there were candidates from only two.* My test for this is to compare the mean turnout of electors in ward elections where there were three party candidates with those where there were two. The method for calculating this is to add up the figures in row 8 of, first, Table 7.1 and then Table 7.2 for wards with three candidates from different parties and divide each by the number of wards with such elections. Repeat the process for ward elections with two candidates from separate parties.

My results are given in Table 7.4.

Table 7.4 Voter turnout (per cent) in wards with two and three party candidates, borough of Northampton, 1919–1938

	1919–1930	1932–1938
3 party candidates	69.64	55.46
2 party candidates	61.23	51.99

In the 1920s there was a mean difference in turnout of 8.4 percentage points between ward contests with three and two party candidates; in the 1930s the difference was 3.5 per cent. In other words there was a marked difference when there were three candidates in the 1920s, a time when the Liberals remained a significant party; however, the difference was less marked by the 1930s, when the Liberal Party had declined sharply both locally and nationally and the third party was as often some other more transient body. Investigating the hypothesis points to what looks like a significant relationship where there were three major parties. Its existence does not *prove* that political parties mobilized voters or that they did so more in one period than in another: we have only observed relationships between sets of figures. But these are at least consistent with the idea that the actions of parties had effects on the level of turnout and that the effect was different in the two decades.

Hypothesis 2   A second hypothesis relates turnout to the number of electors in wards. The underlying idea is that the size of a ward affected the ease with which electors could be canvassed. In the 1960s sample investigated, the differences in the number of electors in wards was considerably greater than in Northampton in the 1920s and 1930s, and because there were only twelve wards in Northampton, and other influences were at work, it is unlikely that any pattern can be identified. Nevertheless I propose to consider whether there was anything evident.

This question can be expressed in the hypothesis that *turnout in small wards was greater than in large wards*. The method I have adopted uses Table 7.1. Wards are placed in three groups – smaller, medium and larger – for two four-year periods and then the level of turnout in the smaller and larger is compared. The first period chosen is 1919–1923 and the second 1927–1930.

Of the twelve Northampton wards in 1919–23, all fall relatively simply into the three groups: three wards were smaller (Delapre, South and Kingsley), six were medium and three were larger (St James', Castle and St Michael's). For the years 1927–30, the distinctions are less clear, with several wards changing group. In this period three wards were smaller (South, St Crispin's, St Edmund's), five were medium and four were larger (Kingsley, St James', Castle and Kingsthorpe).

EXERCISE 7.6

Consult Table 7.1 and do a quick check (without troubling to do calculations) on whether there is a difference in the turnout of the smaller and larger wards in either 1919–23 or 1927–30.

Your quick inspection will have revealed that there is no obvious pattern of differences between the smaller and the larger wards. Expressed as averages (means) the difference between the groups of smaller and larger wards in the two periods was only around 2 per cent, and, while in the earlier period turnout was higher in the smaller wards, in the second period it was higher in the larger wards. In both periods the level of turnout in individual wards varied within both smaller and larger wards. The number of electors in a ward was therefore not obviously related to the proportion of electors turning out in Northampton in the 1920s.

2.3   OTHER INFLUENCES ON TURNOUT

There are many other relationships that could be explored, whether using the electoral data reproduced in Tables 7.1 and 7.2 on their own or in conjunction with other information. If the size of wards was not a factor, was there a difference between older, settled wards and expanding ones with new housing? Is anything apparent when a woman stood for election, or where a sitting councillor stood for re-election, or where the successful candidate was resident in the ward (using information on the residential addresses of councillors taken from the municipal yearbook)? Where a parliamentary election campaign coincided with the local elections (as it did in 1922, 1924 and 1935) was there a change in the level of electoral turnout? Since association with a church had been, and remained, an important basis for political affiliation (notably established church versus dissenting chapels), is there a relationship between the downward trend in turnout and changing involvement (in some way defined) in local churches? Where there was a local or national political issue exciting widespread interest, was there a change in the numbers voting in local elections? You may think of many other questions. Work previously done on the Bath poll books (see Chapter 6) may suggest questions to ask and techniques to be deployed. Wherever something that is possibly relevant is identified, there is a chance that it can be expressed as a hypothesis and the electoral data can be used for testing it. A numerical relationship does not prove a cause but may help towards an explanation.

The more separate observations you make, the more they can help you to understand turnout, but unless you are able somehow to organize these observations they are likely to remain as separate bits of information and you will not know how one observed relationship may be affected by another. In discussing turnout I have been guided by a model which organizes possible factors into broader categories and then postulates relationships between them. It will help, therefore, to be explicit about the model I have used (which is a modified version of one used in studying local electoral behaviour in the 1980s – see Miller, 1986). I have put the factors I have explored into three categories: personal factors, ones that predispose a person to be interested in elections, and ones that actually mobilize a person to go out to vote (or which constrain them from doing so). Under personal factors I put those such as gender, housing and class; under predisposing factors I group such characteristics as interest in local affairs, knowledge of candidates and understanding of political issues. Finally, in the mobilizing category I group factors such as involvement with party, membership of a politically linked organization such as a trade union or church, or active involvement in political issues like the level of the rates or the collection of garbage. My model then postulates causal connections. Personal factors affect predisposing characteristics, and predisposing characteristics interrelate with mobilizing or constraining factors to produce a decision to vote.

I would use the same model to study parliamentary elections, but would then include factors of a national character. Whether I was interested in local or parliamentary elections there would be connections between the two: people mobilized to vote in parliamentary elections may be influenced by this to turn out in local elections, and vice versa. I show these points in Figure 7.3.

Using such a model allows separate observations to be grouped, and it helps also with broader generalizations. My study of Northampton suggests that the personal characteristic of gender appears to have had an effect on turnout. The presence of candidates from three parties

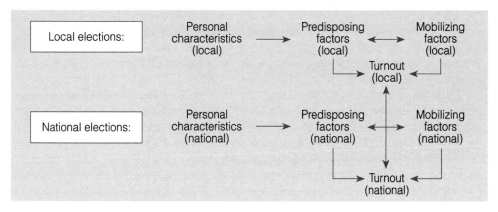

Figure 7.3 A model of voter turnout (Source: adapted from Miller, 1986, p.123)

appears to have had a significant effect in the 1920s, and this, I have hypothesized, was because the parties mobilized voters. On the other hand, the relative size of a ward was not obviously relevant to the mobilization of electors.

My model helps me not simply to categorize factors that are possibly relevant to turnout, but to consider how each factor might interact with another. In Northampton this prompts me to ask whether the apparent relationship between changes in turnout at the time of the change in the franchise was, in fact, the result of changes in mobilizing factors rather than in the personal factor of gender. I have concluded that the presence of three party candidates changed the level of turnout. Could it be that the difference I thought I had established between male and female voting by comparing 1927 and 1928 with 1929 and 1930 was instead the result of a difference in the number of wards being contested by three as against two candidates? Here, then, is another hypothesis: *the difference in the turnout in 1927 and 1928 as against 1929 and 1930 was related to the number of wards contested by three candidates and when an adjustment is made for the numbers of candidates, there is no difference in the turnout.*

To test this the overall turnout for one of the pair of years is recalculated to take account of the larger mean turnout in three- as against two-candidate wards.

EXERCISE 7.7

Consult Table 7.1 and check how many three-cornered ward elections there were in 1927/28 and how many in 1929/30.

You will have seen straight away that there were only two three-cornered contests in 1929 and 1930 out of the 21 ward elections, whereas in 1927 and 1928 this applied in eight wards out of 24. To equalize the number of wards contested by three candidates between the two pairs of years, I have recalculated the turnout in 1929 and 1930 on the assumption that in five further wards there were three-cornered contests, thus equalizing the proportion of three- and two-candidate wards in the two pairs of years. In these five the increased turnout matched the mean difference between three- and two-candidate elections over these four years. On my calculation the adjusted turnout in the two pairs of years was as follows:

	unadjusted	adjusted
Turnout 1927 and 1928	63.26	63.26
Turnout 1929 and 1930	59.95	60.83

The difference in the turnout in the two pairs of years either side of the change in the franchise was no longer so considerable that it significantly exceeded the change in the gender balance of the electors. The proportion of men in the electorate moved down from 49.36 per cent to 46.98 per cent – a change of 2.38 per cent, which can be compared with the change in turnout of 2.43 per cent.

The model helps you to see, in other words, where each of your possible hypotheses and the results of inquiries begin to fit into a bigger jigsaw puzzle. Strengthening explanations tentatively reached will need more inquiry, possibly among new sources relating to your chosen town or district or in the form of comparison, to see what else supports your tentative conclusions (or contradicts them) or what gives you new insights into possibly relevant considerations. For instance, I have compared turnout in Northampton and Leeds to see if there was a similar relationship between the change in turnout and the proportion of men and women in the electorate. What may also have struck you was that while overall turnout in Leeds averaged 51.9 per cent in the 1920s, that in Northampton averaged over 10 per cent more. Why was this? What was different about the two towns? You have the much more detailed data about Northampton with which you can compare a place in which you are interested and which will enable you to pursue those questions of why and what.

QUESTION FOR RESEARCH

Collecting the results of local elections in the 1920s and 1930s for most local authorities is a piece of research in itself, because little use has so far been made of them. Once they have been collected, this chapter has provided examples of questions that can be asked and illustrated relationships that can be explored by adopting a hypothesis-led approach. Some of these can be investigated using local government electoral data on their own; other relationships involve using other information. Comparing what happened in one place with what happened somewhere else (e.g. Northampton) may provide insights.

---

3 THE LIBERAL PARTY IN DECLINE

I could study the way local electors voted and the fortunes of candidates and parties in a similar way to the one I have begun to pursue on turnout. Tables 7.1 and 7.2 provide information that lends itself to the formulation of hypotheses and to a fairly elaborate description of the fortunes of candidates and parties. This can also be handled as a piece of research which proceeds by questioning sources.

If you were doing research on local elections using this approach you would first decide on a focus. It could arise out of the history of a local community – in Northampton you might follow the electoral changes that paralleled the development of the old royal village of Kingsthorpe into an area of new suburban housing, or it might be something like the relationship between Northampton's Doddridge Congregational Church and the political fortunes of the many Liberal and Labour candidates and councillors associated with the church (bearing in mind the then strong connections between the political parties and churches – the Anglican Church with the Conservatives, and the nonconformist churches with the Liberals). It might even arise out of some reading (such as the books or articles listed at the end of this chapter).

What immediate ideas do you have on what would be interesting to investigate?

My own choice concerns the decline of the Liberal Party locally. My reason for this choice lies in a major historical debate that has led historians to give attention to local government electoral data in the early years of the twentieth century. The debate has been about cause and effect in the decline of the Liberal Party nationally and the rise of the Labour Party. One argument has been that the Liberal Party was a potentially effective force after 1910, and it was the splits in the party nationally during the First World War and after – involving most obviously Lloyd George and Asquith after 1916 – that led the party to decline, so allowing Labour to supplant it. The counter argument is that the nature of the cleavages in society changed from chapel versus church to ones based on class. Politics came to be driven by class conflict. The Labour Party grew out of this and was able to exploit the change through the effectiveness of its organization and its election strategy. The debate is outlined in Searle (1992) and Tanner (1990) (which also provide useful bibliographies and indicate such work as has been done on the fortunes of the Liberal Party locally). As the debate has proceeded, attention has been directed to what was happening locally. Tanner (1990) has integrated investigations of local developments into a major study for the period up to 1918. The extent of differences across the country has been recognized. What happened nationally is seen as an aggregation of much local diversity and also the result of the interplay between the local and the national. Tanner points to the need to carry forward the study of what was happening locality by locality in the period between the wars, particularly in the

Figure 7.4   Newspaper advertisement for three Liberal candidates, 1920 (Source: *The Northampton Independent*, 30 October 1920)

areas where the Liberal Party remained a force. My interest, then, is in the fortunes of the Liberal Party in Northampton.

Studying this topic is much helped by Searle's (1992) excellent general account of the history of the Liberal Party from 1886 to 1929. This provides the broader understanding of developments in the Liberal Party against which to set what was happening locally. For Northampton local elections provide a map to guide me. They allow me to identify matters which, on the face of it, look significant and which may be worth investigating. Let me illustrate this by listing some of my reactions to the data in Tables 7.1 and 7.2.

o   From 1919 to 1921 electors were given the choice of Liberal or Conservative candidates as against Labour ones. But starting in the Abington ward in 1922 there was a change in the alignment of the parties from two-party to three-party competition. In the 1930s the predominant pattern of 1919–22 reasserted itself. Were these formal coalitions arranged locally between Liberals and Conservatives? How was the allocation of candidacies organized? Check the local newspaper reports in the years when there seems to be a change in practice or something striking: possibly Abington ward in 1922, the general division of seats in 1932, the Conservative challenge to the Liberals in 1936 and 1937.

o   Liberal candidates in 1921 and 1922 stood under different labels, reflecting the division in the party nationally. How did this division affect the local party organization? Follow this up in the local Liberal weekly, the *Mercury*, during those two years.

o   In the 1920s the Liberals did not contest two wards at all; after the 1932 election the party did not contest a further two. Did these wards have distinguishing features? The party dominated two wards, Kingsley and St James', and on the face of it these were markedly different (St James' was an industrial working-class ward, whereas Kingsley was residential on the edge of town), so what was the basis of the party's support? Conservatives gained a toe-hold in both wards in the 1932 three-seat elections and then defeated the Liberal candidates in 1937. Was there a deliberate strategy being followed by the Conservative Party to undermine the Liberal position? See if there is any reporting on these points in the local daily or weekly papers at the time candidates were nominated in 1932, and then during the local elections in 1936 and 1937. The last point could be pursued further in the Conservative Party papers lodged in the Northamptonshire Record Office.

o   The divisions in the Liberal Party nationally and locally in 1921 and 1922 were not accompanied by more than a small increase in the percentage of voters, or of electors, voting Labour. The number of electors voting for party candidates fluctuated over the twenty years, but the Liberal vote remained significant throughout when Liberal candidates stood. The 1932 elections, where voters had three votes, may be particularly revealing. Read the reports on this election in the local papers; see who the candidates were and how they presented themselves; see what issues the parties were putting before the electorate. Possibly explore the idea that at least by 1934 the local Liberal Party organization was disintegrating, that it could not find good candidates, and that Liberal-inclined electors were left without candidates for whom to vote.

Those are some of my reactions. You will have had others and probably ones that are equally worth pursuing. One, indeed, may be to ask about the fortunes of parties in a community in which you are particularly interested as a comparison with Northampton.

If you were going on to study what happened to the Liberal Party in Northampton, or to do a similar study elsewhere, electoral data have three clear uses. First, they show what the parties' candidates were doing – where they stood, when, and with what success. Second, they show the location and level of electoral support and the trends over time. Space has precluded the inclusion here of the changing percentage of the vote gained by the parties or the swings between them from one year to another, but the raw data are there. Third, they give a lead as to

Five New Civic Fathers.

One Conservative and One Liberal Gain in Northampton Election.

The net results of the Northampton municipal election was one Conservative and one Liberal gain. Councillor A. O. Birt, the Labour candidate at Kingsthorpe, lost his seat to Mr. J. T. Mott (Conservative), and Councillor F. A. Tomkins, who had represented Abington Ward in the Conservative interest for the past three years, was defeated by Mr. H. Fox (Liberal).

NORTH WARD.

W. R. TOWNLEY (Lab.) 1323
Mrs. F. A. Ellard (Con.) ... 980—343
No change.

ST. LAWRENCE'S WARD.

J. L. RAWLINSON (Con.) 799
E. J. Wright (Lab.) 789
F. C. Whiting (Lib.) ...... 618— 10
No change.

ST. EDMUND'S WARD.

W. LEES (Con.) 1008
J. Hill (Lab.) 627
W. H. Garratt (Lib.) ...... 536—381
No change.

CASTLE WARD.

J. V. COLLIER (Con.) ... 1227
J. E. Bugby (Lab.) .... 956—271
No change.

ST CRISPIN'S WARD.

A. P. HAWTIN (Lib.) 1299
F. H. Tomley (Lab.) .... 763—536
No change.

SOUTH WARD.

W. HARVEY REEVES (C) 1087
Mrs. A. E. Cox (Lab.) ... 496—591
No change.

ABINGTON WARD.

H. FOX (Lib.) 1023
F. A. Tomkins (Con.) 978
Liberal gain.

Unopposed Returns.

Kingsley Ward—A. E. RODHOUSE (Lib.)
St. James' Ward—E. LEWIS (Lib.)
St. Michael's Ward—F. C. PARKER (Con.)

TICKLES THE CARBURETTOR!

DOMINION Guaranteed SPIRIT
1/3 PER GALLON.   AT
HOLLINGSWORTH'S
CAMPBELL STREET, NORTHAMPTON.

DELAPRE WARD.

T. WAREING (Con.) 852
W. L. Wright (Lab.) 571
S. Irons (Lib.) .... 535—278
No change.

Figure 7.5   Local election results in *The Northampton Independent* (Source: *The Northampton Independent*, 7 November 1925)

when and where there were important developments – realigning elections or significant developments in the elections overall or in individual wards. All three lead to further inquiry. If I was continuing to study what happened to the Liberal Party in Northampton between the wars, my next step would be to go to the local newspapers to follow up the points I jotted down above. This second step in my research spiral would take me outwards and upwards to further sources. From newspapers I might be led on to using council minutes, party papers deposited in the county archives, oral history, local memoirs and histories like that of the National Union of Boot and Shoe Operatives and Doddridge Congregational Church. The electoral data would thus have pointed me to more precise questions and other sources. Election results for other places would equally serve this purpose.

--- *QUESTION FOR RESEARCH* ---

I have taken one example of research that starts from the electoral data for Northampton. The strategy I adopted was that of questioning sources, which involved consulting one particular source and then moving on to gather information from other sources. In describing the research I have already indicated topics that may interest you.

4 WHERE TO FIND ELECTORAL INFORMATION

Local election results are an under-used source. Despite their limitations there is much you can learn directly from them, and they are a valuable jumping-off point for further inquiry. The first practical thing you have to do is to collect the results in at least the outline form presented in Tables 7.1 and 7.2.

Local newspapers are the key source for local government election results in the 1920s and 1930s. They should appear in the issue closest to the declaration of results, but you will be lucky to find a paper that prints the information in full, year by year. If more than one paper is available it is likely that each will need to be consulted. To collect the local election results for a town or district for the whole period between the wars will probably take at the very least a full day, and that depends on your having the good fortune to be able to use local newspapers in the original form, bound in volumes and all available in one place like the public library. What increases the time it will take are considerations such as the state of the sources, whether you have to use microfilm rather than the originals, to what extent you have to consult different papers to complete the record, the existence of errors in the data as recorded in the papers (indicated by figures not adding up), and the frequency and extent of ward boundary changes.

The date when elections are held will be indicated by the minutes of council meetings. These minutes are printed and published annually (and are commonly available in the local public library or record office), and at the beginning of each council year there is a report on the councillors elected at the local elections. From this you can identify when approximately the election has been held. English boroughs such as Northampton normally held elections in the inter-war years on the first Wednesday in November. The council minutes will tell you much more about the business of the local council, for example which councillors were elected to chair committees and the committees' membership.

Producing runs of election results is affected by changes to ward boundaries. The electoral registers list these boundaries by giving information on electors by street and ward.

A problem in recording election results is the quantity of detailed numerical data and the accuracy needed to record them. The taxing part in compiling these data is, for me, not searching out the information but maintaining my concentration in recording it. However, the effort is worthwhile: the data that you are able to build up are a source with substantial possibilities. If you are able to use computer spreadsheets, these save much time in analysing data once collected but, equally, analysis can be done, as illustrated here, simply by using a calculator.

5   CONCLUSION

For many people pages of numbers are not immediately very interesting, nor do I expect you to be directly interested in the history of Northampton. But I trust that you are persuaded that local elections after the Ballot Act in 1872 are a mine of useful and usable but under-used information, in which patterns of electoral behaviour can be identified. Study of the information is also a starting point for investigating much more about a locality and putting this in a comparative context or linking it to wider historical research. There are many other places besides Northampton waiting to be illuminated by a study of local elections between the wars.

REFERENCES

Bowley, M. (1945) *Housing and the state 1919–1944,* London, Allen & Unwin.

Craig, F.W.S. (ed.) (1974) *British parliamentary election results 1885–1918,* London, Macmillan.

Craig, F.W.S. (ed.) (1983) *British parliamentary election results 1918–1949,* Chichester, Parliamentary Research Services.

Dickie, M. (1987) *Town Patriotism and the Rise of Labour in Northampton 1918–1939,* University of Warwick, PhD thesis.

Dickie, M. (1989–90) 'Northampton's working class homeowners: myth or reality?, *Northamptonshire Past and Present,* VIII, 1, pp.69–72.

Dickie, M. (1992) 'Town patriotism in Northampton, 1918–1939: an invented tradition?' *Midland History,* XVII, pp.109–117.

Fletcher, P. (1969) 'An explanation of variations in "turnout" in local elections', *Political Studies,* XVII, pp.495–502.

Milbrath, L.W. and Goel, M.L. (1977) *Political participation,* Chicago, Rand McNally.

Miller, W.L. (1977) *Electoral dynamics in Britain since 1918,* London, Macmillan.

Miller, W.L. (1986) 'Local electoral behaviour', in *Committee of inquiry into the conduct of local authority business* (Widdicombe Committee), Research volume III, *The local government elector,* Cmnd 9800, London, HMSO.

Rhodes, E.C. (1938) 'Voting at municipal elections', *Political Quarterly,* IX, 2, pp.271–80.

Ross, J.F.S. (1953) 'Women and parliamentary elections', *British Journal of Sociology,* 4, pp.14–24.

Searle, G.R. (1992) *The Liberal Party: triumph and disintegration 1886–1929,* London, Macmillan.

Tanner, D. (1990) *Political change and the Labour Party 1900–1918,* Cambridge, Cambridge University Press.

Turner, J. (1993) 'Sex, age and the Labour vote in the 1920s', in Denley, J., Fogelviks, S. and Harvey, C. (1993) *History and computing II,* Manchester, Manchester University Press.

PART III

RELIGION, CULTURE AND LEISURE

❖ ❖ ❖

CHAPTER 8

FAMILY, COMMUNITY AND RELIGION

*by Kate Tiller (section 1), Terry Thomas (section 2) and
Brenda Collins (section 3)*

In this chapter we examine the roles played by spiritual beliefs and religious institutions within communities. We look at the source materials available for those of you who wish to undertake research projects in this area, and we suggest ways in which these sources can best be used.

Section 1 looks at religious beliefs and practices in nineteenth-century Britain and shows how pervasive religion was in the lives of individuals and families, irrespective of whether they were church- or chapel-goers. Particular attention is paid to the religious census of 1851, local directories, church buildings and local newspapers as sources for exploring the range of activities of local churches and chapels and the extent to which they were involved in the community.

In the nineteenth century the vast majority of the population was Christian – Anglican, Roman Catholic and Nonconformist – and it is only in the last fifty years that one can talk of Britain being a pluralist religious society. Section 2 centres on the inward migration of Hindus, Sikhs and Muslims and raises questions about the extent and influence of their religious organizations within particular communities. What is particularly interesting is that many of the questions relating to the establishment and setting up of these religious networks are similar to those which needed to be asked about Anglican, Roman Catholic and Nonconformist churches and chapels in the nineteenth century.

Section 3 examines religion in Ireland and stresses the prominent role religion plays in contemporary everyday life compared with England, Scotland and Wales and, indeed, other parts of Europe. Again, a number of primary sources – census householders' schedules for 1901 and 1911, national school registers, poll books, and biographies – are suggested as starting points for investigations into the connections between religion and the social structure, education, politics, and popular culture.

1 RELIGION IN NINETEENTH-CENTURY BRITAIN

by Kate Tiller

Religion was a central influence in the lives of individuals, families and communities throughout nineteenth-century Britain. This was the case whether or not those lives involved a formal religious observance, allegiance or membership. The impact of religion was both direct and indirect, its functions in people's lives changed over time, and it did not operate in isolation from other strands of experience discussed elsewhere in this volume. Rather Christianity, as reinvigorated by the evangelical revival of the later eighteenth and early nineteenth century, and as reformed under the pressures of change in an industrializing and urbanizing society, came to provide a dominant ethos touching all aspects of public life and the private lives of virtually all men, women and children, on Sundays and throughout the week.

Victorian Britain experienced a diverse and powerful assertion of Christian concepts which was in marked contrast to the often placid eighteenth century. For some, religion was the primary factor in defining a sense of community, of belonging and of shared values. It could motivate individuals and families to an active sense of participation, intervention and concern in the life around them, whether of a village, parish, small town, urban neighbourhood or street. For others, religion separated rather than attached, generating a more inward-looking identity, an alternative community shared within a household or with fellow religionists and setting its members apart from the local population as a whole. A third scenario might apply to those who embraced religious belief or affiliation less positively but who inevitably encountered them, for example, through the provision of most elementary education by religious denominations. Despite the advances of scientific and mechanical knowledge and the development of secular philosophies such as socialism and utilitarianism, only a small minority of such non-activists in religion positively rejected Christian beliefs for atheism. Rather, responses in this large category of people might be determined pragmatically, according to convenience, social expectations, changes in status or perceptions of economic and social interest.

The aim of this section is to help you recognize the differing forms and functions taken by religion in the places and families which you are studying. What were the factors (for example, urban or rural location, pace of economic change, geographical mobility, occupation or social class), which determined these varying experiences? The principal sources of evidence relevant to your research will be discussed, with examples of how they have been used by historians and suggestions on how you can replicate or build on their work.

1.1 RELIGION AND CHANGE

We need to consider the secular and spiritual shifts which gave religion such a vigorous and overt role in the nineteenth century.

In the spiritual sphere, the carefully unenthusiastic observances of the eighteenth century were overtaken by a revivalism which found many converts. When John Wesley, an Anglican clergyman, began his itinerant open-air preaching in the 1730s, his message evoked in many people dramatic responses that were beyond the ken of organized religion as it operated then. The evangelical message offered the possibility of individual salvation and escape from original sin for all. After the initial heady experience of conversion and salvation the believer had to maintain a state of grace. This could be attained, firstly, though service to the church, for example as a class leader or a local preacher (participation, bearing witness, and continuing active commitment were of the essence); secondly, through tending to the inner soul, for example by tract reading; and, thirdly, through maintaining a methodical discipline and conduct in everyday life, by hard work, self-abasement and lack of pride. It was this last characteristic which gave Methodism its name, originally coined by detractors.

Evangelicalism also became a major force within the Church of England. For clergy and laity alike, practical action in the world was a hallmark and many targets of such action existed – in the sluggish, often neglectful, sometimes corrupt reaches of the Church itself, and in reforms, from Sunday schooling and the emancipation of slaves to prison conditions and child labour. As a state church enmeshed in the Establishment, in patronage and power, Anglicanism was slow to respond to the needs of those growing numbers living outside traditional communities, and only in the 1820s and 1830s was it really stung into action, action which will be very apparent locally. Schools sponsored by the National Society (full title the National Society for Promoting the Education of the Poor in the Principles of the Established Church) sprang up. New churches were built and old ones restored. Bishops clamped down on clerical pluralism and non-residence. The local norm became a resident, trained clergyman, ideally married and setting an example in family life, conducting more services, involved in educational initiatives, in local concerns and (with his family) in pastoral work, and living in a suitably appointed parsonage. For many Anglicans reform was an attempt to protect their Church's unique position as a comprehensive, national church against the encroachments of others who threatened to reduce the Church of England to the position of one denomination in a pluralist world of different kinds of Christianity, of non-Christians and of indifference.

The Nonconformist challenge included 'Old Dissent', the denominations of seventeenth-century origin – the Quakers, Baptists, Independents, Congregationalists and Unitarians – but by the early eighteenth century their zeal was muted and their denominational identities blurred. Under the impact of Evangelicalism later in the century a 'New Dissent' of revived Congregationalism and Particular and General Baptists emerged, but it was Methodism that grew most rapidly of all (Gilbert, 1976, pp.30–2, 36–9). This was a religion that altered individuals' lives and the lives of those who came into contact with them.

Historians have differed greatly on what those effects were. Some have seen Methodism as a radicalizing factor, with its stress on the individual and equality in salvation, offering opportunities for active participation and leadership through its developing structure of classes, societies, circuits and conference, fostering an identity and confidence which translated into purpose and action in the emergent labour movement.

Others have interpreted Methodism, because of its emphasis on sin and maintenance of a state of grace through self-discipline, self-help and hard work, as a cause of personal repression and sexual guilt (Thompson, 1963, ch.XI). It has been associated with authoritarian and patriarchal family relationships and the restrictiveness of a 'thou shalt not …' view of life. Out of such views, 'the English Sunday' with its long list of prohibited activities was born. This aspect of Methodism is epitomized by its dominant figure in the second decade of the nineteenth century, Jabez Bunting. It was he who condemned Sunday school teaching of writing (secular and self-expressive), as opposed to reading (spiritual and a way to the scriptures). (For his powerful signature on a christening register when he baptised a whole family, see Volume 4, Figure 4.7.)

By the mid-nineteenth century, Methodism was passing from a charismatic to a bureaucratic phase; larger, more structured, more established and accepted in national and local life, and inevitably more linked to matters secular. E.P. Thompson argues that Methodism always had these links in that its calls for self-abasement and hard work made it an ideal instrument of social control and work discipline, by employers over employees and by elders over the young. T.W. Laqueur (1985) has questioned this view of the imposition of middle-class ideas on the majority working class. Investigating the role of Sunday schools, a vital arena for any such transmission of values in the period 1780–1850, he examines the industrial town of Stockport and claims Sunday schools came to represent a distinctive provision, whose values were indigenously working class. Patrick Joyce (1982) has studied other northern mill towns and concluded that their institutions, including Sunday schools, were in reality closely tied to middle-class funding and ideas, rather than representing a truly independent creed. Here is rich ground for local research.

It is now some 80 years since Halévy suggested in 1913 that Methodism saved Britain in the 1790s from a revolutionary fate such as France's (see Halévy, 1949, p.424ff.). This third view of Wesleyanism interprets it as defusing dissatisfaction in this world by a strong psychological appeal to those whose lives were being disrupted by change, whether it dislocated their existing community or forced them to migrate to a new place. For them, religion provided identity and security in membership of a like-minded group. The hope of ultimate salvation in the next world further inhibited any active, class-based resistance to their present lot. Any family or community study located within the long nineteenth century, 1789–1914, will need to ask, within its particular context, whether religion acted as refuge, stimulus or externally imposed control, and also how it changed over time.

1.2   SOME KEY SOURCES AND EXAMPLES OF THEIR USE

The initial and most disruptive phase of Britain's Industrial Revolution is commonly dated pre-1850. Is this reflected in the religious dimensions of family and community? To throw light on this possible watershed let us consider the main sources of evidence available for local research.

Four contrasting and complementary sources provide a good place to start. The first is a unique, nation-wide census of religious provision and attendance on one Sunday in 1851; the second is the local descriptions and listings given in commercial directories; the third lies in the many surviving religious buildings, whether for worship, schooling or social events; and the fourth is provided by the rich columns of the local press.

THE RELIGIOUS CENSUS OF 1851

On Sunday 30 March 1851 everybody attending a place of worship in England, Scotland and Wales was counted for a national governmental census of accommodation and attendance at worship. This was the first and only such exercise ever carried out, although some independent local surveys, mainly in urban areas, were to be attempted later in the century (McLeod, 1974). Using the same network of local enumerators and registrars as the 1851 census of population, a further nineteen tons of religious and educational census forms were distributed. The religious forms then went to Anglican clergy, Roman Catholic priests, Dissenting ministers or local leaders such as elders or lay preachers.

The religious census was carried out in an innovative spirit of rigorous statistical and scientific enquiry highly characteristic of the time. The Census Office in London, headed by Horace Mann, which undertook the exercise, attempted an exact measurement of the number of sittings in places of worship as compared with the number of the local population. In the event, this concern with the fixed capital of religious provision in buildings and seats was to prove less interesting, both to contemporaries and later historians, than the second major area of enquiry: that is, exactly how many people actually sat on the available seats.

The information derived from the 1851 religious census can be found in two forms: (1) in the published *Reports* (Parliamentary Papers, 1852–3, LXXXIX, Census 1851: Religious Worship [England and Wales]; Parliamentary Papers, 1854, LIX, Census 1851: Religious Worship and Education [Scotland]), which summarize, tabulate and comment on the returns; and (2) in the original manuscript returns (see Figure 8.5 on p.169) from individual places of worship. Both provide important information about the relative strength of different religious groupings both locally and nationally.

To give its barest bones, the *Report* for England and Wales shows that Protestant Dissenters provided nearly half the church accommodation, that over 40 per cent of those worshipping in the morning and afternoon were Dissenters, that two-thirds of evening worshippers were Dissenters, and that the number present at the best-attended Dissenting services exceeded the number present at the best-attended Anglican services. Further, it was estimated that, of 12,549,326 *potential* worshippers, 5,288,294 stayed away.

These results were much discussed by contemporaries and by historians (see, in particular, Inglis, 1960 and Lawton, 1978). 21,000 copies of the report were sold. Sections of Anglican opinion were outraged and cried foul, claiming distortions, ranging from deliberate exaggeration or rank ignorance on the part of those making Dissenting returns, to the billing of special, popular sermons at local chapels, to the disruption of Anglican attendance by bad weather, a point of dubious validity since it rained on Nonconformists too! However, the collection of information was painstaking – for example, 34,467 places of worship in England and Wales were recorded and, as K.S. Inglis has concluded, 'it may be presumed that any person who could be got to public worship on census day was zealous enough to be described legitimately as an active supporter of his denomination. As an index of sentiment on this particular Sunday it is in a way comparable with registering a vote at an election' (Inglis, 1960, p.77). The result of the 'poll' was undoubtedly unpalatable for the Church of England, because it indicated that Protestant Dissent was on terms of equality in the provision of accommodation and in actual numbers of worshippers nationally, and that everywhere it was significantly strong, sometimes equal or in a majority. The census was thus one important confirmation that the Established Church could no longer claim any monopolistic position and that religious observance was a voluntary matter in a pluralist context. Equally shocking was the finding of the large numbers who did not attend worship. Although Horace Mann's estimates are spuriously precise, the evidence of widespread indifference was irrefutable. Organized religion was failing to reach appreciable sections of the population in terms of class, gender and place. It is in respect of this last point that the religious census provides definite data.

Table 8.1 (p.160) deals with information on accommodation and shows the English counties ranked in terms of percentages of Anglican and Dissenting sittings. Figure 8.1 (p.161) represents the same data geographically and Figures 8.2 and 8.3 (p.162) chart attendance levels.

How should the considerable variations apparent here be interpreted?

One explanation for the variation is that different kinds of place are likely to produce distinctive patterns of religious allegiance and varying degrees of irreligion. It is argued (Everitt, 1970) that the larger the place, the higher its population density and the more rapid its rate of growth before 1851, then the greater the economic and social freedom, and the diversity of ideas, organization and experience it will offer, and the weaker the institutions of established authority, including the Church, are likely to be. On that basis it might seem that the results of the 1851 religious census would resolve themselves merely into a North–South, industrial–agrarian divide. Alan Everitt points out that such broad generalizations are unsound: of thirteen counties with over 100,000 non-Anglican sittings, seven (eight if one counts Gloucestershire despite its woollen mills) were in the South and predominantly agrarian. In the North, agrarian areas like the North and South Ridings were strong in Dissent, whilst Lancashire and Staffordshire had relatively low levels of Dissent yet were heavily industrial. (For this debate, see also Thompson, 1978, pp.258–63).

The religious census clearly revealed higher levels of attendance in Scotland and Wales than in England. These differences were marked and persistent. For example, in Scotland in 1851, 60 per cent of the adult population were church members, three times higher than in England (Obelkevich, 1990, p.349). The 1851 picture for Wales showed the highest levels of observance amongst the three countries yet the lowest levels of allegiance to the Established Church, a fact reflecting both the Church's organizational weaknesses in that country and the intermix of religious issues with those of Welsh language and national identity. Old and New Dissent and

Table 8.1   General religious allegiance in England in 1851

	Total Church and Chapel Sittings	Anglicans		Dissenters		
		Sittings	%	Sittings	%	
1 Herefordshire	68,675	49,312	72	19,363	28	41
2 Rutland	17,299	12,131	70	5,168	30	40
3 Oxfordshire	109,301	74,369	68	34,932	32	39
4 Sussex	160,011	108,076	67	51,935	33	38
5 Surrey	219,094	143,793	66	75,311	34	37
6 Westmorland*	37,239	24,411	66	12,828	34	36
7 Dorset	120,082	77,886	65	42,196	35	35
8 Kent	299,296	194,443	65	104,853	35	34
9 Hampshire	212,161	135,720	64	76,441	36	33
10 Shropshire	143,663	92,435	64	51,228	36	32
11 Suffolk‡	224,229	141,417	63	82,812	37	31
12 Middlesex	552,231	344,487	62	207,744	38	30
13 Berkshire	92,737	56,679	61	36,058	39	29
14 Essex	216,113	132,041	61	84,072	39	28
15 Somerset	287,353	174,723	61	112,630	39	27
16 Warwickshire	201,831	123,624	61	78,207	39	26
17 Worcestershire	138,668	85,155	61	53,513	39	25
18 Norfolk‡	283,420	168,722	60	114,698	40	24
19 Hertfordshire	93,230	55,193	59	38,037	41	23
20 Devon	332,934	191,710	58	141,224	42	22
21 Staffordshire	279,516	161,217	58	118,299	42	21
22 Buckinghamshire	113,209	64,231	57	48,978	43	20
23 Cumberland	99,783	56,803	57	42,980	43	19
24 Gloucestershire	276,606	156,651	57	119,955	43	18
25 Northamptonshire	150,472	84,816	56	65,656	44	17
26 Wiltshire	158,694	87,843	55	70,851	45	16
27 Lancashire	708,217	383,466	54	324,751	46	15
28 Cheshire	229,711	121,882	53	107,829	47	14
29 Leicestershire	156,678	82,964	53	73,714	47	13
30 Huntingdonshire	45,014	23,568	52	21,446	48	12
31 Cambridgeshire	104,196	52,917	51	51,279	49	11
32 Lincolnshire	279,247	142,844	51	136,403	49	10
33 North Riding	161,062	79,740	50	81,322	50	9
34 Bedfordshire	87,814	42,557	48	45,257	52	8
35 Derbyshire	182,581	87,829	48	94,752	52	7
36 Nottinghamshire	150,024	70,928	47	79,096	53	6
37 East Riding	140,793	64,135	46	76,658	54	5
38 West Riding	665,428	276,910	42	388,518	58	4
39 Co. Durham	167,285	66,319	40	100,966	60	3
40 Northumberland	131,646	52,405	40	79,241	60	2
41 Cornwall	261,684	95,155	36	166,529	64	1
Total	8,359,227	4,641,497	56	3,717,730	44	

* The number of sittings in the four Baptist chapels in the county was not reported. These have been estimated at 1,000.
‡ The figures for Anglican sittings in these counties are probably affected by the exceptional size and number of ancient parish churches.

Source: Everitt (1970) p.181

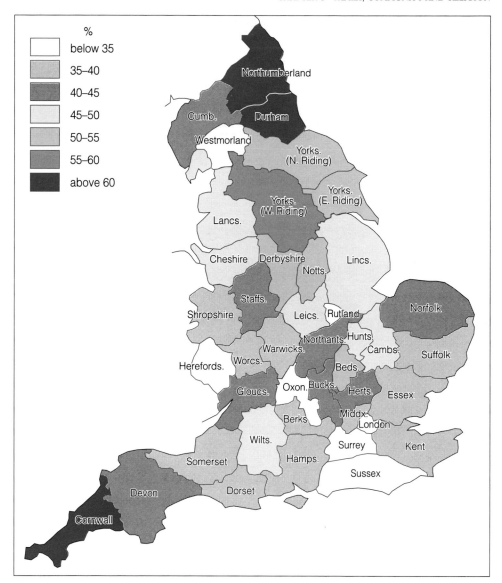

Figure 8.1   Dissent in England in 1851: percentage of Dissenter sittings by county (Source: based on Table 8.1)

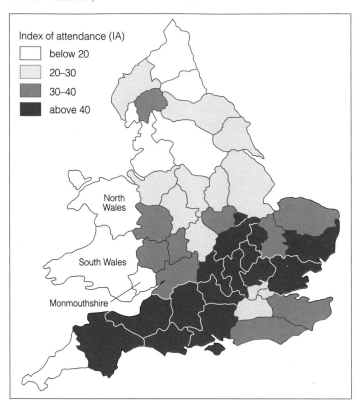

Figure 8.2 Anglican index of attendances: census of religious worship, 1851 (index of attendance = total Anglican attendances as a percentage of local population) (Source: Coleman, 1980, p.20)

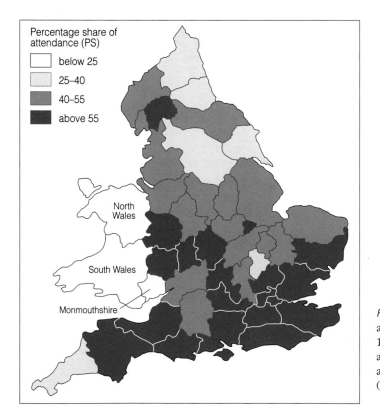

Figure 8.3 Anglican percentage share of attendances: census of religious worship, 1851 (percentage share = total Anglican attendances as a percentage of the total attendances of all denominations) (Source: Coleman, 1980, p.21)

Methodism were extremely strong. Thus national factors may take their place alongside the theological, social, economic and political in analysing religion in family or community.

Consider the differences between Northumberland and Durham, Lancashire and Sussex in 1851 as shown in Figures 8.1, 8.2 and 8.3. In what ways might these differences be related to the above discussion on reasons for variation?

Understanding these varying experiences requires detailed local study. For example, it is interesting to compare experiences within more local regions, such as a county. Figure 8.4 shows the very different balance of Dissenting and Anglican provision in the registration districts of Oxfordshire, a fact masked by the overall average of 31.3 per cent Dissenting sittings. The strongholds of Nonconformity were in Banbury district, followed by Thame, Witney and Henley. Its weakest areas were in the centre of the county in the districts of Chipping Norton, Woodstock, Bicester, Headington and Oxford. These had been weak in Dissent in the seventeenth century, were near to the Anglican stronghold of Oxford and its strong clergy presence, and had high concentrations of landed estates.

Historians have suggested a range of other factors which may have contributed to distinctive local religious patterns. Among these is the geographical and economic basis of an area, with Dissent arising in woodlands, heathlands, moorlands or marshlands – areas which often had larger Anglican parishes, scattered settlements (often with no church), weak manorial structures,

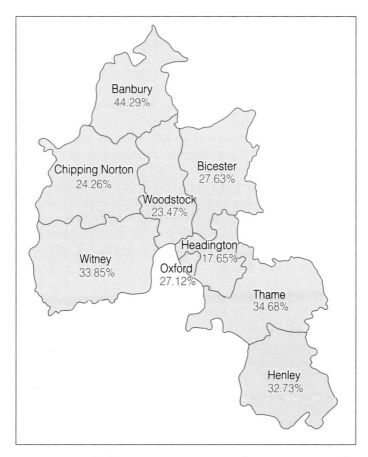

Figure 8.4 Oxfordshire, 1851: percentage of Dissenter sittings by registration district. Average for county = 31.34 per cent (Source: Tiller, 1987, p.xli)

and a greater variety of more specialist employments than fielden areas. Dissent may have occurred outside main settlements, in boundary areas of large parishes, where worshippers would gather. Decaying market towns, with dispersed patterns of property ownership, could provide an encouraging base for Dissenters. Links between town and village could be close, with town meeting houses reflecting the religious colour of the surrounding countryside or acting as a basis for supporting and fostering Dissent in neighbouring village centres.

Another major distinction suggested for rural areas is that between open and closed villages. Open villages had large populations, increasing rapidly by 1851, more proprietors of land, smaller farms, a variety of crafts and tradesmen, shops and pubs, available cheap housing; in short, a degree of variety and independence of which religious diversity and the presence of Nonconformist chapels were a part. By contrast, closed villages were smaller, restricted in growth, dominated by estate ownership and Anglicanism, with large farms, few industries or crafts, few or no pubs, and no Dissenting chapels. In uncovering these variations the religious census offers quantifiable and comparative information. Once this framework is established, literary and qualitative evidence may well take on added significance. For example, Flora Thompson's *Lark Rise to Candleford* (1945) provides particularly effective insights into religion in rural areas. She describes life in north Oxfordshire in the 1880s in the hamlet of Juniper Hill ('Lark Rise') and in the adjoining, closed village of Cottisford, where the parish church lay. Cottisford had no chapel but the open settlement of Juniper Hill did have Dissenters, and it was there that the layman completing the local Methodist census return in 1851 lived. So communities with very different religious institutions and lifestyles could exist in close proximity, indeed to some extent symbiotically, for where did the labourers needed on the large farms of a closed parish find housing or where might a Dissenter in a closed village go to chapel? Similar links as well as sharp differences between parts of the same town or city are often uncovered by local studies.

Overall, in most of the agrarian counties the percentage of church attendances in 1851 was relatively high. But it would be wrong to assume that in a preindustrial, agrarian society Christianity and the status quo were little challenged and that levels of conformity, usually to the Established Church, were high. An analysis of the 1851 religious census of Oxfordshire (Tiller, 1987, p.xxxi), a rural county, reveals that in settlements with only an Anglican place of worship 48 per cent of the population attended worship. In 'mixed' places (those with Dissent), 33 per cent of the population went to the Church of England but 62 per cent attended worship. Thus the Anglican, and probably more traditional, settlements had lower levels of observance by nearly 15 per cent. It seems that the nineteenth-century Dissenters of Oxfordshire were not only reducing Anglican attendance but winning additional numbers to worship. Here the evidence of the religious census sounds a note of caution about assumed characteristics of religion in non-urban places.

EXERCISE 8.1

A generalization worth testing is that the larger the settlement the greater the diversity of places of worship, but probably not the levels of observance. This relates to one of the most protracted debates about religion in modern Britain – did urbanization cause a collapse of religious influence and bring secularization? Look at Tables 8.2 and 8.3. What light do they throw on this debate?

Table 8.2   Census of religious worship, 1851: attendances in the registration counties (excluding the City of York)

	Total IA*	C. of E. IA/PS†	Methodists IA/PS	Independents IA/PS	Baptists IA/PS	Rom. Cath. IA/PS
England and Wales (uncorrected)	58.1	27.6/47.4	14.9/25.7	6.6/11.4	5.1/8.7	2.0/3.5
England and Wales (corrected)	60.8	29.5/48.6	15.2/25.0	6.8/11.1	5.2/8.5	2.1/3.5
Bedfordshire	104.6	41.0/39.3	28.8/27.5	9.2/8.8	20.8/19.9	0.1/0.1
Berkshire	66.0	40.1/60.7	12.8/19.4	6.2/9.4	5.0/7.5	0.8/1.2
Buckinghamshire	87.3	44.3/50.7	17.7/20.2	8.1/9.3	16.1/18.4	0.4/0.4
Cambridgeshire	84.3	37.1/44.0	18.1/21.5	8.6/10.2	17.3/20.5	0.4/0.5
Cheshire	52.3	24.3/46.5	17.5/33.4	4.5/8.6	1.1/2.2	3.0/5.7
Cornwall	68.0	19.2/27.2	43.8/64.5	2.8/4.1	1.3/2.0	0.3/0.4
Cumberland	37.3	20.0/53.7	9.4/25.3	2.7/7.2	0.3/0.9	2.1/5.6
Derbyshire	58.8	23.7/40.8	23.9/40.9	4.3/7.3	4.3/7.3	1.3/2.2
Devon	70.5	40.1/56.9	13.2/18.7	7.6/10.8	5.3/7.5	0.3/0.9
Dorset	77.6	48.2/62.1	13.8/17.7	11.7/15.1	1.6/2.1	0.7/0.9
Durham	42.6	14.4/33.8	19.6/46.0	2.1/5.0	1.4/3.4	3.0/7.0
Essex	73.3	42.2/57.5	6.2/8.5	16.9/23.0	6.0/8.2	0.6/0.8
Gloucestershire	65.5	34.4/52.3	10.5/16.0	9.3/14.2	10.2/15.5	1.6/2.5
Hampshire	67.6	40.5/59.9	10.0/14.8	10.4/15.4	4.6/6.8	1.0/1.4
Herefordshire	49.0	32.3/65.9	8.0/16.3	2.3/4.7	4.0/8.2	0.5/1.0
Hertfordshire	74.7	42.4/56.8	9.4/12.5	10.6/14.3	10.8/14.5	0.4/0.6
Huntingdonshire	94.2	42.3/44.9	20.5/21.8	6.7/7.1	20.6/21.9	–/–
Kent	56.9	38.9/68.5	8.6/15.1	5.2/9.1	5.4/9.4	0.8/1.3
Lancashire	44.1	18.8/42.6	9.9/22.4	4.2/9.5	1.8/4.0	7.2/16.3
Leicestershire	72.0	35.5/49.3	15.6/21.8	6.1/8.4	11.7/16.2	1.7/2.3
Lincolnshire	63.4	27.4/43.3	29.5/46.5	2.3/3.7	3.2/5.1	0.6/0.9
Middlesex	37.2	21.4/60.5	3.0/8.0	6.1/16.3	2.6/6.9	2.1/5.7
Monmouthshire	73.3	16.4/22.4	21.5/29.3	11.2/15.3	20.4/27.9	2.4/3.2
Norfolk	65.3	34.2/52.3	20.5/31.3	3.4/5.2	5.4/8.2	0.5/0.7
Northamptonshire	89.6	45.0/50.3	19.0/21.2	10.2/11.4	13.1/14.7	0.4/0.4
Northumberland	42.0	15.6/37.2	10.7/25.2	1.7/4.0	1.1/2.7	2.7/6.3
Nottinghamshire	58.0	24.0/41.4	19.1/33.0	3.0/5.2	5.8/10.0	1.2/2.0
Oxfordshire	69.0	40.3/58.5	12.9/18.7	4.2/6.1	4.7/6.8	0.8/1.2
Rutland	68.4	42.5/62.1	10.7/15.6	4.4/6.4	10.2/14.9	–/–
Shropshire	59.5	35.4/59.7	16.0/27.0	4.7/7.9	1.9/3.1	1.0/1.6
Somerset	70.3	43.2/61.5	12.5/17.8	6.8/9.7	5.3/7.5	0.6/0.9
Staffordshire	48.8	22.5/46.1	18.1/37.0	3.2/6.6	1.9/3.9	2.6/5.3
Suffolk	82.2	46.7/56.8	8.8/10.8	13.2/16.1	12.4/15.1	0.2/0.2
Surrey	41.9	26.5/63.2	2.7/6.5	5.8/13.8	3.9/9.4	2.2/5.2
Sussex	56.4	38.4/68.1	5.7/10.6	5.5/9.7	4.3/7.6	0.4/0.7
Warwickshire	48.9	27.5/56.3	6.3/13.0	3.4/6.9	4.3/8.8	2.8/5.8
Westmorland	50.1	30.7/61.2	11.9/23.7	2.0/3.9	0.6/1.3	1.2/2.3
Wiltshire	85.7	44.7/52.2	16.0/18.7	10.3/12.1	12.6/14.7	0.6/0.7
Worcestershire	54.9	30.6/55.7	13.9/25.3	2.9/5.3	4.1/7.4	1.8/3.2
Yorkshire (East Riding)	58.8	21.8/37.0	27.8/47.3	4.8/8.1	1.2/2.1	1.6/2.8
Yorkshire (North Riding)	63.6	26.4/41.6	28.8/45.4	3.5/5.6	1.2/1.9	2.4/3.8
Yorkshire (West Riding)	52.9	18.1/34.2	22.3/42.3	5.8/10.9	3.4/6.5	1.5/2.9
North Wales	86.6	15.1/17.4	48.9/56.4	13.8/15.9	7.4/8.5	0.3/0.4
South Wales	83.4	15.6/18.3	23.9/28.7	23.7/28.5	17.7/21.3	0.6/0.7

* IA = Index of attendance (i.e. total attendances as a percentage of local population on Sunday, 30 March 1851).
† PS = Percentage share (i.e. total attendances of one denomination as a percentage of the total attendances of all denominations on Sunday, 30 March 1851).

Source: Coleman (1980) p.40

Table 8.3 Census of religious worship, 1851: attendances in London and the 65 large towns

	Population	Total IA	C. of E. IA/PS	Methodists IA/PS	Independents IA/PS	Baptists IA/PS	Rom. Cath. IA/PS
London	(2,362,236)	37.0	21.0/56.6	3.0/8.1	5.9/15.8	3.0/8.1	2.3/6.3
Ashton-Under-Lyme	(30,676)	45.8	18.4/40.4	10.5/23.0	9.3/20.2	1.4/3.0	3.1/6.8
Bath	(54,240)	79.1	48.7/61.6	11.1/14.0	4.9/6.2	3.6/4.6	2.6/3.2
Birmingham	(232,841)	36.1	17.0/47.1	5.2/14.5	3.3/9.1	4.2/11.6	2.2/6.1
Blackburn	(46,536)	37.7	16.7/44.4	6.2/16.5	5.2/13.8	1.4/3.8	4.1/10.8
Bolton	(61,171)	36.8	15.3/41.7	8.6/23.4	4.2/11.5	0.9/2.5	4.8/13.1
Bradford	(103,778)	42.7	9.8/22.9	16.9/39.6	5.6/13.1	4.9/11.8	3.9/9.1
Brighton	(69,673)	52.5	31.5/60.0	6.4/12.2	4.5/8.5	5.6/10.7	1.3/2.5
Bristol	(137,328)	56.7	25.2/44.9	9.8/17.3	9.0/15.8	4.8/8.4	3.4/5.9
Bury	(31,262)	44.1	17.3/39.3	10.4/23.5	6.1/13.9	2.5/6.0	3.7/8.3
Cambridge	(27,815)	67.8	40.1/59.9	6.9/10.1	2.3/3.3	15.0/22.2	2.3/3.4
Carlisle	(26,310)	35.0	11.5/32.8	9.8/28.0	3.2/9.1	0.3/1.0	6.4/18.4
Chatham	(28,424)	54.3	26.2/48.2	12.8/23.5	6.8/12.6	6.0/11.1	1.9/3.6
Cheltenham	(35,051)	66.2	40.8/61.7	8.1/12.3	5.4/8.1	8.1/12.3	3.2/4.8
Chester	(27,766)	57.4	31.0/54.0	14.0/24.3	6.2/10.8	0.8/1.3	2.4/4.2
Colchester	(19,443)	89.5	43.5/48.6	8.2/9.1	22.7/25.4	10.5/11.7	0.7/0.8
Coventry	(36,208)	40.2	18.2/45.3	2.2/5.4	7.9/19.6	4.2/10.4	6.1/15.1
Derby	(40,609)	59.0	23.6/40.0	14.8/25.1	5.6/9.4	7.8/13.2	5.6/9.6
Devonport	(50,159)	56.5	22.0/39.0	14.3/25.3	10.6/17.9	6.1/10.7	2.0/3.5
Dover	(22,244)	67.1	47.1/70.1	8.2/12.2	4.2/6.2	5.7/8.5	–/–
Dudley	(37,962)	55.3	13.9/25.1	26.4/47.7	3.5/6.2	4.9/8.9	3.5/6.3
Exeter	(32,818)	84.5	54.7/64.7	10.0/11.8	3.6/4.3	7.0/8.3	0.8/0.9
Gateshead	(25,568)	32.9	13.2/40.0	15.4/46.9	–/–	–/–	2.7/8.3
Gravesend	(16,633)	48.6	26.5/54.5	7.6/15.6	7.2/14.7	6.4/13.2	0.8/1.7
Great Yarmouth	(30,879)	56.0	27.4/48.8	19.2/34.2	3.6/6.7	4.0/7.1	–/–
Halifax	(33,582)	41.4	23.4/56.8	17.1/41.4	–/–	0.9/2.1	–/–
Huddersfield	(30,882)	59.6	25.9/43.4	18.9/31.8	9.0/15.1	1.2/2.1	2.2/3.8
Hull	(84,690)	49.6	15.4/31.0	19.0/38.3	7.5/15.2	1.3/2.6	2.4/4.9
Ipswich	(32,914)	71.2	40.8/57.3	4.0/5.6	8.5/12.0	13.5/19.0	1.2/1.7
Kidderminster	(18,462)	53.6	29.7/55.4	12.2/22.8	4.5/8.4	2.2/4.1	2.4/4.5
King's Lynn	(19,355)	51.9	22.6/43.5	15.7/30.2	4.8/10.0	7.0/13.5	1.0/2.0
Leeds	(172,270)	47.4	16.4/34.5	19.8/41.9	3.5/7.4	2.7/5.6	2.9/6.1
Leicester	(60,584)	62.3	28.0/44.9	9.8/15.7	4.8/7.8	14.6/23.5	2.2/3.5
Liverpool	(375,955)	45.2	18.4/40.7	6.0/13.2	1.9/4.3	1.1/2.4	14.7/32.5
Macclesfield	(39,048)	44.0	20.0/45.4	12.9/29.2	2.8/6.5	1.4/3.1	4.7/10.9
Maidstone	(20,740)	60.8	38.2/62.8	9.8/16.0	3.3/5.5	8.0/13.2	–/–
Manchester	(303,382)	34.7	11.9/34.4	7.0/20.2	3.1/8.8	1.3/3.8	8.1/23.3
Merthyr Tydfil	(63,080)	88.5	5.3/6.0	16.8/18.7	27.1/30.6	32.6/36.8	3.8/4.3
Newcastle-upon-Tyne	(87,784)	40.0	16.8/42.0	7.6/19.0	1.5/3.8	2.1/5.3	5.6/13.9
Newport	(19,323)	59.2	11.0/18.6	12.7/21.4	9.8/16.5	10.7/18.0	11.4/19.2
Northampton	(26,657)	63.4	24.5/38.6	11.1/17.4	9.4/14.8	13.9/22.0	–/–
Norwich	(68,195)	46.1	22.1/48.0	6.2/13.5	4.4/9.5	6.6/14.4	0.4/0.8
Nottingham	(57,407)	57.7	17.8/30.8	15.5/26.8	6.3/11.0	8.9/15.5	4.1/7.0
Oldham	(52,820)	31.7	11.7/37.0	8.4/26.7	6.5/20.5	2.1/6.7	1.5/4.8
Oxford	(27,843)	59.3	40.5/68.3	6.1/10.4	3.8/6.4	7.6/12.9	0.2/0.3
Plymouth	(52,221)	55.1	24.5/44.5	7.5/13.7	5.8/10.5	2.8/5.1	–/–
Portsmouth	(72,096)	50.7	22.1/43.5	6.8/13.4	9.6/18.9	12.0/23.6	1.3/2.5
Preston	(69,542)	25.5	5.2/20.4	6.4/25.2	2.6/10.3	1.0/4.1	9.1/35.8
Reading	(21,456)	68.5	35.4/51.7	7.8/11.4	14.4/21.0	8.0/11.6	1.7/2.4
Rochdale	(29,195)	49.8	10.4/21.0	23.8/47.9	4.1/8.2	6.6/13.2	2.3/4.6
Salford	(63,850)	36.6	15.5/42.4	6.9/18.9	5.7/15.5	1.6/4.4	5.6/15.4
Sheffield	135,310	32.1	11.0/34.3	10.9/34.1	3.4/10.5	1.7/5.4	3.0/9.2
Southampton	(35,305)	61.1	33.7/55.2	6.5/10.6	11.1/18.2	2.6/4.2	2.3/3.7
South Shields	(28,974)	46.2	14.6/31.5	18.5/40.0	2.4/5.2	2.1/4.6	1.9/4.0
Stockport	(53,835)	42.8	15.4/36.0	14.2/33.2	6.2/14.4	1.5/3.6	3.7/8.7
Stoke-on-Trent	(84,027)	40.9	12.9/31.6	21.8/53.2	2.6/6.4	0.9/2.1	2.0/5.0
Sunderland	(63,897)	48.5	14.2/29.2	20.1/41.4	4.6/9.5	3.8/7.8	1.5/3.1
Swansea	(31,461)	58.4	11.0/18.8	18.3/31.4	13.4/23.0	11.3/19.4	1.9/3.3
Tynemouth	(29,170)	44.1	17.1/38.9	16.0/36.3	4.1/9.2	1.6/3.7	–/–
Wakefield	(22,065)	71.1	32.3/49.6	19.9/28.0	9.6/13.5	1.9/2.7	2.1/2.9
Walsall	(25,680)	43.3	18.0/41.6	10.8/24.8	2.7/6.3	1.5/3.5	7.4/17.1
Warrington	(22,894)	59.1	31.2/54.5	18.1/30.6	1.2/2.0	1.0/1.8	4.9/8.3
Wigan	(31,941)	53.2	24.5/46.1	5.5/10.4	6.0/11.3	1.8/3.5	15.2/28.2
Wolverhampton	(119,748)	53.1	19.2/36.2	22.5/42.4	3.2/6.0	3.7/7.0	3.7/7.0
Worcester	(27,528)	66.2	46.5/70.3	9.9/14.9	2.8/4.3	2.7/4.1	2.5/3.8
York	(36,303)	62.3	26.9/43.2	19.8/31.8	6.7/10.7	–/–	6.6/10.5

Source: Coleman (1980) p.41; and Table F, Religious accommodation and attendance in large towns, census of religious worship, 1851

Table 8.2 shows that many of the heavily urbanized counties have overall low church attendances, and Table 8.3 helps to confirm this by revealing that few of the rapidly growing industrial towns had church attendances of over fifty per cent. Levels of observance in large towns over 100,000 population were especially low. Note that, in many of the industrial towns, Methodist attendances were much higher than those of the Church of England.

An interesting feature of Tables 8.2 and 8.3 is the evidence of Roman Catholicism contained in the 1851 religious census. Some areas had high percentages of Roman Catholic attendance, especially in Lancashire. In Liverpool and Wigan, Roman Catholic attendances were higher than the combined figures for Dissenters, and Roman Catholic attendances in Preston were almost double those of the Anglicans. In Manchester, nearly a quarter of those attending religious worship were Roman Catholics, and the percentages are high in other parts of the country – Newcastle-upon-Tyne in the North East, Walsall in the Midlands, and Newport in South Wales. In Scotland, approximately 7 per cent of church attenders in Glasgow recorded in the census were Roman Catholics (Best, 1979, p.215).

In fact, the number of Roman Catholics was growing rapidly in the first half of the century. It has been estimated that in England and Wales the Catholic community increased from approximately 70,000 in 1780 to 900,000 in 1851. This was due to general population growth, successful missionary work among the English and, of course, Irish immigration, especially during the 1840s (Gilbert, 1976, p.46).

Returning to the general issue of church attendance in urban areas, studies of the 1851 returns point to lower levels of attendance in large towns over 50,000, and especially those over 100,000 population. Callum Brown (1988, pp.1–14), reviewing the returns for England and Scotland, acknowledges that the mushroom growth of some towns during the Industrial Revolution found existing religious provision gravely wanting, but points to the galvanizing effect that such perceived failures commonly had on local institutions and individuals. Whether the resulting outburst of religious action – church building and restoration, free pews, workmen's services, music and spectacle in worship, Sunday and day schools, district home visiting schemes, missions in poor areas, and religious leadership in local government reform in fields like public health – had achieved much impact by 1851 is a question for your specific researches.

Local studies of the later nineteenth century repeatedly illustrate the formidable institutional provision and pervasive religious idiom of life in British towns and cities. The number, size, location and denomination of places of worship in 1851 and the status of the census signatory may all be clues to levels of activity amongst old-established agencies, to the presence of newer, smaller groupings (perhaps catering to immigrant groups now settling in the town), and to the ability of any of them to attract attendance from a majority of the population. We must ask not only what proportion of local people attended, but also what sort of worship it was. From the numerical basis of the census the investigation will then extend to the role of the religion in individual places and families.

An outstanding study of the place of religion in family and community is James Obelkevich's *Religion and rural society* (1976), based on research into South Lindsey, Lincolnshire, 1825–75. Although the setting is agricultural, the context is one of a breakdown in older patterns of mutual obligation and the emergence of deep social and class divisions. Obelkevich sees religious allegiance and styles as reflecting these changes. Thus, the gentry had 'an ex officio commitment to the Church of England'. The farmers included Anglicans but also Methodists and other Dissenters. Their support was vital to the fortunes of their denominations locally, providing leadership, funds and jobs for co-religionists. Craftsmen and shopkeepers were prominent in Dissent, providing lay preachers and stewards, renting pews in the chapels, asserting their independence and, especially in the case of the Primitive Methodists, injecting an element of radicalism. Labourers were identified with no one denomination, if any. Some turned with fervour to revivalist worship; some, because of their employment (for example, domestic service), had to adopt their employers' allegiances; and many were occasional or non-attenders, adhering rather to non-institutional superstitions and customs of their own.

A parallel approach can readily be taken in researching an urban area (McLeod, 1974). Similar determinants may apply. Although the element of religious choice was greater in certain urban settings, like suburbs and some industrial communities, social and economic pressures to conform could be strong. Take, for example, Edward Akroyd, the Halifax industrialist. He was brought up a Methodist. His father had built a Methodist New Connexion chapel and Sunday school near their Haley Hill mills. Yet by the 1850s and 60s the son was a staunch Anglican, going so far as to have the bodies of his parents exhumed from the chapel burial ground and transferred to his newly-built church (1856–9) of All Souls, Haley Hill. Such new churches (and many were built in this period) visually dominated the workplaces and homes of their builders' employees. Akroyd wanted 'every man, woman and child to feel that henceforth this is their church ... and above all to show that interest by regularly attending its ordinances' (*History of the firm of James Akroyd Ltd*, 1874, p.35).

The effects of commercial success, accompanying changes in lifestyle, social connections and political aspirations (he was elected MP for Halifax in 1865) contributed to Akroyd's switch to Anglicanism. By contrast, the other leading industrial family of Halifax, the Crossleys, remained firmly Congregationalist. However, they too built a church – Square Congregational church of 1855–7, with its 235-foot spire towering over the town centre. They allied themselves with local and national campaigns for equal rights for Dissenters – in voluntary school provision, in entry to universities, in local vestry government, over payment of church rates – and with this went identification with radical Liberal politics. Thus, religious adherence was an important part of broader patterns which encompassed employers and landowners, mill-workers and agricultural labourers alike. Worship, employment, housing, schooling, industrial and social discipline and voting behaviour were part of the same equation to be found in all types of communities.

Let us return to the religious census as a starting point for local studies. The original returns are in the Public Record Office at Kew, but the local studies libraries of most counties or large towns hold microfilms of this census alongside those of the population censuses. A number of printed editions of returns have also been published, which offer a useful introduction to work on this source. The form of a chapel return is illustrated in Figure 8.5, completed with the information for the Baptist chapel in the Oxfordshire village of Hook Norton. Anglican returns also asked when and how the church was consecrated, its endowment, and for post-1800 buildings how, by whom and at what cost it had been erected. A third type of form went to the Society of Friends (Quakers) asking for floor area and attendance, but only on 30 March.

How should the returns be analysed?

Some basic questions occur. How many people attended worship in Hook Norton on 30 March 1851 and what proportion of the population did they represent? This is worth investigating, but, because the returns record attendance at up to three services, a perennial problem arises of people who may have attended more than one service and therefore been counted more than once, either at the same or different places of worship. Horace Mann of the Census Office suggested four possible formulae for adjusting numbers for this factor. For his national figures he adopted that of counting the morning congregation plus half of that in the afternoon and one-third of that in the evening. Unfortunately, the census also shows that Anglican services were held principally in the mornings or occasionally afternoons, whilst the Nonconformists worshipped in the afternoons and chiefly in the evenings. To count only one-third of evening attendances by Dissenters therefore seriously underestimated their activity. Given that as historians we want to

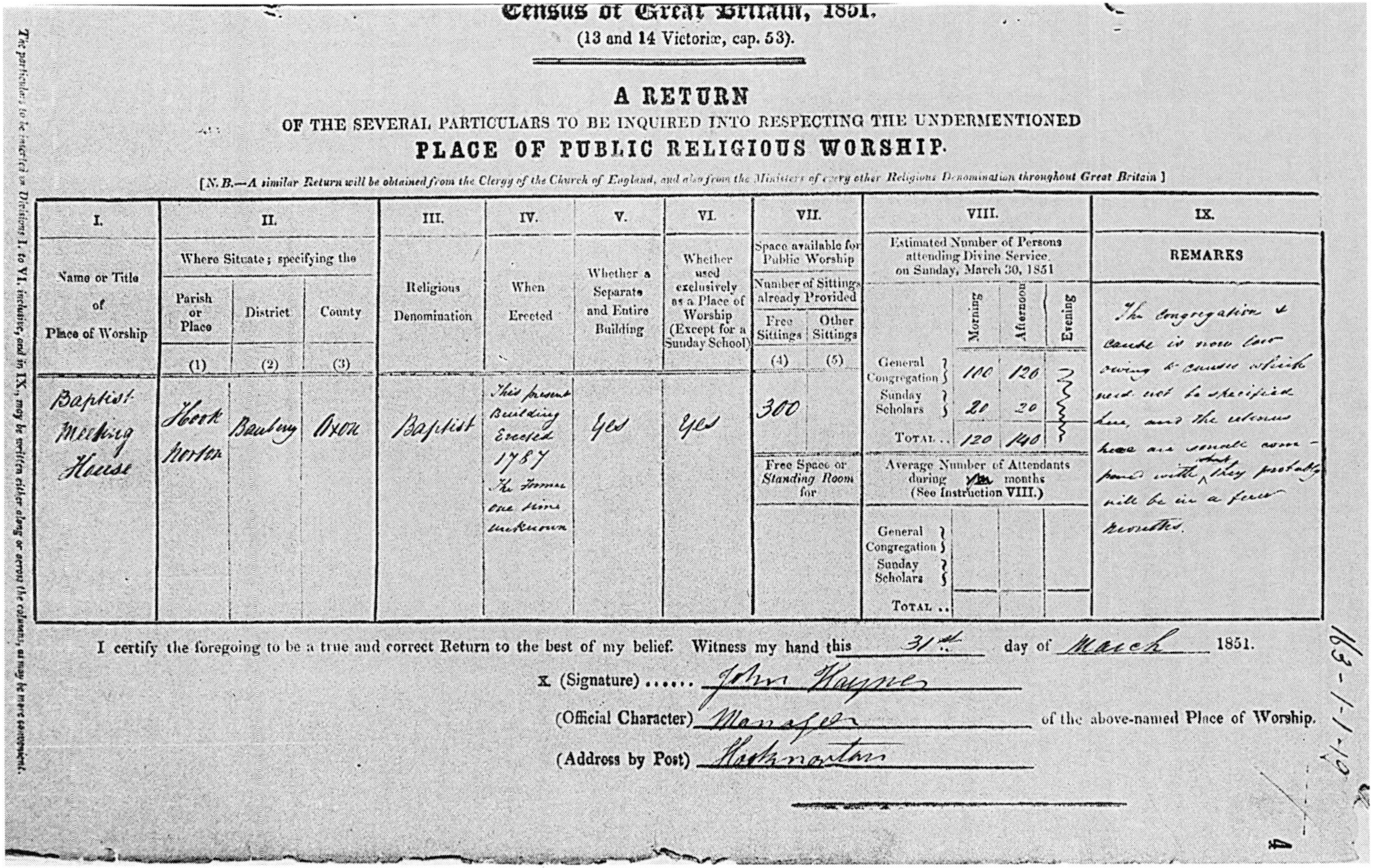

Census of Great Britain, 1851.

(13 and 14 Victoriæ, cap. 53).

A RETURN

OF THE SEVERAL PARTICULARS TO BE INQUIRED INTO RESPECTING THE UNDERMENTIONED

PLACE OF PUBLIC RELIGIOUS WORSHIP.

[*N.B.—A similar Return will be obtained from the Clergy of the Church of England, and also from the Ministers of every other Religious Denomination throughout Great Britain.*]

I. Name or Title of Place of Worship	II. Where Situate; specifying the Parish or Place (1)	District (2)	County (3)	III. Religious Denomination	IV. When Erected	V. Whether a Separate and Entire Building	VI. Whether used exclusively as a Place of Worship (Except for a Sunday School)	VII. Space available for Public Worship: Number of Sittings already Provided: Free Sittings (4)	Other Sittings (5)	VIII. Estimated Number of Persons attending Divine Service on Sunday, March 30, 1851	Morning	Afternoon	Evening	IX. REMARKS
Baptist Meeting House	Hook Norton	Banbury	Oxon	Baptist	This present Building Erected 1787 The Former one time unknown	Yes	Yes	300		General Congregation	100	120		The Congregation & cause is now low owing to causes which need not be specified here, and the returns here are small compared with what they probably will be in a few months.
										Sunday Scholars	20	20		
										TOTAL	120	140		
								Free Space or Standing Room for		Average Number of Attendants during months (See Instruction VIII.)				
										General Congregation				
										Sunday Scholars				
										TOTAL				

I certify the foregoing to be a true and correct Return to the best of my belief. Witness my hand this 31st day of March 1851.

X. (Signature) …… John Haynes

(Official Character) Manager of the above-named Place of Worship.

(Address by Post) Hooknorton

The particulars to be inserted in Divisions I. to VI. inclusive, and in IX., may be written either along or across the columns, as may be more convenient.

163-1-1-10

4

Figure 8.5 Example of a chapel return for Hook Norton Baptist Chapel, census of religious worship, 1851. (Note: the entry in the 'remarks' column reads, 'The congregation and cause is now low owing to causes which need not be specified here, and the returns here are small compared with what they probably will be in a few months.') (Source: Public Record Office) assess the extent of religious activity and enthusiasm between and within different denominations and places, and that to attend two or three times was undoubtedly a mark of support, it is suggested that the most reasonable basis for analysis is to take the total attendance at all services on census day for each and for all denominations. These totals may then be expressed as percentages of total local population (recorded in the 1851 population census) and as an index of attendance (IA). The total for each denomination can also be calculated as a percentage share (PS) of total attendances, as can the number of sittings for each group. Let us try this with an actual example. The raw data for Hook Norton's five denominations are displayed in Table 8.4.

Table 8.4 Church and chapel in Hook Norton*, census of religious worship, 1851

Denomination	Date building erected	No. of sittings	Attendance (General congregation plus Sunday scholars)			Return made by
			Morn.	Aft.	Eve.	
Church of England	Before 1800	365	160 _92_ 252	277 _98_ 375	–	Rev. J.R. Rushton, Perpetual Curate, Hook Norton
Quaker	Before 1800	120	11	–	–	William Minchin, Hook Norton
Baptist	1787	300	100 _20_ 120	120 _20_ 140	–	John Haynes, Manager, Hook Norton
Wesleyan Methodist	1813	260	–	100 _74_ 174	160	Samuel Cooke, Minister, Chipping Norton
Primitive Methodist	1826	100	60	–	100	Charles Waters, Minister

* Note: In 1851, the population of Hook Norton was 1,496.

Following the above processes, percentage shares of both sittings and attendance have been calculated and the results expressed in two pie diagrams (see Figure 8.6). The relative size of the circles shows that there were more sittings available than were filled on census day but that in terms of actual attenders the Parish Church succeeded best in obtaining congregations. The

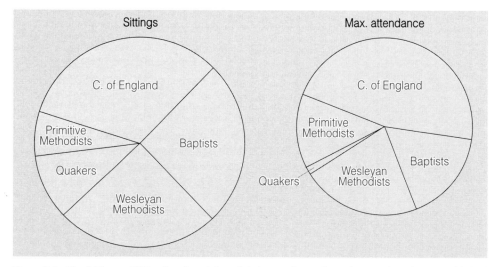

Figure 8.6 Hook Norton 1851 – church and chapel sittings and attendance (Source: based on unpublished research by the author)

Baptist share of attendances and the special pleading on their census return (see Figure 8.5) suggest current troubles, whilst the Quakers' numerical weakness foreshadows their local demise, confirmed from the directories.

Although worshippers' names are unknown, the identity and status of the signatories of returns is worth noting and following up – in directories, census enumerators' books and denominational records. Similarly, the links between the religious structures of the local community and other aspects of its life should be pursued. The number of places of worship in Hook Norton, the size of the village, the number and kind of people and economic activities recorded in contemporary directories, and the strong and lasting local alignments (Tory–brewing–Anglican and Liberal–Baptist) revealed by oral history, all point to an open village structure.

One of the easiest ways to place the detailed snapshot of the 1851 census return in the necessary broader context is to use local directory entries.

COMMERCIAL DIRECTORIES

By the 1830s, directories were being published not just for cities and larger towns but also small towns and villages (see Volume 4, Chapter 4, section 1). A directory entry will typically include a 'potted' history of a place, giving the age of any Anglican church(es), the ownership and value of its living and possibly the value of tithes, major families with whom the church was associated, and the identity of the incumbent. Clues to the strength of the clerical presence will be provided in the list of residents. Did the Rector or Vicar actually live in the parish? Was there a curate or curates? There may have been no Anglican presence at all. Such negative evidence is valuable in itself, for the Church in the early nineteenth century did not have churches, clergy and parish structures in many areas developing away from traditional centres of population or organization. Successive directories may plot the reinvigoration of Anglican organization, either as existing parishes were manned by resident clergy, parsonages built and church buildings restored, or as new parishes were carved out of old, and extra parish or district and mission churches erected.

Alongside this information will be descriptions of the places of worship and activities of other denominations. For example, we learn from Robert Gardner's *History, gazetteer and directory of the county of Oxford* (1852, pp.849–52) that the village of Hook Norton had a '*Baptist Chapel* ... a neat structure, erected by subscription, and endowed with about £50 per annum. It will afford accommodation to about 400 persons, and there are Sunday schools attached to it. The *Wesleyan Chapel* is a good stone building, which will seat about 200 persons, there is also a *Primitive Methodist Chapel*, and a *Friends Meeting House*'. Here both 'Old' and 'New' Dissent were well represented. The Baptist endowment suggests firm, long-term support. Other details worth looking for are mentions of Dissenting or Roman Catholic clergy. Did they exist? Were local Dissenters still reliant on their own lay preachers rather than formally trained clergy? Was the local chapel part of a wider area association or circuit, linking it to city centre or neighbouring town? Did any preachers or ministers make it into the Gentry or Private Residents section of the directory? Or did they appear elsewhere with other employment?

The usefulness of directories is not confined to overtly religious references. Look for information on the panoply of related provisions, especially educational. In 1852 at Hook Norton we find the '*National School* [Anglican] for girls, and the *British School* [Dissenting] ... supported by subscription'. There are also details of various charities, including £11.10s per annum from the Bishop of Oxford to be 'expended upon the poor', Calcott's charity for a Christmas Day sermon followed by distribution of funds 'with the sacrament money to the poor of the parish', and a bequest of 1810 in support of the Sunday school. How might these have affected attitudes to organized religion, not least attendance at Christmas communion?

Finally, in appraising a directory entry remember that the names of individual residents, industrialists, farmers, craftsmen, tradesmen or office holders may fall into place as you explore other sources. For example, at Hook Norton in 1852, one Daniel Warmington is described as 'grocer, draper, tea dealer, and tailor, auctioneer and appraiser, and agent to the Dissenters and General Fire and Life Office, and sub-postmaster'. This and other names from the directory turn up in surviving records of Hook Norton Baptist chapel and the information from the directory helps us to locate them in the overall structure of the local community. Urban directories often give addresses, offering a more precise social geography of identified religious activists.

A great strength of nineteenth- and twentieth-century directories is that they were published at intervals throughout the period. Thus, they may and should be used not just for the analysis of individual entries but comparatively over time. Table 8.5 shows the result of such an exercise for Hook Norton.

Table 8.5 The evidence of directories: organized religion in Hook Norton, 1830–1939

	1830	1844	1852	1864	1876	1887	1895	1915	1939
Church of England	X	X	X	X	X	X	X	X	X
Quaker		X	X	X	X	X			X
Baptist	X	X	X	X	X	X	X	X	X
Wesleyan Methodist	X	X	X	X	X	X	X	X	X
Primitive Methodist			X	X	X	X	X	X	
Strict Baptist/ Calvinist								X	X
Roman Catholic									X

Note: X = entry found in directory.

Anglicanism had a constant presence. The church, which contains Norman fabric, underwent extensive restoration in 1845 during the incumbency of the Reverend J.R. Rushton, who died in 1881 after 40 years as rector. The National School was built in 1855. Old Dissent is represented most strongly by the Baptists, whose chapel was of exceptionally early foundation, 1644. Their present chapel building dates from 1787. They too were building in the nineteenth century, with a Gothic schoolroom of 1873. The third continuous element is Wesleyan Methodism. It was the first such denomination to become established. In 1794 worship took place in a private house, and in 1851 in a chapel built in 1813. In 1875 the Wesleyans built a large, architect-designed chapel, with adjoining vestries and schoolroom, and capable of holding over 400 people. Interestingly, the style chosen was Early English Gothic, an architecture of more established churches.

Other bodies came and went. From Old Dissent the Quakers dwindled into disappearance after 1887. The more radical face of New Dissent, Primitive Methodism, is mentioned in 1852, fifty years after its foundation, and supported a separate chapel for almost seventy years. The schismatic nature of Nonconformity is also shown by the emergence of Zion Strict Baptist chapel. This sternly Calvinistic gathering tolerated no music in its worship. Only after the First World War did Roman Catholicism appear when the chapel of St Theresa of Lisieux, formerly a Primitive Methodist chapel, opened in 1921.

A very different religious option of the same period, unrecorded by the directories but recalled locally, was represented by 'The Barracks', bringing the missionary revivalism of the Salvation Army to the village.

--------- *QUESTION FOR RESEARCH* ---------

The Hook Norton study suggests that you could attempt a similar one dealing with your own particular area by using the religious census of 1851 and local directories as starting points. Clearly, there are some basic questions you can ask. How many people attended places of worship in your locality? What proportion of the population did they represent? How many places of worship were there in the area at different times during the nineteenth century? How do you account for the distinctive religious patterns in your locality? Were economic and geographic factors prominent? Was your settlement open or closed? Also, try to relate your evidence to the more general hypotheses which have been raised. For example, the larger the settlement, the greater the diversity of places of worship; and the larger the settlement, the lower the levels of observance.

Overall, the trend between *c.*1850 and *c.*1918 is that of the establishment and formalization of greater religious diversity. The pattern persisted into the inter-war period but is increasingly hard to discern today. The consolidation of formal religion is clearly expressed in a third major source of local evidence – church and chapel buildings.

BUILDINGS

Everywhere in nineteenth-century Britain new churches and chapels were being built and existing places of worship restored or extended. The many surviving buildings have much to tell family and community historians about the influence of religion past and present. For example, in Hook Norton in the 1980s, the Baptist congregation witnessed a new cycle of fundamentalist revivalism, sweeping away the eighteenth-century box pews arranged for the hearing and seeing of the preaching of the Word in search of a more participatory and expressionist worship. The dwindling fortunes of the Wesleyan Methodists led to the demolition of their chapel, so confidently constructed only a century before, and the development of the site for housing. Elsewhere churches and chapels have passed to other faiths, been turned into garages or shops, or simply decayed. Those doing local research can not only learn much but also contribute to the historical record by recording these threatened buildings (Council for British Archaeology, 1985).

Nineteenth-century ecclesiastical buildings represent very substantial investments of money and time, either by patrons seeking to establish the institutional fixed capital of a local community or by local activists providing their own focus of worship and social activity. Apart from parliamentary grants for church building in 1818 and 1824, state funding was not a factor. It is therefore important to find out from where the resources for local buildings were drawn.

New Anglican buildings varied from elaborate Gothic to the corrugated iron of prefabricated mission churches. Their style and furnishing may well be revealing. For example, the newly developed working-class suburb of Jericho in Oxford had no parish structure or church of its own until the consecration of St Barnabas in 1869. The dedication to St Barnabas, an early Christian martyr, was a favourite of the High Church Oxford Movement and signalled a particular style of ministry. The architecture chosen was that of an early Christian basilica, a conscious counter to current assumptions that Gothic was the correct style for Anglican worship. A plain, rendered exterior masked a richly decorated interior, the main body of the church being wide and open to give uninterrupted views of the true focus of the High Church liturgy – the mass performed in the apsidal chancel, lined with golded mosaics and dominated by a great suspended cross. Here the rituals associated with Tractarian worship – crucifixes, candles, vestments, statues of saints, reservation of the sacrament, processions, the use of incense, the hearing of confession – could find full expression.

If the sacramental and symbolic aspects of religion dominated the High Church experience, the other buildings of St Barnabas also demonstrated all the vigorous interventionism of many Victorian parishes, with a new vicarage, church day and Sunday schools, a parish hall and institute, drum and fife band, football team, women's guilds, winter lectures and summer excursions, all aimed at redeeming a rough neighbourhood. Jericho today is still visually dominated by the campanile of St Barnabas's church. Here and elsewhere, a local church's name, architectural style, continuing liturgy and the range of other buildings associated with its work offer vital clues to understanding the role of religion, both past and present, in a community.

Very many Anglican churches were restored rather than built afresh in the nineteenth century. This reflects the physical as well as spiritual neglect of the previous century, but also positive policies to make worship more accessible. The interiors of many medieval churches were turned around to produce layouts concentrating on the nave rather than the chancel, and on preaching rather than the sacraments. Galleries and pews were focused on the pulpit in the nave. Victorian restorations frequently reinstated the chancel in importance, reflecting more frequent communion services and the need to accommodate an organ and surpliced choir as aesthetic and musical forces were harnessed to winning congregations and enriching the experience of worship. Churches were re-pewed and re-floored, producing more free rather than rented seats and allowing the installation of effective heating systems. Practical and spiritual considerations were thus combined.

Dissenting chapels were also being built or altered. Through this the local historian may trace a congregation's development. Early meetings in dwelling houses may be recorded in the granting of Quarter Sessions licences for meeting houses. To progress to a purpose-built chapel was a sign of local strength. The location of the chapel (traced on the ground or from maps,

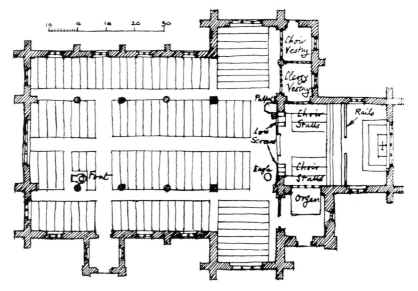

Figure 8.7 A typical Anglican Victorian church. The plan does not represent any particular building, but may be taken as a fairly good example of about 1870, by one of the minor architects of the period. The nave and chancel are somewhat wider than would normally be the case in a medieval building, and the chancel is relatively shallow, being in fact the eighteenth-century altar recess enlarged to accommodate the intruded choir stalls. Pews fill the building to the utmost possible extent; the organ occupies what would have been a chapel or chantry in a medieval church (Source: Addleshaw and Etchells, 1948)

especially early edition 6-inch and 25-inch Ordnance Survey sheets) may be important. Some chapels stand in no-man's-land between settlements, possibly indicating that their congregations were gathered from a surrounding area and/or that they could not gain a site elsewhere because of opposition. Other chapels are in peripheral positions. Did they have to buy land or were they given it? The foundation or dedication stones of chapels will provide clues to their sources of support. Architectural style will relate to how much they had to spend and their desire either to emulate or be different from other churches architecturally. The layout of interiors will express particular religious beliefs – the primary emphasis on the preaching of the Word and the central placing of the pulpit, the relative importance of clergy or elders or the general congregation, or (for the Baptists) adult baptism, using a sunken baptistry within the chapel. As with Anglican and Roman Catholic churches, the search should extend to associated buildings – manse, day or Sunday school, and meeting rooms.

Do not forget the burial grounds linked to churches and chapels. The dates, inscriptions, style and groupings of gravestones are well worth recording. For example, a graveyard survey of Hook Norton Baptist chapel yard revealed 75 stones, some as early as 1719, confirming that the earlier chapel endowed by William Harwood in 1718 had stood on the same site as the current building of 1787. Almost a third of the pre-1800 stones (ten out of 34) record non-Hook Norton families. It seems this was still a congregation gathering members from a wider area. In the nineteenth century, the stones record more local support (four 'outsiders' out of 34, with two of uncertain date), presumably because more chapels were opening elsewhere (see Tiller, 1982).

LOCAL NEWSPAPERS

Religion as a focus of conflict comes over clearly in a fourth and final principal source for research. During the nineteenth century, local newspapers multiplied in number and increased their range and purely local, as opposed to repeated national, coverage (see Volume 4, Chapter 4, section 7). This boom in the local press was particularly marked from the 1850s, so that cities and market towns (and, to a lesser extent, rural areas) will have detailed coverage of local life, both rough and respectable.

In Wigan (Lancashire) local newspapers reveal vividly conflicts apparently centred on religion (Tiller, 1975). Here popular Protestantism and Irish Catholicism provided dominant community alignments. There had been an Irish population before the post-Famine influxes of the 1840s. Church and King popular Toryism of the 1790s coalesced with Orangeism to such a degree as to outweigh class-based Chartism as the popular political cause of the town in the 1830s and 1840s. The resulting Tory Protestantism made every election a flashpoint into the 1870s. Religious labels provided regular and potent slogans in what was in fact an ethnic question, involving a heady mix of nationality, religion, cultural differences, politics and economic interest (the Irish were associated with low wages and strike-breaking). The principal male workforce of Wigan, the colliers, were more than most resistant to the appeals of respectable, organized religion, yet they became a regular part of the fiercely sectarian anti-Irish alignment in the town. The pages of the *Wigan Observer* and *Wigan Times* do contain the religious rhetoric of the respectable working class, like Thomas Halliday who in 1864 urged the Wigan miners to remember that 'in this the nineteenth century the working classes had become convinced that there were blessings in the storehouse of God for them equally as for the rich' (*Wigan Observer*, 16 July 1864). But the typical tone was otherwise. When a speaker at the first Wigan Chartist meeting in July 1839 mentioned the clergy as part of the propertied class robbing the people the meeting was broken up by the deliberate ringing of the bells of the parish church, which overlooked the Market Place. It was the Wigan Operative Conservatives who organized this opposition. Allied with local branches of the Orange Order, anti-Popery was their constant theme. During the 1852 general election campaign an Operative Conservatives' dinner heard this speech (which was reported in the *Wigan Times*):

> *They must return men who would pledge themselves not to yield any further concession to the Pope of Rome. There was a time when we could boast of being a Protestant nation, and then it was that God rewarded our national fidelity with national peace, happiness and prosperity. But when the government of this country became degenerated, and virtually proclaimed themselves to be a joint stock company for the propagation of Popery by the passing of the Emancipation Act of 1829, the annihilation of ten bishoprics in Ireland, the endowment of Godless colleges, the grant to Maynooth, and the endowment of the Roman Catholic priesthood to preach sedition, conspiracy and rebellion – when the government did this, then God sent amongst them the plague, pestilence and famine.*

(Broadside Collection, Wigan Reference Library, p.17)

Following the voting, at which a Liberal narrowly topped the poll, John Blinkhorn, a clogger who had led the Operative Conservatives against the Chartists in 1839, marched a brass band through the middle of Scholes, where many of the Irish of the town lived, playing the Orange air 'Boyne Water' in an 'ostentatious and triumphant' manner. Under this provocation the Roman Catholic Irish turned out, flinging bricks and stones, particularly in neighbouring streets where many colliers 'nearly all Protestants and many Orangemen' lived. The mayor with only 26 police swore in specials on all sides, including many colliers. The Riot Act was read and troops summoned by train from Preston. One hundred and three arrests were made. Blinkhorn was imprisoned but returned to be fêted on his release and to be a leading member of the Ancient Loyal Orange Institution in the 1860s. The primal solidarities uncovered on such occasions persisted not just in churches attacked or pubs stoned, but in opposing networks of defence associations, friendly societies, tea parties, seaside excursions and, perhaps most lasting of all, rival denominational school systems.

All of this, the events and activities, the organizations, the verbatim speeches, the irate letters in correspondence columns, and the court reports appear in the columns of the local press, making it an unrivalled source. So too does ample evidence of how impervious some working-class people were to pleas to ally themselves with respectable religion. If appeals were as inept as that delivered at St Thomas's Anglican church in 1859 condemning the theatre, dancing saloons, drunkenness and revelry and proposing concerts, cricket and fox-hunting, this was hardly surprising. Indeed, the columns are full of rich details (if disapprovingly reported) of the alternative culture, of betting, disorderly houses, and such 'irrational' entertainments as the annual fair with stalls providing 'dubious foods' (pea soup, black puddings and ginger bread), rifle and shooting galleries, an infant Hercules and the 'Wild Woman of the Black Rock'. There were dog fights, whippet racing and even lark-singing matches. Less appealing was the widespread drunkenness and violence, including brutal 'purring' or kicking matches.

Local papers may be used with relish but also with caution. They present many alluring sidetracks which need to be resisted, and the often blatant partisanship of their reporting needs to be identified.

QUESTION FOR RESEARCH

Select a local newspaper or newspapers for one particular year (it would be sensible to choose a year which coincided with the publication of a local directory) and note the extent and range of the activities associated with local churches within your area. (If time is short, select particular months within the year). Remember, local newspapers often have strong political and Anglican or Dissenting leanings, so, if there is more than one local paper, note the differences in items reported.

1.3 RELIGION AFTER 1850

Did religion in late nineteenth-century Britain take on a new, secularized form? Along with many changes in work practices and leisure activities (see Chapters 1 and 9 of this volume), many aspects of local life were affected by legislative reforms based on Benthamite Utilitarianism. This notion of political economy posited that human actions were based on a principle of utility. People made individual choices on the basis of how much pain or pleasure would result for themselves. Each individual would act on the basis of enlightened self-interest. The severely rational, self-confident reformers of this school will be encountered in most nineteenth-century communities, concerned with everything from poor relief to public health, working conditions, charity administration, and improving education. Alongside them were Christian activists, both Anglican and Nonconformist. The result often seems to be the amalgamation of elements of both approaches, even in the same individuals. As the twentieth-century novelist J.G. Farrell sums up the credo of one of his characters, a harbinger of British values to imperial India:

I believe that we are all part of a society which by its communal efforts of faith and reason is gradually raising itself to a higher state ... There are laws of morality to be followed if we are to advance, just as there are rules of scientific investigation ... The foundations on which the new men will build their lives are Faith, Science, Respectability, Geology, Mechanical Invention, Ventilation and Rotation of Crops.

(Farrell, 1973, p.82)

Not surprisingly, some see in the Victorian period the emergence of a new religion – that of progress. Others point to a crisis of faith.

Were the early functions of religion as a response to change – radicalizer, provider of refuge, or imposer of social control – superseded after *c.*1850? Because of the uneven pace of technological advance and the actual implementation of available mechanization, local studies may reveal different patterns. Change could continue. New settlements were still being created and existing ones transformed. In the former category was the railway town of Wolverton in Buckinghamshire. Completing his 1851 religious census return the local Anglican clergyman wrote, 'In a great Railway Station like this, a strike – a quarrel – an increase or decrease of wages – will affect scores and hundreds of persons, so that no certainty exists here. This place too, is inhabited by men of various Countries – men of all habits and opinions – and (*here is the mischief*) Men forever on the move' (Legg, 1991, pp.129–30). Here there was no 'community' and the role of organized religion was unclear. Yet in such unsettled voids religion could still be the formative factor in creating community. In the Deerness Valley of County Durham, coal workings were opened up only from the 1850s. Associated settlements swiftly grew from nothing, at first consisting only of utilitarian terraced housing occupied by immigrant labour working in the mines. Soon each place – East Hedley Hope, Waterhouses, Quebec-Hamsteels, Esh Winning and Cornsay Colliery – had its chapel or chapels, with Methodism, Wesleyan and Primitive, earliest and strongest. There were pubs, schools, Co-op shops, reading rooms and miners' institutes, cricket, football, horticultural societies, leek growing, pigeon and rabbit raising. Some of this fixed capital of community, like the school at Waterhouses, was provided by the mine owners, but Robert Moore in his *Pit-men, preachers and politics* (1974) identifies the communal values imbued by Methodism as the key factor. The villages saw their heyday between 1880 and 1920. They generated their own way of life remarkably quickly, largely because Methodism was not just a religious affiliation limited to formal membership of one denomination but a pervasive source of activities, leadership and generally accepted values. It provided a community consensus, despite the presence of other Christian denominations and despite the inequalities of employer and employed.

This ethical and individual view of the world dominated any political or economic view. It was a world of saved and unsaved rather than of employer and employed. A belief in the equality of men before God served to defuse resentment, at least while relative prosperity lasted. The Methodists provided leadership in the villages, in politics, industrial bargaining and in social mores until the economic fortunes of the coalfield began to falter. Then conflicts of economic interest became undeniable and could no longer be negotiated away as misunderstandings or temporary imbalances in market forces, equally regretted by mutually respecting Liberal Methodist working-class leaders and locally known employers. The 1920s saw prolonged and bitter strikes over wage cuts.

At East Hedley Hope the pit closed in 1936, and finally, after reworking, in 1945. In 1962 the school was demolished, as Chapel Row terrace had been in 1952. In 1963 the Miners' Institute shut, in 1966 the Wesleyan Methodist chapel closed, as had the railway, to be followed by the local post office in the 1970s. In 1911, 808 people lived there in 109 houses; by 1984 there were 91 in 45 houses. The same fate overtook other villages, and the scars of the workings are now planted over in an apparent reversion to ruralism. As Ken Clark (1987, p.104) has written of Esh Winning, '[the colliery] closed in 1968, dying like an aged parent, leaving its mature offspring, the village, to survive on whatever scraps of industry might fall its way'. The Esh Winning Lodge banner of the miners' union made its last appearance at the Durham gala of 1969. On its reverse side was the motto 'All Men are Brethren' and below that a picture of a miner shaking hands with a tail-coated owner. Above and behind this an angel carried a ribbon emblazoned 'Let Us Work Together'. This summed up the character of a settlement created by one kind of work but made into a community chiefly by Methodism.

Wolverton and Esh Winning are examples of new places emerging after 1850. Local studies may also reveal long-established communities subject to continuing change and dislocation. If urban life, now the experience of the majority, was becoming relatively prosperous, then agricultural districts were suffering, from the mid-1870s, a deep and prolonged depression. Flora Thompson's recollections of Cottisford parish in the 1880s again provide helpful insights. Flora attended Anglican Sunday morning service. It was, as Obelkevich shows, the pre-eminent ritual of social stability (1976, pp.143–58), the seating pattern encapsulating traditional social structures:

> The Squire's and clergyman's families had pews in the chancel, with backs to the wall on either side, and between them stood two long benches for the school-children, well under the eyes of authority. Below the steps down into the nave stood the harmonium, played by the clergyman's daughter, and round it was ranged the choir of small school-girls. Then came the rank and file of the congregation, nicely graded, with the farmer's family in the front row, then the Squire's gardener and coachman, the schoolmistress, the maidservants, and the cottagers, with the Parish Clerk at the back to keep order.
>
> (Thompson, 1945, pp.206–7; for further comment on a church seating plan, see Kitchen, 1993)

Flora Thompson summed up the people's attachment to the Church of England as follows:

> If the Lark Rise people had been asked their religion, the answer of nine out of ten would have been 'Church of England', for practically all of them were christened, married, and buried as such, although, in adult life, few went to church between the baptisms of their offspring. The children were shepherded there after Sunday school and about a dozen of their elders attended regularly; the rest stayed at home, the women cooking and nursing, and the men, after an elaborate Sunday toilet, which included shaving and cutting each other's hair and much puffing and splashing with buckets of water, but stopped short before lacing up boots or putting on a collar and tie, spent the rest of the day eating, sleeping, reading the newspaper, and strolling round to see how their neighbours' pigs and gardens were looking.
>
> (Thompson, 1945, p.205)

Congregations do seem to have been heavily unbalanced by social class (higher social classes and their dependents), by age (the old and especially the young, upon whom so many resources were concentrated by organized religion and who seemed to have fulfilled a function of proxy observance for some parents), and by gender (with more female attenders).

The other formal religious option in Cottisford parish was to attend Wesleyan Methodist services. Flora and her brother, bored by Sunday in a respectable working-class family household and having attended the Anglican morning service, would sometimes escape to a very different, entertaining and intriguing religious world. The meeting was held in the main living room of a local cottage, with whitewashed walls, lamp-lit, an open fire, cleared of everyday furniture except for the clock and a pair of red china dogs on the mantelpiece. The congregation were greeted by the householder with a handshake and a 'God bless you', sat down on scrubbed wooden benches, sang Sankey and Moody hymns unaccompanied, heard extempore and direct conversations with God – calling for rain or deliverance of a pig from disease. This direct, individual communication with the deity was at the heart of the religious experience. Flora, who thought God would know all these things already, found it unsophisticated, entertaining, and yet as a spectacle less impressive than the Anglican rituals of the morning. The high point was the arrival of the preacher, a layman, who had often walked miles. These men ranged from impressive sincerity and eloquence to stumbling but also sincere inarticulacy. Some were self-seeking poseurs (where else perhaps could the shop assistant with a bunch of violets in his buttonhole get a hearing?). Yet Flora's final conclusion on Methodism in Cottisford is clear and revealing of the very different functions Dissent of this kind fulfilled as opposed to Anglicanism:

> *Methodism, as known and practised there, was a poor people's religion, simple and crude; but its adherents brought to it more fervour than was shown by the church congregation, and appeared to obtain more comfort and support from it than the church could give. Their lives were exemplary.*

> (Thompson, 1945, p. 215)

Here Methodism had never attained the wealth and security to permit the building of a chapel, yet, despite or perhaps because of that, it clearly retained the sort of appeal associated by some historians with the movement's earlier years.

Flora's practice of going to one denomination in the morning and another in the evening was by no means unusual. But many villagers had no strong commitment to organized religion. The 1851 religious census indicates that 48 per cent of people in Cottisford parish did not go to Church or Dissenting meeting at that time. Flora Thompson comments of their successors:

> *Many in the hamlet who attended neither church nor chapel and said they had no use for religion, guided their lives by the light of a few homely precepts, such as 'Pay your way and fear nobody'; 'Right's right and wrong's no man's right'; 'Tell the truth and shame the devil', and 'Honesty is the best policy'.*

> (Thompson, 1945, p.215)

Honesty, telling the truth, mutual help in adversity, and a degree of sharpness and criticism of anyone getting above, or breaking with, the common experience – these were the features of a strong moral code. This 'popular religion' was a loose combination of unofficial Christianity and large elements of superstition and custom, selectively validated by institutional religion. This occasional and instrumental use of formal religion accompanied by a distinct, independent and stern morality of their own has also been observed in urban, working-class communities.

Town dwellers could be exposed as much or more to proselytizing and good works, but community studies show the strengths of an indigenous code. Robert Roberts (1971), writing of Salford in the early twentieth century, and Elizabeth Roberts (1984), in her study of Preston and

Barrow-in-Furness between 1890 and 1940, both illustrate this. Elizabeth Roberts describes a world in which women were decidedly unequal in the public sphere, in law, politics, employment and pay, but were at the centre of individual households, streets and whole neighbourhoods. They held sway in managing family budgets, in raising children, and in operating a strict code of community behaviour. She found that this distinct lifestyle centred on a 'universal social norm of respectability' with roots in a pragmatic, broadly Christian approach to life. There was New Testament neighbourliness alongside Old Testament justice and punishment; there was rejection of stealing, swearing and adultery; there was suppression of sexuality, there was belief in the saving properties of work and the damning consequences of idleness; and there was the discipline of punctuality, obedience, and a Methodist emphasis on 'cleanliness is next to godliness'. In some households a strong element of class consciousness and political activism came into play. No community is monolithic. There were the dictatorial husbands and fathers, whose womenfolk were allowed little role; there were the homes where drink diluted conformity; there were the graduations within and on the bounds of the working class, of the skilled, semi-skilled and unskilled, and of the shopkeepers. Yet despite these variations, life in the industrial, urban working-class neighbourhoods, which were now the majority experience in England, had the kind of distinct character seen in Preston. It was strongly local in feeling, influenced by 'outside' factors like Board of Health by-laws, or the fortunes of the textile industry, yet by the late nineteenth century stable and stubborn in its self-generating lifestyle. These old working-class social patterns have been slow to change. Elizabeth Roberts believes they only did so after the Second World War.

As we have seen, religion in the late nineteenth century could still have the edge and fervour of earlier evangelicalism. This occurred particularly where major economic, social and physical change for families and communities continued. It was also experienced amongst groups which were part of a continuing cycle of revivalism, often rooted in dissatisfaction with the perceived aberrations, complacency, lack of truth, or unsatisfactory government of the 'parent' body. Schism was a regular part of the religious scene. Primitive Methodism is the 'break-away' most likely to be encountered, and it continued to be associated with radicalism and independence. The Salvation Army, founded in 1865, and proselytizing militantly a gospel of 'Blood and Fire', was another late manifestation of religious revival. Meanwhile, the numbers of Roman Catholics grew steadily. It has been estimated that by the end of the century in England and Wales there were 1.5 million Roman Catholics of whom around just under three-quarters of a million attended mass in 1891 (Gilbert, 1976, p.46).

Having acknowledged these possible sources of variation in local experience it remains the case that after c.1850 religion appears everywhere as the dominant medium for creating a common culture. Religious rhetoric may mask wider concerns. It was inextricably associated with secularized creeds of respectability and progress. The typical alignments which reflect this interplay between the religious and the secular might be summed up as follows:

Anglican	Nonconformist
Conservative/Whig	Liberal
Landowning/some industrial employers	Radical/Lib-Lab
Anti-Papist	Roman Catholic
Anti-Irish	Industrial/middle class
Pro-Establishment of English and Irish Churches	Organized labour Irish disestablishment
National Society schools	British Society schools
Anglican Sunday schools	Dissenting Sunday schools
Drink interest	Temperance Voluntaryism

Beyond this were those who rejected or were simply impervious to the forces of organized religion – some amongst the unreformed upper classes, some amongst a middle-class intellectual élite, but most amongst the working classes. Here two alternative cultures of rough and respectable may be in evidence.

───────────────── **QUESTIONS FOR RESEARCH** ─────────────────

One method of exploring whether religion after 1850 took on a new secularized form would be to extend the approach taken in the previous Question for Research (at the end of section 1.2, p.176) and examine local newspapers for a later year and compare the extent of involvement of the local churches in local affairs.

Besides the four key sources already mentioned, the following can also be useful: records of Established Churches (archdeacons' and bishops' visitation returns and correspondence, parish magazines, parish registers); Nonconformist records (registers, rules, minutes, membership lists); photographs; oral history; written personal testimonies; literature (Anthony Trollope, George Eliot, Mark Rutherford, Edmund Gosse, Mrs Oliphant and many others); ephemera (posters, orders of service, pamphlets, temperance ribbons, membership tickets, Sunday school prizes). For further comments on sources on religion, see Wolffe and Golby, 1993.

1.4   CONCLUSION

The codes of 'secularized' religion and of the indigenous working-class communities, developed in the nineteenth century, were potent and persistent forces. They set patterns which often dominated local experiences up to the Second World War. Only since then have these patterns unravelled as alternative and more individualist beliefs have developed and as functions formerly fulfilled by religion have been superseded. Charity, welfare provision, education, medicine and entertainment are all provided elsewhere than by church or chapel. Pluralism is no longer a matter of a diversity of Judao-Christian denominations. For the first time, immigrants from other cultures and younger generations of native British, whose parents were not products of that essentially nineteenth-century and largely religious mentality, are part of local families and communities. (For further reading on religion in nineteenth- and twentieth- century Britain, see Gilbert, 1976, 1980; Hastings, 1991; McLeod, 1984; Obelkevich, 1976; Stacey, 1960, 1975.)

2   RELIGIOUS PLURALISM IN TWENTIETH-CENTURY BRITAIN: SOME RESEARCH QUESTIONS ON HINDUISM, SIKHISM AND ISLAM

by Terry Thomas

After World War II, religious pluralism in Britain ceased to be just that of a Judaeo-Christian divide. The inward migration of peoples from other continents and countries has ensured that British religious society is more widely diverse than it has ever been.

This inward movement of peoples occurred partly because of economic and social reasons in the migrants' countries of origins, and partly because of the needs of an expanding British economy in the years following World War II. People of the 'New Commonwealth', including Indians and Pakistanis, migrated and settled down in many parts of Britain, and particularly in towns and cities. (For further discussion of migration see Volume 2, Part 1, especially Chapter 3.3 on the 'new British'; see also Chapter 3, section 3 in this volume).

2.1 PATTERNS OF MIGRATION

Three Asian states make up the locus of outward migration as far as this section is concerned. The three states were formerly the subcontinent of India. Following the transfer of power in 1947, two states were created, India and Pakistan. The division was based on an almost exclusive population of Muslims in Pakistan and an Indian state that was predominantly Hindu, but with a large Muslim minority. The Muslim state was made up of West and East Pakistan. West Pakistan consisted of those areas on the western and north-western edge of the old India. East Pakistan was more or less the area of old India known as East Bengal. The division saw a major disruption of peoples, with Sikhs and Hindus fleeing the new Pakistan and Muslims fleeing the new India. The movement of these refugees has itself been a motor of further migration.

Pakistan was thus made up of two major land areas – West and East Pakistan – which were divided by India. The population of the two parts consisted of very different ethnic groups. In 1972, the East seceded from Pakistan to form the new state of Bangladesh. The original two states, independent republics, chose to remain within the British Commonwealth as it was then known. It was this connection which dictated the focus of migration to Britain. The migrations occurred directly from India, Pakistan and Bangladesh or indirectly via East Africa, an area of earlier migration.

_____ *EXERCISE 8.2* _____

Clearly, the inward migration into the urban areas of Britain post World War II differs from the rapid growth in urban population in the nineteenth century. But from your reading of section 1 of this chapter, note down some major problems relating to religious observances which you think are likely to have confronted the early migrants from India, Pakistan and Bangladesh?

It was pointed out on page 167 that, in the early years of the nineteenth century, the existing religious provision was usually inadequate for the rapid shifts in population and emergence of new urban centres. However, although there was a time-lag, many new churches and chapels were built in the nineteenth century to cater for the increasingly urban population.

Stephen Barton (1986) in his study of Muslim migrants suggests there was a similar time-lag between the settling of the first migrants and the building of mosques. The first migrants were primarily males seeking work who lived in 'digs' or boarding houses and who showed little interest in religious matters. It was only from the 1960s on, when their families joined them in Britain, that Muslim religious life flowered in the new communities and that the building of mosques increased.

Table 8.6 Annual registration of mosques, 1966–1985

Year	No.	Year	No.
1966	5	1976	20
1967	4	1977	17
1968	9	1978	21
1969	7	1979	17
1970	11	1980	29
1971	8	1981	31
1972	8	1982	21
1973	8	1983	22
1974	8	1984	31
1975	18	1985	30

Source: Nielson (1987) p.387

_____ *EXERCISE 8.3* _____

Look at Table 8.6 and then refer back to pages 173–5 on church buildings. What questions could we ask about the building of mosques which would throw light on the activities of Muslims within the community?

The answers and discussion follow on below.

The discussion on pp.173–5 stressed the importance of discovering where the resources for church building came from. Virtually no money was made available from the government, but funds were donated by wealthy patrons, and groups within the community. In the case of some dissenting groups, their early meetings were held in houses, and 'progress to a purpose-built chapel was a sign of local strength'.

Again, similarities can be seen with the building of mosques. From the mid-1970s onwards, funds from Middle Eastern oil states were made available for the erection of some purpose-built mosques, often in city centres. However, the vast majority of mosques have come about through local initiatives, in which houses have been converted and sites purchased as money has become available.

Exercises 8.2 and 8.3 show how some questions raised about religion in the community in the nineteenth century can, if suitably adapted, also be relevant for the study of migrant communities in the twentieth century.

_____ *QUESTIONS FOR RESEARCH* _____

Refer back again to section 1 of this chapter and list possible questions which could be used as the starting points for local research projects.

I have come up with a number:

o   When was your local temple, gurdwara or mosque built?

o   Who was involved?

o   How was the money raised?

o   How has the religious network developed for the group you are studying?

o   To what extent are they involved in local politics and administration?

o   What are the range of their activities in the local community?

It would perhaps be unwise to embark upon such a project unless you already have some knowledge of the local and community aspects of one of these religions. If you do have some knowledge, you will probably already have some ideas about local sources. However, some possible sources include: personal memories; oral histories and interviews; audio-recordings; local newspapers, including the relevant specialist and vernacular press; records of local institutions and societies; autobiographies, reminiscences and diaries.

For background reading there is no shortage of material for the study of Hinduism, Sikhism and Islam. There is a whole range of publications from comprehensive encyclopaedias, through studies of individual religions, to monographs on detailed aspects of the religions. Studies such as those by Bhachu (1985), Nyrmla Singh (1985–6) and Kalsi (1992) on the development of Sikh communities in Britain suggest the kinds of questions that you could raise in your projects. If you require lists of caste members, a general source of information is The Inter Faith Network, 5/7 Tavistock Place, London, WC1 9SS, an organization which acts as a 'central information and contact point for people wanting information ... on inter faith affairs'.

3   RELIGION IN IRELAND

by Brenda Collins

One of the more striking features of contemporary Irish society is the strong role of Christian religion in everyday life. Levels of religious practice, as shown in church attendance of both Roman Catholics and Protestants, north and south, are high compared with general European standards. Religious practice is seen to regulate both the public and the private spheres of social behaviour. The origins of the importance of religious identity in Ireland lie in the various religious affiliations of successive groups of settlers in Ireland, particularly during the seventeenth century. The enactment in the eighteenth century of repressive penal laws which restricted the position of Roman Catholics led to the evolution of a religiously stratified social order. Religious differences became associated with social and economic divisions and have also found expression in the continuance of the nineteenth-century debate on Irish nationalism. Within Northern Ireland today, one outcome of this clear definition of boundaries between groups has been intermittent open conflict of a sectarian nature which also has a social and economic dimension. Within the lifetime of the Republic of Ireland, structural accommodation between different religious identities has occurred through a number of different factors, including differential emigration, intermarriage and a declining birth rate among non-Catholics, all of which have reinforced the dominance of Roman Catholicism. In both countries, the use of religion as a social marker is apparent in a wide range of historical sources, some of which are discussed below.

3.1   THE DEMOGRAPHY OF RELIGION IN NINETEENTH- AND TWENTIETH-CENTURY IRELAND

The earliest reliable nineteenth-century estimate of the size of the religious groupings in Ireland was in 1834 when it was calculated that over 80 per cent of the population were Roman Catholics, 11 per cent belonged to the Anglican Church of Ireland, and 9 per cent were Presbyterians. During the Famine years of the late 1840s, the Roman Catholic population declined disproportionately because more of them were in the poorer social groups which suffered excess mortality and higher levels of post-Famine emigration.

In the 1861 census, and each census thereafter in Ireland, a question has been asked on religious affiliation, and this information has been collated in the published census tables for various spatial units (provinces, counties, registration districts, civil parishes, etc.). The totals recorded in 1861 suggest that the number of Roman Catholics had fallen by nearly one third since 1834, while the number of Anglicans and Presbyterians had each fallen by only 19 per cent. This must be set against a background of total population decrease in the aftermath of the Irish Famine from 8.1 million in 1841 to 5.8 million in 1861. As a result, the proportion of Roman Catholics fell to 78 per cent, while the proportion of Anglicans rose to 12 per cent and the proportion of Presbyterians remained unchanged. In 1911, the Roman Catholic share showed a further decline to 74 per cent, while the Church of Ireland and the Presbyterians increased to 13 per cent and 10 per cent respectively.

However, it is not so much their overall proportions but the geographical distribution of the three principal denominations throughout the island which has had the greatest influence on Irish society. Figures 8.8 (a) and (b) indicate the uneven denominational distribution in each province in 1861 and in 1911, and Figures 8.8 (c) and (d) show the same for the two countries in 1961 and 1981.

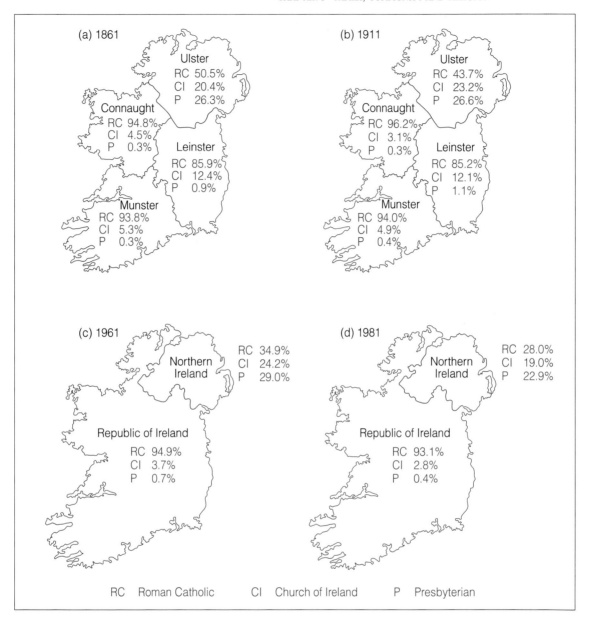

Figure 8.8 Geographical distribution of the three principal denominations in Ireland, 1861, 1911, 1961 and 1981. (Note: The lower percentages for the major religious denominations in Northern Ireland in both 1961 and 1981 are mainly explained by the large number of people who chose not to respond to the (non-compulsory) question in the census)

(a) Religious composition within the provinces of Ireland, 1861 (three major denominations only) (Source: Vaughan and Fitzpatrick, 1978, p.53)

(b) Religious composition within the provinces of Ireland, 1911 (three major denominations only) (Source: Vaughan and Fitzpatrick, 1978, p.68)

(c) Religious composition of Northern Ireland and the Republic of Ireland, 1961 (Source: Vaughan and Fitzpatrick, 1978, pp.49 and 50)

(d) Religious composition of Northern Ireland and the Republic of Ireland, 1981 (Sources: Northern Ireland Census of Population, 1981; Republic of Ireland Summary Report and Statistical Abstract, 1991)

Within Ulster, although Roman Catholics accounted for just over half the population in 1861, they made up a minority of the population in Antrim, Armagh, Down and Londonderry and in the towns of Belfast and Carrickfergus. In two other Ulster counties, Fermanagh and Tyrone, they accounted for not much more than half the population. Elsewhere in Ireland they were in a substantial majority. Presbyterians were heavily concentrated in Ulster (96 per cent of the entire membership), and in Antrim and Down they were the most numerous denomination. The Anglicans were the most dispersed group, 56 per cent in Ulster, one quarter in Leinster, 12 per cent in Munster, and 6 per cent in Connaught. Their greatest concentration outside Ulster was in the city and suburbs of Dublin.

The broad differences between the provinces remained largely the same in the 1911 census. However, after partition the numbers of non-Catholics in the Republic of Ireland decreased. By 1961 their proportion was only 5 per cent of the population, half that of the 1911 population. In Northern Ireland, the Roman Catholic population declined between 1911 and the date of the first Northern Ireland census in 1926 and was stable at around 34 per cent between that date and 1961. The religious composition of both the Republic of Ireland and Northern Ireland in 1981 reflected a rise in the recording of a 'not stated' category and, in Northern Ireland, an increase in the size of other Protestant denominations such as Baptists, Brethren and Free Presbyterians.

In historical terms, the other significant denominations were the Congregationalists, Unitarians, Baptists and particularly the Methodists, whose membership grew from 45,000 in 1861 to 62,000 in 1901. The success of Methodism has been attributed, as in England, to its sense of participation and shared commitment which contrasted with the more aloof rituals of Anglicanism and Roman Catholicism. Its initial growth was in Dublin and then in Ulster among mainly Anglican populations in Fermanagh, Armagh and Belfast. Its appeal seems to have been a response to the economic and sectarian tensions of early industrialization in the first half of the nineteenth century; the Armagh linen-producing district and the Lagan Valley corridor down to the port of Belfast comprised the prime region in Ireland of rapid but piecemeal industrial change from rural domestic textile manufacture to the emergence of a mill- and factory-based workforce. In such circumstances, it has been suggested, fundamentalist religions provided consolation, reassurance and an outlet for the surplus energies of a workforce new to this form of industrial discipline. Perhaps in recognition of this, during the later nineteenth century, Irish Anglicanism itself became more evangelical in orientation. There were two other religious groups whose influence has been disproportionate to their size: the Society of Friends or Quakers, who were a small group of fewer than 3,000 in 1901, and Jews, who numbered about 4,000 at the same date, half of whom lived in Dublin.

3.2 RELIGION AND FAMILY AND COMMUNITY HISTORY IN IRELAND

In this section four main areas of research for those interested in the role of religion in family and community history are discussed.

RELIGION AND SOCIAL STRUCTURE

In the nineteenth century, there were important social distinctions between the members of the main denominations. Most of the major landowners throughout Ireland were Anglicans, and Anglicans were also over-represented in the professions and in business life. In Ulster, while the largest landed proprietors were Anglicans, there was a broad middle stratum farming group who were Presbyterians. Presbyterians also dominated professional and commercial life and relatively few were cottiers or landless labourers. In the Ulster towns, too, Presbyterians were more likely to be found in the skilled trades. Apart from their virtual monopoly of the landed estates,

Anglicans throughout Ireland seem to have been fairly evenly dispersed throughout the social structure. In contrast, the occupational structure of the mass of the population which was Roman Catholic showed a concentration at the bottom of the social scale, as cottiers and labourers in the countryside, and unskilled casual workers and petty traders in the towns. The Roman Catholic middle class in Ulster in the nineteenth century was small and confined to specific areas of commerce and education. In the other provinces, the Catholic middle class was larger, though still under-represented in relation to their total numbers. Methodists and the other lesser sects appear to have drawn on the small tenant farmer class and also, later in the nineteenth century, on the skilled urban working class in the north. The Quakers, from lowly English origins, were, by 1850, a small upper-middle-class business community whose importance in commerce and manufacturing was immense and whose philanthropy and concern for social justice were demonstrated in their contribution to famine relief. The Jews also were part of a commercially successful urban middle class, most of whom arrived in Ireland at the end of the nineteenth century (see Volume 2, Chapter 7, section 1).

―――――――――――――――― *QUESTION FOR RESEARCH* ――――――――――――――――

Although the broad distribution of the various denominations is known, local studies which investigate the relationships between patterns of religious affiliation and other social and economic indicators such as occupation, status, household size and literacy have scarcely been tackled in Ireland (but see Hepburn and Collins, 1981). The published census reports cross-tabulate religious affiliation with other attributes such as occupation and levels of education and provide this information at the level of registration districts. Specifically local studies can also be undertaken of households or individuals using the 1901 or 1911 census household enumeration schedules.

EDUCATION

As in England, in the early nineteenth century most children's education in Ireland took place under some form of religious authority. Elementary education in Ireland was of three main types: paying schools popularly called 'hedge' schools which were often *de facto* Roman Catholic parish schools and varied tremendously in character and quality; schools established by the Kildare Place Society of Dublin, set up in 1811 to fund explicitly non-denominational education; and schools funded by societies connected with Protestant evangelicalism whose aim was the conversion of the pupils in the course of their free elementary education.

In 1831, a non-denominational National School system was set up in Ireland with the aim of introducing mixed education. However, because there were few mixed religion communities outside Ulster and Dublin, the existing school structure continued. Both official Roman Catholic and Presbyterian opinion objected to the exclusion of religious teaching. The outcome was that, in practice, many schools took on a particular denominational ethos – by 1900 only one school in three was classed as religiously mixed and even this definition may have arisen from the enrolment of only one child of another denomination.

―――――――――――――――― *QUESTION FOR RESEARCH* ―――――――――――― ―――

National School registers which are widely available from the 1860s (see Figure 8.9) can be used to build up pictures of communities, as they give religion of child, age, level of attainment, father's occupation, previous school and reason for having left. They enable the investigation of such topics as the relationship between school attendance and social background and also the analysis of family migration patterns at a community level.

EXAMPLE

REGISTER OF_____NATIONAL SCHOOL.

Date of Entrance, 1872.	Register Number.	PUPILS' NAMES IN FULL.	Age of Pupil last Birth Day.	Religious Denomination as stated by Parent or Guardian.	RESIDENCE.	Occupation or Means of Living of Parents.	State the Name and County of the last National School at which the Pupil attended ; and the Class in which he last passed.		
							School.	County.	Class.
July 7	96	Atkinson, John, ...	...	7	Pres.	Bailieboro, ...	Shopkeeper, ...	Hiltown, ...	Down, ...	Infant.
„ 7	97	Coghlan, James, ...	...	7	R.C.	Lisheen, ...	Widow, ...	Never at National School.		
„ 7	27	Brown, John, ...	...	7	R.C.	Ballymore, ...	Farmer, ...	Transferred from	Infants' Roll.	
„ 14	98	Morrison, John, ...	...	11	Meth.	Lisgar, ...	Gardener, ...	Newry D.M.S., ...	Armagh, ...	III.
„ 14	99	Leonard, Edward, ...	...	9	E.C.	Drumbawn	Orphan, ...	Lisball, ...	Cavan, ...	I.

Name of Pupil.	Year ending	No. of Attendances made in the Year.	Class in which Enrolled.	Precise Date of Admission to that Class.	Class in which Examined.	RESULTS OF EXAMINATION.							Extra Branches, Insert Name.				State whether Pupil passed or failed.	If Pupil be struck off, give date.	If Pupil be re-admitted, give date.
						Reading, &c.	Spelling, &c.	Writing, &c.	Arithmetic.	Grammar.	Geography.	Needlework or Agriculture.	Singing.	Algebra.	Geometry.	Mensuration.			
Atkinson, John.	30, 4, 73	119	I.	7, 72	I.	O	X	O	X								Failed.	-	
	30, 4, 74	160	II.	5, 73	II.	X	X	X	X								Passed,	24, 9, 74	
	30, 4, 75	69	III.	6, 74													Absent,		18, 1, 75
	30, 4, 76	133	III.	6, 74	III.	X	O	O	O	X	O		X				Passed.		
	30, 4, 77	97	IV.	5, 76	IV.	X	O	O	O	O	O	X	X				Failed.		
	30, 4, 78	168	V.	5, 77	V.	X	X	X	X	O	X	X	X	X	X	X	Passed,	15, 7, 78	
James.	30, 4, 73	140	I.	7, 72	I.	X	O	O	O								Failed.		
	30, 4, 74	110	I.	7, 72	I.	X	X	X	X								Passed.		
	30, 4, 75	97	II.	5, 74	II.	X	X	X	O								Passed,	7, 5, 75	12, 7, 75

Figure 8.9 Example page for a National School register (Source: Public Record Office of Northern Ireland)

VOTING PATTERNS

In the course of the nineteenth century, the entitlement to vote was extended from a narrow stratum of non-Catholic Irish society to comprise, firstly, denominational emancipation within the same narrow stratum, and, secondly, a much wider social base. By the 1880s the Irish electorate had trebled to over 700,000.

In the last quarter of the century, the numerical strength of the Irish Parliamentary Party (85 of the 103 Irish seats at Westminster) and the commitment of the Liberals to Home Rule which was countered by Tory opposition meant that Irish issues were dominant features of English parliamentary activity. While idealistic support for Home Rule entailed an element of moral principle, opposition to it from the Conservatives in England and Unionists in Ulster arose on pragmatic grounds of the perils arising for prosperity and trade from the separation of the industrial links of Ulster from the supplies and markets of the Empire.

_____ **QUESTION FOR RESEARCH** _____

A wide range of poll books is available for the period from 1832 until the Secret Ballot Act of 1872. They can be used to explore the interaction between landed interests and sectarian support, and to chart the effects of the extension of the franchise at various points, as well as the early stages of the Home Rule debate. Lists of electors were often printed in newspapers, and the addresses and occupations can also be used in wider community studies. A study of appropriate local newspapers can also provide evidence of links between membership of the Orange Order and involvement in local politics (for further examples of work on local politics, see Chapters 6 and 7 in this volume; for poll books and electoral registers, see Volume 4, Chapter 4, section 2).

RELIGION AND POPULAR CULTURE

One everyday impact of religion is seen in the ways in which beliefs structured the calendar of work, particularly in agricultural communities. Oral history can be useful here. An anecdote related by O'Dowd (1991) illustrates the practical usefulness of the church calendar in a legal dispute over unpaid wages. The tale was recorded in Irish for the Irish Folklore Commission in the 1930s.

> *A poor man was working for a man in Crossmolina [County Galway]. Because the employer thought that the poor man was quite simple, he decided not to pay him and felt sure that the poor man would not know anything about his rights or legal proceedings ... In court the poor man stated his case very wisely and told the judge how many days he had worked for the dishonest farmer.*
>
> *'The day after the free day and the day after that; the day of the fair of Crossmolina and the day after that; the day that one does not eat meat and the day after that and so comes the free day again.'*
>
> *The happy ending was that the judge accepted the poor man's story and he received the money due to him.*

(O'Dowd, 1991, p.212)

As well as structuring work patterns in nineteenth- and early twentieth-century Ireland, church communities provided the basis for the activities which occupied the small amount of time which most people had available for leisure. Sunday schools for adults as well as children, and the early twentieth-century affiliation of youth organizations with churches created a childhood identification with the church as the provider of social life. This also imbued church leaders with authority beyond their clerical sphere. Particularly for the Roman Catholic church, this was reinforced by the voluntary system of financial support which underpinned the nature of the priest–parishioner relationship.

There was, in addition, a limited delineation of 'rough' and 'respectable' elements in working-class culture, centring round the alternatives of church and public house. Within popular religion, a social distance between town and country emerged. In Roman Catholicism this was seen in, for example, the Father Matthew temperance campaign of the early 1840s. This was a movement with middle-class patronage in the towns, encouraging self help and thrift. In the countryside it drew heavily on magical symbolism associated with traditional interpretations in order to attract the poorer classes who were more familiar with beliefs in the supernatural than they were with the benefits of saving and self-improvement. Thus, social class and 'respectability' added to the denominational differences in the expression of popular culture.

QUESTION FOR RESEARCH

The greatest potential for the study of religious aspects of popular culture seems to rest with a broad approach using biographies, oral history, parochial histories and community studies.

3.4   CONCLUSION

Religion in Ireland is thus not only a means of explaining God to mankind but also a means of defining many relationships in society. Paradoxically, the social boundaries which are defined in relation to religious adherence enable a coexistence of two separate belief systems. At the local level, the strength of each belief system means that individual Roman Catholic and Protestant people can, if they choose, cooperate effectively on small everyday matters without undercutting their respective sets of beliefs. Local history could scarcely be more relevant.

REFERENCES AND FURTHER READING

Note: suggestions for further reading are indicated by an asterisk.

Addleshaw, G.W.O. and Etchells, F. (1948) *Architectural setting of Anglican worship*, London, Faber.

Akenson, D.H. (1988) *Small differences*, Kingston, McGill, Queen's University Press.*

Ali, M.M. (1986) 'Muslims in Britain: a comprehensive bibliography', *Muslim World Book Review*, 6, 2, Winter, pp.51–64.

Ambler, R.W. (1975) 'The 1851 census of religious worship', *Local Historian*, 11, 7, pp.375–81.

Ambler, R.W. (ed.) (1979) 'Lincolnshire returns of the census of religious worship 1851', *Lincoln Record Society*, 12.

Barton, S. (1986) *The Bengali Muslims of Bradford*, Monograph Series, Community Religions Project, Department of Theology and Religious Studies, University of Leeds.

Best, G. (1979) *Mid-Victorian Britain, 1851–75*, London, Fontana/Collins.

Bhachu, P. (1985) *Twice migrants. East African Sikh settlers in Britain*, London, Tavistock Publications.

Brown, C.G. (1988) 'Did urbanization secularize Britain?', *Urban History Yearbook*.

Burghart, R. (1987) *Hinduism in Great Britain*, London, Tavistock. (Contains the most comprehensive bibliography to date on the subject.)

Clark, K. (1987) *Deerness: a short industrial and social history*, New Brancepeth, Sleetburn Press.

Coleman, B.I. (1980) *The Church of England in the mid-nineteenth century: a social geography*, London, The Historical Association, pamphlet G98.

Collins, B. and Pryce, W.T.R. (1993) 'Census returns in England, Ireland, Scotland and Wales', audio-cassette 2A in Braham, P. (ed.) *Using the past: audio-cassettes on sources and methods for family and community historians*, Milton Keynes, The Open University.

Connolly, S. (1985) *Religion and society in nineteenth century Ireland* (Economic and Social History Society of Ireland, Studies in Economic and Social History), Dundalk, Economic and Social History Society of Ireland.*

Council for British Archaeology (1985) *Hallelujah! Recording chapels and meeting houses*, London, Council for British Archaeology.

Everitt, A. (1970) 'Nonconformity in country parishes', in Thirsk, J. (ed.) 1970.

Farrell, J.G. (1973) *Siege of Krishnapur*, London, Weidenfeld & Nicolson.

Gardner, R. (1852) *History, gazetteer and directory of the county of Oxford*, Peterborough (printer: R. Gardner).

Gilbert, A.D. (1976) *Religion and society in industrial England. Church, chapel and social change, 1740–1914*, London, Longman.*

Gilbert, A.D. (1980) *The making of post-Christian Britain. A history of the secularisation of modern society*, London and New York, Longman.*

Halévy, E. (1949) *A history of the English people in the nineteenth century*, vol.1, *England in 1815*, London, Benn (2nd revised English edn; first published in French in 1913).

Harris, R. (1972) *Prejudice and tolerance in Ulster*, Manchester, Manchester University Press.*

Hastings, A. (1991) *A history of English Christianity, 1920–1990*, London, SCM Press.*

Hepburn, A. C. and Collins, B. (1981) 'Industrial society: the structure of Belfast, 1901', in Roebuck, P. (ed.) *Plantation to partition*, Belfast, Appletree Press.*

Hinnells, J.R. (ed) (1984) *A handbook of living religions*, Harmondsworth, Penguin Books.

Hume, A. (1860) *Remarks on the census of religious worship for England and Wales*, London (printed: Liverpool).

Inglis, K.S. (1960) 'Patterns of religious worship in 1851', *Journal of Ecclesiastical History*, 11, pp.74–86.

Joly, D. and Nielsen, J. (1985) *Muslims in Britain: an annotated bibliography 1960–1984* (*Bibliographies in ethnic relations*, no. 6), Centre for Research in Ethnic Relations, Coventry, University of Warwick.

Joyce, P. (1982) *Work, society and politics. The culture of the factory in later Victorian England*, Brighton, Harvester.

Kalsi, Sewa Singh (1992) *The evolution of a Sikh community in Britain*, Monograph Series, Community Religions Project, Department of Theology and Religious Studies, University of Leeds.

Kitchen, R. (1993) 'Class and community in Wolverton', audio-cassette 1A in Braham, P. (ed.) *Using the past: audio-cassettes on sources and methods for family and community historians*, Milton Keynes, The Open University.

Laqueur, T.W. (1985) 'Religion and respectability: Sunday schools and working class culture, 1780–1850', in Bocock, R. and Thompson, K. (eds) *Religion and ideology*, Manchester, Manchester University Press in association with The Open University.

Lawton, R. (ed.) (1978) *The census and social structure*, London, Frank Cass.

Legg, E. (ed.) (1991) 'Buckinghamshire returns of the census of religious worship', *Buckinghamshire Record Society*, 27.

McLeod, H. (1974) *Class and religion in the late Victorian city*, London, Croom Helm.

McLeod, H. (1984) *Religion and the working class in nineteenth century Britain*, London, Macmillan.*

Michaelson, M. (1979) 'The relevance of caste among East African Gujaratis in Britain', *New Community*, 7, 3, pp.350–60.

Moore, R. (1974) *Pit-men, preachers and politics: the effects of Methodism in a Durham mining community*, London, Cambridge University Press.

Mudie-Smith, R. (ed.) (1904) *The religious life of London*, London, Hodder and Stoughton.

Nielsen, J. (1987) 'Muslims in Britain: searching for an identity?', *New Community*, 13, 3, pp.384–94.[*]

Nielsen, J. (1989) 'Islamic communities in Britain', in Badham, P. (ed.) *Religion, state, and society in modern Britain,* Lewiston/Queenston/Lampeter, The Edwin Mellen Press.

Obelkevich, J. (1976) *Religion and rural society, South Lindsey 1825–1875,* Oxford, Clarendon Press.[*]

Obelkevich, J. (1990) 'Religion', in Thompson, F.M.L. (ed.) *The Cambridge social history of Britain 1750–1950*, vol. 3, Cambridge, Cambridge University Press.

O'Dowd, A. (1991) *Spalpeens and tattie hokers: history and folklore of the Irish migratory agricultural worker in Ireland and Britain*, Dublin, Irish University Press.[*]

Parsons. G. (ed.) (1994) *The growth of religious diversity: Britain from 1945*, vols 1 and 2, Routledge in association with The Open University.

Pryce, W.T.R. (1974) 'The 1851 census of religious worship: Denbighshire', *Transactions of Denbighshire Historical Society,* 23, pp.147–92.

Roberts, E. (1984) *A woman's place. An oral history of working-class women 1890–1940,* London, Basil Blackwell.

Roberts, R. (1971) *The classic slum. Salford life in the first quarter of the century,* Harmondsworth, Penguin Books.

Singh, Nyrmla (1985–6) 'The Sikh Community in Manchester', *Sikh Bulletin,* III, pp.3–26, Chichester, West Sussex Institute of Higher Education.

Snell, K.D.M. (1991) *Church and chapel in the north Midlands: religious observance in the 19th century,* Leicester, Leicester University Press.

Stacey, M. (1960) *Tradition and change: a study of Banbury,* Oxford, Oxford University Press.[*]

Stacey, M. (1975) *Power, persistence and change: a second study of Banbury,* London, Routledge & Kegan Paul.[*]

Tatla, D.S. and Nesbitt, E.M. (1987) *Sikhs in Britain: an annotated bibliography,* Bibliographies in Ethnic Relations No.8, Centre for Research in Ethnic Relations, Coventry, University of Warwick.

Thirsk, J. (ed.) (1970) *Land, church and people: essays presented to H.P.R. Finberg,* Reading Museum of English Agricultural Rural Life, British Agricultural History Society.

Thomas, D. and Ghuman, P.S. (1976) *A survey of social and religious attitudes among Sikhs in Cardiff,* Open University in Wales, 24 Cathedral Road, Cardiff.

Thompson, D.M. (1978) 'The religious census of 1851', in Lawton, R. (ed.) (1978).

Thompson, E.P. (1963) *The making of the English working class 1780–1830,* London, Gollancz.

Thompson, F. (1945) *Lark Rise to Candleford,* London, Oxford University Press.

Tiller, K. (1975) *Working-class attitudes and organization in three industrial towns, 1850–1875,* unpublished Ph.D. thesis, University of Birmingham.

Tiller, K. (1982) 'Village dissenters: Hook Norton Baptist chapel and its chapelyard', *Cake and Cockhorse,* 9, 1, pp.27–31 (Banbury Historical Society).

Tiller, K. (ed.) (1987) *Church and chapel in Oxfordshire 1851: the returns of the census of religious worship,* Oxford, Oxfordshire Record Society.

Vaughan, W. E. and Fitzpatrick, A.J. (eds) (1978) *Irish historical statistics: population 1821–1971,* Dublin, Royal Irish Academy.

Wigan Times, Broadside Collection, Wigan Reference Library.

Wolffe, J. and Golby, J. (1993) 'Religious records as sources', audio-cassette 5A in Braham, P. (ed.) *Using the past: audio-cassettes on sources and methods for family and community historians,* Milton Keynes, The Open University.

CHAPTER 9

CULTURAL LIFE

by John Golby

Just as there are many interpretations and definitions of the words 'family' and 'community', so too the word 'culture' admits to many meanings. However, this is not the place to explore the many ramifications of the word. For the purposes of this chapter, 'cultural life' will be equated with how people spend their spare time within their own localities. Spare-time activities are sometimes equated with leisure, which itself encompasses a whole group of activities ranging from attending concerts to spending evenings in the local pubs. But, in addition to leisure pursuits, spare-time activities include those which may not be regarded as exclusively leisure-oriented, such as membership of the local branch of a trade union, or working as a committee member on a local charitable organization.

Chapters 6, 7 and 8 examined the voting behaviour and the extent of religious observance in various areas of the British Isles. A thorough study of the cultural life of a particular area would build on these chapters and explore, for example, what links there were between how people voted and the denominations of any churches which they attended. But it would delve even further and explore whether the local political parties and the churches provided any other opportunities for their members to meet together. For example, it would ask whether the local branch of the Conservative party ran a social club, where membership was required and where facilities were provided not only for meetings of the local branch of the party but also for social activities such as drinking, and playing billiards and snooker. Again, it would consider whether the parish church, as well as providing church services, encouraged a whole range of cultural activities – perhaps a Mother's Union, a choir, a drama group, or Scout and Guide troops.

So, under the umbrella of the phrase 'cultural life' comes a whole range of activities. Clearly, cultural activities vary to some extent from region to region and, of course, there have been many changes through time. A number of hypotheses have been put forward to explain the reasons for these changes and these will be outlined in the next section. However, the main aims of this chapter are as follows:

1   To suggest various ways by which you can explore the cultural life of an area in which you are interested (e.g. where your particular family and others lived).

2   To get you to start asking questions about how your particular family and others spent their spare time. What was available to them outside of the home? Were the majority of the outside activities which were available for men only? Were some of the spare-time activities connected with work? Is there evidence of participation in spare-time activities by whole family groups? Do the cultural activities in your area help to shed light on whether there was a sense of community and, if so, in what ways?

1   CULTURAL LIFE IN THE NINETEENTH CENTURY

The rapid population growth, urbanization and industrialization in the first half of the nineteenth century not only brought enormous economic and political changes but also affected the social and cultural lives of virtually all sections of the population. However, the extent to which these changes altered the leisure activities of working people has been hotly debated by historians and sociologists. There is no doubt that the concentration of large numbers of people in new towns put enormous strains on the rudimentary local administrations who, fearing social and political unrest, tended to dread and discourage events such as fairs and other public holiday occasions which attracted large crowds and which possessed the potential for spilling over from boisterous celebrations into local riots. In many instances, these local authorities were supported by a growing number of Evangelicals and reformers, who disapproved of many of the old traditional pastimes, especially popular blood sports such as cock-fighting, bear-baiting, and ratting. In addition, manufacturers, particularly those involved in industries becoming increasingly mechanized and dependent on labour forces prepared to accept new work disciplines, disapproved of leisure-time activities which interfered with prompt and regular working hours.

These considerations have led to a number of theories being put forward relating to changes in popular culture in the first half of the nineteenth century. The bleakest suggest that, as a result of the attacks on traditional leisure activities by reformers and Evangelicals and the new demands required of an urban, industrial workforce, there was little time for and little choice of leisure activities. Rapid urbanization, so Malcolmson (1978) concluded, led to traditional customs and activities being 'swept away, leaving a cultural vacuum which would be only gradually reoccupied' (pp.170–1) in the second half of the century. What replaced traditional pastimes, so Stephen and Eileen Yeo (1981) claimed, were new commercial entertainments which involved less robust forms of popular culture and which led to the spread of mass culture. These gloomy views have been contested by Cunningham (1980), who argued that the attacks on popular leisure were not entirely successful and so there was not a sharp discontinuity with the past. Golby and Purdue (1984) have gone even further by suggesting that, although there was a definite expansion of cultural activities in the second half of the nineteenth century, much of pre-industrial popular culture was already commercialized, and that there was a large degree of continuity in cultural activities throughout the nineteenth century.

Those of you working on families in the nineteenth century can test some aspects of these theories by building up pictures of activities within your own communities at specific points in time. I have tried to do this by using material relating to the parish of Eynsham, which had a population of 1,941 in 1851 (see Chapter 3, section 2). My starting point was the 1851 census and local directories of 1851, 1853 and 1854. I then went on to use a local weekly paper, *Jackson's Oxford Journal*, for just one year, 1851. This amounted in all to one afternoon's work in the Central Library at Oxford.

What sort of information would you expect to be able to draw upon from directories and census returns which will be of help in estimating the extent of cultural life within a particular parish or town?

Clearly the answer depends on how detailed the directories relating to your specific parish or town are, but you should be able to discover the number and type of shops, charities and societies which existed as well as the schools in the area. Also, by using them in conjunction with the census returns, the lists of occupational activities can be of great value.

The occupation which tells us most about the cultural life of a town or village in the mid-nineteenth century is that of publican/innkeeper. This is because the pub played such a central role in the lives of many working people. It goes without saying that pubs were first and foremost places for drinking, but to designate them just as drinking houses would be to understate totally the vital social role that they played both in rural and urban areas.

At a time when much working-class housing was cold, damp and cramped, the pub performed the roles of both meeting place and recreation centre. Very often, apart from perhaps a room in a church or chapel, the pub provided the only available centre for a gathering of any size. Consequently, all sorts of activities were carried on in pubs in addition to drinking. Auctions and business transactions were conducted in pubs, wages were paid out in them, local clubs and societies held their meetings in the pub, and doctors even held surgeries there if a convenient room was available.

Pubs varied in size and degrees of respectability from the large posting-house establishment to the front parlour of a small-sized house. At election times, very often the candidates would stay and have their headquarters at the grander establishments. So some pubs were associated with specific political parties. Others attracted specific groups of men: note the titles of some pub signs – the Carpenters Arms, the Bricklayers and so on.

Pub yards were often used for sports and stabling. Remember Alfred Williams's story (Chapter 2, section 2) concerning the group of workers living in an outlying district who arranged to leave their horse and cart in a local pub yard while they did their day shift at the GWR works. Some yards were also used for cock-fighting and ratting, for, despite the Cruelty to Animals Act of 1835, many of the old traditional blood sports survived. Nearly all pubs provided some facilities for pastimes, whether they be quoits, skittles or pitch-and-toss, and these sports were invariably accompanied by gambling. Indeed, pubs were very often the sporting and gambling centres of the locality. Many pubs also provided musical entertainments, even if these were merely impromptu sing-songs. In the larger taverns, where licences for music and dancing were obtained, there were organized events. These entertainments were precursors of the music halls which were to develop rapidly in the 1850s and 1860s.

It is important to keep in mind that there was a long tradition of drinking ale. Alfred Williams, in 1915, referred to past times when farmers met the Great Western Railway workers at the factory gates and took them straight back to their villages where, after meals of 'bread, cheese and ale', they helped with the harvest (Williams, 1969 edn, p.122). In many areas where water supplies were sparse and drinking water often polluted, beer was considered a much healthier and safer drink. Also, in the middle of the century a half pint of ale was cheaper than non-alcoholic alternatives such as tea and coffee, so it is not suprising that there was a tradition of ale drinking both in urban and rural areas. Nevertheless, drink and drunkenness were major social problems in nineteenth-century Britain and many families suffered as a consequence of drink. Consequently, in most towns and villages, as well as public houses, one invariably finds temperance societies and branches of the Band of Hope.

In my work on Eynsham in 1851, I discovered eleven names mentioned in the census which were connected with the drink trade:

William Lord	Publican	105 Acre End Street
George Blake	Innkeeper	143 High Street
Charles Cantell	Publican	151 High Street
Richard Buckingham	Innkeeper	117 High Street
Philip Scholey	Publican	Talbot Public House
Richard Bridges	Publican	20 Queen Street
William Davis	Publican and grocer	80 Newland Street
Ann Faichen	Licensed victualler	Britannia Public House
John Wright	Victualler/drillman	34 Freeland
Charles Goodwin	Brewer/empl. 4 labs	44 Queen Street
William Shillingford	Wool stapler, malster, wine and spirit merchant	35 Queen Street

The local directories were helpful in that they not only, in most cases, supplied the names of the pubs in Eynsham but they also listed three further publicans who were not given that occupational heading in the census:

John Cox, publican of the Crown, Abbey Street
Robert Ford, grocer, mealman and beer retailer of Mill Street
John Harwood, beer retailer and baker, Britannia, Acre End Street.

On checking back in the census, I discovered the names of John Cox living in Abbey Street who had given his occupation as cordwainer; Robert Ford living in Mill Street but who in the census return is listed as a grocer; and John Harwood of Acre End Street listed as baker.

What reasons can you think of for the discrepancies between the information given in the directories and in the census returns?

Perhaps Cox, Ford and Harwood had given up running the drinking establishments at the time when the census was taken. But by far the most likely explanation is that the three men did not regard the running of their pubs as their major occupations. Two other publicans, William Davis and John Wright, also gave additional occupations to the census enumerator, as did the wine and spirit merchant, William Shillingford. Also, the husband of Ann Faichen, listed as the publican of the Britannia public house, had given his occupation as farmer.

For some people, therefore, being a publican was not a full-time occupation. Indeed, running a pub was sometimes seen as a means of supplementing an income rather than as the sole source of a livelihood. It was extremely easy for anyone to set up an establishment selling ale. All the Beer Act of 1830 required was that the proprietor paid the poor rates and obtained an annual licence costing two guineas (£2.10) from the local excise department. So, a grocer like Robert Ford, for a comparatively small sum, could add to his income by selling ale. Further conclusions can also be drawn from this information. The Crown, run by John Cox, cordwainer/publican, was almost certainly smaller and attracted a different social grouping of customers from that of George Blake's Red Lion, which was situated in the square and which was the posting house for the village.

The directories also mentioned a Jonathon Sheldon, corn merchant and maltster of Acre End Street. In the 1851 census, Jonathon was only listed as a corn merchant. So, in 1851 in Eynsham, there was one brewer employing four men, two maltsters (one of whom was also a wine and spirit merchant), and twelve establishments licensed to sell beer. The twelve drinking houses provided beer for a population of 1,941. Thus, there was one drinking place for every 162 inhabitants. Depending on your point of view, this is better or worse than the average for that time of one drinking place to every 186 inhabitants in England and Wales and one to every 225 in Scotland. Compared with these twelve drinking establishments, *Lascelles and Co.'s directory and gazetteer of the county of Oxford* (1853) states that Eynsham had the following shops selling food: five grocers, six bakers, two butchers and two confectioners.

The rest of the information gleaned from the directories was fairly thin. Eynsham had a post office, carriers to Oxford and Witney, a parish church, a Baptist chapel, capable of seating 200, and a Wesleyan chapel. Two National Schools were established in 1847 which had been built on land donated by Mr Samuel Druce who, I discovered from the census, was one of the largest landowners in the area, farming 800 acres and employing 32 labourers. The schools were supported by subscription, charity sermons and a sum from a local charity.

The local newspaper in 1851, *Jackson's Oxford Journal*, did not provide a great deal of additional information. The *Journal* attempted to cover the local news, for all of Oxfordshire and parts of the neighbouring counties of Buckinghamshire and Wiltshire, so perhaps it is not surprising that, on average, there was only one item relating specifically to Eynsham each month. Nevertheless, the reports were helpful in three respects. First, one item helped to lend weight to the view that the local pubs played vital roles in the community as meeting places and centres of entertainment:

19 April 1851

Cricket. The members of the Eynsham Club intend to have their meeting in a few days at the Swan Inn, in this town, to determine the best means of promoting the game during the season of 1851. Several fresh members intend enrolling their names in addition to those of last year.

Secondly, the newspaper reports showed the role played by the churches in the cultural life of the village. A number of annual events were reported: a sermon preached in aid of the children's

Figure 9.1   Eynsham Village Band, 1860s. This photograph found in the County Library indicates that there was a village band in Eynsham around the middle of the century (Source: Oxfordshire County Libraries, Local History Collection)

penny club saving fund; the ceremony giving the children tickets to provide them with clothing through the winter; Easter and Whitsun festivities; the annual Sunday school and day schools treat on 12 June, when the children were entertained to 'cake and tea at the national school rooms at the hands of the Vicar' (21 June 1851); and harvest and Christmas festivals.

Thirdly, the nearest annual fairs were held at Witney and Oxford, although the newspaper did report the activities of an itinerant entertainer, Richard Page, better known as Don Pedro, who provided a spectacle for the villagers by standing on Eynsham Bridge and twice diving into the river about 30 feet below (8 November 1851).

Significantly, but perhaps not surprisingly, I found no references to cultural activities in which women were specifically involved. As was noted in Chapter 3, women's lives were more domestic and private than those of men at this time. For working-class married women, leisure activities outside the home were rare. The pub, at least the respectable pub, was largely a male preserve. Attending local fairs, festivals and markets and accompanying children on special outings were probably the main extent of the working-class married woman's outdoor leisure activities.

_____ ***EXERCISE 9.1*** _____

From the evidence I have collected so far in respect of Eynsham, you may well be entitled to agree with Malcolmson (1978) that there was something of a cultural vacuum in Britain during the middle of the century. Note down any arguments that could be employed to throw some doubts on this conclusion?

_____

First, if much of the cultural life of the village occurred in the bars, upper rooms and back yards of pubs, then it is not surprising that most of the activities are not recorded. Many cultural activities would have been informal ones and it would be unsafe to conclude that there was only one formal club (the cricket club) existing in Eynsham in 1851. Cricket, by 1851, was a well-established game and was played by all classes.

This leads on to a second point. Newspaper coverage of events in Eynsham in 1851 was extremely thin. This is true of many areas of the country at this time. However, in their study of Banbury in the period 1830–60, Harrison and Trinder (1969), through a detailed used of local newspapers, constructed recreational calendars for the town in the years 1843 and 1858. The latter calendar has many more entries, which suggests more cultural activities taking place, but the authors do admit (p.46) that one reason for this could be the fuller reporting of events in Banbury by 1858. Three years earlier the tax on newspapers had been repealed, which gave a boost both to the size and number of newspapers in production throughout the country.

Most events taking place in Eynsham in 1851 would not be reported in the newspaper, and announcements of entertainments, such as the performance of Don Pedro in November 1851, would be, just as they are today, communicated either by printed or handwritten posters in local shops, bars, and on the parish noticeboard. Unfortunately, posters as a primary source are comparatively rare (although you may be lucky to find a collection in your local history library). There must have been hundreds of posters printed every year for any one locality, but few remain. The poster reproduced as Figure 9.2 is quite rare but it does tell us something about the existence of a strong Sabbatarian movement in Eynsham in 1820.

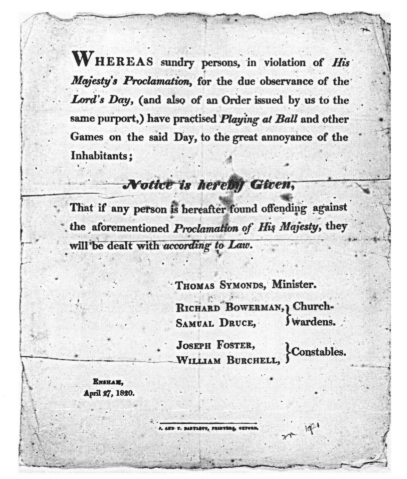

Figure 9.2 Proclamation preventing the playing of games on Sunday, Eynsham, Oxfordshire, 1820 (Source: John Johnson Collection, Bodleian Library)

Finally, one could claim with total justification that I have not done nearly enough research. Trinder, in his scholarly study of *Victorian Banbury* (1982), put together a detailed list of clubs and societies which he found existed in the important Midland market town of Banbury (population in 1851: 8,793) in the period 1830–50 (see Table 9.1).

EXERCISE 9.2

From what you have read so far, comment on what you find the most significant items in Trinder's list.

Table 9.1   Dates of foundation of voluntary societies active in Banbury between 1830 and 1850

Quasi-governmental bodies

Neithrop Association for the Prosecution of Felons	Before*	1819
Banbury General Association for the Prosecution of Felons		1835
Mendicity Society		1834

Philanthropic Societies

Old Charitable Society		1782
Bank for Savings		1818
Visiting Charitable Society		1820
Labourer's Friend Society		1833
Banbury and Neithrop Clothing Society		1831
Medical Aid Society	By*	1838
Dorcas Society		1842
Refuge Society		1845
Small Savings Society		1847

Friendly Societies

Weavers Arms		1832
Conservative Friendly Society		1837
White Horse Friendly Society		1837
Reindeer Club	By	1838
United Smiths	By	1838
Cock & Greyhound, Old Club	By	1838
White Hart	By	1838
Loyal Wellington Oddfellows, Independent Order	By	1839
United Christian Benefit Society		1840
Mutual Aid Society		1843
Reformers' Friendly Society	By	1843
Millwrights Arms		1840
British Queen Oddfellows, Independent Order	By	1843
Fountain of Liberty Oddfellows, Independent Order	By	1843
Rechabites		1844
Tradesmens Benefit Society	By	1844
Buck and Bell	By	1845
British Queen Oddfellows, Manchester Unity Order		1848

Religious Societies

British and Foreign Bible Society Auxiliary		1817
Society for the Propagation of the Gospel	By	1832
Church Missionary Society		1835
London Association for Promoting Christianity amongst the Jews		1842
Society for Promoting Christian Knowledge	By	1846
Protestant Institute		1845
Naval and Military Bible Society	By	1846
China Missionary Society	By	1849
Church Choir		1835

Musical Societies

Amateur Music Society	By	1835
Brass Band		1836
Harmonic Society		1840
Church Singers Society	By	1841
Temperance Brass Band		1844
Choral Society		1844
Philharmonic Society		1847

Educational and Cultural Bodies

National Schools Society	1817
Infants' School	1835
Mechanics' Institute	1835
British Schools	1839
Flori- and Horticultural Society	1847

Political and Social Reforming Bodies

Anti-Slavery Association	1832
Temperance Society	1834
Agricultural Association	1834

Sports Club

Cricket Club	1836

* Before = before earliest directory entry; By = between directories, with no precise date of starting given.

Source: Trinder (1982) pp.200–1; based on Rusher's *Banbury lists and directories*, and contemporary newspapers

There are a large number of friendly societies connected with public houses which once again underlines the social significance of the pub at this particular time.

Although women are not specifically mentioned, it is highly likely that women, most probably those higher up the social scale, were members of some of the philanthropic societies and also members of the surprisingly large number of musical societies existing in the town.

Education for young and old appears to have been a major concern from the 1830s on in Banbury, with the building of an Infants' School, and a Mechanics' Institute. (Remember that in Eynsham two National Schools were built in 1847.)

1.1   VOLUNTARY ASSOCIATIONS

Trinder gave his list the overall title of 'voluntary societies' and he then classified these societies under eight headings. Stacey, who has made two studies of Banbury in the twentieth century, prefers to use the term 'voluntary associations' when discussing formal associations or organiz-ations. In *Tradition and change: a study of Banbury* (1960) she defined what she means by voluntary associations. Basically, they have five characteristics:

(i)   They are formal associations having some kind of constitution by which the affairs of the group are ordered;

(ii)   Membership is voluntary;

(iii) The qualifications for membership are determined by the members themselves;

(iv) The group has some continuity and is not convened merely for a special purpose or occasion;

(v)   The group has some formal name by which it is known.

By definition therefore ad hoc bodies, sets, cliques, and other informal association are excluded ... Among the excluded groups are: the committee raised specially to get money for repairs to the church; the groups of men and women meeting regularly for 'elevenses'; the 'regulars' who 'belong' to the sixty-odd pubs and form a nucleus of their darts teams and thrift clubs [editor's note: Stacey mentions sixty odd pubs in Banbury in 1960, a town with a population of nearly 19,000. In 1851 Banbury had a population of 8,793 and 80 public houses] ... ; the band of collectors whom the representatives of the national charity organizations can call on to help with a house-to-house collection.

(Stacey, 1960, p.75)

Stacey then divided these associations into eight categories:

1   *Sport.* This covers bowls, cricket, football, tennis, cycling, golf, sailing, squash rackets, and table tennis.
2   *Hobbies.* These cover a wide range from pigeon racing and coarse fishing, through the allotment, fanciers, and sweet pea societies to old-time dancing, chess, and tropical fish keeping.
3   *Cultural.* These include art and musical societies, adult education, amateur dramatics, and non-party political organizations ... .
4   *Social.* In this category are some clubs with their own premises and facilities for billiards, table tennis, darts and cards; and societies without premises whose main function is to provide a regular meeting for their members. The Townswomen's Guild is an example of the last type.
5   *Social Service.* A prime function of associations in this category is that members are called upon to fulfil some activity for the benefit of non-members. Rotary, Toc H, and St John Ambulance are included.
6   *Charity.* These associations raise money for the benefit of non-members. Save the Children Fund and Wireless for the Bedridden are examples.
7   *Mutual Aid.* In these associations members band together to insure themselves against personal misfortune. `
8   *Occupational Associations.* These include professional and staff associations and trade unions.

(Stacey, 1960, pp.75–6)

You will probably find it helpful in your research, especially if you are working on the twentieth century, if you utilize the categories delineated by Stacey.

2   CULTURAL LIFE AT THE TURN OF THE CENTURY

Look back again at Trinder's list of voluntary societies in Banbury between 1830 and 1850 (Table 9.1). What categories (use Stacey's eight voluntary association categories) do you think would contain many more entries if you were researching a particular locality at the turn of this century?

Categories 1 and 2, sport and hobbies, would certainly be larger. Even in Eynsham, an agricultural parish whose population had declined in the second half of the nineteenth century from 1,941 in 1851 to 1,757 in 1901, I discovered entries in the local newspapers for 1901 mentioning the following clubs: cricket, football, quoits and draughts. Also, a ladies golf club was formed in 1901, although the golf links, as far as I could make out, consisted of the local football field (*Jackson's Oxford Journal,* 30 March 1901).

There are a number of important reasons for the countrywide growth of sporting activities during, in particular, the last quarter of the nineteenth century. For one thing, by 1901 there was more leisure time available for the majority of the population and this majority also had more money to spend on leisure-time activities than in 1851. The gradual introduction of the five-and-a-half-day working week from the 1850s onwards also did much to encourage sporting activities, as did the Bank Holiday Acts of 1871 and 1875. Another key factor was the vast extension of the railway network during the period 1850 to 1870 (the railway came to Eynsham in 1861) which facilitated travel both for spectators and competitors. It meant that teams could extend their fixtures list rather than just playing against the local villages. This, of course, meant that an increasing number of cultural activities were taking place outside the village. The *Witney Gazette* for 13 April 1901 reported that many of the inhabitants of Eynsham had spent the Bank Holiday in Witney watching the sports day.

Finally, perhaps we can glimpse some signs of the demographic movements taking place within the country and the slight changes occurring in the social status of women. The Eynsham Ladies Golf Club was most probably composed of middle-class ladies (as probably was the Needlework Society which was also in existence in Eynsham at this time), but it does show that women were venturing into an active participation in sports. As well as golf, women were becoming members of cycling, tennis, badminton and hockey clubs.

Although we must remember that there were more newspapers being published in 1901, producing more pages of print and giving a wider coverage of local events, especially sporting events, than ever before, there is no doubt that there was a tremendous expansion of organized sporting activities in the last quarter of the nineteenth century. This is not to say that many men (and a few women) did not participate in or watch sports earlier in the century. Horse-racing, cricket, golf, athletics and rowing, and the gambling which went with these activities, were popular pastimes throughout the century. Indeed, for many working men, sport had long been a central element in their leisure-time activities. Alan Metcalfe, in his study of the mining communities of south Northumberland (1982), goes so far as to state that, 'For the submerged majority of miners, sport provided the meaning of life; it was more important by far, after survival needs had been met, than any other aspect of life' (p.491). Metcalfe also emphasized that what invariably went with sporting occasions was gambling: 'Miners rarely competed just for the fun of competition. They competed for a prize, usually side stakes that were placed by the two protagonists and their supporters. Gambling by the spectators accompanied most competitions' (p.474).

The important change in the second half of the nineteenth century was not necessarily that people became more interested in sport but rather that many sports became regulated, organized and codified. For example, football in one form or other would have been played in villages throughout the century, but only in the second half of the century was the game given rules and regulations which became recognized countrywide. By the end of the century there were football leagues and hundreds of clubs affiliated to county associations. In 1890, fifteen sports had such a wide following that they were governed by national bodies, whereas fifty years earlier only cricket, golf and horse-racing possessed any form of national organization.

Nevertheless, despite the new competitions and organization, the roots of many of these clubs were contained within the old institutions of church, chapel or pub. Mason (1980), in his study of football, discovered that in Sheffield in 1865, eleven out of the thirteen football clubs listed in a local directory gave particular public houses as their addresses. Partly as a result of the strong Muscular Christianity movement of the 1860s, many football and cricket clubs originated from within church clubs. Bailey (1978, p.137), in his study of Bolton, found that one third of the cricket clubs in that town in 1867 were connected with religious institutions. Mason (1980) also estimated that church, chapel and Sunday school teams made up a quarter of all organized football clubs in the 1860s. Some other clubs were founded at the workplace. Arsenal and West Ham football clubs are perhaps the best two examples of this particular development. But there have been a whole host of lesser known works' teams covering a vast range of sports. Alfred Williams, in his memoirs, refers to the powerful men from the frame shed at the GWR works at Swindon who made up a tug-of-war team and competed for trophies throughout the south of England (Williams, 1969 edn, p.73).

It is difficult to overestimate the role that sport has played in the cultural life of Britain. Its links with the family, the community, class and religion are many. Very often entire families support the same team and this support is carried on from generation to generation. Perhaps the reasons why a particular club inspires such loyalty may have been forgotten, but they are often based on factors originally relating to location and, particularly in some parts of the country, religion. Even many people not professing an interest in sport are swept up in at least a temporary enthusiasm when their local team reaches the final of the FA Cup. Imagine all the emotions involved in 1883 in Blackburn – town pride, Lancastrians versus the south and strong class feelings – when the local team, Blackburn Olympic, made up of three weavers, a loomer, a gilder, two iron foundry workers, a clerk, a master plumber, a licensed victualler and a dentist, went down to London and defeated the Old Etonians in the final of the English Football Association Cup.

Whilst most sports took the male out of the home, a number of growing, popular, cultural activities were focusing men on activities within the home or, at least, in their back gardens. An increase in leisure time was leading to a growth in the number of hobbies pursued. McKibbin (1983) cites the contents of the first edition of *Hobbies* magazine (October 1895) which included, 'fretwork and inlaying in wood … photography for amateurs, stamps and stamp collecting, magic lanterns, bazaars and how to decorate them …' (p.129). Domestic gardening had always been popular, and the 1892 Collings Small Holdings Bill was a small, tentative step towards providing allotments for working men. Perhaps surprisingly, many men pursued hobbies which were closely related to their work. But a large proportion of hobbies contained a serious competitive element. Pigeons, canaries, dogs, fish, flowers and vegetables were often reared and grown in order that they should be entered in competitions on which money could be gambled and prizes and cups won.

What is also clear from the newspaper reports is that by 1901 there was a greater variety of places available for sports clubs and other cultural organizations to hold their meetings. The pub was now no longer the only suitable location. Town halls, church halls, schools, mechanics' institutes, and rooms in public libraries all provided alternative meeting places. A wider variety of accommodation, together with improved water supplies and cheap alternative drinks to beer, meant that by 1901, although the pubs still played an important part in the cultural life of towns and villages, they no longer held the position of the all-embracing cultural, social and meeting centre.

From your reading of this chapter so far, what important questions should you be asking if you were researching into the cultural life of your particular area at the turn of the century?

Some suggestions are summarized in Schema A.

Schema A: Questions relating to cultural life at the turn of the century

o Which of the voluntary associations in existence had been formed in the second half of the nineteenth century?

o What percentage of the new associations were concerned with sports and hobbies?

o What percentage of the associations would have female members and what percentage were entirely women's organizations?

---

o   Were these associations as dependent on pubs and churches for places in which to meet? What other meeting places existed?

o   With improved means of transport, did many of the leisure-time activities take place outside of the parish, village or town?

I tried to answer some of these questions with reference to the village of Eynsham by using two local weekly papers for the year 1901, the *Witney Gazette* and *Jackson's Oxford Journal.* (For a village the size of Eynsham, it took two to three hours to accumulate this information.)

The following voluntary associations were formed since 1851:

Young Men's Social Club	The Ancient Order of Foresters
Workmen's Club	Cricket Club
Band of Hope Union	Football Club
Boys' Brigade	Quoits Club
Foreign Missionary Society	Draughts Club
Oddfellow Foresters	Ladies Golf Club
New Inn Clubs	Needlework Society
Swan Club	

In addition, a Children's Union, a Parish Choir and the Parish Bellringers are mentioned, but there is a strong likelihood that these bodies were in existence in 1851.

What percentage of these new associations were connected with sports and hobbies? This is slightly difficult, but if the Young Men's Social Club (attended chiefly by the middle classes (*Whitney Gazette*, 2 March 1901)) and the Workmen's Club are included, then over 50 per cent of the associations were connected with sports and hobbies.

Two of the fifteen associations were for women.

The cricket club held its meetings, including the Annual General Meeting (AGM), at the Red Lion; the Quoits Club met at the Swan Inn; the Ancient Order of Foresters celebrated their AGM at the Red Lion; and the Young Men's Social Club met at the Railway Inn. However, in 1901 a reading room was opened at the Baptist Mission Hall, and this was used by the newly formed Workmen's Club. A draughts tournament was also held there. The January treat for Sunday school children was held in the school room, and the parish church room was refurbished and reopened in 1901. So the availability of these rooms together with the Baptist Mission Hall meant that there was a much greater variety of accommodation in Eynsham in 1901 than fifty years earlier.

Finally, it was difficult to trace records of activities outside the village. I have mentioned Eynsham villagers visiting a sports day at Witney, but as the exercise was one of discovering to what extent people were taking advantage of improved transport facilities, I reversed the process and listed groups who came into Eynsham:

o   Football teams from Oxford.

o   Burford Brass Band, Woodstock Drum and Fife Band, and Coombe Brass Band all visited the village on the Annual Hospital Sunday event in August.

o   The Oxford Temperance Mandolin Band played at the Band of Hope tea party in May.

Burford is a distance of about twenty miles from Eynsham, but I did not find any sports teams or bands which came to Eynsham from outside the county of Oxfordshire. Doubtless a more detailed examination of the local newspapers over a period of three or four years would have extended the lists considerably. But compared with some urban areas, travel appears to have been largely limited to within the county.

Figure 9.3   Eynsham Diamond Jubilee celebrations in the square, 1897. Queen Victoria's Diamond Jubilee was an occasion for festivities throughout the British Isles. Eynsham was no exception. The Red Lion Inn is on the right-hand side of the picture (Source: Oxfordshire County Libraries Local History Collection)

QUESTIONS FOR RESEARCH

Here are some examples of possible small-scale studies based on the questions raised in Schema A.

Work through a newspaper for one particular year which covers your locality. Choose, if possible, a year in which a local directory was issued, so that you can make best use of both sources. If the specific locality in which you are interested is a small village, rather like Eynsham, then you will probably have time to address most of the questions raised in Schema A. If you live in a large town which is covered well by a number of newspapers, then you will only have time to raise one or two questions and these should depend on your particular interests. For example, how many associations met in pubs, or rooms belonging to churches and chapels? What other meeting places existed? What percentage of associations had female members and what percentage were entirely women's organizations?

Try to compare the findings in your area with those in different localities. For example, are the discoveries you have made in your particular village markedly different from mine in Eynsham? Again, if you live in a town, you could compare your finding with, for example, those of Bailey (1978) in Bolton, or Meller (1976) in Bristol. Better still, you could compare a more prosperous district in one part of your town with a poorer area.

Another interesting project would be to do what I have attempted and examine the locality at two particular points of time, one around the 1850s and another at the turn of the century. What sort of changes have taken place and how do your conclusions relate to the wider debates about changes in nineteenth-century cultural life referred to at the beginning of section 1 in this chapter?

3   CULTURAL LIFE IN THE TWENTIETH CENTURY

In section 1 of this chapter, one of the views expressed about changes in cultural life in the nineteenth century was that during the second half of the century many existing cultural activities either disappeared, were commercialized, or were replaced by new mass cultural activities. Whether one agrees or disagrees with this whole argument, a large number of new mass cultural activities clearly did emerge during the twentieth century. The enfranchising of mass electorates, the growth of mass markets, the spread of mass schooling, and the development of mass communications have led to the emergence of what historians and social scientists have called a *mass society*. Mass society, as defined by Biddis (1977, p.14), is one which is 'differentiated from what precedes it by an enlargement in the scale of activities, institutions and loyalties'.

Disagreements occur among historians when they discuss the consequences of the development of a mass society. Some stress the benefits of such a society: for example, the enfranchisement of all adults, the development of a greater social awareness, and, particularly relevant to our discussions, the easier access to cultural activities. Others dwell on the inherent dangers within such a society: the pressures towards conformity, passivity and the loss of individual initiatives; and the increased opportunities for dominant groupings to manipulate society, partly through their control of cultural outlets. This latter view has been taken to its extreme by S. and E. Yeo (1981), who argue that over the last century and a half in Britain the centralization of political and economic power has developed to such an extent that it has infiltrated all cultural forms 'from Butlin's to Brighton and Hove Albion Supporter's Club … from Whitsun in an Oxfordshire village in 1890, to the Canterbury Arms in the 1850s. [Editor's note: the Canterbury Arms was a popular London music hall.] No such cultural form can be seen as natural or spontaneous, or as the simple products of popular demand' (p.137).

Whether the growth of mass cultural activities is a good or bad thing depends very much upon your own personal viewpoint. However, as a historian of the family and the community, it is important to assess the extent to which and in what ways family and community life has been affected by the development of mass entertainments.

As a result of this short discussion in section 3, what questions could you ask when exploring the cultural activities within your community?

I have summarized a number of key questions in Schema B.

Schema B: Questions relating to cultural life in the twentieth century

o   What commercial entertainments outside the home are available in your locality? Have they increased or decreased during the course of the century?

o   To what extent do people travel out of the area for their entertainment? What effect has this had on the local community?

o   How have local voluntary associations fared during the century? Has the growth of mass entertainments, both in and out of the home, reduced the numbers of people involved in formal associations?

3.1 FORMAL ASSOCIATIONS: VOLUNTARY ASSOCIATIONS IN BANBURY, 1948–50 AND 1966–8

In section 1 we made use of Trinder's list of the voluntary societies existing in Banbury around the middle of the nineteenth century. Now we are going to look at the town a hundred years later, largely through the research undertaken by Margaret Stacey (1960, 1975). In 1850, Banbury was an extremely important Midland market town. It has remained a market town but, from the 1930s onwards, large-scale industries were introduced. As a result the population of the town rose from 13,000 in 1931 to 19,000 in 1951, a rate of growth well above that of the nation as a whole. Stacey's research was aimed at investigating the social structure and culture of a town undergoing radical transition. Her first project covered the years 1948 to 1951 and she then followed this up with a second study covering 1966 to 1968.

The purpose of using her studies is to give those of you working on the period since the Second World War a set of figures and conclusions which you can compare with your own researches. Clearly, Stacey's research took many years and there is no way your work can be on anything like a comparable scale. However, in investigating the cultural life of your locality it would be possible to examine one or two of the existing voluntary associations. Concentrating on voluntary associations has a number of advantages in a study relating cultural life to a town or village. First, people who join do so freely and because they are interested in that particular association. Secondly, very often associations are small and so are capable of being examined in some detail. Thirdly, very often associations are connected with other groups, perhaps a local church, which helps in working out some of the cultural networks existing within the locality.

In her first study, Stacey examined 71 voluntary associations and in her second 74. She used the categories detailed in section 1.1 of this chapter. The findings of the study were discussed primarily in terms of the composition of the membership of the committees of these associations, the age range of the members, and their occupational status.

Male/female membership of committees   Table 9.2 shows the male/female membership of the committees of the various voluntary associations in Stacey's first study.

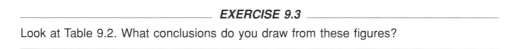

_____ **EXERCISE 9.3** _____

Look at Table 9.2. What conclusions do you draw from these figures?

Table 9.2 Men and women on committees of voluntary associations, Banbury, 1948–51

Type of assoc.	Men only committees		Mixed committees			Women only committees		Total no. of committees	Total members
	No. of committees	No. of members	No. of committees	No of members		No. of committees	No. of members		
				M	F				
Sports	15	143	5	57	13	0	0	20	213
Hobbies	7	61	2	16	2	0	0	9	79
Cultural	1	4	8	57	20	0	0	9	81
Social	5	56	2	20	9	3	26	10	111
Social Service	4	42	2	14	3	2	19	8	78
Charity	1	13	2	12	9	0	0	3	34
Mutual Aid	3	27	2	19	9	1	11	6	66
Occupational	3	33	3	70	8	0	0	6	111
TOTAL	39	379	26	265	73	6	56	71	773
Religious	5	26	16	118	79	6	30	27	253

Source: Stacey (1960) p.78, Table 16

The membership of the 71 associations was predominantly male – 644 men and only 129 women. The same goes for the membership of the committees. The associations listed under the categories sports, hobbies and occupational were particularly male orientated. Only the two charitable associations with mixed committees had a close male-female ratio. However, Stacey abstracted from her totals those associations which had a religious orientation (see final row in Table 9.2), and it is here that there was a much higher proportion of women compared with the other voluntary associations.

Stacey, also found that, apart from the Business and Professional Women's Club, all of the women's associations met in the morning or afternoon. This most probably reflects a feeling at the time that women should be at home when their husbands returned from work, and perhaps we should use this evidence to develop our conclusions concerning the role of married women after the Second World War (see Chapter 3, section 2).

By the time of her second study, the ratio of women to men sitting on the committees of the associations had slightly improved (see Table 9.3).

Table 9.3 Men and women on committees of voluntary associations: Banbury, 1950 and 1966–8 compared

Committees	Committees 1950		Committees 1966–8	
	No.	%	No.	%
All male	39	55	32	43
Mixed	26	36	32	43
All female	6	9	10	14
Total	71	100	74	100

Source: Stacey (1975) p.145, Table 6

Age of committee members of voluntary associations, 1948–50   Stacey concluded that the membership of the associations was predominantly middle-aged and the vast majority of the associations had committees whose average age was in the 40 to 60 band. Even within the category of sports clubs, where one might expect to find a committee with a low age-group, only six out of the twenty clubs had committees in the 30 to 39 age band.

Clearly, the percentage of young people associated with voluntary associations was low. Where there were associations run for young people, the composition of the committees was made up of older people. Even if younger age groups were interested, in 1950 they were too preoccupied with rearing families and were unable to participate in committee work.

Occupational status of committee members of voluntary associations, 1948–50
Membership of the 71 associations was of an above average occupational status, and committee membership was of a higher status than the membership. This was again borne out in the 1960s in the second survey, where a 6 per cent sample survey of the town was also made.

Stacey does point out, however, that manual workers would make up a large percentage of more informal groups like pub darts teams, which were not included in her category of formal voluntary associations. Nevertheless, those lower down the social scale were greatly underrepresented in voluntary associations.

Conclusion   In answer to the 6 per cent sample survey carried out by Stacey, covering the period 1966–68, under one in three of the population stated that they belonged to one voluntary association or more. The examination of voluntary associations was only one aspect of Stacey's surveys of Banbury, and she did not set out specifically to ask to what extent, if any, these associations contributed towards a sense of community within the town. Her overall conclusions were that, if a shared history was one precondition for the development of a community, then there was little sense of community in Banbury. 45 per cent of the population were what she defined as true immigrants; that is, people who were at least seven years of age before they came to Banbury. Also, the high rates of movements of families into and out of the town precluded a sense of community being built up. However, she did concede that, 'For those who are still part of the traditional small-town society, who own, manage or work in its traditionalist shops and smaller factories, who provide the traditional services, who belong to the close-knit and long-standing groups in clubs and pubs ... there is certainly some sense of community, some feeling of belonging ... But these are groups within the town and not the town itself' (1960, p.177).

EXERCISE 9.4

Go back to the questions raised in Schema B. Comment on how the findings of Stacey help in answering the questions relating to voluntary associations.

Stacey concluded from her second survey that under one-in-three of the people of Banbury belonged to voluntary associations, and both her surveys reveal that, within this minority, particular sections of the population were grossly under-represented – women, young people, and lower income groups.

Perhaps, then, the mass society theorists are right and the rest of the population were passively consuming products from the mass media. Or perhaps we need to delve further and explore the extent of informal associations in the town, something we noted had to be done if a full flavour of the cultural life of the community in the nineteenth century was to be experienced.

3.2   INFORMAL ASSOCIATIONS

As we have seen, the problem with concentrating on voluntary associations is that the information culled from them does not necessarily reveal the full extent of cultural activities. There may be four tennis clubs in a town, but that does not mean that the club members are the only active tennis players in the area. Obviously, listing the formal sports clubs in an area is easier than attempting to track down the numerous pub darts, dominoes, pool, snooker, skittles, etc. teams in the locality. But extended oral interviews can help to build up a picture of the leisure activities, including membership of formal and informal associations, within your particular community.

Davies (1992) used oral as well as written evidence in his study of working-class culture in Salford and Manchester in the period 1900 to 1939. He concluded that any study which concentrated on voluntary associations and commercial leisure activities, especially in areas where there was a high level of poverty, would fail to appreciate how working men and women spent their spare time. Just as in the nineteenth century when many leisure activities went unrecorded, so in Salford and Manchester, the poorer sections of the community chose to watch street-entertainers, visit the Saturday night street-markets, have a few illegal low-stake bets, and play football in the local parks. All of these were activities which were free or relatively inexpensive.

Finnegan (1989) also made use of oral techniques, together with observation, questionnaires, local newspapers and other documentary records, in her research into the range and function of musical activities in the new town of Milton Keynes in the early 1980s. Finnegan not only explored the activities of the formal musical associations within the town but also traced numerous informal groups and then attempted to assess the extent to which the local population was connected and involved with music-making, whether as performers, organizers or as audiences.

Perhaps not surprisingly, Finnegan's conclusions were, on the whole, vastly different from those of Stacey. She concluded that music-making in Milton Keynes was not the preserve of men, the middle class, or the middle-aged. Some of the choirs were short of men; brass bands had few older women; but apart from rock groups and some country and western bands, 'there were a few single-sex musical groups. Despite the imbalance of male and female in many groups and the gender constraints on certain activities, most musical pathways depended on the cooperation of both men and women' (p.316). Age was a factor among some of the popular bands, but overall there was a wide age range among musical participants, and many choirs, orchestras and brass bands contained members from several generations. As for music-making being the preserve of one particular class, Finnegan commented on 'the overall *mixture* of people practising it' and concluded that, 'Contrary to some expectations the findings on local musicians and their backgrounds in Milton Keynes in the early 1980s did *not* reveal any clear class-dominated patterns for involvement in music generally' (p.312).

In a new town with a population of some 100,000, it was perhaps not surprising that Finnegan found little evidence of a sense of belonging to a single community. By and large, there was not even an explicit local sense of community brought about by music played within particular localities within the city. Most music-makers did not perform their music within their own localities but travelled across the city to link up with fellow-performers who lived in other parts of the city. However, Finnegan did discover a general sense of belonging and of identity brought about through participation in music, and also quite strong family links, especially in particular branches of music-making. The local brass bands, traditionally strong in family ties, 'seemed to be full of relatives' (p.54). But family connections were also a marked feature in classical music, 'where the established learning system depended on parental support' (p.309),

Figure 9.4   The Cock and Bull Band: one of the many local bands playing in Milton Keynes in the 1980s (Source: Lionel Grech, Milton Keynes Photo Services)

and in operatic societies and in country and western music, 'at least in respect of the learned skill of expert audience participation: the flourishing local club was very much a family affair …' (p.310).

Even more important, the extent of the evidence from all the forms of amateur music-making in the town was such that it ran

> counter to the influential 'mass society' interpretations, particularly the extreme view which envisages a passive and deluded population lulled by the mass media and generating nothing themselves. Nor can music be explained (or explained away) as the creature of class divisions or manipulation, or in any simple way predictable from people's social and economic backgrounds or even in most cases, their age … And far from music-making taking a peripheral role for individuals and society – a view propagated in the kind of theoretical stance that marginalises 'leisure' or 'culture' as somehow less real than 'work' or 'society' – music can equally well be seen as playing a central part not just in urban networks but also more generally in the social structure and processes of our life today.

(Finnegan, 1989, pp.5–6)

What reasons can you give for why Finnegan's conclusions differ from those of Stacey?

First, we can note that Finnegan and Stacey examined different areas of cultural life. Stacey made a horizontal sweep of the town of Banbury, looking at the membership of a wide range of formal voluntary associations. Finnegan took an in-depth look at one particular area of cultural activity in Milton Keynes, involving both formal and informal organizations.

Secondly, Finnegan's work was undertaken thirty years after Stacey's first study.

Thirdly, we must be careful not to exaggerate the differences. For example, although Stacey concluded that the committee membership of voluntary associations in Banbury was dominated by men, she did not investigate the rank-and-file membership of these associations. It is very likely that the proportion of women in associations involving music and drama in 1950 was higher than in some of the other categories, such as sport and hobbies. This has probably always been the case. Note the comparatively large number of music societies in Trinder's list for the 1850s, in which women were almost certainly involved (see Table 9.1). Also, Stacey did observe that the ratio of female to male committee members in voluntary associations had increased slightly between her first and second studies (see Table 9.3).

Fourthly, although Finnegan found all classes and all age groups involved in music-making in Milton Keynes, her conclusions may well have been different, and nearer to those of Stacey, if she had merely attempted to discover the committee membership of the formal music associations within the town. Different approaches can lead to different conclusions, but it is important to look at both formal and informal activities if one is to understand the extent of cultural life within any particular area.

In the preface to her book, Finnegan mentioned that, although when she first went to the new town of Milton Keynes in 1969 many people living elsewhere called it a cultural desert, she found plenty of musical activities going on. It is interesting that Malcolmson, like those living outside of Milton Keynes, wrote in a similar vein, referring to a 'cultural vacuum', when examining the new towns of the early nineteenth century. Perhaps one reason for this emphasis on 'deserts' and 'vacuums' is that, as Finnegan has shown, one has to dig beneath the surface to discover the true extent of cultural activities within an area. Malcolmson, because of the limited source material available to him, was only able to scratch the surface in his search for cultural life in the new towns of the nineteenth century. Consequently, he might well have come to a wrong conclusion similar to that of the people who criticized Milton Keynes in 1969.

Finally, we could reflect on the significance of associations – both formal and informal – in differentiating and integrating people within the community in which they live. This can be important both for long-settled residents and for incomers (like many of those in Milton Keynes).

Phillips illustrates this in his study (1986), drawing on both observation and oral sources, of the small Yorkshire village of Muker in the 1970s and 1980s. He explains how the practice of 'mucking in' to local societies was used to overcome and (sometimes) highlight the differences between natives and incomers. Taking part in small neighbourhood organizations such as the 'Muker Silver Band, the Gunnerside Football Club, the Women's Guild and the Muker Badminton Club ... is the way whereby incomers will be "accepted" by [locals], and is in fact proof of such acceptance' (Phillips, 1986, p.151).

His analysis perhaps raises questions that could be explored more widely and leads us back once again to the importance of trying, wherever possible, to delve below the surface.

QUESTIONS FOR RESEARCH

Set up an oral history project based on members of families from a particular locality and raise the following questions? How do they spend their leisure time? What proportion of this time is spent in the home, watching television or videos, pursuing hobbies, etc.? How many times per week do they consume commercial entertainments outside the home – going to the cinema, watching professional football matches, etc.? Are they involved with any voluntary associations and what is the extent of this involvement? What proportion of their time do they spend in informal activities outside of the home – playing darts, playing in a pop group, etc.? Also, raise questions similar to those used by Stacey in her surveys of Banbury, and enquire about the age, occupational status and male/female membership of the voluntary and/or informal associations to which your interviewees belong.

Another possible project would be to take a particular year in the twentieth century (or even better, compare two different years) and, through the use of local newspapers and local documentary records (church magazines, records of particular clubs, etc.), assess the extent of leisure activities provided by commercial outlets and by formal and informal associations. Clearly, the difficulty in this case, as for those working on the nineteenth century, is to discover the extent and networks of informal associations. However, it is worth noting that some towns do possess registers of the voluntary associations existing within the area. The local citizens' advice bureau is a good starting point in the search for such a register.

Whatever project you choose, ask yourself whether or not your findings contribute to your understanding of your local community and compare them with those of Stacey (1960 and 1975) in Banbury, Finnegan (1989) in Milton Keynes, Davies (1992) in Salford and Manchester, or Phillips (1986) in Muker.

Also ask yourself whether the features of the cultural life in your locality confirm the view of the Yeos (i.e. that the commercialization of cultural activities has led to a mass culture which is not a product of local demand). Have commercial leisure activities reduced people's involvement in local activities and made them merely passive spectators? Or are the informal and formal activities within the area of such a nature that you can conclude, as Finnegan did in her study of music-making in Milton Keynes, that they can 'be seen as playing a central part not just in urban networks but also more generally in the social structure and processes of our life today' (Finnegan, 1989, p.6).

REFERENCES AND FURTHER READING

Note: suggestions for further reading are indicated by an asterisk.

Bailey, P. (1978), *Leisure and class in Victorian England: rational recreation and the contest for control, 1830–1885*, London, Routledge.

Biddiss, M. (1977) *The age of the masses. Ideas and society in Europe since 1870*, Harmondsworth, Penguin.

Briggs, A. (1968) *Victorian cities*, London, Harmondsworth.

Cunningham, H. (1980) *Leisure in the industrial revolution*, London, Croom Helm.[*]

Davies, A. (1992) *Leisure, gender and poverty: working-class culture in Salford and Manchester, 1900–1939*, Buckingham, Open University Press.[*]

Drake, M. (ed.) (1994) *Time, family and community: perspectives on family and community history*, Oxford, Blackwell in association with The Open University (Course Reader).

Finnegan, R. (1989) *The hidden musicians: music-making in an English town*, Cambridge, Cambridge University Press.

Golby, J. and Purdue, A.W. (1984) *The civilization of the crowd: popular culture in England 1750–1900*, London, Batsford.

Harrison, B. and Trinder, B.S. (1969) 'Drink and sobriety in an early Victorian town: Banbury 1830–1860', *English Historical Review*, supplement 4.

Hoggart, R. (1958) *The uses of literacy: aspects of working-class life with special reference to publications and entertainments*, Harmondsworth, Penguin in association with Chatto & Windus.

Holt, R. (1989) *Sport and the British*, Oxford, Oxford University Press.[*]

Humphries, S. (1981) *Hooligans or rebels? An oral history of working-class childhood and youth 1889–1939*, Oxford, Basil Blackwell.

Lascelles and Co.'s directory and gazetteer of the county of Oxford (1853) Birmingham, Lascelles and Co.

McKibbin, R. (1983) 'Work and hobbies in Britain 1850–1950', in Winter, J. (ed.) *The working class in modern British history*, Cambridge, Cambridge University Press.

Malcolmson, R.W. (1978) *Popular recreations in English society 1700–1850*, Cambridge, Cambridge University Press.

Mason, T. (1980) *Association football and English society 1863–1915*, Brighton, Harvester Press.

Meacham, S. (1977) *A life apart: the English working class 1890–1914*, London, Thames and Hudson.

Meller, H.E. (1976) *Leisure and the changing city 1870–1914*, London, Routledge.

Metcalfe, A. (1982) 'Organized sport in the mining communities of South Northumberland 1800–1889', *Victorian Studies*, 25, 4, pp.469–95.

Phillips, S.K. (1986) 'Natives and incomers: the symbolism of belonging in Muker parish, North Yorkshire', in Cohen, A.P. (ed.) *Symbolizing boundaries: identity and diversity in British cultures*, Manchester, Manchester University Press. Reprinted in Drake, M. (1994).

Stacey, M. (1960) *Tradition and change: a study of Banbury*, Oxford, Oxford University Press.

Stacey M. (1975) *Power, persistence and change: a second study of Banbury*, London, Routledge.

Stedman Jones, G. (1983) *Languages of class: studies in English working-class history 1832*, Cambridge, Cambridge University Press.

Thompson, P. (1975) *The Edwardians: the remaking of British society*, London, Weidenfeld and Nicolson.*

Trinder, B.S. (1982) *Victorian Banbury*, Chichester, Phillimore.

Walton, J.K. (1992) *Fish and chips and the British working class, 1870–1940*, Leicester, Leicester University Press.

Walton, J.K. and Walvin, J. (eds) (1983) *Leisure in Britain 1780–1939*, Manchester, Manchester University Press.

Williams, A. (1915) *Life in a railway factory*, London, Duckham. New edition published 1969, Newton Abbott, David and Charles.

Yeo, S. (1976) *Religion and voluntary organizations in crisis*, London, Croom Helm.

Yeo, E and Yeo, S. (eds) (1981) *Popular culture and class conflict 1590–1914*, Brighton, Harvester Press.

PART IV

REFLECTING ON THE ISSUES

CHAPTER 10

CONCLUSION

by John Golby (section 1) and Ruth Finnegan (sections 2 and 3)

1   FAMILIES AND COMMUNITIES

by John Golby

The major aims of this volume have been to trace relationships between the family and the community, and to suggest various localized and manageable research projects which explore these relationships. We hope that at least some of the proposed projects connected with work and other activities within the community, including local politics, religion and leisure activities, will have excited your imagination and that you are now keen to go ahead with your investigations.

Your own particular researches should prove to be the most enjoyable outcome of your work on this series of volumes. You are now in the driving seat and you have an opportunity to add to our knowledge of family and community history. Whatever strategies or techniques you adopt (from quantitative analyses to basing your project on family letters), whatever particular community you are investigating, or whatever period you are concentrating on, there is still much for us all to learn.

Perhaps your researches may reinforce our views concerning some aspect of family or community history because they verify and confirm the findings of previous local or wider comparative studies. However, it will be very unusual if *all* of your conclusions mirror precisely those of other similar studies. In his work on the English working class in the period 1890–1914, Standish Meacham wrote, 'Yet no working class district was quite like any other. Local geography and local industry lent each one distinction, sordid or otherwise. In York, the smell might be from the slaughterhouses; in South London, from the jam factories' (1977, p.31). We are not expecting your research to go into such minutiæ as investigating smells. In fact, it is very unlikely that Standish Meacham spent much research time on this particular aspect of history. What he was trying to emphasize was that no community was or is exactly the same as any other. Even within a comparatively small geographical area, there can be significant differences. Elizabeth Roberts, in her oral history study of women in three towns in central and northern Lancashire, concluded that the experiences of these women and their families varied widely, especially in respect to housing and work opportunities. Even in the matter of diet there were marked local differences (Roberts, 1984, p.7).

So, while it is meaningful and important to explore the interconnections and similarities between your own research and that of others, it is also essential that you attempt to isolate the differences. Indeed, highlighting differences is just as important, if not more so, than verifying the results of previous studies. History is just as much about the particular and unique as it is about exploring patterns and connections.

All the volumes in this series have concentrated on helping you to acquire the necessary skills to embark on a research project. They have introduced you to a wide variety of primary sources, and they have also attempted to provide a historical background and to give you some understanding of the various major debates and findings in the areas of family and community history. You should now have all the resources to produce a research project. What you should do with your research into family and community history is a topic which will be discussed in the next section.

2   WHAT SHOULD YOU DO WITH YOUR RESEARCH INTO FAMILY AND COMMUNITY HISTORY?

by Ruth Finnegan

Your own research and its relation to that of others has been a key theme throughout the volumes in this series. But why *should* you report your findings? True, there are undoubtedly personal satisfactions in conducting research: the thrills of detection and triumphs of surmounting obstacles; the rewards of finding things fall into place or relating a single case to wider patterns; the emotion of discovering something of one's own; or the consciousness of deploying the skills of analysis, criticism and synthesis. But is there more to it than just personal enjoyment? The assumption in these volumes is that there is: that the outcome will be not just undertaking a piece of research, but also *communicating* it; and furthermore that this is a worthwhile thing to do.

Let us consider this a bit further, starting as usual with personal questions before moving on to the wider issues.

Why might *you* go to the trouble of writing up and communicating your research to others?

Your own reasons are personal to you, but here are some likely ones:

1   Like so many others, you've been fascinated by your discoveries and want to share them with other people (anyone who'll listen perhaps …).

2   You relish communicating and expressing yourself: the fruits of your researches in family or community history are as good an occasion for this as any – better than most, quite likely.

3   Pulling together and communicating your findings is a final touch which gives you even greater insight into what you have discovered.

4   If your research has been about a particular locality, group or family, you may want to pass something on for its future, as well as present, generations.

5   You would like to contribute to the further development of historical knowledge.

There are some common reasons *against* writing up and communicating research too (real ones – but note also the comments in brackets):

1   You may encounter so many obstacles that you don't feel in a position to provide a serious report: the results do not turn out as you'd hoped or the whole thing gets in a mess. (That happens to even the best of researchers! But negative results too are worth reporting, if only to save others needless trouble; and research that turns out unexpectedly may lead to new insights. Sometimes

it *is* only sensible to cut your losses – but having learnt lessons from your abortive attempt, you will be in a stronger position to carry your *next* project through successfully.)

2 You feel you are not yet ready, and have more to do first. (Although this may be true, don't forget the danger of *never* being ready – deadlines sometimes help! Research can be reported in small bites, so you don't have to move immediately into the definitive work.)

3 No-one else (you suspect) will be interested in your research. (Don't be too sure – at any rate finish reading this chapter).

4 Completing, writing up and communicating research results is hard work: often harder than the agreeable process of searching out sources or gathering data. (True, but who thought historians had easy lives?)

There is also an ethical issue. Small-scale studies, once set in perspective, can contribute to our historical understanding, provided their investigators are willing to share their results. Thus, Peter Laslett (1987) argues strongly that historians of the family have a *duty* to both their own and earlier generations to provide informed perspectives on the past. The same could be said of community history, indeed of all the research projects suggested in these volumes.

How can this be done? There are many possible forms. One option is to produce a book or booklet, whether through self-publication or a commercial publisher. Another is to contribute to local newspapers or to a variety of periodicals, from those of your local family or local history society to regional or national journals (Volume 4, Chapter 10 gives detailed advice). It is also worth considering other formats – photographic and pictorial forms, maps, lectures, seminars, local radio, and audio or video presentations (see Volume 4, Chapter 11; also Calder and Lockwood, 1993; Kirkup and Clegg, 1993).

And what kinds of projects are worth reporting? Follow the Chinese adage: 'Keep your eye on what is big, but try your hand on what is small' (quoted in Kao, 1982, p.25). In other words, as is suggested throughout these volumes, go for small-scale studies set in the context of comparative work by other researchers.

3 THE STUDY OF THE PAST AND THE RESPONSIBILITIES OF THE HISTORIAN

Your actions in conducting and reporting your research are, of course, those of a historian. So it is appropriate to conclude this volume by stepping back to reflect a little further on the uses of the past and the contribution of historians, thus putting your own activities into perspective.

Why *do* people study the past? We can start with your own views.

Why are you, or others, interested in family or community history?

There are many answers. Here are several possible responses – worth pondering, if only to compare them with your own experience.

First, we don't want to lose the past. One poignant consequence of parting from friends or family, or seeing one's contemporaries die (envisaging one's own death too) is losing those shared memories. But we try to retain and recreate them through historical study, to a degree keeping the past alive. A classic Chinese historian put it picturesquely, but his sentiments are ones many would share:

So long as the office of historiographer is carried on, so long as books continue to exist, then though men die and enter into darkness and empty silence, their deeds remain, shining like the stars of the Milky Way

(Liu Chih-Chi (661–721 AD); quoted in Kao, 1982, p.47)

Secondly, our experience of our own identity lies partly in our memory, in our consciousness of the past. As the reminiscence movement shows so clearly, recognizing an individual's memories plays a significant role in validating their life – notably with older people, but in a way with everyone (see Bornat 1989, Finnegan, 1992, pp.128ff.). This applies not just to individuals but also to families and groups. Uncovering their own history can bring a sense of identity and recognition for those who have felt rootless, faced discrimination, or somehow been defined out of sight. Recent attention to the history of women, of ethnic groups, of Africa, of working-class families, has led to the historical 'discovery' of groups which in the past were assumed to be either too unimportant to deserve historical attention or to 'have no history'. Researching the histories of previously 'invisible' groups has made their experience both more valued and more 'real'.

Forging a sense of identity and meaning through studying the past is hardly unique to modern times. But is this, perhaps, especially important now, when – it is argued – people are coping with massive change and uncertainty, or finding it hard to retain personal meaning when struggling with uncontrollable outside forces? Some analysts suggest a connection between current crises and the huge expansion in family and local history over recent years (see Sayers, 1987; Schürer, 1991; Hey 1993, Chapter 1). Certainly, an interest in 'roots' and 'heritage' is a striking feature of present day society. As Peter Burke notes:

> In order to orient themselves in a period of rapid social change, many people find it increasingly necessary to find their roots and to renew their links with the past, particularly the past of their own community – their family, their town or village, their occupation, their ethnic or religious group.
>
> (Burke, 1992, p.19)

The psychologist Stephen Sayers (1987) goes further, proposing the historical hypothesis that genealogical interest is specially important when people's identities are in doubt. He notes the aristocrats' preoccupation with genealogy in just that period (1550–1650) when their identity was under threat, and suggests a similar link between the modern interest in family history and the transformations and uncertainties of today (1987, p.152, citing Plumb, 1969, pp.31–34; for a modified view, see Hey, 1993, p.1; Drake, 1994, p.1).

Finally, there is the common human longing to somehow locate ourselves and our interests within the continuities of the past. How can we see meaning in our small bit of the vast millennia of the past, or find continuity in the endless cycles of generations? This challenge is a pressing one, and it should not be avoided by reflective human beings. Some responses lie of course in the cosmologies of the world's great religions. They refer us, for example, to God's purpose working through the ages, the transmigration of souls enacting out destinies over the eras, or ancestors whose names are revered as part of present realities. There are the alternative responses, too, of overarching social theories like nineteenth-century evolutionism, Marxism, or the 'Whig' view of history as one-way progress to the present.

But this search for what is in some sense eternal in the transiencies of the present is not just confined to the big theories. It takes place through personal and down-to-earth experience too.

One example is people's sense of the continuity of a *place*. It could be a particular house or area, for example, whose meaning for individuals and families can be deepened yet further as they discover and celebrate the past continuance behind the present. Perhaps equally likely, given the population movements over the last centuries, is that links with place are appreciated more indirectly: through old names for new places, or the recurrent use of the same house name despite the moves. We know too of the deep emotion with which people sometimes search out and visit the places from which their forebears came, perhaps many generations back.

Or take the (apparently) trivial matter of people's *names*. In some cultures, the spirit of a grandparent is thought to be reborn in a descendant with the same name, a direct link into the world of the ancestors. This is not the contemporary British or Irish custom. But something of that feeling of continuance comes through when we find first names repeating through many generations. And we expect the same surname to continue through paternal branches of the family, and that the maternal surname too will sometimes be commemorated through a child's second name. Recurrent naming practices were once quite explicit in Scottish families, the same names echoing down the generations (see Table 10.1). Remember too how we name children 'after' friends or relations from an earlier generation.

Table 10.1 Scottish naming cycle

	named after	
Eldest son		Father's father
Eldest daughter	"	Mother's mother
Second son	"	Mother's father
Second daughter	"	Father's mother
Third son	"	Father or father's brother
Third daughter	"	Mother or mother's sister

Rosemary Aubert's evocative poem 'Me as my grandmother' (Aubert, 1977, p.45) expresses something of this deep consciousness of the recurrent cycles of human life.

Me as my grandmother

Sometimes
I look up quickly
and see for an instant
her face
in my mirror,
random tightness
turns my mouth
into a facsimile of hers,
eyes caught oddly
in the glass
make me
into her
looking at me

Now that she's dead,
I understand
that it is right
that I should age
and wrinkle into her
It brings her back,
it puts me into
the cycle of family.
We look at all time
with just that
one same face.

Such reasons behind the search for family or community history are certainly intelligible ones (relevant for you too?). We can draw out their implications further by returning again to the more general question of why people should be interested in the past at all.

One answer is that the process of memory is fundamental to human beings and to their life together. So it is hardly strange that interest in the past is apparently universal in human society. It is more than just an individual matter. For the continuance of human culture depends on our devices for 'defying individual mortality and bridging generations' (Bullock, 1985, p.18; see also Middleton and Edwards, 1990). Shared human memories of the past and their systematic formulation in historical study are crucial for this continuance.

The ways people think about the past take different forms, of course, varying in particular places, cultures, or historical periods (see Davis, 1992; Tonkin, 1992; Tonkin et al., 1989). Sometimes the emphasis is on stark chronicles of events; on individuals' lives; on genealogies of the powerful; on myths about the origins of the current social order. Sometimes the study of history is presented as scientific and objective, sometimes as a model for good behaviour or a celebration of the past. Often the primary sources lie in written documents; but there are other kinds of sources too (particularly in the many cultures where literacy has taken a less dominating role than in modern western history, and more recently here in the west too), not least the resources of unwritten human memory. But there is always some way, it seems, by which the past is studied and recalled (for further discussion of history and its study, see Volume 4, Chapter 2 by Arthur Marwick, sections 1–2).

There is another obvious reason for studying the past. The past moulds the present. Think of the effects of earlier political events, demographic trends, human–landscape interactions, family traditions passed from generation to generation, the identity of communities based on their perceptions of a shared past. Indeed, as Alan Bullock argues (1985), it is *only* by understanding these historically-imposed constraints that we can free ourselves from the 'tyranny of the past', and gain a sense of alternative options, the freedom to help to shape the future. Or, as Arthur Marwick puts it, 'quite simply, societies need history' (Volume 4, p.17).

It is not just 'objective' past events that influence the present; it is also people's *attitudes and views* about the past. This comes out in family myths or in the way people's *beliefs* about their long attachment to a particular community can mould its identity (see, for example, Phillips, 1986; Strathern, 1981). Shared images about the past can shape – and justify – the present.

Similarly, we are often profoundly influenced by historical interpretations which explain and sanction the present by reference to the past. The elaborate genealogies familiar not only in the Bible but in many other cultures of the world are one example. Throughout history, royal and aristocratic genealogies have been used to explain and support the position of their present-day descendants (the status-seeking interests of some genealogists are scarcely unique to recent times!). Other historical theories may seem less explicitly related to the contemporary order. None the less, the 'myths we live by' (as it is put in Samuel and Thompson, 1990) can be equally potent for our interpretation of the world around us. We need only recall the influence of images like the 'Golden Age' of the Family or of the Community when, unlike our fallen world now (so goes the story), all was harmony and stability; or of the contrary but still powerful idea of the linear progress of family and community life since the supposedly more primitive times of the past. Our assessment of such theories affects our view of the *present*, not just the past.

There is also the additional twist, of course, that there are often *contrasting* interpretations of the past and of how it should be studied, or struggles between several interested parties. Since our historical perceptions affect our vision of the present world, whose version prevails makes a difference. It is a matter of more than just academic interest that the traditional historical focus on aristocrats, the powerful and those at 'the centre', is now increasingly being extended to the experiences of ordinary families and of peripheral localities. As Jim Sharpe has it:

> *History from below helps convince those of us born without silver spoons in our mouths that we have a past, that we come from somewhere. But it will also, as the years progress, play an important part in helping to correct and amplify that mainstream political history which is still the accepted canon in British historical studies.*

(Sharpe, 1991, p.38)

Such extensions directly affect our interpretation of both past and present. Whether most people know it or not, the ways we look at the past are bound up with the present (and with its power relationships too). The values we live by are intertwined with our images of the past.

It matters, therefore, what view of the past people hold. This is where historians come in, and why they carry responsibilities for how they reconstruct the past. Peter Laslett is surely right when he writes of the duty of

the historian of the family, like all investigators of society and of its history ... to search after truth to the utmost of his capacity, or hers, recognising that it may be impossible to avoid some degree of bias but doing all that can be done to reduce it.

(Laslett, 1987, p.263)

Because of this crucial importance of the historian's role, it can be argued that it should not just be those in political and economic power who control the interpretations of the past (and, hence of the present and future); nor should history just be 'owned' by a small élite of professional academics. It should be taken up by all citizens with the opportunity and capacity to engage in historical study and reclaim it as their own. Consciously or unconsciously we all pass on history and see ourselves through history. The emphasis in these volumes on careful and detailed small-scale studies in the perspective of wider understanding – keeping your eye on the big but turning your hand to the small – suggests a route to fulfilling that citizen's responsibility: enhancing our understanding of the past and, through this, leading to a deeper and more informed appreciation of the present.

REFERENCES AND FURTHER READING

Note: suggestions for further reading are indicated by an asterisk.

Aubert, R. (1977) *Two kinds of honey: poems,* Ottawa, Oberon Press.

Bornat, J. (1989) 'Oral history as a social movement: reminiscence and older people', *Oral History,* 17, pp.16–24.

Bullock, A. (1985) 'Breaking the tyranny of the present', *Times Higher Education Supplement,* 24 May, pp.18–19.*

Burke, P. (1992) *History and social theory,* Cambridge, Polity Press.

Calder, A. and Lockwood, V. (1993) *Shooting video history,* Milton Keynes, The Open University.

Davis, J. (1992) 'History and the people without Europe', in Hastrup, K. (ed.) (1992).

Drake, M. (ed.) (1994) *Time, family and community: perspectives on family and community history,* Oxford, Blackwell in association with The Open University (Course Reader).

Finnegan, R. (1992) *Oral traditions and the verbal arts: a guide to research practices,* London, Routledge.

Hastrup, K. (ed.) (1992) *Other histories,* London, Routledge.*

Hey, D. (1993) *The Oxford guide to family history,* Oxford, Oxford University Press.

Kao, G. (ed.) (1982) *The translation of things past: Chinese history and historiography,* Hong Kong, Chinese University Press.

Kirkup, G. and Clegg, J. (1993) 'Presenting your findings through audio-vision', audio-cassette 6B in Braham, P. (ed.) (1993) *Using the past: audio-cassettes on sources and methods for family and community historians,* Milton Keynes, The Open University.

Laslett, P. (1987) 'The character of familial history, its limitations and the conditions for its proper pursuit', in Hareven, T. and Plakans, A. (eds) *Family history at the crossroads,* Princeton, Princeton University Press.*

Lowenthal, D. (1985) *The past is another country,* Cambridge, Cambridge University Press.*

Meacham, S. (1977) *A life apart: the English working class 1890–1914,* London, Thames and Hudson.

Middleton, D. and Edwards, D. (eds) (1990) *Collective remembering,* London, Sage.

Nicolaisen, W.F.H. (1991) 'The past as place: names, stories, and the remembered self', *Folklore,* 102, 1, pp.3–15.*

Phillips, S.K. (1986) 'Natives and incomers: the symbolism of belonging in Muker parish, North Yorkshire', in Cohen, A.P. (ed.) *Symbolising boundaries: identity and diversity in British cultures,* Manchester, Manchester University Press. Reprinted in Drake, M. (1994).

Plumb, J.H. (1969) *The death of the past,* London, Macmillan.

Roberts, E. (1984) *A woman's place: an oral history of working-class women 1890–1940,* Oxford, Basil Blackwell.

Samuel, R. and Thompson, P. (1990) (eds) *The myths we live by,* London, Routledge.*

Sayers, S. (1987) 'The psychological significance of genealogy', in Bennett, G., Smith, P. and Widdowson, J.D.A. (eds) *Perspectives on contemporary legend,* Sheffield, Sheffield University Press.*

Schürer, K. (1991) 'The future for local history: boom or recession?', *The Local Historian,* 21, pp.99–108.

Sharpe, J. (1991) 'History from below', in Burke, P. (ed.) *New perspectives on historical writing,* Cambridge, Polity Press.

Strathern, M. (1981) *Kinship at the core: an anthropology of Elmdon a village in north-west Essex in the nineteen-sixties,* Cambridge, Cambridge University Press.

Tonkin, E. (1992) *Narrating our pasts. The social construction of oral history,* Cambridge, Cambridge University Press.

Tonkin, E., McDonald, M. and Chapman, M. (eds) (1989) *History and ethnicity,* ASA Monograph 27, London, Routledge.

EXERCISES: ANSWERS AND COMMENTS

Exercise 1.2

These are some of the ideas I came up with:

1   What paid employment did the heads of the families undertake? What occupations did the other members of the family living in the same house have? Did the mothers work, and if so, did they go out to work or work at home? Clearly, CEBs are an essential source if you are basing your studies in the nineteenth century. If you are working in the twentieth century, birth and marriage certificates together with oral evidence are major sources (see Volume 4 for further information on these sources).

2   Into which social classification would you put the occupations of the household heads? Certain broad ways of classifying these are outlined in Chapter 5. Other more detailed classification schemes are given in Volume 4, Chapter 3, section 2.1.1.

3   What work opportunities were there in particular localities? Were the localities which you are researching dominated by one particular industry? Again, census returns are a key source here; directories are also very useful.

4   How large were the industries in your area? Were there many small workshops? What were relations like within the workshops and factories? Indeed, what were the work experiences of the families you are investigating? Sources you can use in relation to these questions include newspapers, directories, CEBs and personal sources such as reminiscences, letters and diaries.

5   Was there continuity of work, or did family members change jobs fairly regularly, or were there periods of irregular work? What were the opportunities for 'moonlighting'? These are difficult questions to answer, especially for those working on the nineteenth century, but they can certainly be explored if you are using oral evidence.

Exercise 2.1

The work histories of the Manchester Arnisons illuminate particularly well the feature of the irregularity of work and multi-occupations. Edith's recollections about her father, Joseph Arnison, demonstrate very clearly how many different kinds of jobs her father undertook. In addition, he was described on his marriage certificate as a coal miner, though the story goes that he met his future wife while working in his brother-in-law's public house. He attracted her attention initially because he was wearing a white shirt instead of the usual workman's blue one. Edith herself also had to turn her hand to many jobs. Besides the work she did as a machinist, she also helped out in her mother's tripe shop in the evening. Her mother cleaned other people's houses during the day. Using census and other records such as the birth certificates of Joseph's thirteen children and army records, it might be possible to build up a more detailed picture of his various jobs.

Exercise 2.2

There are a number of features of this part of the Arnison family history that could be developed to illuminate larger-scale themes which could, in their turn, be used to cast light both on this individual family history and on others.

Examples I picked out were inheritance customs (the way in which the property at Kirkoswald was left to elder sons); patterns of inheritance (Nathan was apparently left nothing by his father, but all the rest of his siblings got their £30); demographic experience (the size of the Arnison families); commercial and business practices (the way in which Nathan Arnison learnt the drapery business and bought property, the development of the solicitors' business in Penrith) and even local politics (Robert Arnison became mayor of Sheffield). Volume 4, Chapter 4, sections 1 and 5 on trade directories and business records would provide useful support to the investigation of how companies were set up and grew; the material later in this volume (Chapter 5 on social mobility and Chapters 6 and 7 on local politics) would also be helpful in this kind of research.

Exercise 2.3

The most telling source for this kind of experiential evidence is, of course, the oral material recorded with Edith Seddon (née Arnison) and her younger sister, Alice. Shortage of space here means that many anecdotes about their own and their parents' working lives have had to be left out. However, they were able to supply many details about what their father wore to work, what hours he worked, what rules governed the household where his work was concerned ('The pony was fed before us children') and, very occasionally, what good times were had at work ('My father drove his cart along the street, throwing oranges to all the children'). Jim Arnison's autobiography also contains a great deal about his father's working life and, in particular, his work as President of the local Boilermakers' Union. If the union records are available, then this would be another useful source.

No letters survive from the Manchester Arnisons' past – one suspects they wrote very few. But the Penrith Arnisons left many letters behind, both formal and informally written, which refer, albeit indirectly, to their working lives. The obituaries in the local paper contained some useful insights into their professional lives. Work done by Major William Burra Arnison, Clerk to the Guardians of the Penrith Union, will have been documented in their records.

Exercise 2.4

Clearly in a town of 50,000 and with a workforce of 10,000, the factory in one sense dominated the town. Many of the other inhabitants of the town must have been, at least indirectly, dependent on the prosperity of the works. Even for those who had no connection with the factory, the 'dreaded' factory hooter, first sounded at 5.20 a.m., would waken the townspeople and those living in outlying parts.

Although the majority of workers lived in the town itself, many travelled considerable distances, some as far as 12 miles, and used different means of transport. Most walked, some used the 'factory trains', some by 1915 rode bicycles, and some workmen shared costs by coming in together by horse and cart. (Incidentally, the arrangements made for stabling the horse and storing the vehicle with the proprietor of a local pub tells us something about the part that pubs played in the community. This will be explored further in Chapter 9.)

There is an interesting reference to the links between town and country. In the past, at haymaking and harvest times, farmers would meet some of the men who lived in the outlying villages, take them back and, for the price of a meal and a couple of shillings a night, the men would help with the harvesting. By 1914 this work practice had died out.

Some of the men living in outlying parts kept pigs and worked in their gardens *before* setting out for work.

The factory hooter was sounded at 5.20 a.m., 5.50 a.m., 5.55 a.m. and finally at 6 a.m. Non-management workers were given five minutes' grace, but were fined if they arrived for work after five past six.

The sort of information you need to treat with care is, of course, that contained in the old stories that are passed down from generation to generation, with their tendency to become taller at each telling. It is also important to remember that Williams was first and foremost a country-man, and in this section (as throughout the book) he shows his prejudices in this respect and makes wide generalizations. For example, 'country mothers are far more painstaking in the matter of providing meals than are many of those in the town'. Again, later on, he remarks that the food the countrymen bring in to eat at lunchtime is plainer and simpler but fresher and cleaner. Nevertheless, diets did differ in town and country and from region to region (see Burnett, 1966).

Exercise 2.5

The introduction of piece work clearly led to conflict between management and men. Many men were put on part-time work, some were transferred to other workshops, and some were dismissed. There was little trade union organization within the works except among the most skilled workers. Fitters, who served apprenticeships, did belong to a trade union and, significantly, it was from among this trade that foremen were recruited.

Although the GWR works were massive, the factory was divided into a series of specialized workshops which had little contact with each other. There was a rivalry between the managers of the various workshops, and, to a lesser extent, between the foremen, but for the vast majority of the men who had no chance of promotion, they were indifferent to what was going on within the works.

Transfers from one workshop to another were extremely rare, and it was forbidden for men to move around the factory. Consequently, men rarely got to know other working men apart from those doing the same skilled, semi-skilled or unskilled jobs. As Williams writes, 'the workman's sphere is very narrow and limited. There is no freedom ... '.

There was a hierarchy in the works, not just on a manager, foreman, worker basis, but between different trades. The carriage finishers, who had served apprenticeships, obviously had to wear clean clothes because of the work they did; however, they possessed their own uniform – cloth suits, linen collars, spotless white aprons and bowler hats – which distinguished them from other craftsmen. Although they were by no means the best paid group in the works (see Table 2.3), they, at least in Williams's eyes, possessed an air of respectability and lived in the better parts of Swindon. The fitters were the élite of the works. As well as belonging to trade unions and serving apprenticeships, they had their own 'uniform'.

Exercise 3.1

1 The numbers of female domestic servants peaked in the 15–24 year age group, with about half the total. Female domestic servants heavily outnumbered their male counterparts.

2 Ireland had, relatively speaking, fewer domestic servants in the younger age groups and dramatically more in the higher ones. Note that 8 per cent, or 1 in 12, of Irish women *over* 65 years of age appeared, in the census at least, to be indoor domestic servants. Miss Collett put forward the following suggestions to explain this.

> *The process of elimination of the unfit and infirm does not seem to go on in Ireland with the same completeness as in England, and the elderly and incompetent appear to be retained with more tolerance in Ireland. Perhaps also in Ireland capable servants are more inclined to stay on with mistresses to whom they are accustomed, without much thought whether they could earn higher wages elsewhere.*

(Board of Trade, 1899, p.9)

Perhaps you can think of alternative explanations and carry out the necessary research to see how accurate they – or those of Miss Collett – are.

Exercise 3.2

Today this is known as a 'snowball sample', the analogy being with a snowball that increases in size as it is rolled along. Miss Collett defended her method on two counts. First, she believed it 'gave a better guarantee that the information filled in would be trustworthy, a matter of special

227

importance in the case of an enquiry which has been necessarily conducted by means of schedules to which no signatures were required'. Second, although she recognized that the method 'wouldn't result in a set of returns that accurately represented the different classes of servant keeping households', she believed this didn't matter, so long as she got an adequate number from each class. For she could then use the census returns to 'weight' the different sets of returns. She recognized, however, that she had a 'special difficulty in the case of one-servant households'. In fact there were two. One was that her sampling method was unlikely to throw up an adequate number of such households. And second, even if it were to do so, Miss Collett felt it would be 'impossible to obtain satisfactory returns of wages from mistresses employing the roughest and most unskilled class of servants'. She therefore went to another source, the Metropolitan Association for Befriending Young Servants. This body had established registries for domestic servants across London. From these, in 31 different districts, Miss Collett obtained the 'initial wages of 1669 girls of the least trained class' (Board of Trade, 1899, p.2).

Exercise 3.3

Clearly, here are two very different views about married women taking employment outside the home. The first comes from an interview with a Lancaster housewife recalling attitudes early in this century. Notice that Mrs S interprets the question about work as one which involves going out to a place of work. She adds that there were not many opportunities for married women to work outside the home and, in any case, the attitude of her tradesman father was that it would reflect badly upon him if his wife were 'to go to work'. Incidentally, in the 1901 census only 13.2 per cent of women classified as 'occupied' were married or widowed (Braybon, 1981, p.25).

The second extract is from an answer given by a 43 year old wife of a farm labourer in Argyllshire to a Mass-Observation questionnaire of January 1944 which asked, 'Should married women be able to go out to work after the war?' The woman's attitude is quite different from that of Mrs S: although she recognizes that many men still believe that the place of women is in the home, she argues that women should be allowed to retain the jobs they have undertaken during the war. In 1943 some 43 per cent of working women were married (Central Office of Information, 1944), that is, nearly 1 out of every 2 working women were married (Summerfield, 1989, p.196).

Exercise 3.4

I have noted the following:

o The percentage of married women working in Eynsham was higher than the national figure.

o The vast majority of the married women in Eynsham pursued occupations that could be carried out in their own homes (glovers alone account for 42.5 per cent of those in employment).

o Most of the occupations were gender-based, probably casual, and certainly without career prospects.

o The majority of these working women were married to poorly paid agricultural labourers and, presumably, the incomes of the wives were very important for family survival.

Exercise 3.5

1 Here are nine possible sources (there are others):

o Published census returns: for comparative material about work patterns or specific occupations (Chapter 2, section 1, and Chapter 3, section 1).

o   CEBs: to collect comparative information about occupations in different families (Chapter 2, section 1), or within a particular community (Chapter 3, section 2); or about a specific occupation (Chapter 3, section 1).

o   Local newspapers: for information about the background of a particular occupational group (Chapter 3, section 3); to trace industrial disputes (Chapter 2, section 2).

o   Memoirs and autobiographies: for the nature of work, industrial relations, etc., particularly the experiential aspects (Chapter 2, section 2).

o   Occupational records (Chapter 2, section 3 explores police records and their uses, but comparable sources may be available for other occupations).

o   Interviews and oral recordings: for personal experience, views of particular roles (Chapter 2, sections 1 and 3).

o   Maps: to provide the location and basis for certain calculations (Chapter 3, section 1), or for the distribution of particular occupations (Chapter 3, section 2).

o   Business records: to trace the history of a particular firm, and relate it to wider theories (Chapter 3, section 3; see also Chapter 4).

o   Trade directories: for information on a specific locality, useful not just for locating individuals but for comparisons over time and place (Chapter 2, section 2 and Chapter 3, section 3).

For further details on these sources see Part II of Volume 4.

2   You will have your own answer, but other notable sources include the Scottish Statistical Accounts (described in Chapter 4) and – mentioned in Chapters 1–3 but not treated in detail – letters, photographs and buildings (see also the sources described in Volume 4, together with advice on their critical assessment).

3   This is up to you, but don't forget the practical point that a source, however good in *theory*, is no use to you unless you can somehow get access to it.

Exercise 3.6

Your answer will partly depend on your definition of 'methods' and 'strategies' (they overlap); here are some possibilities:

o   Interviews and oral recordings (e.g. Chapter 2, sections 1 and 3)

o   Computer analysis (e.g. of police recruits, Chapter 2, section 3)

o   Quantitative calculations (Chapter 3, section 1)

o   Starting from a question or source (e.g. Chapter 3, section 2)

For further discussion of research methods and strategies, see Volume 4, Chapters 1,7, 8 and 9.

Exercise 3.7

Possibilities include:

o   Any one of the four ideas and debates discussed in Chapter 1, section 3.

o   General trends to which specific cases can be related (see the examples in Chapter 1, section 2, and Chapter 3, sections 1 and 2 – this comparative approach can be applied to other topics too).

o   Questions raised about one type of work here could be followed up for (a) a different type of work or (b) a different period or area, and the results compared to the findings here.

o   Further suggestions (often involving some link to a general theory and/or the possibility of *comparison)* appear in the Questions for Research.

Exercise 5.1

1 69.

2 394.

3 3,126.

4 Classes I and II = non-manual; Classes III–V = manual; therefore the number of fathers in Classes I and II with sons in Classes III–V = 33 + 9 + 8 + 458 + 216 + 161 = 885.

5 The number of sons in Classes I and II with fathers in Classes III–V = 13 + 5 + 1 + 287 + 87 + 77 = 470.

Exercise 5.2

1 0.

2 315.

3 44 per cent.

4 7.7 per cent.

Exercise 5.3

Because the categories are drawn up differently, what counts as inter-generational occupational movement in one scheme does not in the other. For Miles and Vincent, the train driver's son who became an insurance clerk was upwardly mobile, but not for Glass. Other problems are: (a) their geographical coverage was different (and neither covered Ireland, north or south); (b) aggregate figures may not tell us about *local* differences; and (c) both focused on men.

Exercise 5.5

1 See the information summarized in Table 5.1 (also Schemas A, B and C in this chapter).

2 Some examples include McKay's (1985) study of shale-oil workers (type C in Table 5.1) using CEBs, civil registers and newspapers (Chapter 4, section 3) and Erickson's comparative (1959) study of recruitment among steel and hosiery industrialists 1850–1950 (type D in Table 5.1) using (among other sources) local newspapers, marriage notices, parish and civil registers, directories, and school records (Chapter 3, section 3). (It is useful, whenever you meet or use the terms 'class', 'social mobility', etc., to ask what classification is being used.)

3 This is up to you, but among the factors you would need to consider would be (a) what kind of study do you want to carry out – quantitative? experiential? local?, and (b) what kinds of sources will you be using?

Exercise 6.1

The mean assessments per vote were Whately, £54.3; Tite, £33.4; abstainers, £47.9. There was obviously a marked difference between the mean assessment of the supporters of the two candidates, with (on this measure at least) the Conservative supporters being 63 per cent better off than the Liberal supporters. Note that those who abstained were comparatively well-off too.

Exercise 6.2

1 Some 519 of Roebuck's 1,153 supporters in 1841 voted for him in 1847, i.e. 45.0 per cent.

2 Some 58 of Roebuck's 1,153 supporters in 1841 voted for other candidates in 1847, i.e. 5.0 per cent

3 Some 576 of Roebuck's 1,153 supporters in 1841 did not take part in the 1847 election, i.e. 50 per cent.

4 Of those who took part in both elections, Roebuck's support remained very solid indeed. However, 50 per cent of his 1841 supporters did not take part in the 1847 election, indicating a not inconsiderable turnover of the electorate. This raises questions about the stability of the community, whether a turnover such as this was unusual, and what the causes were.

Neale (1972, p.59) remarked that Roebuck '*retained* the support of 1,093 of the electors' (my italics). However, as your calculations will have shown, this is something of a misnomer since the physical replacement of the electorate was so high. Indeed this physical replacement would appear to be one of the fundamental determinants of voting behaviour at this time.

Exercise 7.1

You will have spotted that in Kingsley ward the eligible voters more than doubled, with an increase of 3,153.

Exercise 7.2

The smallest was Castle ward (majority of 72), the largest St Michael's (362) and Kingsley (354). You may have noted, however, that the year after the franchise was equalized – whether wholly due to the legislation is not revealed – there was a bigger change in Kingsley than in St Michael's: in Kingsley a male majority in 1928 became a significant female one in 1929. This may indicate a different age structure in the population of the two wards. In contrast to St Michael's, a late Victorian housing development, Kingsley was a growing area with new housing. The difference between the two wards may indicate that Kingsley had more women under thirty.

Exercise 7.4

My (expanded) table looks like this:

Year	Wards contested	Voting percentage			Men as percentage of electors		
		electors	votes	%	electors	men	%
1927	12	41 970	25 918	61.75	41 970	20 718	49.36
1928	12	42 936	27 898	64.98	42 936	21 188	49.35
Mean				63.36			49.36
1929	10	38 515	22 873	59.39	38 515	18 080	46.94
1930	11	42 596	25 407	59.65	42 596	20 026	47.01
Mean				59.52			46.98

My conclusion is that there is a drop in turnout of 3.8 per cent between the pairs of years 1927/1928 and 1929/1930. This coincides with the change in the franchise which resulted in men constituting 2.4 per cent less of the total electors. The change in turnout is greater than the change in the distribution of men and women electors, but the two changes are in the same direction and in that sense there is a parallel with what happened in Leeds.

Exercise 7.5

As the table below shows, neither the mean turnout nor the overall rank order indicates any relationship between the distribution of dwellings by rateable value and the turnout in local government elections.

Ward	Mean turnout 1923–27	% of dwellings with rateable value below £13	Ward	Mean turnout 1923–27	% of dwellings with rateable value below £13
North	66.10	92.80	South	57.50	68.27
Delapre	59.07	91.28	St Michael's	66.96	63.54
St James'	62.03	88.13	Kingsley	60.94	54.31

ACKNOWLEDGEMENTS

Grateful acknowledgement is made to the following sources for permission to reproduce material in this book:

Chapter 1

Figures   Figures 1.1, 1.2: Oxfordshire County Libraries, Centre for Oxfordshire Studies.

Tables   Table 1.1: Deane, P. and Cole, W.A. (1967) *British economic growth 1688–1959*, Cambridge University Press; Table 1.2: Daly, M.E. (1981) *A social and economic history of Ireland since 1800*, The Educational Company of Ireland.

Chapter 2

Figures   Figure 2.1: Monica Shelley; Figure 2.5: Rural History Centre, University of Reading; Figure 2.6: Swindon Museum and Art Gallery, Borough of Thamesdown; Figure 2.7: West Mercia Constabulary.

Table   Table 2.1: Marshall, J.D. and Walton, J.K. (1981) *The lake counties from 1830 to the mid-twentieth century*, Manchester University Press.

Chapter 3

Figures   Figure 3.2: Pennington, S. and Westover, B. (1989) *A hidden workforce, homeworkers in England 1850–1985*, The Macmillan Press Ltd; Figure 3.3: Oxfordshire County Libraries, Centre for Oxfordshire Studies; Figure 3.4: Hulton-Deutsch Collection; Figure 3.5: Courtesy of Dr Pnina Werbner, University of Keele.

Table   Table 3.8: Halsey, A.H. (1988) *British social trends since 1900*, Macmillan.

Photographs   p.42: Buckinghamshire County Record Office.

Chapter 4

Figures   Figure 4.2: New Lanark Conservation Trust; Figure 4.3: Archives and Business Records Centre, University of Glasgow; Figure 4.4: Trustees of the National Library of Scotland; Figure 4.5: Dr John McKay.

Tables   Table 4.2: McKay, J. (1985) *The social history of the Scottish shale oil industry 1850–1914*, unpublished Ph.D. thesis, Open University; Tables 4.4 to 4.7: Glenrothes and East Kilbride Development Corporation Archives.

Chapter 5

Figures   Figures 5.1, 5.2: Monica Shelley.

Tables   Tables 5.2 , 5.3, 5.4: Miles, A. and Vincent, D. (1991) 'A land of "boundless opportunity"? Mobility and stability in nineteenth-century England', in Dex, S. (ed.) *Life and work history analyses: qualitative and quantitative developments*, Routledge; Tables 5.5, 5.6, 5.7: Pearce, C. (1969) 'Social mobility through marriage in Ashford (Kent) 1837–70', unpublished paper from ESRC Project, *Ashford (Kent) 1840–70: a social demographic study*; Table 5.8: Glass, D. (1954) *Social mobility in Britain*, Routledge and Kegan Paul; Tables 5.9, 5.11: Goldthorpe, J.H. (1980) *Social mobility and class structure in modern Britain*, Oxford University Press; Table 5.10: Payne, G. (1987) *Mobility and change in modern society*, Macmillan Ltd, also by permission of Sheridan House Inc.

Chapter 6

Figures   Figures 6.1, 6.2, 6.3: Kentish Express & Ashford News; Figure 6.4: Potts Collection, Banbury Public Library, 1837, Volume 4, p.22; Figure 6.5: Potts Collection, Banbury Public Library, 1841, Volume 5, p.15; Figure 6.6: Potts Collection, Banbury Public Library.

Chapter 7

Figures   Figure 7.2: (top) Northamptonshire Libraries and Information Service, (bottom) Northampton Borough Council, Print Services Unit; Figure 7.3: Miller, W.L. (1986) 'Local electoral behaviour', in *Committee of inquiry into the conduct of local authority business* (Widdicombe Committee), Research Volume III, *The local government elector,* Cmnd 9800, reproduced with the permission of the Controller of Her Majesty's Stationery Office; Figures 7.4, 7.5: Photographed by Mike Levers at the offices of the *Chronicle and Echo* in Northampton by kind permission of the Deputy Editor.

Table   Table 7.3: Rhodes, E.C. (1938) 'Voting at municipal elections', *Political Quarterly,* IX, 2, p.275, Basil Blackwell Ltd.

Chapter 8

Figures   Figures 8.2, 8.3: Coleman, B.I. (1980) *The Church of England in the mid-nineteenth century: a social geography,* The Historical Association; Figure 8.4: Tiller, K. (1987) *Church and chapel in Oxfordshire 1851: the returns of the census of religious worship,* Oxfordshire Record Society; Figure 8.5: Public Record Office, ref. HO 129/163/4 BC/3956 © Crown Copyright, reproduced with the permission of the Controller of Her Majesty's Stationery Office; Figure 8.7: Addleshaw, G.W.O. and Etchells, F. (1948) *Architectural setting of Anglican worship,* Faber and Faber; Figure 8.9: Deputy Keeper of the records of Northern Ireland.

Tables   Table 8.1: Everitt, A. (1970) 'Nonconformity in country parishes', in Thirsk, J. (ed.) *Land, church and people,* Supplement, *Agricultural History Review,* volume 18, The British Agricultural History Society; Tables 8.2, 8.3: Coleman, B.I. (1980) *The Church of England in the mid-nineteenth century: a social geography,* The Historical Association; Table 8.6: Nielsen, J. (1987) 'Muslims in Britain: searching for an identity?', *New Community,* 13, 3, pp.384–94, Commission for Racial Equality.

Chapter 9

Figures   Figures 9.1, 9.3: Oxfordshire County Libraries, Centre for Oxfordshire Studies; Figure 9.2: John Johnson Collection, Bodleian Library; Figure 9.4: Lionel Grech/Milton Keynes Photo Services.

Tables   Tables 9.2, 9.3: Stacey, M. (1960) *Tradition and change: a study of Banbury,* Oxford University Press, © Dr Margaret Stacey.

Chapter 10

'Me as my Grandmother', by Rosemary Aubert, is reprinted from *Two kinds of honey* by permission of Oberon Press.

Covers

Front (clockwise from top left)   Railway station scene: detail from *Country Connection* by Don Breckon. Copyright: Solomon and Whitehead (Guild Prints) Ltd; Villager with boys: Garland Collection, West Sussex County Record Office/Photo: Beaver Photography; Aerial view of Kettering: Northamptonshire Libraries and Information Service, Local Studies Department; Street party: London Borough of Tower Hamlets, Globe Town Library Local Studies Collection/Photo: Godfrey New Photographics; Soldier on leave: Rural History Centre, University of Reading.

Back (clockwise from top left)   Female factory workers: from D. Biggar and T. McDonald *In sunshine and in shadow,* Belfast, Friars Bush Press; Children gleaning at harvest time: Rural History Centre, University of Reading; Shell fish at cottage door and ladies working: The Sutcliffe Gallery; Part of envelope containing letter from Joseph Hartley, 1861: courtesy Michael Drake; Raunds – Peace Day 1919: Northamptonshire Libraries and Information Service, Local Studies Department/Copyright: Mrs P. Keedle; Three ladies in Llanfair Caereinion, Powys, *c.*1900: courtesy of the late Miss Blodwen Jones, from Pryce, W.T.R. (1991) *The photographer in rural Wales,* Llanfair Caereinion, The Powysland Club; Aerial view of west London.

INDEX

DATE DUE